AF593537

THE ARCHAEOLOGY OF RAILWAYS

N.B. Mention in this book of any railway, railway structure or railway artefact does not imply any right of access, nor that it is safe to visit it. Readers are particularly warned against trespass on railways in use.

THE ARCHAEOLOGY OF RAILWAYS

P.J.G. Ransom

WORLD'S WORK LTD

By the same author:

Railways Revived
An Account of Preserved Steam Railways
Faber & Faber Ltd

The Archaeology of Canals
World's Work Ltd

Copyright © 1981 by P. J. G. Ransom

Designed by David Gibbons

Maps by Reginald and Marjorie Piggott

Index by Richard Raper

Published by World's Work Ltd
The Windmill Press, Kingswood, Tadworth, Surrey

Printed in Great Britain by BAS Printers Limited
Over Wallop, Stockbridge, Hampshire

SBN 437 14401 1

CONTENTS

LIST OF ILLUSTRATIONS

Illustrations are by the author, except where acknowledged

Colour illustrations

Black and white illustrations

FOREWORD

by
Viscount Downe
Chairman, Friends of the National Railway Museum

Professionally my world is in the higher technology reaches of electronics, where the developments of three years ago are seen like relics from another age. Paradoxically this has increased my amateur interest in history: the march and countermarch of nations, and equally the slow movement in country village life; the men and women who become individuals as I read and see the physical associations which they left behind them. The past can come to life to a surprising extent, the artifacts can display their usefulness, and people can become as recongisable and human as our contemporaries today. A study of the past is a delightful pastime, but it can also be of great value in thinking about the present and future. History does repeat as situations and stresses recur to be met by human nature which changes little. John Ransom is so right when he says: 'A knowledge of the past is essential to an understanding of the present.'

Nevertheless there are discoveries which have changed life as it was understood: primary examples being the wheel, gunpowder, and the railway. The way in which life was revolutionised by rail transport is difficult to visualise. It made transport fast and generally available. Its path made towns and cities, its absence doomed important communities to stagnation and decline. The arrival of the train affected people commercially and intellectually, the old days could not return, a new age had arrived.

This interaction of the railway upon people and the balancing drive of people to extend and benefit from the railway is an interesting study in its own right. The study of the physical remains from those events is no less fascinating and no less important. This book goes further and puts them into context. I like to think that John Ransom has provided us in these pages with a time machine for our imagination. It is allowing us to share in the results of his wide research upon the physical relics of the formative age of the railway; to follow paths to precisely map referenced places where the actual events took place; to look and perhaps to close our eyes for a moment and almost see the happenings of years before the birth of the oldest person we will ever meet. We are told of the place, the inanimate survivor and why it is important and interesting. In reading I found a great temptation to leave my transitory semiconductors to their own devices and follow the paths so beguilingly laid out. We may even meet along the way. I hope so.

CHAPTER 1

THE PRESENT AND THE PAST

On the Flying Scotsman

Ten minutes out of Edinburgh Waverley, the High Speed Train that is in 1980 the up *Flying Scotsman* is already travelling fast. Inside, its muffled steady roar is intensified at intervals by the bridges which approach, pass overhead in the blink of an eye, and are swept away astern. Passengers are settling down to newspapers or knitting, or just to looking out of the window. Even among the latter it takes sharp eyes to spot that, immediately after one of these overbridges, there come the stone abutments of another, the deck of which has been removed.

These abutments mark the course of a railway far older than that upon which the *Flying Scotsman* is running. It was the first railway in Scotland: the Tranent-Cockenzie Waggonway built as long ago as 1722 with rails of wood as was then the practice. Down its two-mile track, waggons of coal ran by gravity from mine to harbour; horses hauled the empties up again. By the time the North British Railway was built between Edinburgh and Berwick in the 1840s, the waggonway had been relaid with iron rails carried on stone blocks; the bridge had to be provided for it, and was in use until the 1880s.

During the time that the observant passenger has been pondering this, the *Flying Scotsman* has travelled far on its way. The line it is running on follows a route recommended by George Stephenson: it is suitable for fast running for it has easy gradients and few sharp curves. Stephenson favoured such routes, even though they might be indirect. The line shows this characteristic too, for it follows the coast so that in the early part of its journey the *Flying Scotsman*, though heading eventually south, is actually travelling slightly north of east. The great Brunel had favoured a rival route, more direct but more steeply graded, through the Border hills, which was to have been worked by atmospheric traction, that great Victorian engineering fiasco. It is as well that the Stephenson line prevailed.

Passing Morpeth, our sharp-eyed passenger may spot, particularly if the train slows down for signals, a wall map of porcelain tiles on the up platform. It is headed 'North Eastern Railway' and shows that former company's system; the map has been there since about 1910. At Newcastle upon Tyne, as the train draws to a halt, not even the most unobservant passenger can fail to notice that it has entered one of those typical spacious Victorian city stations at which a very large glazed roof covers track and platforms alike. What is not obvious, however, is that Newcastle Central is the prototype of them all, and dates from 1851. Then, farther south, as the train approaches Darlington, a lineside sign announces 'Stockton & Darlington Railway 1825'. The *Flying Scotsman* crosses the site of that pioneer railway and then, for a short distance, runs along or very close to the course of a branch of it. Dating from 1829, this is the oldest part of the whole line from Edinburgh to London.

Near York, the River Ouse and York Minster appear on the left. All true railway enthusiasts, however, are looking out to the right. In a siding stand cattle vans and other goods vehicles of types familiar yesterday but not today, close by are semaphore signals of distinctive 'somersault' pattern, and a cast iron bridge bears aloft a chaldron waggon of primeval appearance. They indicate the presence of the National Railway Museum. Of course, the majority of exhibits are out of sight, housed under cover in what was once a locomotive shed but, with luck, among the other outdoor exhibits there may be, temporarily, a gleaming crimson or apple green steam locomotive, brought out to work a steam special.

As the High Speed Train, that entirely modern form of transport, continues swiftly on its way to London, the observant passenger sees a succession of reminders of the past. Open spaces mark former wayside stations, closed when passengers changed their habits of travel, and the trackbeds of closed branches curve away from the main line. There are reminders of the steam age: locomotive tenders converted into snow ploughs, steam cranes at work in sidings, and warning notices which still command engine drivers to whistle rather than hoot. There are vehicles built by the old railway companies which remain in use by railway engineers: Great Western goods brake vans, London & North Eastern Railway coaches. The teak bodies of the latter, which once were varnished, are now disguised by grey or yellow paint. And prominent above the platform barrier at King's Cross, on the occasion of the journey which suggested this introduction to railway

archaeology, a sign with painted pointing hand indicating in which direction passengers might find the City & South London Electric Railway. That pioneer tube has long since lost its identity in London Transport's Northern Line, but my notebook confirms that I was not dreaming. The sign must, I suppose, have been uncovered temporarily during alterations.

The 'up *Flying Scotsman*' I wrote earlier. It is always 'up' to London, in railway language, and has been since the days of horsedrawn mail coaches on the roads. Edmund Vale, in *The Mail Coach Men of the Late Eighteenth Century*, explains that the metropolis was regarded as the high place of the kingdom; adjacent to it were the 'upper grounds' (a coachman's ground being the distance he covered), beyond them the 'middle grounds' and beyond them again the 'lower grounds'. Hence, 'up' to London and 'down' to the country. The terms were adopted early by railways and appeared in Bradshaw by 1842. There are other old coaching terms which survive in railway use: 'coach' and 'carriage', of course, and (I suspect) to 'book' tickets; and certainly 'guard'. On a train as on a mail coach, the driver drives and the guard is in charge but the mail coach guard really was an armed guard.

The *Flying Scotsman* is old-established, too. There has been a 10 am departure from King's Cross to Edinburgh, and a corresponding up train, since 1862; the name *Flying Scotsman* was at first unofficial, though it was famous by the 1890s, and was adopted officially in timetables and on carriage-roof destination boards in 1923. It is not alone as a long-lived train name. *Cornish Riviera*, for instance, dates from 1904. Oldest of all is the *Irish Mail*, which train first ran in 1848. This name, for the Euston–Holyhead service, is another echo of coaching days.

Traces of the past

That journey to London by the *Flying Scotsman* has illustrated something of what this book is about, which is railways in terms of surviving traces of the past. Much more can be shown by now returning, as it were, to Edinburgh, and considering briefly the railways of that city in their present

1/1 The abutment of a vanished bridge over the East Coast Main Line at grid reference NT 403742 marks the course of the Tranent–Cockenzie Waggonway. This was completed in 1722; when the main line was built by the North British Railway in the 1840s the bridge had to be provided for it. It was used until the 1880s. The course of the waggonway is described in chapter seven.

1/2 (next page) The up Flying Scotsman *enters Newcastle Central on 16 August 1980. The train is now indistinguishable from other services worked by High Speed Trains, but there has been a* Flying Scotsman *between King's Cross and Edinburgh in one form or another for almost 120 years. Newcastle Central is even older: it was built in 1850–1, the first station to have arched all-over roofs of the type which was soon to become familiar.*

D
9
E

state, taking them in clockwise progression.

One accepts today that the railway from Edinburgh to London is the East Coast Route, followed by the *Flying Scotsman*, via Newcastle, York and Grantham to King's Cross. But it was not always the only route. John Buchan, in *The Three Hostages* (published 1924), describes two of his heroes, in a hurry to reach London, 'having a late tea in the Midland express, having nearly broken their necks in a furious motor race to catch the train at Hawick'.

In the 1980s one can no more catch an express to London at Hawick than a rocket to Mars; and even before the line was closed in 1969 one would not have wasted much effort, if in a hurry, in rushing to catch one there. For in the years preceding closure the train service over this route, from Edinburgh Waverley via Hawick to Carlisle, and onwards by still-existing lines of the former Midland Railway to Leeds and St Pancras, had become excessively dilatory. Railway company politics and decline of traffic due to road competition had combined over many years with topographical difficulties to inhibit improvements. Today, the trackbed of the 'Waverley Route' still winds its way between the hills for ninety miles or so from the outskirts of Edinburgh to the outskirts of Carlisle, but its rails have long since been taken up. Yet in Buchan's day it ranked equally with the East Coast Route.

The Waverley Route included the southern part of the course of Edinburgh's earliest railway, the Edinburgh & Dalkeith, opened in 1831. The practicability of steam locomotives was not then everywhere accepted, and the Edinburgh & Dalkeith, like earlier lines, hauled its traffic, both passenger and freight, by horses. Except on an incline with a gradient of 1 in 30: up this, trains were hauled by cable, through a short tunnel, and into its original Edinburgh terminus at St Leonards. Though disused, trackbed and tunnel mouth can still be seen.

In the heyday of railways, passengers from Edinburgh to London had a wide choice of routes. Not only were there the East Coast Route and the Midland Route (of which the Waverley Route formed part), but there was also the West Coast Route, from Edinburgh Princes Street station via Carstairs, Carlisle and Crewe to Euston. Decline of railway traffic as a result of road and air competition in the twentieth century, and unification of the old railway companies into the single nationalised system in 1948, resulted in concentration of traffic formerly carried by competing routes onto the one considered most suitable, in this case the East Coast. So, although the West Coast Route from Edinburgh is still complete, trains from Edinburgh run over it as far south as Liverpool, Manchester and Birmingham, but no longer to London.

To say that the West Coast Route south from Edinburgh is still complete is not strictly accurate, for its trains no longer leave from Princes Street station but from Waverley (as the Ordnance Survey still marks it; British Rail timetables now refer to it simply as Edinburgh). The decline of traffic led to diversion of surviving trains starting from Princes Street to start from Waverley, followed by closure of Princes Street station in 1965. The course of the railway approach is now the West Approach Road, a convenient fast route for motorists, as they approach the city from the west, to avoid congested inner suburbs.

The earliest main line to enter Edinburgh was none of these, but the Edinburgh & Glasgow Railway, authorised in 1838 and opened in 1842 from Glasgow to its original Edinburgh terminus at Haymarket. It was typical of early direct trunk routes built in the image of the Liverpool & Manchester, the first trunk line to link two cities. At Haymarket the original station building remains in use, although the line was extended as early as 1846 to what was later called Waverley station.

Trailing into the line of the Edinburgh & Glasgow Railway on the outskirts of Edinburgh comes the line from North and North East Scotland which crosses the Firth of Forth by the Forth Bridge—the supreme monument of the railway age and one which, because of immense difficulty of construction, was completed fairly late in it, in 1890. Previously, travellers bound from Edinburgh to the North took a train to Granton and crossed the Forth by ferry to Burntisland, whence the railway continued northwards. So, while the principal railways of Edinburgh today have generally an east-west alignment, there runs at right angles to this a substantial but disused railway tunnel nearly half a mile long. Scotland Street Tunnel is a relic of the Edinburgh, Leith & Granton Railway and through it, between 1847 and 1868, travellers to the North commenced their journey.

But the tunnel remains and not only its prominent northern end but also its southern end can be found. A door communicating with it can be seen on the north side of Waverley station (which lies in a cutting) under the seventh blind arch from the west end, according to a survey made by A. Graham for the National Monuments Record of Scotland in 1971. The same survey records the intriguing fact that at the EL & G's Trinity station an extra, outdoor ticket window was provided at which the Newhaven fishwives—itinerant costumed fish vendors who were once a picturesque feature of Edinburgh—might book their tickets and so keep the booking office proper free from contamination by the smell of fish!

We have now encountered the principal types of historic railways, and seen how they, and their features, appear today. Apart from mention of the National Railway Museum, we have seen little of what traces remain of the trains which ran on them. But here again Edinburgh is fortunate in having, in the Royal Scottish Museum, the locomotive *Wylam Dilly*. She and *Puffing Billy*, in the Science Museum,

London, are the two oldest surviving steam locomotives: they were built in 1813–14 to run on the Wylam colliery waggonway near Newcastle upon Tyne. Preserved steam locomotives of more recent build are to be seen in or near Edinburgh from time to time, for Edinburgh-to-Aberdeen and Edinburgh-to-Stirling are among the routes over which British Rail permit steam specials.

To be sure of seeing preserved steam locomotives and contemporary rolling stock one must go slightly farther afield, however, to the Falkirk depot of the Scottish Railway Preservation Society. To find preserved steam locomotives in full operation it is necessary to go farther still, to the Lochty Railway in Fife, to the Strathspey Railway in the Highlands, or to the North of England for the North Yorkshire Moors Railway, the Worth Valley Railway or the Lakeside & Haverthwaite Railway. On all these railways, steam trains still operate regular public train services. The SRPS is establishing its own line at Bo'ness.

Railway archaeology

C. F. Dendy Marshall, in his encyclopaedic *A History of British Railways down to the Year 1830*, first published in 1938, considers that the railway concept contains three elements: the wheel, the prepared track, and the means of lateral constraint. It cannot be expressed better. Archaeology is defined as the study of antiquities. Here I take the archaeology of railways to be the study of railways in terms of surviving traces and relics of the past, whether they be on the ground, in museums, or in action. By and large this book refers only to the British Isles and, because the condition of railway relics is liable to change—particularly as later developments obscure the courses of closed lines, it should be born in mind that references to the present refer in the main to the period 1979–80 when the book was being prepared.

A member of the staff of one of the museums contacted during preparation of this book expressed misgivings that his job was concerned so exclusively with the past. But a knowledge of the past is essential to an understanding of the present, and knowledge of the past which does not derive in part from study of its physical remains is incomplete. Furthermore it is essential in planning for the future, for progress is ever a step back for every two steps forward, and it is important that we should remember what we have lost, so that we may recover it at a later date.

While studying the material on which are based the case histories of certain steam locomotives appearing in chapter five, I was concurrently in process of selling a motor car. At an age of $4\frac{1}{2}$ years and with a mileage of 29,000 I judged it no longer sufficiently reliable for winter use in the severe climate in which I happen to live. These figures made a striking contrast with those for the steam locomotives which emerged from successive sets of notes: their usual ages at withdrawal were about 40 years, their mileages $1\frac{1}{4}$ million. Building vehicles of limited life in order to keep the price down may yet come to be seen as a false economy.

Railway archaeology is a colossal subject. One could compile a two-volume book on the archaeology of railways in South Wales alone—and probably a five-volume one on North East England. I have therefore had to be selective. In this book, after an outline of the history of railways, come descriptions of surviving traces of its most interesting periods and aspects. These include waggonways and tramroads—the era of the horse railway, which may be taken as extending from 1604 until 1830, lasted longer than that of the steam railway, from 1830 to 1968—and of the first great main lines of the steam railway era. There is something about relics of the steam age, not only locomotives both static and working, but also the buildings and equipment they required, and about traces of the multiplicity of railway companies of Victorian and Edwardian times, and of the big four companies into which most of them, in Britain, were amalgamated at the grouping of 1923, and which lasted until 1948. The last chapter is devoted to localities of special interest. I do not claim to be encyclopaedic, but I hope that all principal features will be found here, and a selection of lesser but representative ones. Descriptions are, to a large extent, based on personal observation.

The manner in which relics of the old companies survive is sometimes as inconsequent as it is delightful. While preparing this book I had time to spare, between trains, at a busy but old-established station on British Rail's Inter-City network, and so I set out to explore it in search of anything which might be of interest. I investigated fruitlessly a large island platform, walking its full length, which was considerable, and then turned my attention to another platform which adjoined the main station buildings. Though everything was basically old and, as is the present practice, well cared-for, nothing definite appeared which could be linked with any specific company. Then, as a last resort, I entered a waiting room. To judge from an abundance of mirrors and panelled woodwork, it had once been a refreshment room; but the counter had been removed and the room was furnished with railway wooden bench seats, long, solid and old. On the back of one were carved, in Gothic script, the initials of its original owner: MR—the pre-grouping Midland Railway. But next to it was a greater rarity, a seat bearing the initials MS & LR—Manchester, Sheffield & Lincolnshire Railway. It was in 1897 that that company changed its name to Great Central.

Railway modernisation

Since much of this book, with *Archaeology* in its title, is about steam locomotives and branch lines and suchlike which were commonplace until quite recently, some explanation is needed. It lies in the fact that, in the fifteen years between 1955 and 1970, the British railway system saw more, and more fundamental, changes than at any similar period since the 1830s and 1840s, the boom years for railway construction.

During the Victorian era and until 1914, the years of prosperity, railways were pre-eminent and scarcely challenged. The period between the wars brought both industrial depression and road competition from motor vehicles, changed conditions to which railway managements were slow to adapt and which in any event themselves limited the finance available for alterations. Furthermore, the grouping of 1923 was followed by a shaking-down interregnum of six or seven years during which little of fundamental importance was attempted and no sooner had the big four companies started to get into their stride than progress was interrupted by the Second World War. This was followed by nationalisation in 1948 which again was followed by a six- or seven-year shake-down period. So in 1954 the railway system was still being run on much the same principles as it had been for a century or more. It was dependent on steam traction; electric and diesel power, though they had been practicable for many years, were used only to a limited extent. The network was still laid out as it had been when the alternative was horsedrawn transport: that meant that lines were widespread and stations frequent, on the principle that travellers would make the greatest possible part of their journey by rail, for however slow a train might be it was still much quicker than the fastest horse. In the era of

motor road transport, this was no longer relevant.

Modernisation came mostly as a result of two main steps: the British Transport Commission Modernisation Plan of 1955 and the Beeching Report of 1963. The contents of these were such that it would have been better if their order could have been reversed: for while the BTC plan dealt mainly with the details of how railways were to be modernised in terms of gradual replacement of steam by diesel and electric traction, of semaphore signals by colour lights, and so on, the Beeching Report, eight years later, got down to the brass tacks of whether and where railways should be modernised at all—in terms of improved services for passengers in quantity and freight in bulk between main centres, and, notoriously, of closure of a great many

under-used lines and stations.

What had happened was that although British Railways had, just, been breaking even up to 1955, they then commenced a financial nose dive. The reasons for this I enlarge upon in chapter two; the effect was to call into question the desirability of putting more and more public money into a concern that was making greater and greater losses. This was a much less

1/3 The north entrance of Scotland Street Tunnel, Edinburgh. The tunnel runs beneath Scotland Street, in the background, and continues southwards for nearly half a mile to Waverley station. From 1847 until 1868 it was part of the principal route from Edinburgh to the North: by train to Granton, and then by ferry across the Firth of Forth to Burntisland. A diversion was completed in 1868 and since then the tunnel has been disused.

familiar story then than now! Looking back, although memories of the Beeching period still arouse the ire of many railway enthusiasts, it is difficult to appreciate now how generally controversial a subject railways were at that time. Nowadays the great debate is about education rather than transport, the butt of comedians is the Post Office rather than the railways and the nationalised industry which gives most concern is (exquisite irony) the nationalised motor manufacturer, British Leyland.

At any rate, change on British Railways, having been long delayed, was severe in its impact. In 1955 there were some 19,000 steam locomotives; by mid-1968 they had been totally replaced by diesel and electric locomotives and trains (with the sole exception, never to be omitted, of the three narrow gauge steam locomotives of the Vale of Rheidol tourist line). Between 1961 and 1972 the route mileage of British Railways was reduced from 17,830 to 11,444 and the number of passenger stations fell from over 7,000 to 2,362.

The modernisation programme or something similar was both inevitable and essential but, like any big programme prepared late, carried out in haste, and altered while in progress, it had its deficiencies. In detail, its effects often appear capricious. To give but one example, Tavistock, a substantial town, has lost its two railways, but Causeland and Sandplace Halts, on the Liskeard to Looe branch not far away, still get sixteen trains a day although they appear to serve little but a wooded valley. There were indeed lines closed which should have been kept open and there were lines kept open which might well have been closed. In one of the latter instances it is plausibly rumoured that the deciding factor was the number of marginal parliamentary constituencies traversed by the line in question.

On lines which remain open the effect is sometimes strange too. In 1904 the fastest scheduled trains between Paddington and Worcester took 135 minutes, twice a day, non-stop. In 1954 the fastest schedule was 150 minutes. In 1980 the fastest schedule is once again 135 minutes, twice a day—with many stops at intermediate stations as the sole benefit from modernisation.

Writing in 1980 it is curious to reflect that, although it is now twelve years since the end of steam locomotives on British Rail, it is only twenty years since the last new BR steam locomotive was built. That was *Evening Star*, completed in 1960. As things turned out, she was to have a working life of only five years. When rapid change brought a sudden end to old techniques which had long persisted, it turned surviving examples of much that was lately familiar into traces of the past. That is why they are described here. *Evening Star* is now as much a relic of the past as *Puffing Billy*.

Railway preservation

One effect of the modernisation programme was to give a great stimulus to railway preservation. Previously there had been a tendency for locomotives, rolling stock, and indeed railways, to be preserved (if at all) because they were very old, or very famous, or both. Rapid disappearance of both old and not-so-old steam locomotives under the modernisation plans resulted in a comprehensive programme to preserve representative examples of different classes to form the nucleus of the national collection. As well as this, a great many steam locomotives were purchased for preservation either by individuals or, more often, by funds or societies set up for the purpose. Simultaneously, closure of innumerable branch lines prompted a great many schemes for their preservation, that is to say their continued operation with, mainly, steam locomotives. Elsewhere, redundant steam locomotive sheds and similar locations were adapted as preservation depots, where preserved locomotives and rolling stock are maintained and from which (after a few years' pause for reflection, following 1968) British Rail allows them to emerge to work steam specials. It is almost entirely because of these activities that steam locomotives have survived to be described, here, in the present tense.

Some preserved railways are remarkably good at re-creating the atmosphere of railways as they were. Peer forward with me through the window of a Severn Valley Railway train as it rounds a curve: a line of red-and-cream coaches leads the eye towards locomotive *Hinton Manor*, with dark green taper boiler, arched nameplate prominent above the running board, large pendulous cylinder and connecting rod lazily swinging back and forth. Carriage wheels clatter quickly and high-pitched over the joints of short, light, branch line rails. Twenty five years slip away: these were the sensations, this the scene, when one exchanged the main line at Shrewsbury for the lesser line to Welshpool and the hills beyond. Is it Hanwood next stop, or Yockleton?

Movement and travel are so closely associated with steam locomotives that to preserve one wholly static (though better than cutting it up) is to eliminate one of its essential features. The point was brought home to me recently when visiting a museum which housed several locomotives and was in many respects excellent; but the only sign of movement was on a model railway tucked away in a corner. The National Railway Museum's solution to this particular conundrum is to maintain some of its locomotives in working order and to send them out to haul steam specials. During 1979 ten locomotives in the national collection were considered to be potentially steamable, and others were in course of restoration. Of those ten, five were based at the NRM itself and five were on loan to other reputable preservation organizations. As well as loaning items from its collection, the

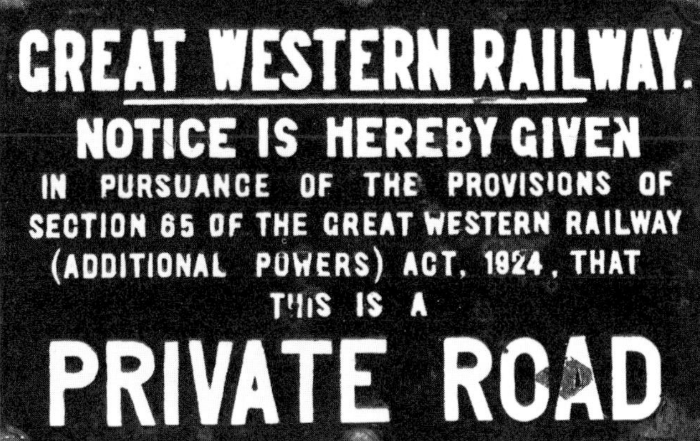

1/4, 1/5, 1/6 Traces of old companies: notices photographed on British Rail in 1979–80. Often, on cast iron notices, the name of the company is painted out, but no such inhibition is evident in the Great Western private-road notice photographed at Moreton-in-Marsh. The LNER notice was photographed at Falkirk Grahamston, and was replaced by a modern notice shortly afterwards; similar LNER notices survive at nearby Linlithgow. Enamel warning notices were unusual: the LMS example is at Dalmally.

NRM rotates some of its exhibits between its main museum and its reserve collection, so that with this, and with locomotives going out to work steam specials, there is quite often movement within and around the museum. Nevertheless, even these policies bring complaints, I understand, from people who have travelled far to see one particular exhibit, only to find it missing.

More important, there is constant controversy between those who feel that the only thing to do with a steam locomotive is to make it go, and those who feel that to do so, because it necessitates gradual replacement of worn components by new ones to an ever greater extent, is in the long run to destroy a locomotive's historic integrity. Or perhaps, since those in the first category are so much in the majority, there is not a controversy, but ought to be.

Fuel is added to the fire by the fact that although steam locomotives were built for a long life, they were also designed to achieve it by constant replacement of components as they wore out. Consider the example of the NRM's London, Midland & Scottish Railway 4-6-2 express locomotive *Duchess of Hamilton.* She was built in 1938 and withdrawn in 1964. Surviving records show however that her present boiler was fitted in 1959, that it was the *ninth* boiler fitted to this locomotive, and that this boiler had been fitted to *six* other locomotives previously.

So, since alterations were constantly made to locomotives and parts replaced during their working lives, why should not that process continue when they are preserved? But if it is, then how far should it go? Dame Margaret Weston, Director of the Science Museum, told the railway preservation symposium held in Manchester in September 1980 that she would not be prepared to have the remains of George and Robert Stephenson's *Rocket* restored to working order. Earlier Mr A. E. Jarvis of Merseyside County Museums had touched on the same

point in connection with his museum's locomotive *Lion*. *Lion* was built in 1838, was steaming during 1980 at the celebrations for the 150th anniversary of the Liverpool & Manchester Railway and was a very fine sight too: the oldest steamable locomotive. Her boiler, though not the 1838 original, is thought to date at least from the 1840s, and its shell is in good condition. Mr Jarvis expressed the opinion that when, eventually, the boiler wears out, a new boiler should be fitted to the locomotive to enable it to continue to run and the old boiler should be preserved separately. In the author's opinion this would be a mistake: when *Lion*'s boiler wears out, I suggest, the time will have come to call a halt to alterations to *Lion*, to preserve her static, and to put the finance and effort needed for a new boiler towards building a complete working replica of a locomotive of the same period—say the Stephensons' *Planet*, the true ancestor, in design, of all later conventional British steam locomotives. On the other hand the early locomotive *Cornwall*, which was recently loaned by the NRM to the Severn Valley Railway to be restored to working order, seems an excellent choice for the purpose. For *Cornwall*, though authentically old, is a hotchpotch: an 1897 rebuild of an 1858 rebuild of a wholly untypical locomotive of 1847. There is more about all these locomotives later in the book.

At the other extreme come those steam locomotives which provide the motive power for the scheduled trains of preserved railways. Here, clearly, maintenance of advertised services implies that locomotives must be properly maintained in full working order with parts replaced as necessary. This in turn does happily mean the survival of the crafts, techniques and skills of steam locomotive maintenance and operation which would otherwise have been lost. Indeed, on railways such as the Festiniog it has encouraged continued development of steam power and the techniques associated with it, which would otherwise have ceased.

In between these extremes there are a great many locomotives preserved, of greater or lesser historic importance and greater or lesser suitability for hauling steam trains or specials. Fortunately there are enough, in total, for those in which historic importance is paramount to be preserved static but intact, and for others to be maintained in working order, modified if necessary.

Ancient monuments and listed buildings

For a long time, in its haste to modernise, British Rail seemed to wish to obliterate all traces of its history. But for some years now there have, happily, been signs that it is prepared, while still looking forward to the future, to respect the best of its past. This is fortunate, for although BR was able, as a result of the Transport Act 1968,

1/7 (left) Motor road competition has reduced the route mileage of railways in Great Britain from a peak of 20,443 miles in 1927 to about 11,000 miles at the present time. The courses of closed and dismantled railways are a familiar sight in the countryside: this was the Border Counties line (Riccarton Junction to Hexham) near Saughtree. The site of the railway is used as a farm track, one boundary fence is maintained as a field boundary but the other has vanished, and a former platelayers' hut is now used by a farmer. The last passenger train ran here on 13 October 1956.

1/8 (next page) Coal in the tender of a locomotive in the National Railway Museum emphasises that some of its locomotives are maintained in working order and emerge from time to time to work specials. The building was formerly a locomotive shed of the 'roundhouse' type: tracks for stabling locomotives radiate from two turntables, one of which is seen here. The National Railway Museum, opened at York in 1975, is the definitive museum of railways in Britain; it is an outstation of the Science Museum.

to hive off responsibility for historic relics (locomotives, rolling stock, small relics etc) to the Department of Education and Science, it must inevitably continue to maintain an enormous number of historic buildings and structures simply because they remain in use.

Some of them in any event get statutory protection through having been scheduled as ancient monuments or listed as buildings of special architectural or historic interest. Readers already familiar with these terms will perhaps bear with me through a few sentences of explanation. Ancient monuments are scheduled by the Secretary of State for the Environment, in England, and by the Secretaries of State for Wales and Scotland, under a series of Acts of Parliament of which the earliest was the Ancient Monuments Act 1882 and the latest is the Ancient Monuments and Archaeological Areas Act 1979. The acts define the term 'ancient monument' so widely as potentially to include almost every building or structure of historic interest of any kind made or occupied by man from ancient to modern times; they do however specifically exclude occupied dwelling houses. Ruined abbeys and castles are the sort of things generally known as ancient monuments, but the Department of the Environment has extended its scope in this respect to include industrial archaeology and industrial monuments, within the existing legal framework. The principal effect of scheduling is to prohibit destruction, damage, repairs or alterations to a monument without 'scheduled monument consent' given by the appropriate secretary of state. An exception is made, however, where works are urgently needed for safety and notice is given to the secretary of state as soon as reasonably practicable. This is particularly relevant, for instance, to a railway viaduct which is scheduled but carries heavy traffic. Grants towards preservation of ancient monuments are sometimes given.

Lists of buildings of special architectural or historic interest are prepared by the secretaries of state under various Acts of Parliament. The effect of listing a building is that alterations to it must preserve its character as far as possible, and demolition is not allowed unless the case for it has been fully examined. Anyone wishing to alter or demolish a listed building has to get listed building consent from the local planning authority. In theory listed buildings are classified in four grades: grade I, grade II*, grade II, and grade III. In practice grade III is no longer used and the great majority of listed buildings are in grade II. A few listed buildings (about four per cent of the total) are considered to be buildings of exceptional interest and are listed in grade I. In railway terms this means stations such as Paddington, St Pancras and King's Cross.

There is, clearly, an element of overlap between ancient monuments and listed buildings where railway structures and buildings are concerned. With stations, the usual but not invariable practice is to list them as historic buildings rather than to schedule them as ancient monuments.

There are 43 ancient monuments of railway significance in Great Britain and further schedulings are expected.

Many of these monuments do not belong to British Rail; although BR owns 42 ancient monuments, 26 of them are memorials, ruins and so on which happen to be on railway property. Examples of railway ancient monuments include parts of the course of the Penydarren Tramroad, on which Richard Trevithick ran the first successful steam locomotive in 1804, the principal viaducts of the Settle & Carlisle line, relics of the Stockton & Darlington Railway, and the preserved Bowes Railway, Tyne & Wear, which is operated, as it has been since the 1820s, by cable haulage.

British Rail has a total of 511 listed buildings. The figure breaks down as 139 stations, 11 hotels, 142 other buildings, 27 memorials, gates, etc., 171 viaducts, bridges etc., and 21 tunnels. These are 1979 figures; the total had increased from 146 in 1971 and will be greater still by the time you read this. Grants towards maintenance of listed buildings are sometimes made by the Historic Buildings Council—in 1978 for instance BR commenced a five-year programme of cleaning and repairs to the buildings at St Pancras, the cost of £40,000 a year being split equally between this council and BR.

The rapid increase in the number of listed buildings on BR is an indication of increasing public concern for the national heritage. This has happily been reflected in the attitude of British Rail's management led by chairman Sir Peter Parker, who is himself concerned that BR should wherever possible preserve or restore, provided this is consistent with other obligations. One of the consequences of this was his appointment in 1977 of Mr Bernard Kaukas as Director-Environment, with the task of examining and co-ordinating those facets of railway business which decide whether it is providing a product acceptable to customers (or, as Kaukas himself puts it, of being a sort of cultural ombudsman).

The most obvious practical result of this has been a programme of cleaning station buildings. Removal of a century of soot has in places had spectacular results—though the programme has been made worthwhile, I regret to admit, by the absence of smoke-producing steam locomotives! The programme is also good business for BR: cleaning the exterior fabric of a station is much cheaper, and produces much quicker results, than building a new one, but has almost as great an effect in engendering confidence in the permanence of the train service. On the Inter-City network, clean, rather than dirty, stations are now normal—Carlisle, Preston, Crewe, Hereford, Bristol, Sheffield, York, Newcastle, to mention only a few noticed during recent safaris.

I would like to be able to be equally complimentary about lesser stations, but this unfortunately is not possible. I get the impression that the recent improvement in condition of large stations is matched by deterioration in the condition of small ones—except where they still have a staff, in which case they are usually fairly well kept. A great many such stations have become unstaffed halts, served by 'pay trains' on which passengers buy tickets from the guard. The buildings of such stations are usually either derelict or

1/9 On the Festiniog Railway, old techniques live on, and see further development. In the late 1860s this 1 ft. 11½ in. gauge railway adopted Fairlie's Patent locomotive, with double-ended boiler carried on bogies, as the solution to its problem of how best to carry heavy traffic over a tortuous narrow gauge line. Double Fairlie Merddin Emrys, *on the left, was built originally in 1879, and has been many times rebuilt after the manner of steam locomotives.* Earl of Merioneth *on the right was completed in 1979, to the same basic principle, with many new innovations and some old parts. They are seen together at Porthmadog in October 1979, about to double head a special train.*

demolished, replaced by small shelters. Both tend to be equally badly vandalised. In this respect they are rivalled only by telephone kiosks and bus stops and, I suppose, being less in the public eye are even more vulnerable. BR's only immediate solution seems to be to demolish as much as possible. I am inclined to the opinion that there is scope for leasing or selling redundant station buildings for use or conversion for dwelling houses or other purposes, to a far greater extent than is done at present. In addition to financial benefit for BR, constant presence of people would reduce vandalism of buildings remaining in railway use. Paradoxically, where stations were closed long ago, their buildings often survive, adapted for other purposes—but on stations remaining open the buildings have often gone.

The traditional small country station, staffed, well kept and fully signalled with semaphores, has become extremely rare on BR: to have perpetuated such stations is one of the least appreciated but most important achievements of preserved railways. That it is not totally unappreciated, however, is evident from the institution in 1979 of a 'Best Preserved Station in Britain' competition, won on that occasion by Oakworth on the Worth Valley Railway.

The pleasures of discovery

Certainly railway archaeology offers the pleasures of discovery, in seeking out historic railway relics, even though it may be difficult to explain exactly why one is travelling (say) from Stirling to Worcester by the slowest practicable route with the maximum number of changes. On a train, one is much better off in the front seat of a local diesel than in an express.

Some exploration, however, cannot be done by train. I recollect with particular pleasure driving south from Merthyr Tydfil in search of traces of the Penydarren Tramroad one Sunday at the end of September. Late but glorious sunshine made the valley of the River Taff seem as romantic as the Cevennes, and each little mining village vied with the next in brilliance of hues with which its houses were decorated. (I doubt whether South Wales is always like this, but so it is now implanted on my mind.)

Halting at Edwardsville, near Quaker's Yard, I looked over the wall beside the main road. Below it in the sun lay the line of the Taff Vale Railway, and the ring of hammers against steel indicated that a permanent way gang was doing a Sunday job nearby. Below it again, woods stretched down to the river. There, according to my map reference, should be traces of the tramroad; but there was nothing to be seen, and no apparent means of access.

I drove on, parked at the site of an old level crossing, and walked back along the course of a closed branch line in search of the viaduct by which the Taff Vale line crossed the river of its name. Beneath it, I knew, the tramroad had also passed. Realising that the trackbed which I was walking along would bring me out near the viaduct at rail level, I scrambled down a little path through the bracken and beneath the trees towards the river, to emerge suddenly onto a narrow road in the shadow of the viaduct. This road passed beneath the viaduct; it might have been the course of the tramroad, or it might not: there was nothing to show. It led to a farm; I came to a closed gate, diverged up a footpath, sensed that I was getting too high, and cut downwards again to find a rough trackway, evidently a continuation of the earlier road.

As I walked along this in the direction of my map reference, it became clear that the location of this trackway was indeed right for the course of the tramroad, its curves easy enough, its gradients not too steep. Then, half hidden in the dirt, appeared a large stone: in its top surface was a B-shaped recess, and a hole bored into it, made for plate-rail ends and locating peg. This was a tramroad stone-block sleeper. Within a few yards came many more, and I was able to follow them for three quarters of a mile or so, the actual blocks (for it is unlikely that many were replaced) which carried the rails upon which ran the first successful steam locomotive, 175 years before.

1/10 On British Rail, introduction of pay trains, on which passengers buy tickets from the guard, has resulted in many country stations—where they survive at all—becoming unstaffed halts, their buildings either derelict or demolished. Fortunately the traditional country station, well kept and signalled by semaphores, lives on, on some of the preserved railways: here, trains are passing at Hampton Loade on the Severn Valley Railway on 9 August 1980. Locomotive no. 4930 Hagley Hall *spent several years in a scrapyard before restoration, and gets extended mention in chapter five.*

PLATFORM
1
BRIDGNORTH
4930

CHAPTER 2

THE HISTORICAL OUTLINE

Origins

It is a popular misconception among those who read only railway history that the world began in 1830. That was the year when the Liverpool & Manchester Railway was opened. On further consideration they may perhaps go back as far as 1825 and the opening of the Stockton & Darlington.

But these dates are by no means the beginnings of railways: they are those at which the steam locomotive came into its own. By then, the Industrial Revolution was already far advanced, and there had been railways of various sorts for a couple of centuries, relying on horses, gravity and manpower.

Horse railways in Britain, at their greatest extent, had a total route mileage of some 1,500 miles; but their individual lengths were short, usually a few miles only, and they were widespread. Their history has been little recorded. C. F. Dendy Marshall, mentioned earlier, gathered together all he could. Bertram Baxter, in *Stone Blocks and Iron Rails* (1966) gave a detailed historical and topographical description of, principally, those lines which, from the 1760s onwards, were laid with rails of iron. Earlier lines had rails of wood, and these, their origins, extent, scope and significance, have been ably treated in Dr M. J. T. Lewis's scholarly *Early Wooden Railways*, published in 1970.

Waggonways of wood

So familiar is the concept of iron and steel rails to railway-minded people, and so difficult is it for them to associate the term 'rail' with anything else, that it is worth noting that its use in connection with wood or timber survives in everyday speech in terms such as 'a post-and-rails fence'.

Railways originated on the Continent of Europe. Roman roads included rutways which were probably, in part, of deliberate construction, and these existed in Britain and elsewhere in the Roman Empire. After the collapse of that empire they went out of use. Today's railways are descended from wooden railways constructed underground in the mines of central Europe during the early sixteenth century, and possibly earlier still. They may have been first used in England by German miners in the Lake District late in the sixteenth century.

The first wooden railway built on the surface in Britain was completed in 1604: two miles long, it ran from the coalfield of Wollaton, west of Nottingham, to a point near that town where it was convenient for coal to be sold. Roads in the district were in bad repair. The railway does not seem to have lasted for many years, as the coal pits were unprofitable. In 1605, however, a similar line was built at Broseley in Shropshire, and Huntingdon Beaumont, who had built the Wollaton line, soon afterwards constructed three others in Northumberland.

All these early lines were connected with coal mines and it was in North East England that such railways first became commonplace. Wood fuel was becoming scarce in London and Londoners turned to coal brought by sea from the North East. Wooden railways connected coal mines with the nearest navigable water—usually the River Tyne or the River Wear. Nevertheless, because of the Civil War and the unsettled times associated with it, it was only towards the end of the seventeenth century that wooden railways were built to any great extent: by the end of the century, there were probably, in total, more than forty miles in use.

In the North East these lines were called waggonways. According to Lewis, the term 'railway' is first recorded in 1681, and 'railroad' in 1702. 'Tramroad' later familiar, is dated by Baxter no earlier than 1790.

Wooden railways were being built in Shropshire as well as in the North East, and by about 1700 the idea was spreading farther afield. In South Wales, for instance, the first line was built near Neath in 1697, and in Scotland the Tranent-Cockenzie line was built in 1722. As the use of waggonways spread, so the skill with which they were constructed increased. Shallow cuttings and embankments on early lines were succeeded by larger earthworks on later ones, notably the Tanfield Waggonway, which ran south east from the Tyne near Gateshead and was opened between 1725 and 1738. Where possible, waggonways were laid out so that loaded waggons could descend gentle slopes by gravity, to riverside staithe or harbour, and horses were used to pull empties uphill.

The Tanfield line had to cross a watershed and therefore necessitated extensive civil engineering works to make horse-haulage uphill as easy as possible.

One of the earliest wooden railways not connected with coal mining was built in 1731 for Ralph Allen, postmaster of Bath, to connect his stone quarries at Combe Down with the River Avon. It is also one of the earliest for which a precise description of its equipment survives. It had rails of oak and descended 500 feet in $1\frac{1}{2}$ miles (which included some sections level or nearly so). Its 'carriages' were minutely described by J. T. Desaguliers in 1734 in *A Course of Experimental Philosophy* (Allen's name appears in the list of subscribers to the book). Desaguliers's illustrations are reproduced here as illustrations numbers 2/1 and 2/2. Waggons descended by gravity, and were drawn uphill, or along the 'plain', by two horses. The line was dismantled after Allen's death in 1764.

The track gauge of Allen's line was 3 ft. 9 in. between the rails, and in this it probably followed Shropshire practice. Narrow gauges were employed there, where mine adits emerging on hillsides were level enough for the same narrow track used within the mine to continue on the surface to the bank of the River Severn. In the North East, track gauges between 4 ft. and 5 ft. were used on the surface, and are the forerunners of the standard railway gauge of 4 ft. $8\frac{1}{2}$ in.

Primitive though it may sound to us today, the typical Newcastle waggonway was no ramshackle affair but, for its period, a highly developed example of engineering. After the trackbed had been formed, transverse sleepers (the term is contemporary) some 6 feet long and 4 to 8 inches diameter were laid at intervals of 2 to 3 feet. On these were laid rails of timber, sawn precisely to 4 or 5 inches square and about 6 feet long, secured to the sleepers by wooden pegs. To make worn rails easy to replace, the technique evolved of pegging a second set of rails on top of the first. The whole track was well ballasted, over the sleepers, and superannuated workmen were employed to keep clear grooves in the ballast, along the inner edges of the rails, for the flanges of the wheels. They also sprinkled ashes on the rails in steep places to prevent their becoming so slippery that waggons went out of control. Operation and maintenance of waggonways were a skilled business, and new ones were opened with ceremony: Lewis mentions that when a new waggonway was opened it was customary for the first waggon down it to be lined with tin and filled with punch, so that en route those concerned might celebrate.

The Newcastle waggon or chaldron waggon had four flanged wheels of wood or, later, cast iron, and a pivoted wooden brake lever called a convoy which bore direct on one of the wheels and was applied, down long gradients, by the weight of a man sitting on its end. The shape of the waggon body became distinctive, with some or all sides and ends splayed outwards from the floor. This contained a trapdoor: when a laden waggon arrived at a staithe it was positioned directly over a chute leading to the hold of a waiting ship or barge, and the trapdoor opened to deliver coal direct. Sloping sides to the waggon meant that no coal was left behind. Until the 1790s it was usual for there to be one man and one horse for each waggon, the horse walking behind down gradients where the waggon ran by gravity.

Where a steep slope on the route of a waggonway could not be avoided, a rope-operated, double-tracked, inclined plane was used, laden descending waggons more than counterbalancing empty ones ascending. The first such inclined plane in Britain may have been installed in 1755 on a branch of Ralph Allen's railway.

At first, wooden railways were built on the land of the proprietor or, by permissive way-leaves, over the land of others. In 1758 Charles Brandling, wishing to lay a waggonway to Leeds from his colliery at Middleton, obtained an Act of Parliament to confirm his agreements with other landowners. So Brandling's waggonway became the first railway established by Act of Parliament, an Act which was repealed only in 1978.

In the nineteenth century the Act of Parliament was to become the usual way to incorporate a company to build a railway, but for the time being, the late eighteenth century, Parliamentary involvement in construction of railways came through Acts to authorise construction of canals. The seventy years or so from 1760 onwards were the canal era. During the previous two centuries rivers had been steadily improved for navigation; now a network of artificial canals was built, linking navigable rivers to each other and with mining and manufacturing districts and agricultural areas. A canal was more economic to operate than a horse railway, for a single horse could haul a much greater load in a boat or barge than in a waggon or waggons. But it was more expensive to construct, particularly in hilly districts, and many horse railways were authorised by canal Acts to be built as feeders to canals, or as temporary links in their routes pending completion of difficult engineering works such as tunnels or aqueducts. Throughout their era, horse railways and waggonways, though essential, remained secondary in importance to transport by water—by sea, river and canal.

Iron rails

The growth of railways during the canal era was much assisted by the introduction of iron rails. These were first cast in 1767 at Coalbrookdale, Shropshire; wooden railways had been used there since 1750. The iron rails were of rectangular cross-section, 4 inches wide and $1\frac{1}{4}$ inches thick, and they were pegged on top of wooden rails in place of upper rails of wood. By 1785 there were twenty miles of iron railways serving the Coalbrookdale mines and furnaces, and similar

Fig. 2.
Fig. 3
Fig. 1.
Fig. 4.
Fig. 5.

2/1 (opposite) 2/2 (right) Carriages (sic) of Ralph Allen's wooden waggonway at Bath, as illustrated by J. T. Desaguliers in 1734. The design is remarkably advanced for the period. Wheels were of cast iron, one of the earliest instances in which the material was used for this purpose, and braking arrangements were elaborate, as was to be expected on a line where waggons carrying four tons of stone ran by gravity down a line with an average gradient steeper than 1 in 16. The two rear wheels (in the downhill direction) were braked by blocks attached to levers, seen in the side elevation, which were themselves held down by chains attached to pulleys (H) rotated by handspike-operated winch (h) and ratchet (i, r) arrangements. The front wheels could be locked by retractable bars projected between the spokes; these were operated by rods from levers (1) at the rear of the waggon. Wheels could revolve, or not, independently of one another, and the sides were dismountable. The figures 7, 8 and 9 in illustration 2/2 are extraneous, as are, obviously, figs 1, 2 and 3 in illustration 2/1.

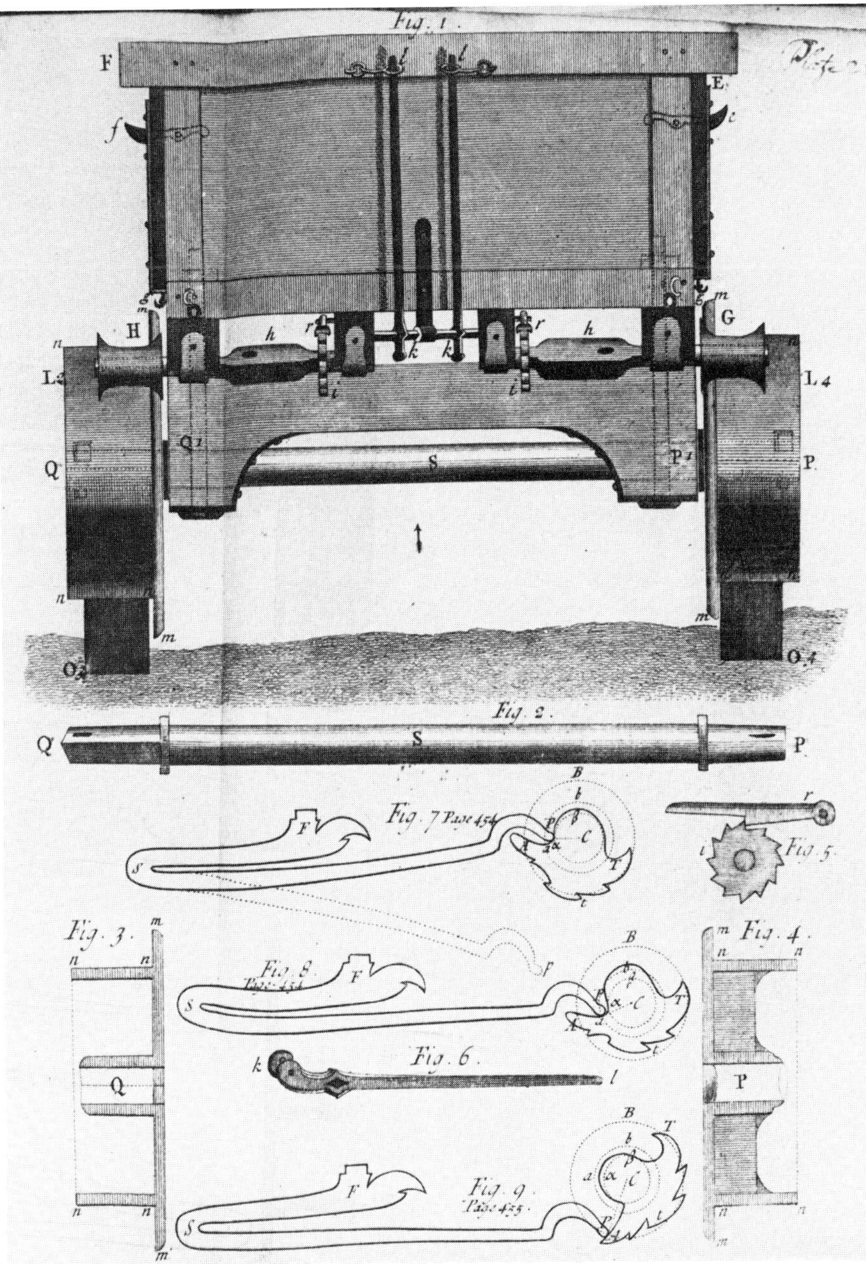

railways elsewhere in the district. When the Trent & Mersey Canal extended its Caldon branch by a three-and-a-half mile railway from Froghall to Caldon Low, Staffordshire, this form of construction was used. Branch canal and railway were together authorised by Act of Parliament in 1776 and opened in 1778; the railway connected the canal terminus at Froghall with limestone quarries. This was the first time an iron railway was authorised by Parliament.

Rails entirely of cast iron came into general use at the beginning of the 1790s; precisely when and where they originated remains a subject of controversy. Of necessity they were by modern standards very short, generally from 3 to 4 feet long; each joint rested on a sleeper. Two main types of iron rails were introduced. One was the edge rail, used with flanged wheels, and apparently first laid in South Wales and on the Loughborough-to-Nanpantan section of the Leicester Navigation's rail-and-canal Forest Line opened in 1794. On the latter line for the first time the rails were of the pattern graphically called 'fish-belly': the lower edge described a longitudinal curve to give strength where it was most needed.

The other type of cast iron rail was the L-section tramplate or plate rail, used with plain wheels. This type was extensively promoted by engineer Benjamin Outram. The term 'plateway' describes railways laid with rails of this type, and so, properly speaking, does the term 'tramroad' (which may or may not be linked with the name Outram), although the latter term, and also 'tramway', are frequently used to describe all railways of this period. Much later, 'tramway' came to be associated with passenger-carrying street tramways, at first horsedrawn or steam, then electric.

The use of stone block sleepers instead of wooden ones, and of cast iron chairs to locate the rails upon them, followed later in the same decade. Stone blocks were more substantial than wood and did not decay, but generally they were not long enough to tie two lines of rails to gauge, as did wooden sleepers, and a separate row of blocks supported each line of rails.

In 1797, for the first time, a Tyneside wooden waggonway was rebuilt with iron rails, the first of many so treated in subsequent years. At their peak, around 1800, there were probably about 150 route miles of wooden railways on Tyneside, and as many again elsewhere. These were mileages soon to be greatly exceeded by that of iron horse-railways. In South Wales alone there was an extensive network. These lines began as feeders to the canals built in the South Wales valleys at this period, and ended by far exceeding them in extent, stretching eventually as far north as Hereford and Kington. The first were built as edge railways, then converted to (and later ones built as) plateways, probably as a result of the activities of Outram. In the North of England, with its long experience of flanged wheels, edge railways remained general.

Other important lines constructed during this period include the Peak Forest Tramway and the Penrhyn Railway. The Peak Forest line formed the upper part of the Peak Forest Canal Co.'s canal-and-rail route from Dukinfield, where it joined the Ashton Canal east of Manchester, in a south-easterly direction to limestone quarries near Doveholes. The interchange point between canal and rail was at Buxworth, and the tramway, a plateway, was completed in 1796. The Penrhyn Railway, completed in 1801 with the unusually narrow gauge of 2 ft., was to be the first of several slate quarry-to-port lines in North Wales.

The first railway companies

In the 1790s a canal was proposed from the Thames at Wandsworth to Croydon. Because water supply for this was inadequate—the canal would have drawn too much water from the River Wandle for the mills on it to operate—engineer William Jessop recommended that the entire route should be built as an iron railway instead. Jessop, a great canal engineer, also had much experience of tramroads built in connection with them. So in 1801 Parliament passed an Act authorising the line and incorporating the Surrey Iron Railway Company. No doubt at this date the use of iron rather than wooden rails was still so recent a development as to be worth emphasising in the company's name. The Surrey Iron Railway was the first railway company incorporated by Act of Parliament, and the line was the first railway, intended for public transport, which was independent of a canal.

The line was built as a plateway and opened in 1803; the same year a further Act incorporated the Croydon, Merstham & Godstone Railway, to extend the line southwards. This company—like many later railway companies—never completed its plans in full, but its line was opened in part in 1805.

Both lines had been thought of as the first links in a horse railway from London to Portsmouth. Already people were beginning to think in terms of horse railways—or even a horse railway system—very much

more extensive than those already existing. The time for this was not yet ripe, but iron railways for local transport were built in increasing numbers. Their engineering became ever more refined, and more and more lines were built as public railways. Fifteen Acts of Parliament were passed for them in the twelve years from 1802 onwards. Such lines were considered to be public highways: anyone might run a waggon on them, provided it was of suitable construction and the operator paid the appropriate tolls. One of these railways was the first public railway in Scotland, the Kilmarnock & Troon: a plateway, it was opened in 1810.

2/3 Eighteenth century waggonways in North East England used chaldron waggons of this type to convey coal from mine to riverside staithe. Where gradients permitted, waggons ran by gravity, with the driver sitting on the convoy *or brake lever and the horse following. A trap door in the floor enabled the waggon to be discharged. The artist of this picture, or more probably the engraver, has failed to understand the principle of flanged wheels on rails.*

2/4 (next page) The Church Pit, Wallsend, was drawn by T. H. Hair as late as 1839 or thereabouts, but scenes of this sort had been common in the North East for very many years previously. The chaldron waggons are typical. The one in the foreground appears to be about to be dispatched down a gravity-operated cable-worked inclined plane. It looks as though rails are still of wood, and the three rails shown would diverge into a passing loop half way down the plane.

Trevithick's steam locomotives

By the beginning of the nineteenth century, stationary steam engines had been known and used for some ninety years. The first example of Newcomen's steam pump, the first practical steam engine, had been built in 1712. Its design had been greatly improved by James Watt in the 1760s, and from it had evolved the beam engine to power machinery. By the end of the century people were attempting to adapt the steam engine to drive self-propelled vehicles.

Richard Trevithick was the first to design a workable locomotive. After building working models, he patented in 1802 a steam engine which could be used as a stationary engine, or to power a road or rail vehicle. Its principal features were a cylindrical horizontal boiler and a single horizontal cylinder let into it. The piston, propelled back and forth in the cylinder by pressure of steam, was linked by piston rod and connecting rod to a crankshaft bearing a large flywheel. In the railway version a geared drive to the wheels was added. The first locomotive was built by the Coalbrookdale Company in the same year. Very little is known about it apart from a drawing which survives in the Science Museum, London. The engine does not appear to have been successful; a fatal accident may have caused the project to be abandoned. At any rate, one feels that had successful trials taken place, there would certainly be a record of them: this is indeed the case with the next Trevithick locomotive.

This locomotive was built by the Penydarren Company, of Dowlais,

Drawn by T. H. Hair

South Wales, under Trevithick's supervision, and was tried out on the Penydarren Tramroad. This was a plateway, nine and a half miles long, completed in 1802. The locomotive ran for the first time on 13 February 1804. 'It work'd very well, and ran up hill and down with great ease' wrote Trevithick. The locomotive was tried out on several occasions but although it ran satisfactorily its weight was too great: it broke too many of the cast iron tramplates to be used regularly. The engine was subsequently used as a stationary engine.

A third Trevithick locomotive was built, about 1804, at Whinfield's foundry, Gateshead. Christopher Blackett of Wylam, Northumberland, had an option to purchase it on completion. Blackett had inherited his Wylam estate in 1800; it included a colliery, linked by the five-mile long Wylam Waggonway to the Tyne near its navigable limit at Lemington. The waggonway, of wood, had been built about 1748. When the locomotive was complete, it was tried out on a temporary track at the builder's works. It seems to have run satisfactorily but Blackett evidently then saw that a locomotive weighing over five tons would be too heavy for his wooden track, and he did not purchase it. This locomotive too was converted into a stationary engine.

Blackett did, however, relay his waggonway about 1808 as (unusually on Tyneside) a plateway, possibly with the continuing intention of using steam power. This, as we shall see, he was soon to do successfully.

In the meantime Trevithick made one further attempt to promote his locomotive, also in 1808, when he operated a locomotive hauling a carriage on a circular railway in London as a public spectacle. There was no direct result.

So the first regular application of mechanical power to railways came not through the locomotive but in a different way, through construction of steam-powered winding engines to haul waggons up inclined planes. In locations where the flow of traffic meant that loaded waggons were travelling, principally, up hill, and empty ones down, gravity-operated self-acting inclined planes were clearly impracticable. The first steam-powered inclined plane was built on Tyneside in 1809; it was followed during the next twenty years by many more.

About two years earlier there had been another innovation which passage of time was to show to have been of greater importance. This was carriage of passengers by rail, on a regular basis. Railway passenger traffic began on 25 March 1807, on the line of The Oystermouth Railway or Tram Road Company, to give it its full title. This had been incorporated by Act of Parliament in 1804, and the line probably came partly into use in 1806. It was a plateway running westwards along the coast from Swansea to Oystermouth. Passengers travelled in a horsedrawn carriage operated by a contractor.

The steam locomotive in service

The first wholly successful application of steam power to railways came in 1812, prompted by the rising cost of horse fodder during the Napoleonic wars. John Blenkinsop was viewer—manager or superintendent, that is—of Middleton Colliery, and also part-owner. In 1811 he patented, as a means of conveying coal or other articles, a rack railway, powered for preference by a steam engine. The reason for the rack was the general uncertainty among engineers of the period whether a steam locomotive with smooth wheels on a smooth rail would have sufficient adhesion to propel itself and a load, or whether the wheels would merely spin round. This doubt was not so ludicrous as it seems: consider how easily, on a wet or greasy rail, a locomotive's wheels do slip, how essential is a supply of sand to drop upon the rails. In Blenkinsop's time too, when rails were still of brittle cast iron, it was particularly important to minimise axle loads.

The Middleton Waggonway was relaid with iron edge rails which incorporated a rack to one side, and in 1812 a locomotive was built by Fenton Murray & Wood of Leeds. Detailed design was probably by Matthew Murray of that firm, which became the first to build locomotives on a commercial basis. Murray's locomotive had two vertical cylinders within the top of the boiler, and the pistons drove the rack wheels through rods and pinions. The first public trial took place on 24 June 1812 and was a complete success. The locomotive seems to have gone into service immediately and was joined in due course by three more.

These locomotives continued at work until the mid-1830s when the price of horse fodder fell and the line reverted to horse traction. Locomotives of the same type were used for shorter periods at at least two other locations.

While Blenkinsop and Murray were building their steam rack line others were tackling the adhesion problem in different ways. William Chapman patented in 1812 a locomotive carried on several wheels, some or all of which were to be mounted on a pivoting bogie or bogies. A locomotive to his patent was built and tried out on the Heaton Colliery Waggonway, near Newcastle upon Tyne. It hauled itself, and its load, along by a chain laid in the track—without conspicuous success.

And at Wylam, Christopher Blackett was initiating the series of experiments which were to lead to the first successful adhesion locomotives.

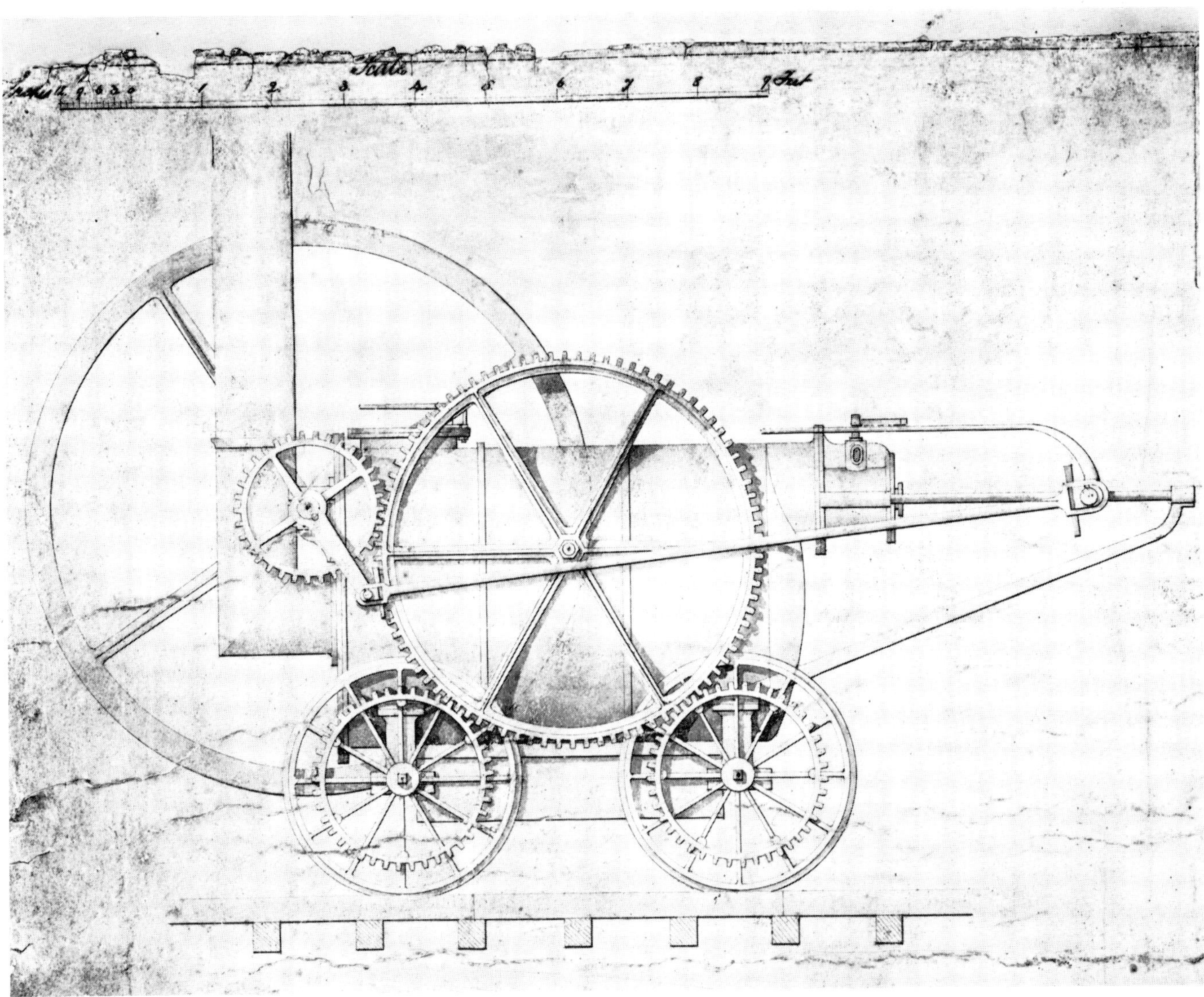

2/5 Richard Trevithick designed the first locomotives to run on rails and four were built to his designs. This is one of the original drawings, preserved in the Science Museum, of the third locomotive, which was built at Whinfield's Foundry, Gateshead in 1804–5. It was intended to run on wooden rails, which are clearly shown. The firedoor was alongside the chimney and there was a return flue furnace. No means of coupling the locomotive to a train is shown, nor is there any place for the driver to stand. It is the author's guess that, like any other waggonway horse, this iron horse was intended to be hitched to a waggon by traces, and that the driver was expected to walk beside it, and stop it to feed it from time to time. On trial, however, it proved too heavy for wooden track and was converted into a stationary engine. The overall design is similar to Trevithick's two earlier locomotives and, primitive though it now appears, it is nevertheless remarkably polished for a first attempt.

The Wylam locomotives

The rise in fodder prices had prompted Blackett also to experiment again with steam power, and in October 1812 he requested his viewer at Wylam Colliery, William Hedley, to construct a steam locomotive. In this task Hedley was assisted by Jonathan Foster, principal enginewright, and Timothy Hackworth, who later became famous as a steam locomotive engineer but at the time was aged about twenty four and held the post of foreman smith.

Hedley held the theory that, if the wheels were coupled, the weight of a locomotive alone would provide sufficient adhesion, even where smooth wheels ran on smooth rails, to haul a train of loaded waggons. To prove his theory he arranged to have built first a model, then a full-size test carriage. This was propelled by men riding on it and turning handles. On test it was loaded with various weights of iron and attached to varying numbers of waggons, and it proved Hedley's theory correct.

A locomotive was then built on the frame of the test carriage. It had a single cylinder and a flywheel and it did not work satisfactorily, for it did not generate sufficient steam. In common with other early locomotives, the fire was contained in a large horizontal tube, within the boiler, which led direct to the chimney at the opposite end to the firedoor. To increase the surface available for transmission of heat from fire to boiler water, and so generate more steam, Hedley built his next locomotive with a return-tube boiler: that is to say, the fire tube doubled back to a chimney at the same end as the firedoor. This same locomotive had two vertical cylinders outside the boiler. Piston rods extended upwards to pivotted beams, which were in turn connected by rods to a crankshaft beneath the frames, from which gears drove and also coupled the wheels.

The first locomotive of this type was put into service probably in the spring of 1814, and it was successful enough to be followed by others. Originally carried on four wheels they were soon altered, so as to spread the load on the tramplates, to run on eight; the arrangements for doing so evidently owed something to Chapman's ideas. Later still, when the Wylam Railway was relaid as an edge railway in 1830, they were converted back to run on four wheels. At least two of these locomotives ran until the 1860s and were eventually preserved: *Puffing Billy* and *Wylam Dilly*. The names were not carried when they were in service, and which was built first is not known.

George Stephenson

An interested spectator of the locomotive trials at Wylam, and friend of those carrying them out, was George Stephenson. Stephenson, whom events were to prove a natural genius, had been born on 9 June 1781 in a cottage alongside the Wylam Waggonway. His earliest memories must therefore have been of the horsedrawn waggons creaking past the door along the wooden track, and his father was fireman of the pumping engine at the colliery. The family moved in 1789,

2/6 One of Blenkinsop and Murray's rack locomotives hauls a train on the Middleton Railway. High cost of horse fodder caused by the Napoleonic wars caused introduction of locomotives of this type in 1812: the first commercially successful steam locomotives. The boiler has a single-pass furnace and the two cylinders are set upright within it along the centre line, with geared drive from connecting rods to rack pinion.

though it remained in the district, and by 1813 Stephenson was living and working at Killingworth, north east of Newcastle. In his work he had followed in his father's footsteps as a pumping engine fireman, and then rapidly overtaken him, learning to read and write in his free time at the age of eighteen, and working his way up to the appointment of enginewright at Killingworth High Pit colliery in 1812.

Here he built his first locomotive, the *Blucher*, which was completed in July 1814 to work on the Killingworth Railway. Like Blenkinsop and Murray's locomotives, it had two vertical cylinders let into the boiler, from the pistons of which rods drove a train of gears. But these drove not rack pinions but the plain flanged wheels which carried the locomotive. *Blucher* was the first successful flanged-wheel adhesion locomotive. An improved version was built the following year, in which connecting rods drove the wheels directly; these were coupled together by a chain.

Just how many locomotives George Stephenson eventually designed and built even he does not appear to have known: according to Dendy Marshall, when speaking in 1825 he said he had made about 55 engines, of which he thought 16 were locomotives. He realised early on that improvements in permanent way were needed as much as improvements in locomotives, and in 1816 patented, jointly with William Losh, an improved form of track which was installed on the Killingworth Railway. Stephenson also conducted a series of experiments in 1818 to establish the resistance to which railway vehicles were subject when in motion. From the results he became convinced, says his biographer Samuel Smiles, not only that to use steam power on rough-surfaced ordinary roads was impracticable, but also that steam railways needed to be made as level as possible by civil engineering works, as the resistance of vehicles increased markedly when the gradient steepened.

In 1819 he was invited to lay out an entirely new railway to link a colliery

which was to be sunk at Hetton-le-Hole, Co. Durham, with the River Wear at Sunderland. This, the Hetton Colliery Railway, was completed in 1822 and was about eight miles long. It was the first railway built to be worked independently of animal power, for it used steam power or gravity throughout. It was laid out in sections: the first 1½ miles from Hetton were worked by locomotives, this was followed by 1½ miles worked by fixed engines and cables, ascending to a summit about 250 feet above sea level; this in turn was followed by about 2½ miles of self-acting inclined planes, 2 miles of locomotive haulage, and a final ½-mile self-acting plane. This pattern was typical of Stephenson railways laid out over the next decade.

Another important step forward in the development of railway track took place in 1820 when John Birkinshaw patented the manufacture of rails using malleable iron passed while hot between profiled rollers. This meant that, while the top edge could be of bulbous form to provide a running surface, the length of rails could be increased to about eighteen feet. The stable track that resulted was an essential preliminary to the general introduction of locomotives.

William James

Men of vision were now thinking in terms of railways on a more and more extensive scale. Foremost among them was William James, who had been born in 1771, and was a land agent and surveyor. Being, as he was, a land agent for the nobility at this period involved a knowledge not only of agriculture but also of mines and their associated railways. James was involved with horse railways and railway projects by 1800, is said to have seen Trevithick's Penydarren locomotive at work in 1804, and by 1808 was considering formation of a General Rail-road Company. This was premature, and for a few years James's ideas for railways seem to have lain fallow while he looked after the estates of others and amassed a fortune for himself. He instigated completion of the Stratford Canal between 1812 and 1816, and its link at Stratford with the Upper Avon Navigation which he purchased in 1813. At this period he is said to have been worth £150,000 and to have had an income of £10,000 a year from land agency.

About 1819 he returned to railway schemes with a vengeance. He surveyed a line to extend the route of the Stratford Canal to Moreton-in-Marsh and proposed that this should itself be extended by way of Oxford and Thame to London: the Central Junction Railway or Tram-road, it was to be called. He met Stephenson at Killingworth and became a staunch proponent of the locomotive. He foresaw that locomotives would be developed and their speed increased from the 8 or 10 mph then usual to 20 or 30 mph, and he realised the potential of railways worked by such locomotives for carrying passengers. James surveyed, or planned, locomotive-worked railways between Liverpool and Manchester (in 1821–2), Canterbury and Whitstable, Bishop's Stortford and Cambridge (to

2/7 Dramatic appearance of a Wylam train, hissing and rumbling out of (one may assume) the dusk of a wintry Northumberland evening, is graphically depicted in Thomas Hair's etching. The scene is post-1830, when the line was converted from plateway to edge railway as shown here. The locomotive's return-tube furnace was fired from the front.

link the navigable rivers Stort and Cam) with extensions perhaps to Lynn, Lincoln and Norwich, and many other lines probable and improbable.

He completed none of his railways, although he made a start on the Stratford & Moreton and some of them were built by others, notably Stephenson. For James over-reached himself with his railway schemes, to the neglect of his other businesses; and by 1824 he was bankrupt. His son and daughter were convinced he was the victim of conspiracy. Whatever the truth, his lasting achievement was to impress the idea of long-distance steam passenger railways firmly on the public mind. And, it seems likely to the author, on George Stephenson's mind also.

The Stratford & Moreton Railway Company was incorporated by Act of Parliament in May 1821, to build a railway between the two towns of its name, with a branch to Shipston on Stour. Construction commenced the following year under John Urpeth Rastrick. Rastrick, born in 1780, was a noted engineer, a builder of bridges, and partner in the engineering firm of Foster, Rastrick & Co. of Stourbridge, and he had in due course other important contributions to make to early steam railways. In the meantime, six weeks before the Stratford & Moreton Act, Parliament had authorised another railway which, though built at the same period, was to have far greater effect on the course of history: the Stockton & Darlington.

The Stockton & Darlington Railway

The need for good transport between collieries near Bishop Auckland, Co. Durham, and the port of Stockton, on the tidal Tees, had been apparent for many years; the form which it should take—canal, canal-and-tramroad, tramroad all the way—had been equally controversial, and all three were at various times surveyed. Eventually, after a survey by South Wales tramroad engineer George Overton (who had laid out the Penydarren Tramroad among others) an Act of Parliament was passed on 19 April 1821 to incorporate the Stockton & Darlington Railway. The company was authorised to build a horse railway with a main line from the Tees at Stockton, westwards to Darlington, and then in a generally north west direction to Shildon and collieries at Witton Park;

2/8 The Hetton Colliery Railway, opened in 1822, was George Stephenson's first independent commission, and the first railway built with the intention that no animal power should be used: it employed a mixture of locomotives, stationary engines and gravity. Two early Stephenson locomotives are shown in this view of the colliery.

there were to be some short branches also.

Prominent among the promoters was Quaker businessman Edward Pease. George Stephenson, accompanied by Nicholas Wood, viewer of Killingworth Colliery, visited him, and convinced him that a locomotive-worked edge railway would be preferable to a horsedrawn plateway in the South Wales manner. Stephenson was asked to re-survey the route and in due course was appointed engineer.

In his survey George Stephenson was assisted by his son Robert Stephenson, then aged eighteen. The father had ensured that the son received a very much better education than he himself had had, so much so that Robert Stephenson may be said eventually to have caught up with his father, and father and son went forward together.

Some alterations to the Stockton & Darlington Railway route suggested by George Stephenson were included in a further Act of Parliament, passed in May 1823. This also included the memorable clause that the company might 'make and erect . . . loco-motive

or moveable engines' and use them on its railways. Construction of the line had already started, the first track being laid at Stockton in 1822. Malleable iron rails rails were used, carried in cast iron chairs. These were laid on wooden blocks from Stockton to Darlington, and stone blocks west of Darlington. Cheaper cast iron rails were used on some parts of the line. From Stockton to Shildon, a distance of about twenty miles, the line had no steep gradients and was suitable for horse or locomotive traction; west of Shildon, over the remaining five miles or so, it surmounted successive ranges of hills, at Brusselton and Etherley, by inclines up and down.

In 1823 George Stephenson, with Pease as one of his partners, founded the firm of Robert Stephenson & Co. in Newcastle. Intended as a specialist locomotive builder, the firm in its early years also made stationary engines and did other engineering work. Its location in Forth Street, Newcastle, was used continuously for locomotive building until about 1960.

In 1824 however, Robert Stephenson left for South America on a three-year engagement as engineer to gold and silver mines, and Timothy Hackworth, who had helped to build the Wylam locomotives, came temporarily to Newcastle to take charge of Stephenson's locomotive works. So it was under his supervision that the first two locomotives for the Stockton & Darlington were built, when the order was received the same year.

In May 1825 Hackworth agreed to come to the Stockton & Darlington Railway to be superintendent of 'the permanent and locomotive engines'. He moved to Shildon and soon

2/9 (above) 2/10 (right) Despite experiments with locomotives, horses were still the conventional motive power for railways when the Stockton & Darlington Railway was incorporated in 1821, and its share certificates were embellished with this engraving of a typical horse railway of the period. This was no doubt what the shareholders at first expected to get: what they eventually got was, as the world knows, something rather different. The certificate in full is shown in illustration no. 2.10.

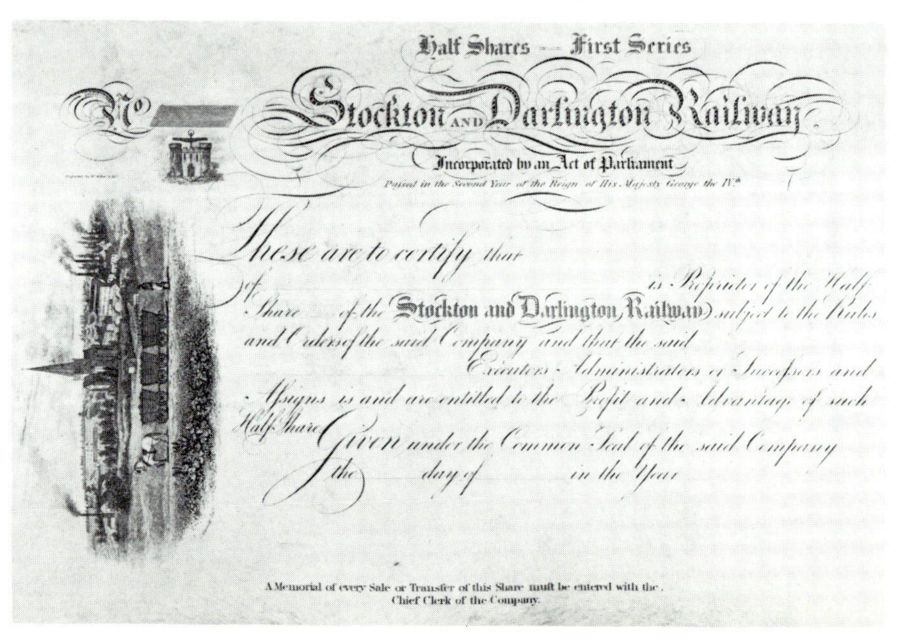

Half Shares — First Series

No

Stockton and Darlington Railway

Incorporated by an Act of Parliament

Passed in the Second Year of the Reign of His Majesty George the IVth

These are to certify that
of   is Proprietor of the Half Share   of the Stockton and Darlington Railway subject to the Rules and Orders of the said Company and that the said
Executors Administrators or Successors and Assigns is and are entitled to the Profit and Advantage of such Half Share
Given under the Common Seal of the said Company the   day of   in the Year

A Memorial of every Sale or Transfer of this Share must be entered with the Chief Clerk of the Company.

became, in effect, manager of the railway. The first locomotive, *Locomotion*, was delivered in September 1825. She was similar to Stephenson's locomotives at Killingworth and Hetton: her boiler had a single fire tube and two vertical cylinders let into the barrel in line; the four wheels were coupled by rods rather than a chain, probably at Hackworth's suggestion.

The Stockton & Darlington opened

On 27 September 1825 the Stockton & Darlington Railway was opened with much public ceremony. Descriptions of the occasion are well known. *Locomotion*, George Stephenson driving, was coupled on to a train of chaldron waggons, some laden with coal, some fitted with seats for passengers, at Shildon. Included in the train was the company's passenger coach, conveying the directors. Some of the coal waggons had originated at a colliery at the far end of the line, reaching Shildon by horse traction and inclined plane. *Locomotion* hauled this train successfully to Darlington, destination of some of the coal waggons which were detached, and then onward to Stockton. The crowds of onlookers were immense.

The Stockton & Darlington Railway was the first public railway laid out for steam traction from the start. It was also the old-style colliery-to-port waggonway at the peak of its development. To power most of its traffic, horses were used. It also used powered and self-acting inclined planes. It used gravity elsewhere too—trains were soon equipped with 'dandy carts' in which the horse might ride when the train ran down-grade by gravity. Passenger and parcel traffic started on 10 October 1825. The coach, *Experiment*, was horsedrawn; mounted on a waggon frame was a body similar to that of contemporary road coaches, except that it was double-ended so that the vehicle need not be turned: horses could be attached to either end. This first coach was operated under lease from the railway; following its success at least five others, owned by other proprietors, were put on the line in the next two years.

The company's early experiences with steam locomotives, once opening-day euphoria had worn off, were unhappy. *Locomotion* broke a wheel within a month and in 1828 the boiler exploded, killing the driver. She was rebuilt. More worrying in the long term was the general reluctance of *Locomotion*, and three other engines like her delivered within a year, to make sufficient steam. The locomotives were inadequate for a twenty-mile run, and the company seriously considered abandoning steam in favour of horses and gravity. Hackworth, however, had encountered the problem of a locomotive which would not steam previously, during Hedley's early experiments at Wylam. Taking the boiler from a fifth and even less satisfactory locomotive (not of Stephenson build), he enlarged it and installed a return fire tube.

This boiler then became the basis of the locomotive *Royal George*. She was mounted on six wheels, all coupled: this made her the first 0-6-0; the cylinders were vertical, inverted and outside the boiler, and pistons and connecting rods drove the rear wheels directly. *Royal George* entered service late in 1827 and was entirely satisfactory. Steam was retained and Hackworth developed and further improved the design in subsequent locomotives.

Railway promotion in the mid-1820s

Following the progress of the Stockton & Darlington Railway has meant jumping ahead chronologically. After the activities of William James, the mid-1820s were a time of intense activity in railway promotion. As many as sixty railways were projected during the years 1824–5. In the latter year the firm of George Stephenson & Son, Railway Engineers, was formed, with an office in Newcastle to draw up plans from surveys. Several trunk routes were considered. This again was premature: not many proposals reached the stage of Acts of Parliament, and of those that did, some were not built. Their principal effect was to cause canals to improve their often circuitous lines and to stir canal engineers to do their finest work. Among them, men such as Thomas Telford were still more skilled than their railway counterparts, and did their greatest work on, for instance, the Birmingham & Liverpool Junction and the Macclesfield Canals, which were built largely to counteract the threat of railway competition. I have discussed them in greater detail in *The Archaeology of Canals*.

During 1824–6 some sixteen railway Acts were passed, however. Some of these were for railways to be linked with canals, such as the Monkland & Kirkintilloch (1824) which was to feed the Forth & Clyde Canal with coal traffic, and the Cromford & High Peak, which was to link the Peak Forest and Cromford Canals and so complete a direct route across the Derbyshire uplands between Manchester and Nottingham. Other lines were purely railway, such as James's Canterbury & Whitstable (1825) for which Stephenson became the engineer, the Nantlle Railway in North Wales (also 1825), the Edinburgh &

Dalkeith and the Dundee & Newtyle. The Monkland & Kirkintilloch was built quickly and opened in 1826, to be operated partly by horses and partly by locomotives. In the same year there were completed the Springwell Waggonway, south of Newcastle and under the same ownership as Killingworth, which was laid out by Stephenson and incorporated a typical mixture of more or less level sections and inclined planes; and, a year after the Stockton & Darlington, the Stratford & Moreton. Ironically, although planned by James as a locomotive line, it used horses for motive power, and continued to do so for many years.

The Liverpool & Manchester Railway

In 1826, however, there was another event which was to prove of far greater importance than any of these: the incorporation of the Liverpool & Manchester Railway. Its Act was passed on 5 May 1826.

William James, backed by Liverpool merchant Joseph Sandars, had surveyed a route between Liverpool and Manchester in 1821, and surveyed a better line, with Robert Stephenson as assistant, the following year. A bill for this line, re-surveyed by George Stephenson, was rejected by Parliament in 1825, as a result of opposition by landowners and waterway proprietors, but after a further survey of a more southerly route by Charles Vignoles, the Act was obtained in 1826 and George Stephenson was appointed engineer.

One gets markedly different impressions of the state of transport between Manchester and Liverpool at this period according to whether one is reading the history of railways or that of canals. According to railway history, and I suspect that it originates from evidence given before Parliamentary committees by the railway promoters, there were then two waterway routes between Manchester and Liverpool, which were monopolistic, inefficient and slow. In fact, there were three routes, and the two principal ones, the Bridgewater Canal and the Mersey & Irwell Navigation, competed hotly against one another. So did the many independent waterway carriers. The waterways were efficient enough and, by the standards of the time, fast enough to carry traffic which, in imported cotton for instance, had increased approximately twenty-three-fold over forty years. Ownership and control of the waterways were concentrated around Manchester however, and I get the impression that it was, as much as anything, a desire of Liverpool men to get a slice of this increasing action that led to promotion of the railway.

Manchester was certainly looking for further improvements to transport routes—but not necessarily through Liverpool, where port dues on imported goods were ever a bone of contention. There was already a proposal for a ship canal to the Dee, the seed of an idea which eventually bore fruit in the 1880s as the Manchester Ship Canal. When the Liverpool & Manchester Railway eventually opened, canal protagonists were to a large extent vindicated when the railway failed, initially, to capture more than one-third of the goods traffic between its termini. It was fortunate indeed for the investors of Liverpool that, during the period when the railway was being built, locomotive technology advanced sufficiently for the L & M steam trains to take the passenger traffic from the roads. From that unexpected success the Liverpool party went on to be prominent in railway promotion elsewhere.

The Liverpool & Manchester Railway was built under the direction of George Stephenson. Thomas Telford, inspecting it on behalf of the Government in response to a request for financial aid, considered the works very ill-organised by comparison with the system of large scale contracting under chief and resident engineers which he had originated for canals and roads. With self-taught Stephenson ever quick to learn (and, regrettably, ever reluctant to give credit to sources of learning), such methods were adopted for subsequent railways and it was soon forgotten that they had an earlier origin. Similarly, at Rainhill a main road was carried over the railway on a skew bridge, which was described in T. T. Bury's 1831 account of the line as 'being constructed upon a new principle'. Perhaps it was this that led recent historians to suppose that it might have been the first stone skew bridge. The principle was new, but no newer in England than 1797, when the first skew canal bridges were built, and by the 1820s they were not rare.

By any standard, though, the Liverpool & Manchester Railway was a remarkable engineering achievement, with its crossing of the notoriously unstable peat bog of Chat Moss, its nine-arched viaduct across the Sankey Valley, its deep and two-mile long rock cutting at Olive Mount, and its approach to the docks at Liverpool through an inclined, cable-worked, tunnel over a mile long. By such extensive engineering works a main line was achieved which, outside Liverpool, had no gradient steeper than 1 in 880, except for two $1\frac{1}{2}$-mile inclined planes of 1 in 96. The original track comprised 35 lb/yard fish-bellied rails in 15 foot lengths, carried for part of the route on stone blocks and elsewhere on wooden sleepers. The railway was laid with double track.

The Bolton & Leigh Railway

Even while the Liverpool & Manchester Railway was under construction, another railway was opened which was to connect with it. This was the Bolton & Leigh Railway, incorporated in 1825 to link Bolton with the Leeds & Liverpool Canal at Leigh. It was opened in 1828 and the following year the Kenyon & Leigh Junction Railway was incorporated to extend the line to meet the Liverpool & Manchester at Kenyon Junction. Engineer of the Bolton & Leigh was George Stephenson, and its first locomotive was supplied for the opening by Robert Stephenson & Co. Robert Stephenson himself had returned from America at the end of 1827, assumed control of the works, and started rapidly to develop and improve locomotive design. The Bolton & Leigh locomotive, *Lancashire Witch*, was the first of several Stephenson locomotives which had the cylinders not vertical but inclined at about forty five degrees, with direct drive to the wheels. This enabled her to be, probably, the first locomotive with steel springs on all wheels. To encourage her to steam she had twin parallel furnace tubes and eccentric-driven bellows.

Rainhill

At this period, nevertheless, the future of the locomotive was still far from certain. So was the type of motive power to be used on the Liverpool & Manchester. The directors realised they would have too much traffic to work it with horses, but were unsure whether to use stationary engines or locomotives. They dispatched engineers J. U. Rastrick and J. Walker to North East England as a deputation to examine the railways there, and this deputation reported in favour of the proven technique of cable-haulage with, on the L & M, stationary engines at one-and-a-half mile intervals.

Then, to establish whether or what sort of locomotives might be satisfactory, the L & M board decided to hold a competition—for a prize of £500—for a locomotive which would be a decided improvement on those then in use. This competition took the form of the Rainhill Trials, held during October 1829. Before judges J. U. Rastrick, Nicholas Wood and John Kennedy (and a collossal concourse of spectators) each competing locomotive, hauling a load of three times its own weight, was expected to run twenty times up and down the completed track on the $1\frac{3}{4}$-mile Rainhill level between the two inclines, at an average speed of at least 10 mph. This was equivalent to a return trip between Liverpool and Manchester. Locomotive weight was restricted to six tons to minimise wear and tear on the track which was, by later standards, very light.

It seemed likely at one stage that there would be ten or more competing locomotives, but only five arrived at Rainhill and of these two were withdrawn. These were *Cycloped*, which was powered by horses walking on a sort of treadmill, and *Perseverance*, which had been damaged en route to Rainhill and was, after repairs, too slow, and unable to run continuously for long enough. This left the field open to three: *Sans Pareil*, *Novelty* and *Rocket*.

Sans Pareil was built by Timothy Hackworth and was, in effect, a lighter version of *Royal George*, carried on four wheels only, all coupled. Nevertheless she was the heaviest entrant (in fact over-weight, but allowed to compete) and she had the heaviest load to haul. After a promising start she suffered a cracked cylinder. That the cylinder had been cast by Robert Stephenson & Co., builder of *Rocket*, did nothing to promote a spirit of harmony!

Novelty was built by John Braithwaite and John Ericsson of London, and was the popular favourite: the neatest, lightest and, on test, the fastest entrant. Her design was unusual but, in the context of the competition, effective. Her boiler had, in side elevation, the shape of a T laid on its side: ⊢. The fire was at the lowest part, and hot gases were directed through a tube within the horizontal part of the boiler, which was of small diameter. This tube turned back on itself twice so that gases traversed the length of the boiler three times before emerging into a vertical exhaust pipe. Bellows produced an inadequate forced draught.

That *Novelty* did not complete the trials was due, however, to hasty design and construction—she had been built in six weeks and had not been tried out before arriving at Liverpool. In use the water pipe from feed pump to boiler proved inadequate, and the water level in the boiler fell below that of the boiler tube which became overheated and was damaged. To reach it for repairs it was necessary partially to dismantle the boiler, and in re-assembly steam-tight joints were made with a cement which normally took a week to harden. Because of the competition, the locomotive was steamed within twelve hours. The inevitable result was that, while *Novelty* was running at fifteen mph towards the end of her second return trip up and down the course, the joints started to blow so badly that it was impossible for her to continue.

So the winner of the Rainhill Trials was, as every schoolboy knows, *Rocket*, the boiler of which became the prototype for every conventional steam locomotive built subsequently. *Rocket*, entered by Robert Stephenson, was built by him at Newcastle for a partnership comprising himself, his father and Henry Booth, who was secretary and treasurer of the Liverpool & Manchester company. It was Booth who had earlier hit on the solution to the problem of designing a boiler to produce sufficient steam for a locomotive: to increase the heating

These were the contestants in the Rainhill Trials, as depicted by the contemporary Mechanic's Magazine.

2/11 (above) Rocket, *entered by George and Robert Stephenson and Henry Booth, incorporated Booth's idea for a multi-tubular boiler. It was this feature, coupled with reliability consequent on the Stephensons' long experience of constructing and operating steam locomotives, that enabled* Rocket *to win. Robert Stephenson was at this date developing locomotive design rapidly; he had moved the cylinders from their traditional vertical position to one inclined at thirty-five degrees, and was soon to make them almost horizontal.* Rocket *was in due course altered to match later locomotives.*

2/12 (opposite above) Sans Pareil, *built by Timothy Hackworth was based on Wylam and Shildon ideas. The design includes a return-tube boiler, and steam was exhausted up the chimney by a blast pipe to draw the fire as fiercely as possible. Cylinders are vertical, like those of earlier locomotives, but they are inverted for the pistons to drive the rear pair of wheels directly by connecting rods. This, however, effectively prevented springs being used to carry the locomotive.*

2/13 (opposite below) Novelty *was, at the start of the trials, the popular favourite. She was built and entered by Braithwaite and Ericsson and the design was based on contemporary road steam carriage ideas. The vertical component of the boiler is clear and Braithwaite (or Ericsson) is feeding coke into it; the small-diameter horizontal part of the boiler runs the length of the locomotive beneath the footplate. Drive from the vertical cylinders was via bell cranks and connecting rods to the left-hand pair of wheels. Problems resulting from necessarily hasty construction and lack of trial runs led to* Novelty*'s failure at Rainhill, though in any event it seems unlikely that, with draught induced by bellows, she would ever have produced adequate steam. As a vehicle, though, she looks likely to have punished the L & M's light track far less than either of the other two competitors.*

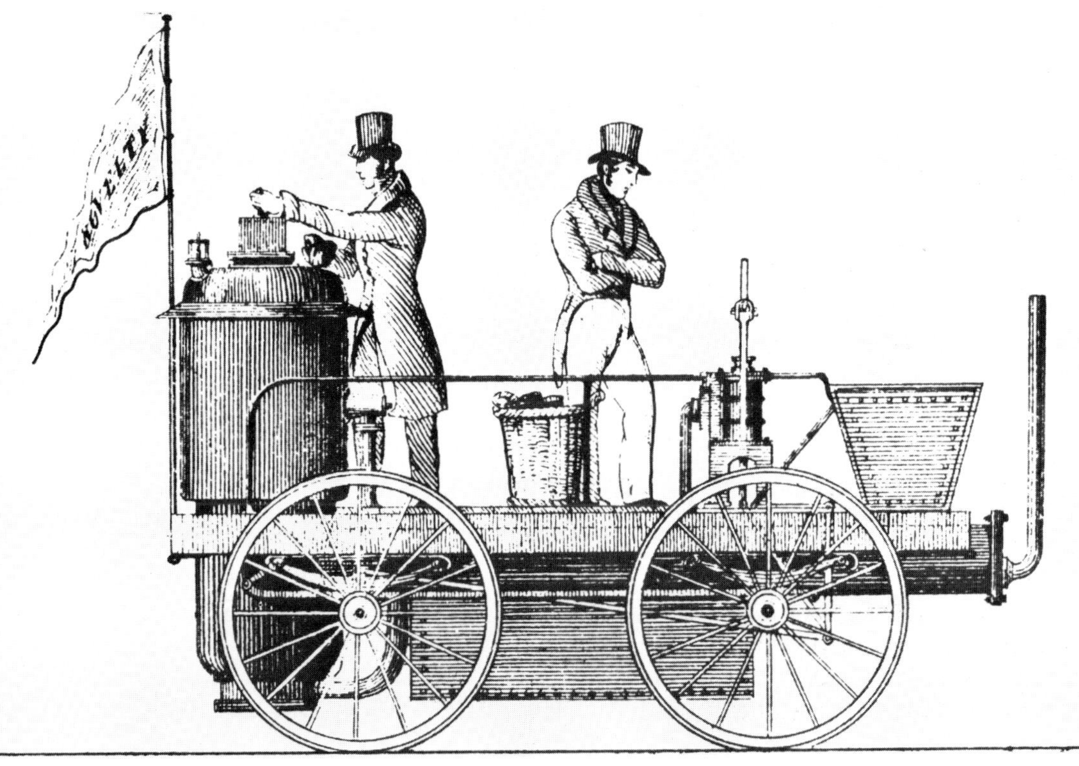

Old names live on: this is London Transport's South Kensington station in 1979. The Metropolitan Railway and the District Railway were absorbed by the London Passenger Transport Board in 1933, but their names still appear. The history of railways in Britain was one of repeated amalgamations of small railway companies into larger ones (or, in this instance, the LPTB) culminating in nationalisation in 1948. Notices and signs bearing the names of former companies were often painted out or removed, but despite this so many remain in existence that to find them is not difficult.

During the late 1950s, there was a strong body of opinion that railways should be converted into roads. Despite closure of an immense mileage of railways during the 1960s however, very few railways in fact proved suitable for conversion. One that did was the approach to Princes Street station, Edinburgh. This was closed in 1965 and the railway was subsequently converted into West Approach Road, seen here at grid reference NT 238726. The main line passed beneath the photographer; cars bearing right are heading for the trackbed of the Leith branch.

Steam trains still run regular services on preserved railways such as the Worth Valley, from Keighley to Oxenhope in West Yorkshire. This is operated almost entirely by volunteers. Here, a train is arriving at Haworth station on 3 May 1980; the locomotive is one of the few surviving examples of the many 0–6–0 pannier tanks of the former Great Western Railway. She is maintained, however, in the maroon livery used by London Transport for steam locomotives, for she was sold by British Rail to London Transport and used for some years to work maintenance trains on the Underground at night when electricity is switched off.

surface by replacing a single 12 in. diameter fire tube made of $\frac{1}{2}$ in. thick iron by a multiplicity of tubes of 2 or 3 in. diameter made of $\frac{1}{16}$ in. thick copper. This was the principle of *Rocket*'s boiler, with the fire contained in a water-and-steam jacketed firebox to the rear of the barrel. Her cylinders drove on the front pair of wheels and were steeply inclined towards the rear; the back wheels were carrying-wheels only, making the locomotive a 0-2-2. During the Rainhill Trials, *Rocket* alone among the competitors did all that was asked of her, and a great deal more.

In winning the Rainhill Trials, *Rocket* decisively proved that it was preferable to power the L & MR with locomotives rather than stationary engines. The wider implications of the performances of *Rocket* and *Novelty* were not lost on the public either. During the trials, both the locomotives achieved speeds over 30 mph and ran regularly between 20 and 30 mph. In a world where locomotives normally ran at 8 or 10 mph, and horsedrawn road coaches averaged about the same speed, this was revolutionary. Coaches, too, had only achieved that sort of speed during the previous few years, as a consequence of extensive road improvements and increasingly complex organisation (for a scheduled coach service, a fresh team of four horses had to be provided promptly at the end of each stage of about ten miles throughout the route).

Now it appeared that Liverpool and Manchester, half-a-day's journey apart, were going to be separated by only a little over one hour. The three- or four-day journey from Edinburgh to London could be reduced by steam locomotives, pointed out *The Scotsman* newspaper, to one of twenty hours. That would put Edinburgh in the same position, relative to London, as Leicester and Birmingham were with horse transport. The effect would be comparable anywhere a steam railway was built.

And it happened like that, as steam railways were built over Britain during the next thirty years. This sudden surge in the speed of travel, with corresponding reduction in journey times, was one of the most marked changes in the history of transport, and indeed of mankind.

Railways opened in 1830

Towards the end of the 1820s, two other railways as well as the L & M were approaching completion. The Canterbury & Whitstable was opened first, on 3 May 1830. Most of the six miles from Canterbury to Whitstable were laid out as cable-operated inclined planes, but, to operate over one and a quarter miles of level track at the Whitstable end, Robert Stephenson & Co. supplied the locomotive *Invicta*. Fare-paying passengers were carried on the C & W from the first, and so to *Invicta* fell the distinction of being the first steam locomotive to haul regular passenger trains.

The first fifteen-and-a-half mile section of the Cromford & High Peak Railway was opened soon afterwards, on 29 May, and the remainder of it in July of the following year. The C & HP used a mixture of inclined planes and horse traction and by the time it was completed must already have been starting to look old-fashioned, for on 15 September, 1830 the Liverpool & Manchester Railway had been opened.

The L & MR was opened by the prime minister, the Duke of Wellington, with a grand procession of trains from Liverpool to Manchester. (The company had purchased *Rocket* and several more locomotives like her.) The day was marred, however, by the tragic fatal accident to William Huskisson.

Huskisson was a Liverpool Member of Parliament and had helped the company to obtain its Act. L. T. C. Rolt in *George and Robert Stephenson* suggests that the presence of the Duke of Wellington was to some extent a political contrivance, designed to effect a reconciliation between the two men, for they led differing factions of the Tory party between which reconciliation was badly needed if it was not to be defeated by the Whigs. When the ducal train stopped at Parkside, approximate half-way point, to take water, Huskisson and other passengers got out, although they had been requested not to. The duke had just beckoned to Huskisson, who responded, and it seemed that the hoped-for reconciliation was about to take place, when *Rocket* and train approached on the other track. In the confusion which ensued, Huskisson was run down: he died the same evening.

Public passenger trains started the following day; goods trains did not commence until December. As I have already mentioned, it was for passenger traffic that the L & MR had its unexpected but great success. George Stephenson, writing in September 1831 to a potential investor in the Leicester & Swannington Railway, stated that during several weeks that summer the L & MR had carried upwards of 15,000 passengers and had occasionally taken more than 3,000 in a day. Since the line opened, 300,000 passengers had been carried with only one fatal accident.

Liverpool & Manchester Railway trains were controlled by railway 'policemen' giving hand signals. The first fixed signals, vertically pivoted boards-and-lamps, were introduced on the L & MR in 1834. They were held at right angles to the track, to indicate 'danger', for five minutes after the passage of a train, and then pivoted to 'clear': the time interval system.

Locomotives develop

The L & MR's Stephenson locomotive *Northumbrian*, an enlarged version of *Rocket* with the cylinders almost horizontal, had the firebox incorporated into the boiler for the first time and had a smokebox at the front, to produce what became the conventional locomotive boiler. Then, late in 1830, Robert Stephenson & Co. built *Planet* for the L & MR. Cylinders had been moved forward and located, horizontal, beneath the smokebox, which made the locomotive ride smoothly: the steam locomotive had achieved the layout which was to remain basic as long as steam locomotives were built.

In *Planet* the pistons drove the rear axle: she was a 2-2-0. For goods traffic a 0-4-0 version was introduced, with coupled wheels. Then, because four-wheeled engines were hard on the L & MR's light track, on later engines to spread the load a pair of trailing wheels was added, 2-2-2 or 0-4-2.

Meanwhile, on the Stockton & Darlington, Timothy Hackworth was continuing to develop his design of heavy goods locomotive, and locomotives of this type were built until the mid-1840s. Steam had taken over main line work on the S & D from horses by 1833, though horses were still being used on branch lines in the 1850s.

Local railways in the 1830s

From the 1830s onwards the Stockton & Darlington Railway was extended by means of separate companies incorporated for the purpose. Elsewhere, the Newcastle & Carlisle Railway had been incorporated in 1829. Originally intended as a horse railway, with a route as extensive as seventy eight and a half miles, it was opened, with steam, by stages from 1835 onwards. The first public railway in Ireland, the Dublin & Kingstown, was incorporated in 1831, though not wholly opened until 1840. Two short lines, the Warrington & Newton and Wigan Branch Railways, were opened in 1831 and 1832 respectively: at first, in effect, branches of the Liverpool & Manchester, they later became components of the West Coast main line from London to Scotland. The Dundee & Newtyle, Glasgow & Garnkirk and Edinburgh & Dalkeith Railways were all opened in 1831, the Leicester & Swannington in 1832–3. Here, for the first time, some Stephenson locomotives had all six wheels coupled. The Stephenson locomotive, for goods, had caught up with the Hackworth type, and these 0-6-0s were the forerunners of the type which became the standard British goods locomotive for a century. In the extreme South West, the Bodmin & Wadebridge Railway was opened in 1834.

Some horse railways were opened remarkably late—the Whitby & Pickering, for instance, and the Festiniog, both in 1836. The latter, like the Penrhyn Railway, was of very narrow gauge, less than 2 ft. But mostly, waggonways and tramroads were starting to be upgraded into steam railways. This often meant re-alignment to avoid sharp curves and weight-restricting bridges. In many places traces of early alignments can still be seen close to later ones. The Tanfield Waggonway was converted into an iron railway during 1837–9 and became a branch of the North Eastern Railway in 1854; the last wooden railways in North East England were superseded in the mid-1840s, though the term 'waggonway', to describe a colliery-owned mineral railway, lasted much longer. Some horse railways simply closed—the Surrey Iron Railway, for instance, although it was sold to the London & Brighton Railway, never saw much commercial success and was abandoned in 1846. Meanwhile the steam railway had first come to London in the form of the London & Greenwich Railway, opened between 1836 and 1838.

The first trunk railways

The 1830s and early 1840s were above all the era when the first trunk railways were built and opened. The success of the Liverpool & Manchester Railway, the first to link two great commercial centres, prompted their building and in particular the revival of earlier ideas for a line southwards, to link Liverpool and Manchester with Birmingham and indeed London.

After lengthy surveys and long and bitter Parliamentary battles, there were passed on the same day, 6 May 1833, Acts of Parliament for the London & Birmingham Railway and the Grand Junction Railway. The London & Birmingham was to link the places of its name; the Grand Junction to run from Birmingham to Warrington, where it would make an end-on junction with the little Warrington & Newton and so gain access to Liverpool and Manchester. Engineer of the London & Birmingham was Robert Stephenson, who laid out a line which had a ruling gradient no steeper than 1 in 300, apart from a cable-worked incline out of the Euston terminus. On the Grand Junction the engineer was, during surveys and the early stages of construction, George Stephenson. Under him were J. U. Rastrick on the southern part of the line and Joseph Locke on the northern. Locke had been Stephenson's pupil and devoted assistant on the Liverpool & Manchester Railway and elsewhere, but over the Grand Junction there was an awkward rift between them which

Horsedrawn chaldron waggons on a wooden waggonway are clearly shown in this view of a Newcastle coal pit about 1800, even though the artist has had more success with his spirited horses than with the perspective of the waggons. In the right background a beam engine is draining the pit, and in the left distance a laden waggon is descending a waggonway by gravity. There is a considerable descent to the River Tyne in the distance.

Late horse railway: with very narrow gauge of under two feet, the Festiniog Railway was opened as a horse-and-gravity tramroad as late as 1836, and this print is dated 1849. The viewpoint is now the entrance to Boston Lodge works, and the scene is entirely recognisable, with William Madocks's great embankment leading to the still small town of Porthmadog in the distance. Masts of ships in the harbour can be seen. The horses have just been attached to a train, which has run down from Blaenau Ffestiniog by gravity, to haul it across the level embankment. Accurate depiction of waggon wheels has defeated the artist, and so has the colour of the slates with which they are loaded. A girl in Welsh costume is travelling in the first waggon.

(Left) Entrance to the Locomotive Engine House, Camden Town. The locomotive is one of the type designed by Edward Bury, with typical copper-capped firebox (see also illustration no. 4/20, Old Coppernob*). This is one of J. C. Bourne's famous lithographs of the London & Birmingham Railway, published in 1838–9. Bourne lived from 1814 to 1896 and was therefore only in his mid-twenties when he did his London & Birmingham drawings.*

ended with Locke becoming sole engineer-in-chief in 1835. Locke was about thirty years old at this time: a young man, like many other builders of railways.

There were firm proposals, too, for lines south and west out of London. The London & Southampton, first proposed in 1831, obtained an Act of Parliament in 1834. The Great Western, to connect London and Bristol, reached that stage in 1835. That flamboyant character Isambard Kingdom Brunel was its engineer: another young man (he was twenty seven when appointed in 1833 to do the surveys) and probably the most brilliant of all nineteenth-century engineers. As is well known, it was at his instance that the Great Western was built not to the standard gauge of the northern lines of 4 ft. 8½ in., but to the grand Brunel broad gauge of 7 ft. 0¼ in.

In 1835 also an Act of Parliament was passed for the London & Croydon Railway. This, at first in effect a branch from the London & Greenwich, was to become part of the route from London to Brighton, for the London & Brighton Railway was incorporated two years later, to extend it from Croydon to Brighton.

The year 1836 brought Acts of Parliament for constituents of a whole network of railways in central and

2/14 Platelayers and others on the Liverpool & Manchester Railway, as depicted in A. B. Clayton's lithograph of 1831. The scene is Chatsworth Street Cutting, Edge Hill, Liverpool, where trains exchanged locomotives for cable haulage through the inclined tunnels in the background. The right hand tunnel led up to Crown Street passenger station, the centre one down to Wapping goods. The Moorish Arch was an architectural fancy which concealed the winding engines for the inclines. See also the colour illustration on page 254.

(Top) The opening ceremony of a new railway was to become a familiar part of the Victorian scene. This is the opening of the Brighton-to-Shoreham branch, the first part of the London & Brighton Railway to be completed, in 1840. The main line to Brighton was opened the following year.

(Above) The four greatest railway bridges crossed respectively the Menai Strait, the Tamar Estuary, the Firth of Tay and the Firth of Forth; and of these, Robert Stephenson's Britannia Tubular Bridge across the Menai Strait was the first to be built. It was completed in 1850 for the Chester & Holyhead Railway, and was a vital link in the route between London and Dublin. Because a suspension bridge would not have been sufficiently rigid for trains to cross, Stephenson, aided by shipbuilder William Fairbairn, developed the concept of a bridge of wrought iron tubes, through which the railway passed. In the background is Telford's suspension bridge of 1826 for the Holyhead road.

The railway in Victorian England: Epsom Downs station, London Brighton & South Coast Railway, presents an animated scene on Derby Day, 1878. The royal train has just arrived at the nearest platform with the Prince and Princess of Wales. Elsewhere, long trains have arrived behind remarkably small locomotives, which are painted in Stroudley's 'improved engine green'. One of them, a 'Terrier' 0–6–0T, appears to be called Sutton*, which identifies her as the locomotive of this class which, intended only for London suburban work, was to work an excursion throughout from Liverpool Street to Brighton a couple of years later. The preserved locomotive now called* Sutton*, however, (see illustration no. 5/6) is a different member of the same class.*

northern England. They included the Birmingham & Gloucester, the Birmingham & Derby, the Midland Counties (Derby and Nottingham to Leicester and to the London & Birmingham at Rugby), the North Midland (Derby to Leeds), the Manchester & Leeds, the York & North Midland (the last two in fact to join the North Midland at Normanton, Yorkshire) and the Great North of England, which was intended to run from York to Newcastle. An Act was also passed for the Ulster Railway, from Belfast to Portadown and Armagh.

Opening of the Grand Junction and London & Birmingham Railways

Throughout all this flurry of promotion and the feverish activity of construction which followed, not a mile of trunk railway had been opened since the Liverpool & Manchester. It was not until 1837 that the first of its successors was opened, and this was the Grand Junction Railway, opened for passengers, parcels and light goods on 4 July of that year. Heavy goods traffic did not commence until the following February. The railway was eighty two and a half miles long from Birmingham to Newton Junction (it had absorbed the little Warrington & Newton Railway) and passed through or near Wolverhampton, Stafford, Crewe (then a place of little importance) and Warrington. It included 100 underbridges, 2 tunnels, 2 aqueducts carrying canals over the line, 50 overbridges and 5 viaducts.

The track, originated and installed by Locke, was the forerunner of what was to be the usual form of track on British railways for a great many years. He used double-headed rails (ie, of vertical dumb-bell cross-section) held in chairs mounted, on part of the line, on wooden sleepers. Most of the line was on stone blocks and the wooden sleepers were originally intended as a temporary expedient to be replaced by stone. In fact they gave a more resilient ride and the eventual outcome was replacement of stone by wood.

There was little ceremony at the opening—too many of the railway's officials had sadly vivid memories of the Huskisson accident at the opening of the Liverpool & Manchester—but enormous crowds turned out to see the trains. The first left Birmingham for both Liverpool and Manchester (dividing at Newton Junction) at 7 am and with the arrival at Birmingham at 11.30 am of the first train from the North, the era of long distance train travel was well and truly launched.

The London & Birmingham Railway took longer to complete. In building it Robert Stephenson had to contend with several ranges of hills which lay across its route; these necessitated deep cuttings at Tring and Roade, and tunnels at Watford and, notoriously difficult to bore, Kilsby. The railway was opened in stages between 20 July 1837 and 17 September 1838 when it was completed.

With the London & Birmingham open there was now through rail communication between London, Birmingham, Liverpool, Wigan and Manchester, and when the North Union Railway was opened a few weeks later it extended the continuous line northwards from Wigan to Preston. The Grand Junction promoters had always thought of their line not only as a link between Liverpool and Birmingham but also, on a still grander scale, as the first component of a through route from London to Scotland and Ireland. As early as 1835 they had Locke surveying a route between Preston and Carlisle and onward to Glasgow. Between Preston and Carlisle Locke favoured an inland route, direct over the fells, in contrast to a circuitous but comparatively level coastal route proposed soon after by George Stephenson.

Locke seems to have been the first engineer to appreciate the true capabilities of steam locomotives on lines that were more steeply graded than the Stephensons' near-level routes. He too considered a level line best; but he also reasoned that if, between two places, interest on the additional cost of the necessary civil engineering works was likely to exceed added fuel costs for working trains over a more steeply graded line, then the latter was preferable. In this he may be taken as the forerunner of the second generation of railway engineers who, from the mid 1840s, built their main lines with gradients as steep as 1 in 50, and with, in consequence, fewer great engineering works than earlier lines.

Although this, and completion of a railway over the fells, were both still some years ahead, the opening of the Preston & Lancaster Railway did extend the railway system northwards as far as the latter town in 1840. The same year the Chester & Crewe Railway was opened, making Crewe a junction, which became a more important one when the Manchester & Birmingham Railway was completed from Manchester to Crewe in 1842. To the green fields of Crewe the Grand Junction then moved its locomotive works, hitherto in a cramped location beside the L & MR at Edge Hill; the new works was opened in 1843. It was not only to repair locomotives, carriages and wagons, but also to build them, and for its people to live in a new town was built.

To extend the Chester line to the port for Ireland, the Chester & Holyhead Railway was incorporated in 1844. George Stephenson had surveyed it in 1838, Robert Stephenson was appointed engineer.

Trunk lines in the South

While all this was going on, early trunk lines elsewhere were being built. The London & Southampton was opened between 1838 and 1840, and changed its name to London & South Western in 1839. Among its directors was William Chaplin, former magnate among coaching proprietors, who was astute enough to throw in his lot with the new form of transport, and so prospered. Other coaching men were ruined. Still other proprietors of an earlier form of transport, the Croydon Canal, doubtless considered themselves fortunate to sell out in 1836 to the London & Croydon Railway, which used much of the canal's course for its line. This was opened in 1839. In the long run, few canals were actually converted into railways in this way, but many were purchased by railway companies which generally attempted to stifle competition and transfer traffic, so far as possible, to rail. Canals, however, were in general far more seriously affected by railways than railways were by canals, and readers are referred to *The Archaeology of Canals* for more about the inter-relationship between the two.

The London & Croydon Railway was notable for two technical innovations, one successful, the other not. It was the first railway to install

2/15 The Liverpool & Manchester Railway attracted the attention of many contemporary publishers of lithographs. Like 2/14, this one was prepared by A. B. Clayton and is less well known than other views. Accurate depiction of a Rocket-*type locomotive (particularly the connecting rod) and of the gauge of the track has eluded the artist, but the precipitous rock sides of Olive Mount cutting look convincing.*

Railways at the turn of the century, as depicted on coloured postcards of the time. The card above probably portrays the colour of Midland Railway livery accurately, and can be compared with the colour illustrations on pages 190 and 191 which show a preserved Midland Railway locomotive and coach. The colours in the card, far right, are not accurate: when the photograph on which it is based was taken, Leek & Manifold Valley Light Railway coaches were painted primrose yellow. The publisher, however, has put them into the crimson lake livery of the operating North Staffordshire Railway in which they were later painted. The course of this railway as it appeared in 1980 is shown in illustration no. 6/32. The centre illustration shows Cannon Street station, London, with the overall roof which it then had.

(Left) In the latter days of steam: the West Coast Route passes through the gorge of the River Lune during its climb to Shap summit, and standard class 7 4–6–2 no. 70041 is hauling a Liverpool to Glasgow express in July 1965. With steam locomotives, the darker the smoke, the more the coal recently shovelled onto the fire: here it looks as though the fireman, as well as the locomotive, is working hard. (See also illustrations on page 114.)

2/16 Construction and operation of railways with inclined planes reached a peak of efficiency in the late 1820s and 1830s. This view shows a gravity-operated plane on the line from South Hetton to Seaham Harbour, opened in 1833, with descending waggons hauling up the empties.

semaphore signals, at the period when other railways tended to use arrangements of vertically pivoting discs and crossbars. It also attempted to use atmospheric traction. A large cast iron tube was laid between the rails, having a continuous slot along the top sealed by a leather flap. Trains were attached by an arm through the slot, to a piston within the tube, and the air in the tube ahead of them was exhausted by a stationary pump, so that atmospheric pressure propelled piston and train forwards. The principle was simple, the trains quick, clean and silent, but to keep the slot sealed and sufficiently air tight was beyond contemporary technology.

The route of the London & Croydon Railway was extended from Croydon to Brighton by the London & Brighton Railway, engineered by Rastrick and opened in 1841. The South Eastern Railway, branching from it at Redhill, was opened to Dover in 1844, and the London & Croydon and the London & Brighton companies amalgamated to form the London, Brighton & South Coast Railway in 1846.

The Great Western, the Midland, and the battle of the gauges

The first section of Brunel's broad gauge Great Western was opened from London to Taplow in 1838. The line was completed to Bristol in 1841 (except at the London end where a temporary terminus sufficed until Paddington station was opened in 1854). In 1841 the Bristol & Exeter Railway, extending the line further west, was already open to Bridgwater—it was completed to Exeter in 1844—and the Cheltenham & Great Western Union Railway was open from Swindon as far as Cirencester. A Great Western branch from Didcot to Oxford was opened in 1844.

By the junction at Swindon, then a small market town, was established the Great Western Railway's locomotive works. Swindon was expected to be a place at which trains would change engines, for locomotive superintendent Daniel Gooch expected to use locomotives with seven foot diameter driving wheels for the London-to-Swindon section, where the steepest gradient was 1 in 660, and to change them for smaller-wheeled locomotives over the western part of the line with its gradients of 1 in 100. In practice the seven foot wheeled locomotives were able to work right through, but the works remained at Swindon and went on to fame. The Great Western was the first railway to install electric telegraph alongside its line, in 1839; the first to use electric telegraph to signal all trains was the Norwich & Yarmouth, opened in 1844.

The Bristol & Gloucester Railway, broad gauge, was opened in 1844. At Gloucester it met the standard gauge Birmingham & Gloucester, opened in 1840, and the inconvenience of break of gauge—that is, of having to transfer passengers and goods between trains on what would otherwise have been a through route, rapidly became apparent. Before considering its consequences, however, it is necessary to consider the progress of the other railways on the south-west to north-east line, all of which, it will be remembered, had been incorporated in 1836.

First to be opened was the Nottingham-to-Derby section of the Midland Counties Railway in 1839, promptly followed by the Birmingham & Derby, which had altered its name to Birmingham & Derby Junction and its route to run northwards from Hampton-in-Arden on the London & Birmingham Railway. It opened a branch into Birmingham itself in 1842. The Midland Counties was completed down to Rugby on the L & BR in 1840, and the North Midland (Derby to Leeds) and the York & North Midland were completed the same year. The North Midland Railway had been engineered by George Stephenson, who settled close to it, near Chesterfield, for the rest of his life, and the York & North Midland had for its chairman George Hudson. Hudson, lately lord mayor of York, was a provincial politician at the start of a meteoric career in railway promotion, to which he was to bring the ethics of provincial politics. And in those pre-secret ballot days, a man's vote was regarded as a negotiable asset, to be purchased by the highest bidder.

None of these railways was very prosperous, and the B & DJ and Midland Counties were soon competing against one another in a manner which might have become ruinous. Instead, largely at the instigation of Hudson who had been made a director of the North Midland, that company, the Midland Counties and the Birmingham & Derby Junction were amalgamated by Act of Parliament in 1844 to form the Midland Railway. Preceding the formation of the London, Brighton & South Coast, this was the first large scale amalgamation of small railway companies into one large one, something which subsequently became common.

In 1845 the standard gauge Birmingham & Gloucester and the broad gauge Bristol & Gloucester agreed to amalgamate, and the Great Western then offered to take over both, with a view to extending the broad gauge to Birmingham. Now this would not have suited the Midland at all, for much of its traffic originated at the port of Bristol, and when the Great Western's offer proved too low for the shareholders of the two Gloucester companies, the Midland immediately made a better offer which was accepted. So the Birmingham & Gloucester and the Bristol & Gloucester (once a Great Western satellite) were amalgamated into the Midland, and the standard gauge in due course was extended to Bristol.

Controversy over railway gauges—the 'Battle of the Gauges'—raged during 1845 and 1846 and included a series of comparative trials of trains on the broad and 'narrow' gauges. Broad gauge trains were faster and smoother, but the 4 ft. 8½ in. gauge with its greater mileage extant (2,013 miles in 1844, compared with 223 miles of broad gauge) carried the day. In 1846 an Act of Parliament made it illegal to build railways in Great Britain to gauges other than 4 ft. 8½ in., unless they extended already existing broad gauge lines. Many Great Western lines were in due course equipped with mixed broad and standard gauge track, using three rails.

2/17 Atlas *was completed in 1834 by Robert Stephenson & Co. for the Leicester & Swannington Railway. She was a development of their Patentee type with, for the first time on a Stephenson locomotive, all six wheels coupled. Hackworth had previously adopted this arrangement in his idiosyncratic locomotives built for the Stockton & Darlington Railway, but* Atlas, *incorporating what had become the conventional locomotive boiler, with the firebox between the centre and rear pairs of wheels, was the first of what was to be the usual British goods locomotive for a century or so.*

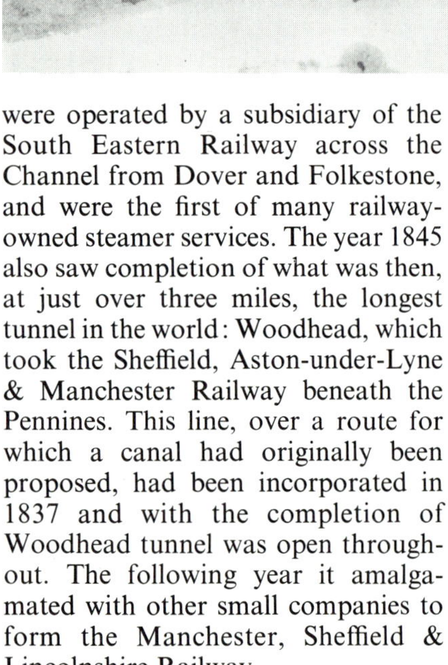

2/18 (above) 2/19 (right) J. C. Bourne's lithographs of the London & Birmingham and Great Western Railways are the most famous illustrations of these great lines when new, and one is reproduced as a colour illustration on page 55. In the Elton Collection at Ironbridge Gorge Museum there survive, however, original sketches made by Bourne on site, and these have a spontaneity which the finished lithographs lack. Here are two. In illustration 2/18, men are at work building the London & Birmingham Railway: masons, navvies, builders of bridges, a man climbing a ladder and carrying two buckets suspended from a yoke. Wash drawings of Great Western locomotives and carriages (2/19) convincingly depict the broad gauge. Why one of the locomotives lacked a chimney we shall never know.

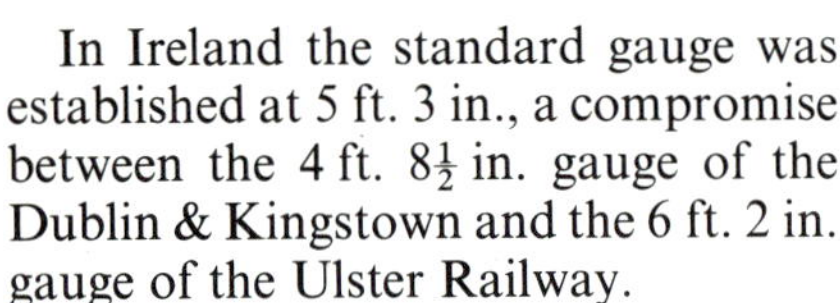

In Ireland the standard gauge was established at 5 ft. 3 in., a compromise between the 4 ft. $8\frac{1}{2}$ in. gauge of the Dublin & Kingstown and the 6 ft. 2 in. gauge of the Ulster Railway.

In the North of England, the Manchester & Leeds Railway was completed between Manchester and Normanton in 1840; it later became the principal constituent of the Lancashire & Yorkshire Railway. The Great North of England was opened between York and Darlington in 1841; it approached Darlington over a branch (which it had purchased) of the Stockton & Darlington. The line north from Darlington was built not by the GN of E but by Hudson's Newcastle & Darlington Junction Railway, and by 1844 there was through rail connection between London and Gateshead, which faces Newcastle across the Tyne.

Elsewhere the first section of the Eastern Counties Railway, from Shoreditch to Romford, was opened in 1839; it was extended to Colchester in 1844, and had already leased a branch to Bishop's Stortford, built by another company, in 1842. In South Wales the first steam railway, rather than tramroad, was the standard gauge Taff Vale Railway from Merthyr Tydfil to Cardiff; its first section was opened in 1841. Scotland's first trunk line, the Edinburgh & Glasgow, was opened in 1842.

The first railway-owned steamship services commenced in 1845. They were operated by a subsidiary of the South Eastern Railway across the Channel from Dover and Folkestone, and were the first of many railway-owned steamer services. The year 1845 also saw completion of what was then, at just over three miles, the longest tunnel in the world: Woodhead, which took the Sheffield, Aston-under-Lyne & Manchester Railway beneath the Pennines. This line, over a route for which a canal had originally been proposed, had been incorporated in 1837 and with the completion of Woodhead tunnel was open throughout. The following year it amalgamated with other small companies to form the Manchester, Sheffield & Lincolnshire Railway.

The Railway Mania

By 1842 there were over 1,600 miles of steam railway open in Britain. By the end of 1844 there were 2,235 miles. During that year's session of Parliament, railway promoters applied for bills to construct a further 900 miles of route. Not all were successful. In 1845, however, there were authorised by Parliament a further 2,170 miles of railway in Great Britain, and 646 miles in Ireland (in which country there were only 70 miles of railway already open). Far more had been proposed. In November 1845 it was estimated that capital expenditure on railways open or under construction, or earmarked for the latter, totalled £138 million; the capital cost of lines then proposed was more than £563 million.

This was the Railway Mania. Early trunk railways had been promoted largely in the provinces. Once they were seen to be successful, City financiers became interested. Then, as the market in railway shares boomed and more and more companies were formed, so did every Tom, Dick and Harry who could get in on the act. The result was a colossal speculative bubble.

Like all such bubbles it burst, early in 1846. Those who had got rich quick found themselves poor again even quicker. The reign of George Hudson, nicknamed The Railway King, whose activities had done much to inflate the bubble, did not long outlast it. In 1848 his kingdom, the railways which he controlled, extended from Bristol to Gateshead. Then the financial malpractices by which it had largely been built up came to light in one company after another, and by the middle of 1849 he had resigned all his railway chairmanships. Vilification and ruin followed, but his railways remain.

2/20 Typical of the engineering works of the early trunk lines was Defford bridge which carried the Birmingham & Gloucester Railway over the River Avon. There is an element of 'artist's impression' about this lithograph, for it is dated 1839 and, although it depicts a passenger train, the line was not opened until 1840.

The railway network expands

From the period of the Railway Mania, despite its excesses, and the years which followed, there date nevertheless many main lines which continue to be important today. For the next eighty years the railway system was to continue to expand, though at a decreasing rate, at first by construction of strategic lines, later by filling in the gaps. Railways were built not to any centrally established plan, but by companies which were, in the spirit of the Victorian age, to compete against one another in the public interest. Such a policy led to much duplication, indeed triplication, of routes between principal cities but competition did indeed work in the public interest, by keeping down fares and rates, as long as total traffic was sufficient for total capacity. Where it was not, it led to impoverishment of the companies concerned and corresponding deterioration in train services.

This was also an era when more and

more companies merged, either when large companies took over smaller ones, or when equals amalgamated to form new, large companies. A wholly comprehensive account is impracticable here: some of the most important examples are selected.

The first important long distance route to be completed was the West Coast Route from London to Scotland. In 1844 the Grand Junction Railway had subscribed to the capital of the Lancaster & Carlisle Railway, and in 1845 to the Caledonian Railway, to continue the route northwards. Engineered by Locke, they included the climbs over Shap and Beattock summits. In 1845 the Grand Junction took over the Liverpool & Manchester, and then in 1846 it amalgamated with the London & Birmingham to form the London & North Western Railway. Into this amalgamation came also the Manchester & Birmingham and Trent Valley Railways. The line of the latter, engineered by Robert Stephenson, was opened between Rugby and Stafford in 1847, giving a more direct route to the North West than that via Birmingham.

The following year, 1848, the West Coast Route, London to Glasgow and Edinburgh, was open throughout. It included the Lancaster & Carlisle Railway, opened the previous year. Locke's inland route had been preferred to George Stephenson's coastal line, but much of the region through which the latter would have passed was eventually served by the Furness Railway. Its first section near Barrow was opened in 1846. North of Carlisle the Caledonian Railway originally connected with earlier lines to gain access to Glasgow, though it had its own line to Edinburgh. In 1848 railway communication was also extended further north, by companies which later amalgamated with the Caledonian, to Stirling, Perth, Forfar and Montrose.

The new West Coast Route had an

2/21 The Newport, Abergavenny & Hereford Railway's Crumlin viaduct, completed in 1857, indicates how ambitious were the works that railway engineers could undertake by the 1850s. The viaduct lay on a branch running westwards from the NA & H main line, at right angles to the general hill-and-valley lie of the land: the attraction of its difficult route was to give the standard gauge railway system access to the South Wales coalfield. The viaduct was 1,700 feet long and 200 feet high.

unexpected accolade in the autumn of 1848 when Queen Victoria, wishing to return south from Balmoral and learning that the royal yacht was fogbound at Aberdeen, travelled by rail throughout from Montrose to Euston. Her first railway journey had been made earlier, in 1842, on the Great Western. A sadder event, in 1848, was the death of George Stephenson. Despite his fame he was not a great innovator himself: his achievement was to assimilate the ideas of others, to be the channel by which they were combined and translated into concrete form. During his lifetime he saw the waggonway develop into the trunk steam railway, and he more than anyone was responsible for that development.

The West Coast Route was extended from Montrose to Aberdeen in 1850. The same year the Chester & Holyhead Railway was opened, Robert Stephenson having spanned the formidable obstacle of the Menai Strait with his Britannia Tubular Bridge. The Chester & Holyhead was eventually incorporated into the London & North Western, as were all West Coast companies south of Carlisle. One company which might have been amalgamated with the LNWR, but was not, was the North Staffordshire Railway. It opened its first section from Stoke-on-Trent to Norton Bridge on the Grand Junction in 1848 and then built up a network of lines in and around the Potteries. Although one of them

became part of the through route from London to Manchester via Stoke, which was owned at both ends by the LNWR, the North Staffordshire maintained its independence until the grouping.

The East Coast Route from London to Scotland came into being in 1850 also. Its principal southern component, the Great Northern Railway, opened its line that year, northwards out of London (from a temporary station at Maiden Lane) to Peterborough, whence trains reached York via Boston, Retford, Doncaster and the York & North Midland Railway. The direct route via Grantham was opened two years later, as was the London terminus at King's Cross. North of York was the York, Newcastle & Berwick Railway, an amalgamation of earlier lines, which spanned the Tyne at Newcastle and the Tweed at Berwick by magnificent bridges; beyond Berwick the North British Railway ran to Edinburgh. In 1850, through trains took twelve hours.

North from Edinburgh the Edinburgh Leith & Granton Railway's line ran to Granton Harbour whence there was a ferry across the Firth of Forth to Burntisland, and from Burntisland the Edinburgh & Northern Railway had built northwards. By 1850 the EL & G and the E & N had amalgamated into the Edinburgh, Perth & Dundee Railway. Trains from Burntisland ran to Tayport whence there was another ferry service across the Firth of Tay to Broughty Ferry, from which point railways already in existence led to Dundee and Montrose. The ferries across the two firths were the earliest train ferries, for wagons were shunted aboard*. Passengers, however, had to board them on foot.

Another important technical innovation of this period was the introduction of fishplates to clamp rail ends together at joints. Until then, abutting rail ends had generally been held in a common chair. Fishplates were patented in 1847. Construction of new lines with stone block sleepers ceased at about the same time.

* Earlier, in the tramroad era, there had been some instances of waggons carried on boats.

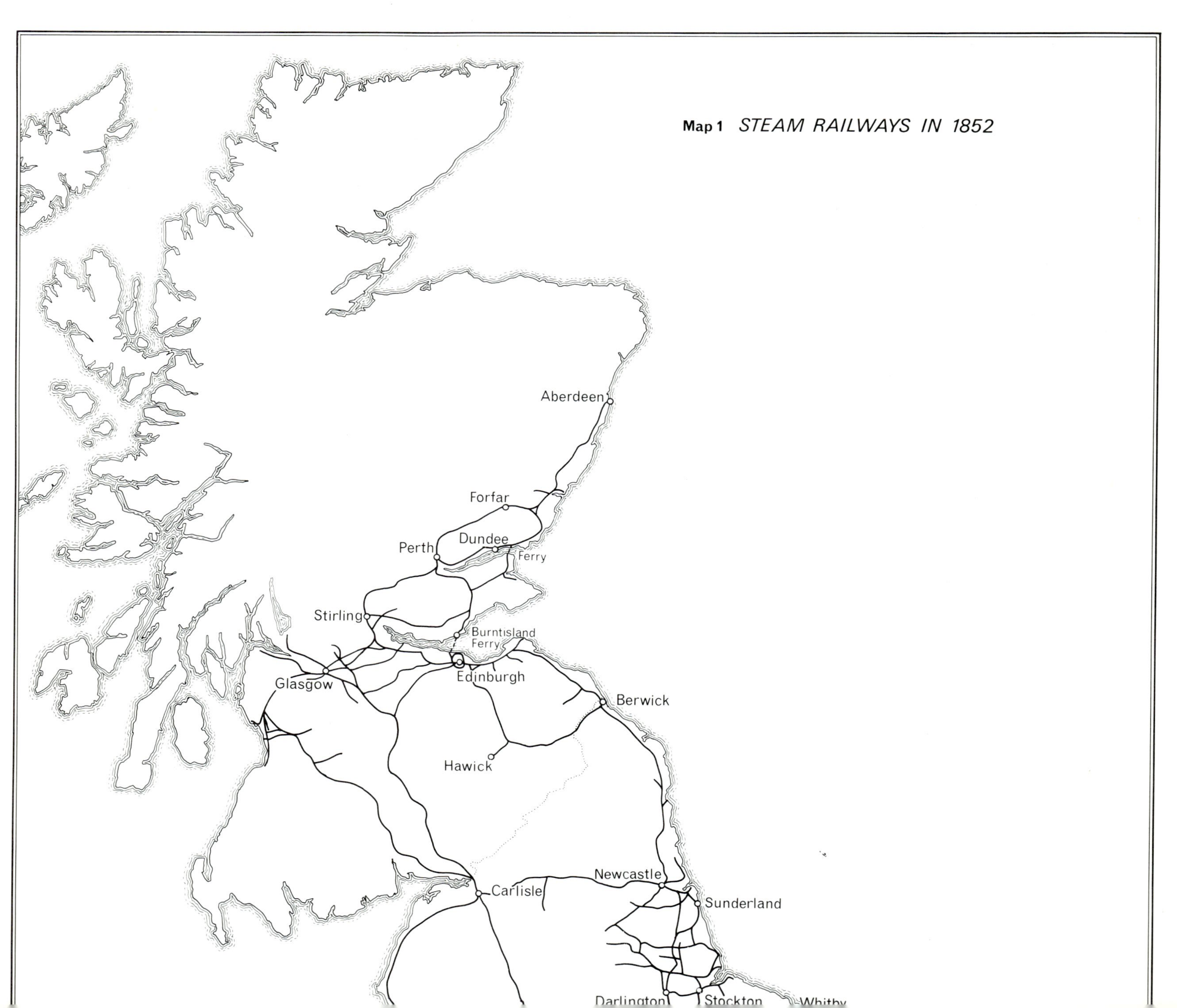
Map 1 STEAM RAILWAYS IN 1852
Aberdeen
Forfar
Dundee
Ferry
Perth
Stirling
Burntisland
Ferry
Glasgow
Edinburgh
Berwick
Hawick
Newcastle
Carlisle
Sunderland

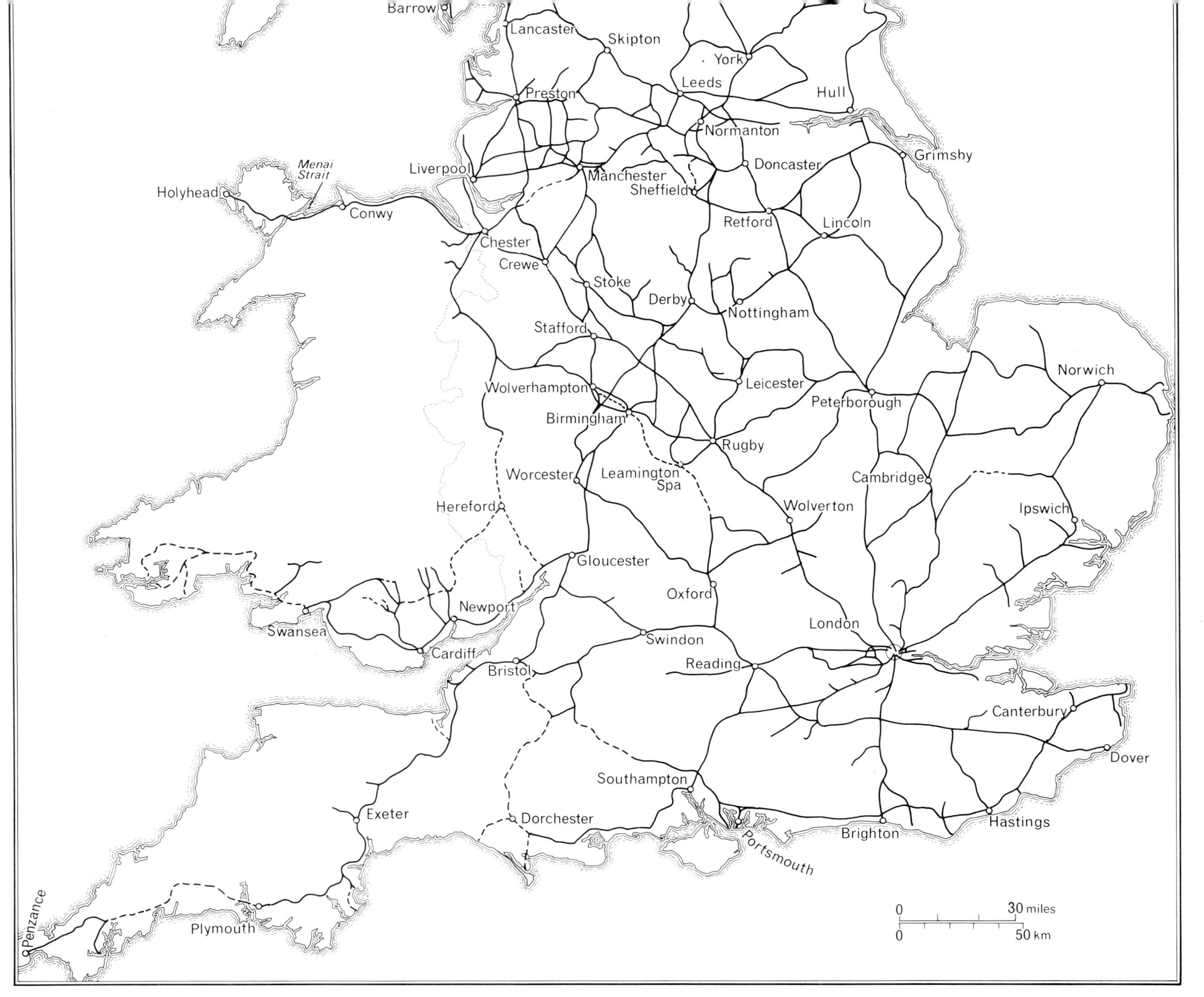
Barrow
Lancaster
Skipton
York
Leeds
Hull
Preston
Normanton
Grimsby
Liverpool
Manchester
Doncaster
Sheffield
Menai Strait
Holyhead
Conwy
Retford
Lincoln
Chester
Crewe
Stoke
Derby
Nottingham
Stafford
Norwich
Leicester
Wolverhampton
Peterborough
Birmingham
Rugby
Worcester
Leamington Spa
Cambridge
Hereford
Wolverton
Ipswich
Gloucester
Oxford
Newport
London
Swansea
Swindon
Cardiff
Reading
Bristol
Canterbury
Dover
Southampton
Exeter
Dorchester
Brighton
Hastings
Portsmouth
Penzance
Plymouth
0
30 miles
0
50 km

By the end of 1850, railway route mileage in Great Britain was 6,084 miles. South Wales was brought into direct rail communication—broad gauge—with London, via Gloucester, in 1852 by the completion of Chepstow bridge over the River Wye. The broad gauge, which had reached Plymouth in 1849, was extended into Cornwall by the opening of Brunel's Royal Albert Bridge over the Tamar at Saltash in 1859. The line was completed to Penzance in 1867. Most of these lines were built by satellites of the Great Western, which later absorbed them. Meanwhile the standard gauge London & South Western Railway had been extending from Basingstoke, on the London–Southampton line, via Salisbury to Exeter (reached in 1860) and later it was projected into North Devon and North Cornwall, and to Plymouth, partly by taking over and narrowing earlier broad gauge lines.

Standard gauge track reached Paddington in 1861, when the main line from Reading was made mixed gauge. This was a consequence of the amalgamation of the standard gauge West Midland Railway with the Great Western; the WMR itself had been formed by amalgamation in the previous year, of the Oxford Worcester & Wolverhampton, the Worcester & Hereford, and the Newport Abergavenny & Hereford Railways. All these had been opened during the 1850s. New construction and amalgamation during the same period gave the GWR a route from Oxford north west by Banbury, Birmingham, Wolverhampton and Shrewsbury to Chester. Beyond Wolverhampton it was always standard gauge and, from Wellington to Shrewsbury inclusive, owned jointly with the London & North Western.

The North Eastern Railway was formed in 1854 by amalgamation of, on the one hand, the York, Newcastle & Berwick and the York & North Midland, and on the other, the competing Leeds Northern which ran direct from Leeds to Stockton. The Stockton & Darlington, and the Newcastle & Carlisle, were amalgamated with the North Eastern in 1861. The Great Eastern was another railway formed by amalgamation, in 1862 (though its London terminus at Liverpool Street was not opened until 1874). These railways came to have as near a monopoly of rail transport in their territories—North East England and East Anglia respectively—as did any in Victorian and Edwardian times.

The North British Railway expanded far beyond the limits of its original Berwick–Edinburgh line. It had purchased the little Edinburgh & Dalkeith horse railway in 1845, rebuilt it for locomotives and linked it to its own line, and built a long branch down to Hawick, reached in 1849. This was extended to Carlisle as the Border Union Railway, opened in 1862. Later publicists were to promote the whole line as the Waverley Route, after the novels of Sir Walter Scott, whose former home was close to it. In 1862 also, the NBR absorbed the Edinburgh, Perth & Dundee Railway and, in 1865, the Edinburgh & Glasgow.

Construction of railways in Ireland had started more slowly than in Britain and was then further hindered by the Great Famine of 1847 and its aftermath. The railways of Ireland never occupied as important a place, historically or technically, in relation to the railways of the British Isles as did Irish canals and inland waterways among the waterways of these islands.

Nevertheless, the Great Southern & Western Railway opened the first section of its main line from Dublin to Cork in 1846, and had 211 route miles open by 1850; and the Midland Great Western Railway, authorised in 1845, was open throughout from Dublin to Galway by 1851. Through running between Dublin and Belfast commenced in 1853; the route eventually became the main line of the Great Northern Railway of Ireland, which was formed by amalgamation in 1876. By then there were in total over 2,000 miles of railway operating in Ireland; the eventual peak mileage was 3,442 in 1920.

In England, the line of the Midland Railway between Rugby and Normanton had been part of the original trunk route between London and the North East, and it had seemed likely that it would become part of the route to Scotland when the line was in due course extended. Construction of the Great Northern, however, had changed this, and relegated the Midland to wholly provincial status. The reaction of the company was, first, to seek its own route to London. In 1858 it opened its line south from Leicester via Bedford to Hitchin, whence it had obtained running powers over the Great Northern to King's Cross. Then, ten years later, it achieved its own entry to London, opening the line from Bedford to St Pancras in 1868. In the meantime it had in 1867 completed a line from Ambergate, north of Derby, via the Peak District to Manchester.

North west of Leeds, the Midland had already been extended by absorption of smaller companies, to Bradford, Skipton and Lancaster. Diverging from this route near Settle, it built the Settle & Carlisle line. This was laid out, in part, high among the Pennines—the only practicable route—and was opened for freight in 1875, for passengers the following year. With its completion the Midland from St Pancras to Carlisle became the principal component of the third of the great Anglo-Scottish main lines, for north of Carlisle the North British took its trains onward to Edinburgh over the Waverley Route, and the Glasgow & South Western (its line south via Kilmarnock had been completed as early as 1850) took them on to Glasgow.

Construction of lines through difficult upland country was typical of the 1860s and 1870s, by which period most important lowland routes had been built. Aberdeen had been linked to Inverness in 1859: the Great North of Scotland Railway had built north west from Aberdeen as far as Keith, local companies completed the route via Forres to Inverness. But Inverness to the South via Aberdeen was roundabout; in 1863 a more direct route

south from Forres over Druimuachdar summit (still, at 1,484 feet above sea level, the highest point on British Rail) to Dunkeld and Stanley Junction north of Perth was completed. The companies concerned amalgamated in 1865 to form the Highland Railway.

Railway communication was then extended further north, reaching Strome Ferry on the west coast in 1870 and both Wick and Thurso in 1874; these lines were in due course taken over by the Highland Railway. Further south, Callander in Perthshire had been reached by a branch of the Caledonian Railway about 1865; this was extended farther west by the Callander & Oban Railway which, always under the Caledonian wing, was opened by stages and eventually reached Oban in 1880.

2/22 (above) Railways were built, to a large extent, by power of human muscle. Here navvies are excavating a cutting and loading the spoil into tip wagons running on temporary track. These will convey it to the point at which it will be dumped to form an embankment. The picture dates from 1884, but the scene was familiar from the 1830s until the 1890s.

2/23 (next page) The first city underground railway was the Metropolitan, opened from Paddington to Farringdon Street, London, in 1863. It was built beneath the streets by 'cut and cover' methods, and is seen here in 1865 at the station now called Great Portland Street. Locomotives condensed their exhaust steam, and smoke escaped from the tunnel through vents. The eight-wheeled coaches had rigid wheelbases.

PORTLAND ROAD

In mid-Wales a series of small companies, which were either constructing railways or had recently opened them, came together in 1864 and 1865 to form the Cambrian Railways Company. Its main line ran from Whitchurch (on the LNW Crewe–Shrewsbury line) to Aberystwyth, with a long branch up the Cambrian Coast to Pwllheli, reached in 1867.

In many places Parliament granted one railway company running powers over the tracks of another. Elsewhere railways came to be owned jointly by two or more companies. One such was the Shrewsbury & Hereford, opened in 1853, jointly owned by the LNWR and the GWR from 1862. Some joint lines became entities of their own, such as the Somerset & Dorset Joint Railway owned by the Midland and the London & South Western from 1875, and the Midland & Great Northern Joint Railway, an amalgamation of several local companies mostly in North Norfolk, which was taken over by the main line companies of its name in 1893 with a view to competing with the Great Eastern.

Underground and narrow gauge railways

While the trunk lines were being constructed many branch lines were also built, often by local companies later taken over by larger ones. Then, to relieve congested streets in large cities, underground railways were built. The first, the Metropolitan Railway from Paddington to Farringdon Street in London, was opened in 1863, and rapidly extended. It reached South Kensington from Edgware Road in 1868 and the route was further extended by the Metropolitan District Railway, opened to Westminster in the same year. Completion of what is now known as the Circle Line was delayed until 1884, however, by rivalry between the two companies.

These lines were, of course, worked by steam locomotives. But in 1879 Werner von Siemens demonstrated the first satisfactory electric railway locomotive in Berlin. The first electric railways in the British Isles were that of

2/24 The Festiniog Railway successfully introduced steam locomotives for its narrow gauge of 1 ft. 11½ in. in 1863, and started to run passenger trains in 1865. Here is one of them, seen at Blaenau Ffestiniog. At that date, construction of new railways of other than 4 ft. 8½ in. gauge was illegal, except that existing 7 ft. 0¼ in. gauge lines might be extended. Successful and cheap operation of such small trains by the Festiniog attracted great attention.

Magnus Volk, along the sea front at Brighton, and the Giant's Causeway Railway between Portrush and Bushmills in Ireland. Both were opened in 1883.

Another form of specialised railway developed at this period was the narrow gauge railway. Its exceptionally narrow gauge kept the Festiniog Railway as a horse-and-gravity tramroad until 1863. To construct locomotives for a gauge under 2 ft. had been considered impossible or at least very difficult, but in that year two very small locomotives were put to work on the FR. They were successful and were followed by others, and by passenger carriages for a passenger train service to be introduced in 1865. Success was crowned by the introduction of powerful double-ended locomotives, to Fairlie's patent, and the 1 ft. $11\frac{1}{2}$ in. gauge Festiniog was shown to be both successful and profitable at a date when construction of new railways of other than 4 ft. $8\frac{1}{2}$ in. gauge was still generally illegal. It was an object lesson in how to build and operate railways cheaply, particularly in mountainous areas where the sharp curves which the narrow gauge allowed enabled expensive civil engineering works to be minimised.

As has sometimes happened with British ideas, the lesson was applied overseas (from the Rockies to the Himalayas) rather than at home. Some narrow gauge lines derived from the Festiniog were built in Britain: the 2 ft. 3 in. gauge Talyllyn Railway opened in 1865, the 1 ft. $11\frac{1}{2}$ in. gauge North Wales Narrow Gauge Railways opened during 1877 to 1881, the 3 ft. gauge Ravenglass & Eskdale and Southwold Railways opened in 1875 and 1879 respectively, and the 1 ft. $11\frac{1}{2}$ in. gauge Lynton & Barnstaple Railway opened in 1898. The first section of the 3 ft. gauge Isle of Man Railway was opened in 1873 and this gauge also became almost a second standard for local railways in Ireland.

Developments in passenger carriages and locomotives

It was, however, another pioneering venture by the Festiniog which time has shown to be of greatest significance in a wholly British context. This was the introduction of the first successful passenger carriages carried on bogies. Railway vehicles carried on two small swivelling and pivoted bogies or trucks, each with four wheels, had been usual in America for many years (being most suitable for the roughly-laid tracks there), and vehicles of American type, probably on bogies, were used on the Waterford & Limerick Railway for a short time after its opening in 1848. They were replaced by the more usual four- and six-wheeled carriages of the period; some eight-wheeled rigid wheelbase carriages were built by the Great Western in 1852. By the early 1870s the Festiniog Railway was already using a Fairlie's patent locomotive carried on

2/25 In 1857 a historic locomotive was preserved in public for the first time when the Stockton & Darlington Railway mounted its no. 1 Locomotion *on a plinth outside its principal station, North Road Darlington. After a subsequent long stay on exhibition at Darlington Bank Top station,* Locomotion *has now returned to North Road and is exhibited in the railway museum into which most of the station has been converted.*

bogies; its earliest passenger carriages were very small four-wheelers, but the particular suitability of much longer carriages on bogies to carry a useful load on a narrow gauge line with sharp curves must have been clear, and the Festiniog's first two bogie coaches, designed by its engineer C. E. Spooner, were placed in service in 1872.

Since then, bogie coaches have been in continuous use on British railways. Next after the Festiniog Railway came the Midland Railway, about to open its route to Scotland. In 1874 it agreed with George Mortimer Pullman, who had been operating luxury sleeping cars and other vehicles on American railroads since 1859, that he should operate Pullman sleeping and day cars on its line. Of American design, these were of course on bogies. The same year, the Midland built some ordinary coaches on bogies, and subsequently they were gradually adopted by other companies.

This was a period of great development in passenger coaches. Since the beginning there had generally been three classes of passenger accommodation, though third class was often relegated to slow trains. In 1872 the Midland and the Great Eastern Railways started to include third class accommodation on all passenger trains, and in 1875 the Midland abolished second class altogether and improved its third class accommodation. This example was followed elsewhere, but only very slowly. In 1873 the first sleeping car was introduced, on the East Coast Route, and in 1879, on the Great Northern Railway, the first dining car. Passengers had to make their entire journeys in these vehicles, for there were as yet no corridors or connections between vehicles. Coaches still consisted of several separate compartments according to the design derived from stage coaches and inherited from the Liverpool & Manchester and Grand Junction Railways. The first compartment coach with a side corridor and a lavatory at each end was introduced by the Great Northern in 1881, but it was still on six wheels; gangway connections to adjoining coaches were not introduced until 1888. Lighting was originally by oil lamps, later by gas; the first electrically-lit coach appeared on the London Brighton & South Coast Railway in 1881.

The period from the railway mania until the 1880s was one of expansion of the railway system rather than great technical advance in locomotives. Rigid wheelbase locomotives of the 2-2-2, 4-2-2, 0-4-0, 2-4-0, 0-4-2 and 0-6-0 wheel arrangements were used. Bogies for the carrying (non-driving) wheels of locomotives came into use in the 1850s and 1860s and the inside-frame inside-cylinder (ie, frames between the wheels, cylinders between the frames) 4-4-0 was introduced by the North British Railway in 1871. The first 2-6-0s were introduced by the Great Eastern in 1878. During this period the driver's cab evolved from non-existent, through a front weather-board with spectacle glasses, to a full cab; also steam operated brakes, displacement lubricators, steel tyres and fireboxes and injectors for boiler feed all came into use.

It was during the 1850s that some early locomotives, because of their historic interest, were preserved. The South Eastern Railway, having inherited the locomotive *Invicta* from the Canterbury & Whitstable, preserved it in its Ashford Works from 1853 onwards. The first to go on public display, however, was the Stockton & Darlington Railway's famous *Locomotion*. In 1857 it was placed on a pedestal outside the S & DR's Darlington, North Road, station. Hedley's even older locomotives at Wylam worked there on the waggonway until the 1860s. *Puffing Billy* was then first lent to, and subsequently purchased by, the Patent Office's South Kensington Museum, a precursor of the Science Museum. *Wylam Dilly* was purchased by Hedley's sons and eventually passed to the Royal Scottish Museum. What was left of *Rocket* was presented to the Patent Office Museum in 1862.

Points and signals were first interlocked, so that signals could not indicate clear while points were incorrectly set, in the late 1850s. Time interval working had largely given way by the 1870s to block working, in which each track of a double line is divided up into sections, onto which only one train is allowed at a time. Signal boxes at the ends of sections communicate by electric telegraph, and a section is considered to be blocked unless it has been confirmed to be clear. Construction of extended single track railways in the 1860s was contemporary with introduction of the train-staff-and-ticket system: on single lines, engine drivers have to carry with them a wooden staff for each section or—so that successive trains may follow one another safely—a ticket authorising them to proceed after they have seen the staff. Tyer's electric train tablet apparatus, introduced in 1879, and the electric train staff systems, developed soon afterwards, gave greater flexibility. Rails of steel were common on main lines by the 1870s.

The Regulation of Railways Act 1889 made interlocking and block working compulsory and also, on passenger trains, automatic continuous brakes. That is to say, if a train becomes divided, brakes are applied automatically on all its vehicles. Two systems became standard: the automatic vacuum brake and the Westinghouse automatic air brake. In the former brakes are applied by atmospheric pressure, in the latter by compressed air. After the 1923 grouping, vacuum brakes were made standard by all four British main-line companies, and it is only in recent years that (more effective) air brakes have been reintroduced on British Rail's most modern stock.

2/26 The Stephensons' Rocket *is seen here as received by the Patent Office Museum, South Kensington, in 1862. Obvious alterations since new are lowering of the cylinders and addition of a smokebox and front buffer beam. The picture repays comparison with illustration 2/11.*

2/27 (right) 2/28 (opposite) The railway was part of everybody's life in Victorian Britain, whatever their class in society. In 2/28 a workmen's train arrives at London Victoria.

Estuary crossings

In the early 1870s proposals to cross the three big estuaries which still interrupted railway routes came to fruition. In 1870 the North British Railway obtained an Act of Parliament to bridge the Firth of Tay, followed in 1872 by the Great Western which obtained powers to tunnel beneath the Severn estuary, and so obtain a more direct route between London and South Wales than that via Gloucester. To cross the Firth of Forth was too great a task for one railway company, and when the Forth Bridge was authorised in 1873, the Forth Bridge Railway Company was formed jointly by the Great Northern, North Eastern, North British and Midland companies.

The Tay Bridge was completed and opened in June 1878. Eighteen months later, in December 1879, inadequate design and indifferent workmanship combined to result in notorious disaster, when part of the bridge, with a train upon it, was blown down by a fierce gale. Work on a replacement started about 1881; on the Forth Bridge, which had the same designer, contracts were cancelled and work to a new design started in 1883.

The Great Western, after the greatest difficulty with flooded workings, eventually completed the Severn Tunnel in 1886. The second Tay Bridge was opened the following year, and the Forth Bridge was opened ceremonially by the Prince of Wales in 1890.

The Golden Age

With the opening of the Forth Bridge commenced the golden age of steam railways, which lasted until 1914. At its start, the railway system was nearly complete, and railways were almost unchallenged for inland transport in the British Isles for distances of more than a few miles (the railway companies had, willy nilly, purchased enough canals to prevent the canal network from functioning as a general competitor). At its end, other forms of transport were appearing but had not developed sufficiently to be a serious threat. Steam railways, operated by some twenty five large companies and many more small ones, were to all intents and purposes synonymous with inland transport.

Competition between companies was rife and took its most glamorous form in the races to the North. During 1888 East Coast and West Coast schedules from London to Edinburgh were reduced by successive stages from 9 hours to 7¾ hours, before being standardised at 8½ hours by both routes. In 1895, with the Forth and Tay Bridges and connecting lines open, the East Coast Route was well placed to compete with the West Coast for traffic to Aberdeen. Successive accelerations reduced the time from London to Aberdeen from 12 hours 20 minutes to 8 hours 40 minutes. The night after an East Coast train achieved that time, the West Coast companies made a demonstration run in 8 hours 32 minutes. During the course of it, LNWR 2-4-0 *Hardwicke* averaged 67·2 mph from Crewe to Carlisle, including the ascent of Shap.

An event of a totally different sort which equally caught the public imagination was the final conversion of Great Western lines from broad gauge to standard. This had been going on by stages since 1868; the last broad gauge train eventually left Paddington on 20 May 1892 watched by a large crowd. People were sorry to lose the broad gauge with its large comfortable trains: this was the first expression of popular sentiment at the loss of a railway feature. Lay interest in railways was growing during the 1890s and to cater for early railway enthusiasts, *The Railway Magazine* was founded in 1897.

With the broad gauge replaced by standard, and old locomotives and rolling stock replaced by new, the Great Western was encouraged to compete more than ever with the London & South Western for traffic between London, Exeter and Plymouth. Out of this came the remarkable occasion in 1904 when GWR 4-4-0 *City of Truro*, hauling an Ocean Mails special from Plymouth to London, averaged 70 mph from Exeter to Bristol, with a maximum of 102 mph.

By the late 1880s the only extensive gaps in the railway map of Britain were in the West Highlands of Scotland. After several abortive proposals, the West Highland Railway was promoted by the North British to link Glasgow and Fort William. The WHR was authorised in 1889 and opened in 1894, its line crossed above the Callander & Oban at Crianlarich and a connection was put in but since the two lines belonged to different companies which were elsewhere in hot competition, it saw little use.

Possible construction of a railway northwards from Glasgow in the general direction of Inverness had earlier prompted the Highland Railway to obtain powers, in 1884, to shorten its own route by building a line direct from Aviemore to Inverness. This was eventually completed in 1898. It had also obtained powers in 1893 to extend from Stromc Ferry to Kyle of Lochalsh, a better located port; the extension was opened in 1897. Meanwhile the extension of the West Highland Railway westwards had been authorised on the previous year; it was opened to the new west coast port of Mallaig in 1901. Much pioneering use of concrete was made in its structures.

The other extensive piece of new construction in the 1890s was the London Extension of the Manchester, Sheffield & Lincolnshire Railway—or, as it was soon to become, the Great Central Railway. This was the brainchild of Sir Edward Watkin, already-elderly tycoon whose railway interests included not only the MS & L but also the Metropolitan Railway. From its underground beginnings, the Metropolitan had gradually built northwestwards from Baker Street, coming to the surface and extending into Middlesex and Buckinghamshire, encouraging commuters to 'live in Metroland' and reaching Aylesbury and eventually Verney Junction on the LNWR branch from Bletchley to Oxford.

The London Extension of the MS & L was authorised in 1893, to leave the MS & L proper south of Sheffield and run by Nottingham, Leicester and Rugby (all places well served by long-established railways) to Quainton Road, north of Aylesbury, where it joined the Metropolitan.

Great Central trains then had running powers over the Metropolitan as far as Harrow (the section later became a joint line) whence was constructed a new line to the GCR's own terminus at Marylebone. Coal trains started in 1898; the extension was opened for general passenger and goods traffic in 1899—the last new main line.

The Great Western was notorious for the roundabout course of some of its routes, and during the 1900s it built many cut-off lines to shorten them. The first to be completed, in 1903, from Wootton Bassett, near Swindon, to Patchway, produced a direct approach to the Severn Tunnel. Next, in 1906, opening of the Castle Cary to Langport section completed the direct line from Reading to Taunton for expresses to Devon and Cornwall. Upgrading of the branch line between Stratford-upon-Avon and Honeybourne, and new links southwards to Cheltenham and northwards to Birmingham, at last gave the GWR, in 1908, a main line between Birmingham and Gloucester able to compete with the Midland. In 1910 the GWR shortened its route from London to Birmingham by completing the direct line from Old Oak Common, not far from Paddington, to Aynho, south of Banbury. Part of this had been built as a joint line with the Great Central, which needed access to London independent of the Metropolitan's heavy suburban traffic.

Elsewhere, in South East England long standing competition between the London, Chatham & Dover Railway and the South Eastern Railway had created two interlaced networks of competing lines with their own London termini; these were more extensive than the traffic warranted and eventually, in 1899, a managing committee was set up to work the two companies' lines together, as the South Eastern & Chatham Railway.

The Midland Railway, still expanding, acquired in 1903 the Belfast & Northern Counties Railway (of which the oldest section, the Belfast & Ballymena, dated back to 1848), and, in 1912, the London, Tilbury & Southend Railway.

Light railways

Although railways were widespread by the 1880s, many country districts still lacked rail communication: the expenses of obtaining an Act of Parliament to authorise a line, and building it to meet government safety requirements which, based on many years' experience, had become very strict, was often too great for the likely financial returns. After several

2/29 (left) A broad gauge train of the Great Western Railway, running on mixed gauge track, shows how very much wider the Brunel gauge of 7 ft. 0¼ in. appeared than the standard gauge of 4 ft. 8½ in. With quadruple track, the slow lines on the left are standard gauge only—the scene is near London shortly before the end of the broad gauge in 1892. The origin of the existing wide spacing between the standard gauge fast lines on this section is clearly shown—see also illustration no. 4/8.

ineffectual attempts at legislation, the Light Railways Act 1896 was passed. This cheapened procedure by enabling light railways in Great Britain to be authorised by Light Railway Order, and reduced construction costs by relaxing main line safety standards in return for stringent speed restrictions.

The next thirty years saw many light railways built, although they were never as widespread in Britain as in many Continental countries. Some were built to standard gauge, some to narrow; some were built and worked by existing companies, some were wholly independent. Among them were the standard gauge Rother Valley Railway opened in 1902, and extended and re-named the Kent & East Sussex Railway shortly afterwards, with the 1 ft. $11\frac{1}{2}$ in. gauge Vale of Rheidol Light Railway and the standard gauge Dornoch Light Railway (operated by the Highland Railway) also opened in 1902; the 2 ft. 6 in. gauge Welshpool & Llanfair Light Railway opened in 1903 worked by the Cambrian, and the Leek & Manifold Valley Light Railway of the same gauge opened in 1904 worked by the North Staffordshire; and the standard gauge and independent Derwent Valley Light Railway completed from York to Cliff Common in 1913.

Tubes, trams and suburban electrification

The first deep level tube railway, the City & South London, was opened in 1890; planned for cable traction, it pioneered the use of electricity underground. The next tube railway in London was the Waterloo & City, owned by the London & South Western and opened in 1898. It was followed during the 1900s by several others, and the underground lines of the Metropolitan and Metropolitan District Railways were electrified by 1905. Electrification of the Metropolitan was accompanied by the installation of the first colour light signals.

The first serious competition for steam trains from a newer form of transport came from the electric tram. There had been, in cities, street tramways with horsedrawn or steam trams for many years. In the 1900s they were electrified, and greatly extended, sometimes under light railway orders. Steam railways rapidly lost traffic from their innermost suburban stations. Some railway companies set about meeting this competition by electrifying their own suburban lines. Among

2/30 (centre) Pre-grouping branch line: a North Eastern Railway train enters Rowley station. Despite its poor quality, this photograph is of interest in showing, in its original location, the station building which was, much later, taken down and re-erected in Beamish Open Air Museum—see illustration no. 6/18.

2/31 (right) Pre-grouping main line: a down West Coast Route express leaves Carlisle, headed by Caledonian Railway Dunalastair class 4–4–0 no. 389. The inside cylinder, inside frame 4–4–0 was the typical British passenger locomotive of the latter part of the Victorian period.

2/32 H. N. Gresley, chief mechanical engineer of the LNER, is remembered best for his A4 class streamlined Pacifics, several examples of which are preserved (see illustration no. 5/21). An important design of his which has not survived was the P2 class 2–8–2, of which the first, Cock o' the North, *was built in 1934, incorporating ideas by André Chapelon, noted French locomotive engineer.* Cock o' the North *is seen here leaving Edinburgh Waverley for, probably, Aberdeen in the mid-1930s.*

the earliest to do so were the Lancashire & Yorkshire, the North Eastern and the London, Brighton & South Coast Railways. Advantages of electric traction compared with steam included better acceleration leading to faster schedules, better availability of stock, elimination of the need for a fireman as well as a driver, and cleanliness.

As early as 1905, the LBSCR was experimenting with a petrol-driven railcar for branch lines. On roads, motor vehicles were coming into use at the same period. Railway companies, notably the Great Western, were among the earliest operators of motor buses.

Heavier trains, more powerful locomotives

During the 1890s and early 1900s, trains, particularly expresses, were rapidly getting heavier in relation to the numbers of passengers carried. By 1893 for instance, there were dining car expresses on all three Anglo-Scottish routes, and that on the West Coast Route had corridor coaches throughout. The first bogie sleeping car of modern layout went into service on the East Coast Route in 1894, and buffet cars were first introduced on the Great Central Railway in 1899. The Pullman Car Company in Britain passed into British ownership in the mid-1900s and concentrated on providing luxury daytime accommodation.

Heavier trains needed larger and more powerful locomotives. In Britain, the first Atlantic, 4-4-2, locomotives appeared on the Great Northern Railway in 1898, the first passenger 4-6-0s on the North Eastern and Highland Railways in 1900; they had been preceded in 1894 by the Highland Railway's first 4-6-0s intended for goods trains. The Great Western Railway built the first 2-8-0s (for goods trains) in 1903, and the first Pacific, 4-6-2, in 1908; the chief asset of the latter locomotive, however, proved to be only its publicity value, and it was later rebuilt as a 4-6-0.

The most important technical advance in locomotive design at this period was the introduction of superheating, first on the LBSCR in 1908, and then on the LNWR in 1910.

The idea was adopted from Continental practice: en route from boiler to cylinders, the steam is passed through horizontal U-tubes which are located within large diameter boiler fire tubes and so are exposed to the hot gases from the fire. The effect is to increase both temperature and energy of the steam, which in turn reduces consumption of both water and coal.

The First World War and the grouping

The First World War was a disaster for railways. They were worked more intensively than ever before; simultaneously they lost many of their staff to the armed forces and standards of maintenance declined sharply. Furthermore, the war gave a marked impetus to the development of motor cars and lorries, and afterwards a great many war surplus vehicles were sold for commercial use. Railways were ill-placed to compete.

There were bright spots. H. N. Gresley, locomotive superintendent of the Great Northern Railway, introduced his first Pacific locomotive *Great Northern* in 1922, the first of a highly successful design. In the same year the LSWR completed rebuilding Waterloo, the largest terminus in Britain. Generally however, railways were badly run down. During the war they had been controlled by the Government and such unification had been seen to be beneficial.

Shortly after Government control ceased, Parliament passed the Railways Act 1921. This required the amalgamation of most of the railway companies into four large ones on a broadly regional basis, the 'grouping', it was called.

The new companies were formed and operating by 1 January 1923. Of main line companies, only the Great Western Railway retained its identity; but it also took over the Cambrian and Taff Vale Railways and lesser lines within its area. Largest of the new companies, with a route mileage just under 8,000 miles, was the London, Midland & Scottish Railway. Its principal constituents were the London & North Western (including the Lancashire & Yorkshire with which it had recently amalgamated), Midland, North Staffordshire, Furness, Caledonian, Glasgow & South Western and Highland Railways. The new London & North Eastern Railway incorporated the Great Northern, Great Eastern, Great Central, North Eastern, North British and Great North of Scotland Railways. The Southern Railway, smallest of the big four, was formed principally from the South Eastern, London Chatham & Dover, London Brighton & South Coast and London & South Western Railways.

In each case many smaller railways which had remained independent were grouped into whichever new company was regionally appropriate. A few small companies were not included; the most important of these were the tube and underground lines in London. They, and London's bus and tram operators, were eventually incorporated into the London Passenger Transport Board, formed in 1933.

The grouping affected railways in Ireland only where they were owned by a British company. Following partition however, all railways wholly within the Irish Free State were amalgamated into the Great Southern Railways in 1924. The principal railways affected were the Great Southern & Western, the Midland Great Western and the Dublin & South Eastern. The Great Southern Railways became, in turn, part of CIE, *Coras Iompair Eireann*, the national transport undertaking, in 1945. Railways which crossed the border—notably the Great Northern Railway of Ireland—remained independent.

With the benefit of hindsight nearly

2/33 W. A. Stanier and his staff designed a class of streamlined Pacifics, of striking appearance, to haul, initially, the LMS Railway's Coronation Scot *express which was introduced in 1937. Here, one of them is approaching Berkhamsted with the down* Mid-day Scot. *Streamlined casings were eventually removed from these locomotives to improve accessibility for maintenance;* Duchess of Hamilton *(see page 182) was originally streamlined in this manner.*

Map 2 *PASSENGER RAILWAYS IN GREAT BRITAIN IN 1910*

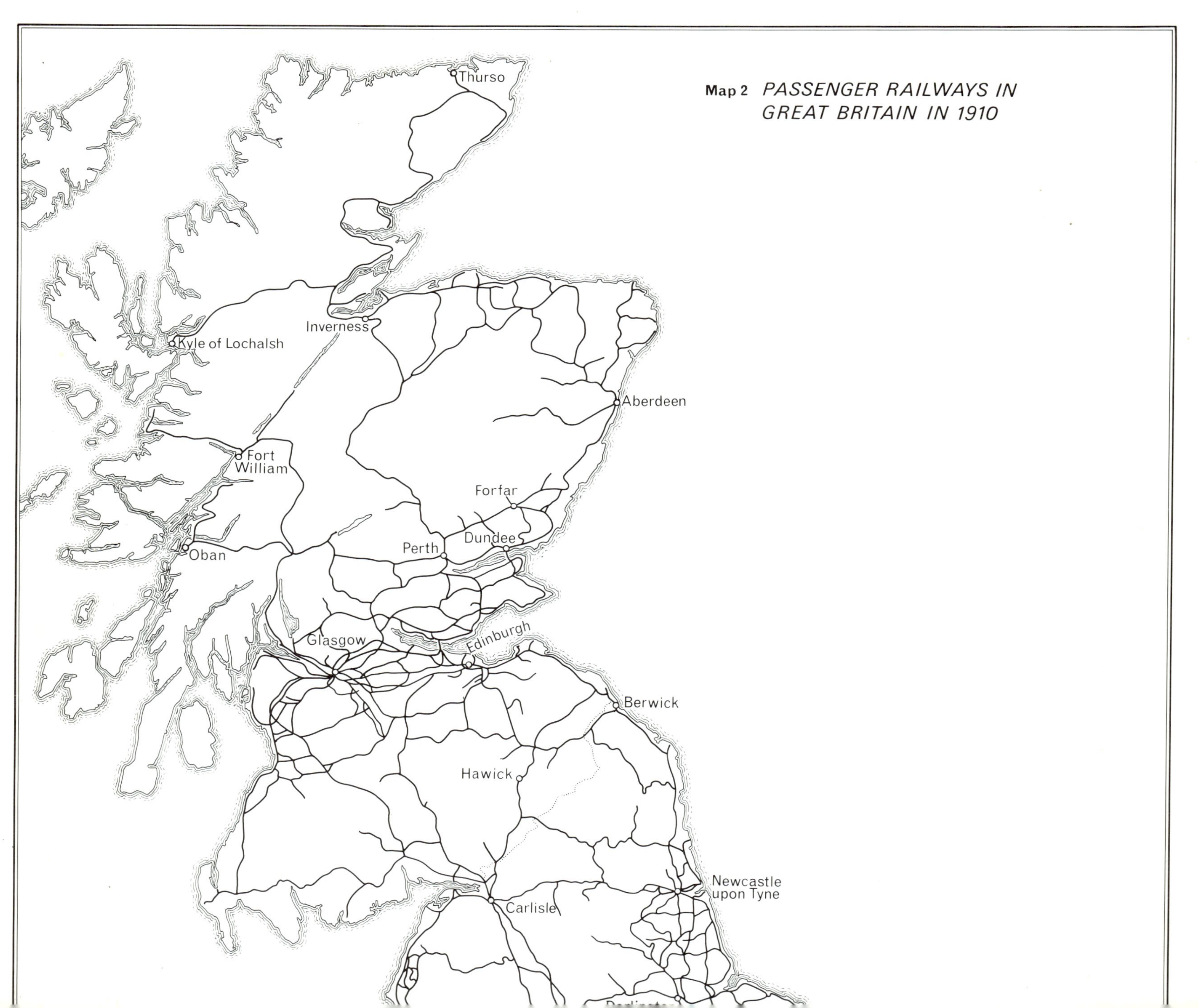

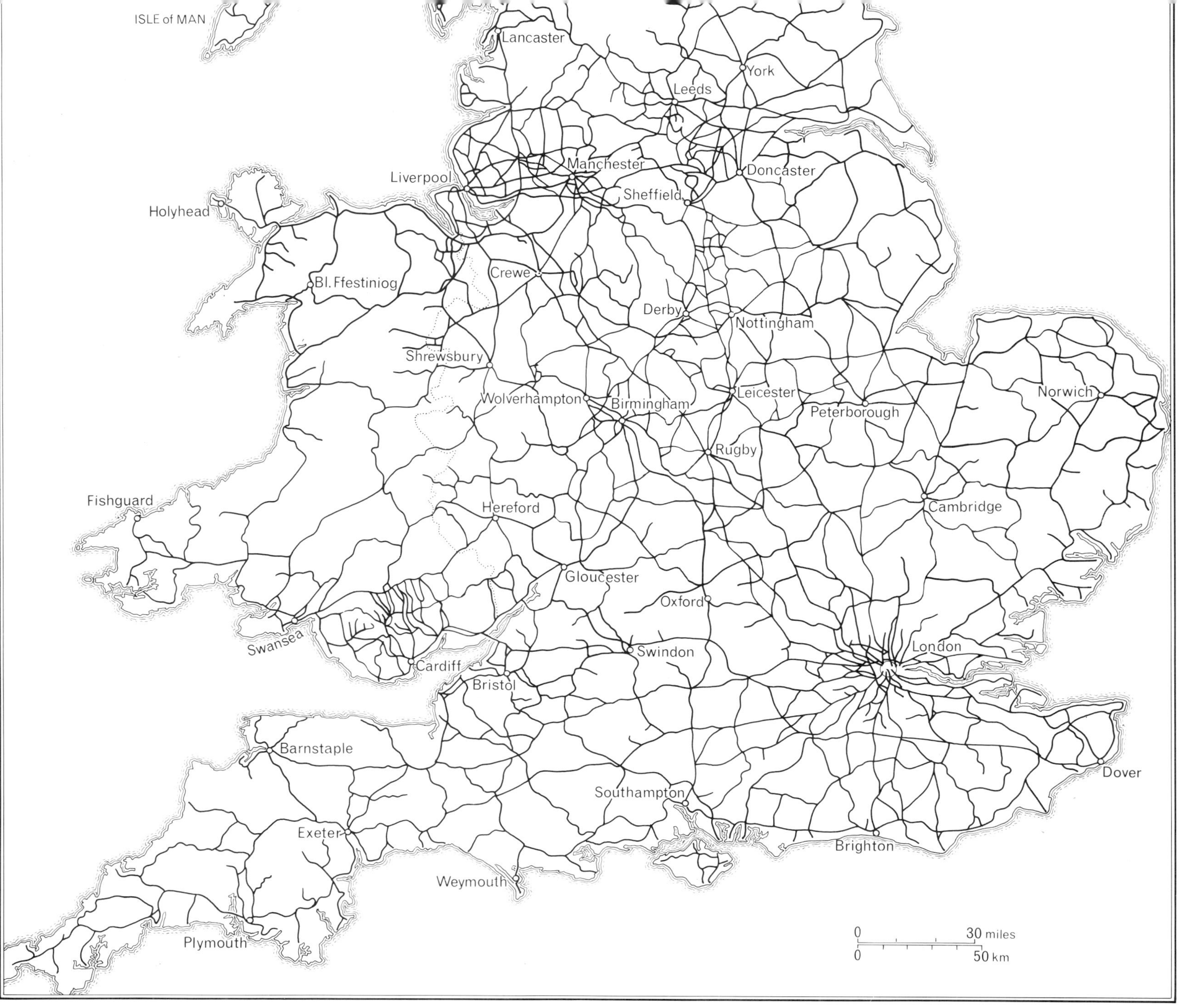
ISLE of MAN
Lancaster
York
Leeds
Manchester
Liverpool
Doncaster
Sheffield
Holyhead
Crewe
Bl. Ffestiniog
Derby
Nottingham
Shrewsbury
Leicester
Norwich
Wolverhampton
Birmingham
Peterborough
Rugby
Fishguard
Hereford
Cambridge
Gloucester
Oxford
Swansea
London
Swindon
Cardiff
Bristol
Barnstaple
Dover
Southampton
Exeter
Brighton
Weymouth
Plymouth
0 30 miles
0 50 km

sixty years later, it is difficult to see that the grouping in Britain achieved very much. The Great Western alone retained pre-grouping esprit-de-corps; and, with a few hiccups, it paid a dividend until nationalisation in 1948. The other three big companies, unwieldy colossi, took years to settle down; they did, eventually, become notable in their various ways. The LMS, the most unwieldy of all, was eventually forged into a single entity in the thirties by the draconian accounting measures of its chairman Lord Stamp; the Southern achieved widespread electrification for passenger trains, mostly of London suburban lines but also as far afield as Brighton and Portsmouth; and the LNER became famous for its high speed steam trains developed by (as he became) Sir Nigel Gresley.

Railways in the 1920s

In 1923 these things lay in the future. The first railway development of importance, after the grouping, was establishment in 1924 of the first public train ferry service to the Continent, for goods wagons. It had been preceded by a military version during the First World War. The railway system was still expanding to a limited extent: the standard gauge Totton, Hythe & Fawley Light Railway, for instance, was opened down the west side of Southampton Water in 1925.

The year 1926 saw the opening of the first section of a very different sort of light railway, the Romney Hythe & Dymchurch. During the golden age it had become fashionable for wealthy owners of estates to build passenger-carrying miniature railways on them, using model locomotives; similar lines had also been built to give public rides at seaside resorts and international exhibitions. From 1915 onwards the moribund 3 ft. gauge Ravenglass & Eskdale Railway had been relaid as a miniature line on the 15 in. gauge. The Romney Hythe & Dymchurch Railway in Kent represented this trend at its zenith: 15 in. gauge, double track and $8\frac{1}{4}$ miles long (later extended to $13\frac{3}{4}$ miles), it was a main line in miniature, using locomotives based on the Gresley Pacifics of the LNER.

Upper quadrant semaphore signals, which indicate clear when the arm is inclined about forty-five degrees upwards instead of downwards, originated on the Metropolitan Railway and were adopted as standard by the LMS, LNE and Southern Railways. The GWR continued to use lower quadrant semaphores. Operation of points and signals by electric power had been introduced, and during the 1920s and 1930s lever frames in signal boxes began to be replaced by route setting panels: by one or two movements, a complete route can be set up, including points, signals and interlocking.

The late 1920s were a very bad time for railways. The general strike of 1926 not only affected them directly, but also interrupted supplies of good locomotive coal. Industrial depression and growing road competition combined to reduce traffic. On the LMS, for instance, passenger receipts fell from £26 million in 1925 to £17·8 million in 1932. Railway route mileage in Britain reached its peak in 1927, at 20,443 miles. From then on, railways started to close because they could not meet road competition successfully. Slow-speed narrow gauge and light railways were among the first to go. The Derwent Valley Light Railway, despite early use of internal combustion rail buses, had been closed to passengers in 1926, and the Southwold Railway closed to all traffic in 1929. The GWR, which had purchased the Corris Railway in 1930, closed it to passenger traffic early in 1931, and did the same for the Welshpool & Llanfair Light Railway shortly afterwards. The Lynton & Barnstaple Railway, which had been grouped into the Southern Railway, was closed completely in 1935, and the Welsh Highland Railway, also of 1 ft. $11\frac{1}{2}$ in. gauge, from Porthmadog to Dinas Junction (it incorporated the North Wales Narrow Gauge Railways and had been completed only in 1923), was closed to all traffic in 1937. Ordinary standard gauge lines suffered too. On one day, 22 September 1930, seventeen branch lines were closed to passengers and, with some stations on other lines, a total of ninety-nine stations lost their passenger trains that day. The total was only exceeded, on a single day, at the height of the Beeching era.

The trend, however, was not wholly towards closure. Railways, often of specialised type or purpose, continued to be built, as indeed they are to this day. The Southern Railway opened its branch from Wimbledon to Sutton in 1930 with electric trains, and the Metropolitan opened its branch to Stanmore, also electrically worked, in 1933. In the same year the Great Western completed cut-off lines to avoid Westbury and Frome so that expresses need no longer slow down for these stations.

The 1920s saw the building of large 4-6-0 locomotives for express passenger work by the Great Western, Southern and LMS Railways—respectively the Castle class (introduced in 1923), the Lord Nelson class (1926), and the Royal Scot class (1927). In 1927 too, the GWR enlarged its 4-6-0 design still further to produce the King class.

The same year also saw the start of another trend when for the first time a voluntary organisation—the Stephenson Locomotive Society—acquired a withdrawn locomotive for preservation. The object of their action was the noted LBSCR 0-4-2 *Gladstone*, subsequently restored by the Southern to LBSCR condition and displayed at the York Railway Museum, which had been founded in 1922.

Sleeping cars with third class accommodation (four berths per compartment) were introduced in 1928 by the LMS, LNE and GW Railways. During the 1930s passenger coaches with steel panelling over a wooden-framed body,

2/34 When the Talyllyn Railway Preservation Society started to run the Talyllyn Railway in 1951, the rails were the originals of 1865 (one short section excepted) and the sleepers, many of them rotten, were mostly hidden beneath the layer of turf which had covered the ballast. Relaying the track was a long task, and this photograph, taken at Easter 1957, shows the one part of the line which was still, then, in basically its 1951 condition. The train proceeding cautiously over it is hauled by 0–4–2 saddle tank locomotive no.3, built for the Corris Railway in 1878 and obtained by the TRPS in 1951 to augment the TR's own limited locomotive stock.

carried on steel underframes, came into use, at first on the LMS, which also introduced wide windows with sideways-sliding upper opening sections.

Early diesel motive power

The internal combustion engine has greater thermal efficiency than the steam engine, and small petrol and diesel locomotives for shunting and industrial use were built in limited quantities during the 1890s and 1900s. The War Department used several hundred on 60 cm gauge military light railways in France during the First World War, and some of these were used subsequently in Britain by, for instance, the Festiniog Railway, which obtained two for shunting. The first regular passenger service by diesel railcar in the British Isles was introduced in 1931 by the 3 ft. gauge County Donegal Railways, which already had several years' experience with petrol railbuses, having purchased and re-gauged the Derwent Valley vehicles.

British main line companies were slow to adopt diesel power, although it was available to them—in 1929 for instance Armstrong Whitworth supplied diesel trains, with electric transmission, to the Buenos Aires Great Southern Railway. In 1933 however, the Great Western Railway obtained its first, streamlined, diesel railcar, the first to be put into regular service by a British main line company.

It was followed on the GWR by others, though not in great quantity. Of more immediate importance was the adoption, in 1932–3 by the LMS, as a by-product of a drive for economies in goods train marshalling, of diesel shunting locomotives which were subsequently built in large numbers to replace steam shunting locomotives.

High speed in the thirties

On main lines, the 1930s saw increasing use of new classes of 4-6-0 locomotives for mixed traffic (ie, suitable for goods or passenger trains), replacing old 4-4-0s. Much more spectacular, however, as the LMS and the LNER got over the worst of the problems of the 1920s, was the outbreak again of competitive high speed running to the North, which was prompted by the need to compete with the private car.

An essential preliminary was the introduction, by LMS chief mechanical engineer W. A. Stanier, of that company's first 4-6-2 express locomotive in 1933. It was the LNER, however, which introduced the first high speed streamlined train, the *Silver Jubilee*, in 1935. Gresley had first examined the high speed diesel trains put into service between Berlin and Hamburg in 1933. He decided to stick to steam, and designed his streamlined A4 class 4-6-2. The *Silver Jubilee* train, hauled by an A4, was allowed four hours for its 268-mile run between King's Cross and Newcastle: on trial, it reached a record speed of 112·5 mph.

In July 1937, to mark the coronation of King George VI, streamlined expresses were put on between Euston and Glasgow (by the LMS) and King's

Cross and Edinburgh (by the LNER), called *Coronation Scot* and *Coronation* respectively. For the LMS, Stanier had produced an improved and streamlined 4-6-2, the Princess Coronation class (later engines became, more euphoniously, the Duchess class). On trial, a speed of 114 mph was reached.

Introduction of the high speed expresses on the LNER had rapidly made clear a need for improved brakes: development of these required trial runs at high speed. One of these runs, in July 1938, was chosen for an attempt to beat the LMS speed record. During the course of it the A4 no. 4468 *Mallard* ran at over 120 mph for almost three miles, and achieved a momentary top speed of 126 mph. This record for steam traction remains unbeaten. A vivid personal recollection of the record breaking run, by P. T. W. Remnant who, as a young engineer, travelled on the train, appeared forty years later in *The Railway Magazine* for July 1978.

To publicise new stock and a streamlined locomotive for the *Flying Scotsman* train, the LNER got out GNR 4-2-2 no. 1 of 1870, which had been preserved since withdrawal in 1907, by way of comparison. She was restored to working order and hauled a train of GNR six-wheeled coaches from King's Cross to Stevenage on 30 June 1938. There the *Flying Scotsman* trains of 1870 and 1938 were photographed alongside one another. Later that year, no. 1 was used to haul the first enthusiasts' rail tour, which was organised by the Railway Correspondence & Travel Society.

While the northern lines were concerned at private car competition, the Southern Railway was having to meet competition for its Continental traffic from early air services. To counter this, the through overnight sleeping car train, the *Night Ferry*, was put into service between London and Paris in 1936, using the Dover–Dunkirk train ferry. News of its eventual withdrawal, in 1980, came as the manuscript of this book was being typed.

The Second World War and nationalisation

Hardly had the big four companies begun to make real progress, however, than they were embroiled in 1939 in the Second World War. From the railway point of view, this had much the same bad effect as had the first: overintensive use coupled with declining minimal maintenance, with blackout and bomb damage as added complications. Again, railways came under government control. The immediate post-war years, 1946, 1947, saw austerity and shortages of fuel and materials if anything more acute than in war time itself. The most important technical developments of the period were the introduction in 1941 by the Southern Railway of its first 4-6-2 locomotives, the Merchant Navy class, given both striking appearance and technical novelty by CME O. V. S. Bulleid; and the development after the war of prototype main line diesel electric locomotives by the LMS and Southern Railways.

By then, return of a Labour government in 1945 with, for the first time, a large majority in Parliament, had made nationalisation of public transport inevitable. State ownership of railways had been considered at intervals since as early as 1844; it was eventually brought about by the Transport Act 1947.

The Act established the British Transport Commission and a series of public bodies called executives—the Railway Executive, the London Transport Executive, and so on—through which it was to act. The list of 'bodies whose undertakings are transferred to the commission' included the big four railway companies, the London Passenger Transport Board, and a surprisingly long list of others. Many of these were joint committees relating to lines owned jointly by two of the big companies, but it also included a few independent railways such as the Kent & East Sussex Railway. A very few railways such as the Talyllyn and the Derwent Valley Light, which had not been sufficiently important to come under government control during the Second World War, were omitted. Nationalisation of railways was almost all-embracing, but not quite. It came into force on 1 January 1948. The old companies were eventually dissolved in 1949, by which date the Great Western had had a continuous existence since 1835.

The nationalised railway system was called British Railways. It had a route mileage of 19,863, a staff of more than

2/35 The up Cambrian Coast Express, *Aberystwyth to Paddington, is heading across Llanbadarn level crossing near the start of its journey about 1960; the locomotive is former-GWR Manor class 4–6–0* Barcote Manor. *The picture is full of steam age paraphernalia—level crossing gates worked from the signal box, an oil lamp to illuminate the wicket gate for pedestrians, tablet changing apparatus. The fireman is picking up the tablet for the single-line section ahead.*

700,000 people, and 20,445 locomotives, the great majority of them steam. The system was divided into six regions: London Midland, Eastern, North Eastern, Scottish, Western and Southern. The London Midland corresponded generally to English and Welsh lines of the LMS, the Eastern and North Eastern to the English lines of the LNER, the Scottish contained all LMS and LNE lines in Scotland, and the Western and Southern Regions corresponded to the GWR and SR respectively. There was therefore much geographical overlapping and subsequent adjustment of regional boundaries in England and Wales, and the Eastern and North Eastern Regions were eventually merged. The lines in Northern Ireland which the LMS had inherited from the Midland were transferred to the Ulster Transport Authority.

Whatever the political merits or otherwise of nationalisation, the manner of carrying it into effect was inept. The relative responsibilities of the BTC and the Railway Executive had not been clearly defined, and members of both were appointed by the government. M. R. Bonavia, in *The Organisation of British Railways*, gives a horrific account of consequent jealousies—of how, at the lowest level for instance, when the BTC required the Railway Executive to send it copies of its minutes, the Executive responded by producing an official set of minutes, which was sent, and a further set of 'Memoranda of Decisions at Meeting', which was not. They were known to staff, from the colour of their paper, as the white and the green minutes respectively! During the early years of British Railways there was little strong direction, at the time when Britain's biggest-ever railway undertaking needed it most.

The first technical advance by BR, which followed experiments by the LMS in the late 1930s, was the adoption as standard of heavy section (109 and 98 lb per yard) flat bottom rail in place of the 95 lb or so bullhead rail which had been in general use. British Railways did have great problems because of government restrictions on investment, and it was not until 1951 that a standard design of coach was introduced. Rather than any great technical innovations, it incorporated the best features of the coaches of all four pre-nationalisation companies. The only main feature not found previously was the use of steel, rather than timber, for the body framing. Uninspired, the Mark I standard coaches nevertheless laid the foundations for a process of improved design which continues to this day.

Motive power developments were less auspicious. Forgotten or perhaps ignored, it seemed, was the limited progress with diesel and electric power which had been made by the big four companies and the much greater progress abroad. Instead, twelve classes of standard steam locomotives were designed, locomotives of conventional type which combined the best of existing features in the interests of high availability, ease of maintenance and low first cost. Within these limited objectives they were good designs. The first BR standard steam locomotive, no. 70000 *Britannia*, a class 7 4-6-2, was completed late in 1950 and the other classes, nearly all mixed traffic types, followed quickly.

Railway preservation

The same period was marked by withdrawal of many locomotives dating from before the 1923 grouping. Some were officially preserved by the Railway Executive, such as former GWR no. 4003 *Lode Star* of 1907 and the venerable LMS/Midland 2-4-0 no. 20002 of 1866, both of them preserved in 1951.

Of greater long term importance in 1951, though this may not have been apparent at the time, was the preservation of the Talyllyn Railway. At that date it was both in appalling condition and an incredible antique: its two locomotives, four coaches and single brake van all dated from the 1860s. It was about to close, but was instead preserved as a going concern by the Talyllyn Railway Preservation Society.

This was the first time a society of amateurs preserved a railway by means of a public appeal for funds and voluntary labour.

The Talyllyn Railway was preserved at the instigation of the late L. T. C. Rolt and his friends, and the TRPS was formed by them. I wrote its story in *Railways Revived*, but in amplification of this I must give credit here to Mr O. H. Prosser, who has recently sent me a copy of a letter he received from Rolt in September 1949 in reply to one of his own. This makes it clear that Prosser had then already suggested to Rolt the idea of a Talyllyn Railway Preservation Society, and that Rolt had not previously envisaged such a body.

The eventual success of the Talyllyn is well known, and it led to the establishment of many other preserved operating railways. Next after the Talyllyn came the Festiniog—closed in 1946, re-opened from 1955 onwards by the combined efforts of Alan Pegler (who had purchased control of the company) and of the Festiniog Railway Society.

Approaching change

At this period, the British Railways system was profitable. The British Transport Commission, of which railways were by far the largest undertaking, had revenue surpluses in 1951, 1952 and 1953—it was £7·6 million in 1953. Since railways generally had an old-fashioned air, one cannot help but suspect that this situation was due as much to contemporary inadequacies of other forms of transport as to inherent merits of rail. In any event, closure of unremunerative lines and stations—which had all but ceased during the war—was now continuing at a gradually increasing rate. Between the beginning of 1948 and the beginning of 1954, about 1,000 miles of line were closed to passengers.

A harbinger of greater change was the financial collapse, despite long experience of diesel railcars and heavy traffic during the war years, of the Great Northern Railway of Ireland. In 1950 the company proposed closure of its entire undertaking. This was then purchased by the governments of Northern Ireland and the Irish Republic, acting together; it was operated by the Great Northern Railway of Ireland Board on which CIE and the Ulster Transport Authority were equally represented. Eventually, most GNR (I) branch lines were closed and the Dublin–Belfast main line, the only remaining cross-border route, was divided between CIE and UTA.

In Britain, the Railway Executive was eventually abolished in 1953. In 1954 electrification of the former Great Central route from Manchester to Sheffield was completed; this revival of a pre-war LNER project had involved boring a replacement Woodhead tunnel and provided Britain with its first main line on which both passenger and goods trains were electrically hauled. The year 1954 also saw the introduction of the first British Railways lightweight diesel multiple

2/36 In 1960, an N class 2–6–0 built for the South Eastern & Chatham Railway is hauling a local train of Southern Railway coaches near Folkestone Warren. The flat bottom rail is a British Railways innovation.

unit (DMU) trains, in a belated programme to replace steam trains by diesel on branch lines in six areas. The West Riding of Yorkshire was the first to receive them. Such things had long been commonplace on the Continent.

In the same year that it put its first DMUs into service, British Railways introduced two new standard classes of steam locomotive, completing the range of twelve. They were the class 9F 2-10-0 for heavy freight trains, and the class 8P 4-6-2 for express passenger trains. The former was perhaps the most successful of all standard classes, and 251 locomotives were built; but the latter was destined to contain only a single isolated prototype, no. 71000 *Duke of Gloucester*. For elsewhere, French Railways, having completed electrification of the main line from Paris to Lyons in 1952, achieved on it in 1954 a world speed record of 151 mph, and then went on in 1955 to reach 205 mph on the electrified main line south of Bordeaux. In Ireland, CIE in 1954 ordered, from British builders, sufficient diesel locomotives to complete conversion of most of its railways from steam to diesel.

Modernisation of British Railways

In 1955 came, at last, a comprehensive plan for the modernisation of British Railways. It was announced by BTC chairman Sir Brian Robertson in January and its aims were to exploit the natural advantages of railways as bulk transporters of passengers and goods. The principal means by which these were to be achieved were: upgrading of track, civil engineering works and signalling to permit speeds of at least 100 mph; electrification of some lines and replacement of steam by diesel traction in specified areas elsewhere; fitting of goods wagons with continuous brakes, and replacement of many small goods stations and marshalling yards by fewer, larger, ones.

Particular proposals included electrification from Euston to Birmingham, Liverpool and Manchester and from King's Cross to Doncaster and Leeds; widespread replacement of semaphore signalling and mechanical operation of points by colour lights and power signal boxes; extensive use of diesel multiple unit trains, and construction of 2,500 main line diesel locomotives. Though belated, the plan was bold. At that time BR had about 6 main line diesels and some 19,000 steam locomotives. Over 6,000 of the latter still dated from before the grouping. It was intended that the plan would be completed over fifteen years—by 1970, that is—at a cost of £1,200 million. The Government gave its blessing but no money: the plan was to be financed by borrowing. Remarkable omissions from the plan, when considered with the benefit of hindsight, were any hint that the steam locomotive might become virtually extinct within the time span involved, or that there would be any marked reduction in the route mileage of the railway system, apart from a brief mention that certain loss-making branch lines and steam train stopping services might be replaced by road transport.

The plan was only just in time. Roads, as old fashioned as railways, were about to be improved: late in 1955 construction of the first 345 miles of motorway, over ten years for £85 million, was announced.

In December 1955 the English Electric Co. completed, as a speculation, a 3,300 hp diesel electric express locomotive—the prototype Deltic—which was put into experimental use on BR. The following month the BTC announced contracts with several manufacturers for a total of 141 main line diesel locomotives and 30 power units, of various types, for a pilot scheme of comparative trials; none of them was to be of more than 2,300 hp.

Hardly had implementation of the modernisation plan commenced however, than the BTC started to fall into serious financial trouble, due to increasing costs (particularly wages), increasing competition, and inflation. For 1955 a working surplus was converted into an overall deficit by central charges. In 1956 there was a working deficit on British Railways of £16·6 million, in 1957 it rose to £27·1 million. In the latter year there were in addition interest and central administration charges of £41 million. And although passenger traffic in 1957 was the highest since nationalisation, that was a consequence of petrol rationing brought about by the Suez crisis. Reluctant rail passengers were only too willing to revert to road as soon as possible.

In Britain, for many years, two classes only of passenger accommodation had generally been provided, called first and third class. First, second and third classes survived on boat trains for the Continent, in conformity with Continental practice, for there were through bookings to consider. In 1956 both Continental railways and British Railways reduced the number of classes to two, first and second. The general effect in Britain was that former third class accommodation was re-classified as second.

Progress, and otherwise, in the late fifties

At this period there were still a few developments with steam. For example, Bulleid 4-6-2s of the Southern Region were rebuilt to retain their best features and lose their less satisfactory ones, and some class 9F 2-10-0s were fitted with mechanical stokers. A new motive power depot, authorised before the modernisation plan and laid out largely for steam, was opened at Thornaby-on-Tees. The late-afternoon express between King's Cross and Edinburgh, called *The Talisman*, was introduced in 1956, powered by A4 4-6-2s; the West Coast Route responded the following year with *The Caledonian*, London to Glasgow, powered by Duchess class 4-6-2s. On one notable occasion (5 September 1957) no. 46244 *King George VI* improved markedly on the schedule of 6 hours 40 minutes for 401 miles by arriving with the up train at Euston 37 minutes early.

That long-familiar accompaniment to a railway journey, the clickety-clack of wheels on rail-joints, began to disappear in the late 1950s with the introduction of long-welded rails. In 1958 the BTC decided to install them on main lines throughout the country. By the end of the same year there were more than 2,000 vehicles to form diesel multiple unit trains in service, and BR's first four-wheeled diesel railbuses were introduced—too late, unfortunately, to make the branch lines for which they were intended remunerative. Construction of second class coaches with separate compartments ceased.

Delivery of the main line diesel locomotives to form the pilot scheme had started, but long before they had all been delivered the BTC had decided to increase their numbers greatly, in an attempt to realise quickly the economies that were expected to result from the change from steam to diesel. This attempt was not to be wholly successful, for many of the early designs of main line diesel locomotives proved to be underpowered or otherwise unsatisfactory, and these locomotives themselves had short lives. However, by the end of 1958, 100 main line diesel locomotives were in service, and 600 more were on order.

The Netherlands Railways had already run their last steam train on 7 January 1958: the first European national railway system to cease using steam locomotives. Laggard Britain was at least able to take advantage of improved methods of electrification. It had been intended to electrify lines outside the Southern Region (which was committed to the Southern Railway's third rail system) with overhead wires at 1,500 volts dc. This system had been used between Manchester and Sheffield. Developments on the Continent made it possible to electrify more cheaply at 25 kV 50 Hz ac, and the decision to adopt this sytem was taken in 1956. During the same year the BTC decided to accelerate the scheme to electrify the LM Region main line from Euston to Birmingham, Liverpool and Manchester; proposed electrification of the East Coast main line from King's Cross was relegated to a date later than 1963, later modified to 1970 (and eventually, it seems, to oblivion).

The first section of the M1 motorway was opened in November 1959. It enabled the time by motor coach between London and Birmingham to be reduced to two and a half hours, including the crowded city streets at each end of the run. The fastest times by train had been two hours for many years, and many trains took longer; and the fares by train were higher than those by coach.

In 1959 too, the Mini had been introduced. Whereas a short time before one had assumed an average speed of 30 mph when planning a car journey, suddenly in the late 1950s it seemed that Everyman in a mass-produced car was going to be able to average 60 mph along a motorway. The motor car, the privilege of the few, was becoming the privilege of the many. There was a considerable, and vociferous, body of opinion that held that the proper future for railways lay in their conversion into roads.

This proposal was, in general terms, fallacious, if only because of the much greater width of land required for a motorway or main road than for a railway. There were, however, some instances where roads were built along the courses of closed railways. Notable ones included the construction of part of the Heads of the Valleys Road in South Wales along the course of the closed LNWR line between Abergavenny and Merthyr, and of part of the A1(M) Darlington Bypass on the course of a closed branch line of the North Eastern Railway.

During the summer of 1960 diesel multiple unit Pullman expresses were introduced between St Pancras and Manchester; Paddington, Birmingham and Wolverhampton; and Paddington and Bristol. The first two routes were imaginative gestures to retain and encourage traffic while electrification works on the West Coast main line caused deceleration of trains between Euston and the places served. The first 25 kV ac locomotives were delivered late in 1959, and the Manchester–Crewe line was electrified in September 1960, the first section of the London Midland scheme to be completed.

Branch lines and wayside stations were indeed being closed at an increasing rate. Between 1955 and 1958 nearly eighty branch lines were closed, with closure of another thirty pending at the end of 1958; during the same period 350 little-used stations were closed. Notable among the lines closed were the Welshpool & Llanfair in 1956, the last un-preserved narrow gauge line in Britain to carry public freight traffic; and almost the whole of the system of the Midland & Great Northern Joint Railway, closed in 1959. Both closures prompted preservation schemes. Nor in many instances did introduction of diesel trains increase passenger traffic on branch lines sufficiently to save them. It was stated that passenger traffic on the Buckingham-to-Banbury branch, for instance, increased by 434 per cent after diesel railcars were introduced in 1956 (which does rather suggest that the line must have been extremely poorly patronised previously), but the branch was closed nevertheless in 1961.

A forerunner of things to come was the simultaneous closure of many wayside stations on main lines too—in the first case, the closure to passengers of thirty stations on the lines between Glasgow Buchanan Street and Perth, Perth and Aberdeen, and Perth and Dundee, on 11 June 1956. An improved service of fast trains to surviving stations was introduced at the same time. Much earlier than this however, before the Second World War, the LNER had closed simultaneously all the wayside stations between York and Malton, twenty one miles apart.

Another early example of an economy scheme of a type which has since become familiar was the demotion, in January 1960, of fifteen passenger stations on the Hull–Hornsea and Hull–Withernsea branches into unstaffed halts, with the introduction of conductor guards on trains, to issue tickets. It was later named the pay-train system. The purpose-built unstaffed halt was not new, the Great Western, for instance, having opened a great many during the years before and after the First World War.

Two ancient railways closed at this period were the Swansea & Mumbles which, as the Oystermouth Railway, had pioneered railway passenger traffic in 1807 but had subsequently transformed itself by stages into an electric tramway, which was closed in 1960, and Stephenson's Hetton Railway, which had remained a colliery line and was last used about the end of 1959. Closure of the 3 ft. gauge West Clare line in Ireland, in 1961, despite full dieselisation, brought to an end the use of the 3 ft. gauge for public railways in that country.

Standard gauge preservation

A small but pleasant feature of railways in the late fifties and early sixties was the restoration to working order by British Railways of several museum-piece locomotives, principally to haul special trains. The first of these was Great Western record breaker *City of Truro*, restored to working order in 1957; she was followed by three pre-grouping Scottish locomotives, from the Caledonian, Highland and Great North of Scotland Railways, and former Midland Railway 4-4-0 no. 1000. All were repainted in the liveries of their original owners.

Such activities could not outlast the eventual withdrawal of everyday steam power by British Railways, but in the meantime standard gauge operating preserved railways were becoming established. The first two to be reopened, almost simultaneously in 1960, were the Bluebell and the Middleton Railways. The Bluebell is the Horsted Keynes–Sheffield Park section of the former LBSCR branch between East Grinstead and Lewes. This line had been closed in 1955 and, following discovery of an old Act of Parliament requiring a train service over it, reopened in 1956. It closed a second time in 1958, not without publicity. The Bluebell Railway Preservation Society was eventually able to reopen its section through the medium of a light railway order made to a limited company set up to lease, and eventually purchase, the line from BR. The Middleton Railway is the direct descendant of that early waggonway which was authorised by Act of Parliament in 1758 and equipped with rack rails and steam locomotives as early as 1812. The Middleton Railway Preservation Society was formed in 1959 and later converted into the Middleton Railway Trust; it is notable, almost uniquely among preserved lines, for having concentrated for many years on freight traffic.

Earlier than this, enthusiasts for industrial railway locomotives were starting to preserve them in their gardens. A pioneer was J. B. Latham, secretary of the Industrial Locomotive Society, who in 1957 purchased the 1 ft. 11½ in. gauge 0-6-0 saddle tank *Triassic* when the Rugby Portland Cement Co. Ltd ceased to use its railway system of that gauge at Southam, Warwickshire. Another pioneer was Captain W. G. Smith, who in 1959 purchased privately from British Railways the former Great Northern Railway 0-6-0 saddle tank locomotive no. 1247, withdrawn that year, and restored her to her original livery for preservation in working order. She was operated from time to time on British Railways' lines. Yet another pioneering venture was a public appeal set up in 1960 by T. R. Gomm to purchase GWR 4-4-0 no. 9017 from BR. The fund was successful in raising the £1,500 required, and the

2/37 The first part of the M1 motorway was opened in 1959, and anyone in a mass-produced car could cruise along it at 60 mph or more. Near Welton, south of Rugby, it ran alongside the West Coast Main Line, and express trains hauled by Pacifics designed twenty-two years earlier began to seem sadly old-fashioned. The locomotive is no. 46242 City of Glasgow. *However, comparison of the width of the double track main line railway with one carriageway alone of the motorway effectively disposes of the then popular notion that railways should, in general, be converted into roads; and the stylised petrol pump on the motorway* Fuel *sign now has its own antique appeal!*

locomotive was purchased in 1962 and taken to the Bluebell Railway where she has since worked.

Change in the sixties

Construction of new steam locomotives for BR ceased in March 1960, when there was completed at Swindon the class 9F 2-10-0 no. 92220. Her superbly appropriate name *Evening Star* was chosen as a result of a competition among railway staff.

Almost simultaneously came the first indications of more great changes to come on the railways. Continuing high expenditure on modernisation of a railway system which was falling deeper into debt was causing great public concern. The Guillebaud Committee, which had been set up by the BTC and the railway trades unions, recommended that increases equivalent to as much as eighteen per cent were needed to bring pay of railwaymen up to the rates paid for equivalent work elsewhere. In those days, when high inflation rates were known only as something which happened in Germany after the First World War, such a percentage increase was phenomenal.

The government of the day accepted it however, but with the proviso that the railway industry should be modified to a size and pattern suited to the conditions and prospects of the time. In pursuit of this aim, the Transport Act 1962 wrote off much of the railways' debt and disbanded the British Transport Commission, distributing its various activities among new boards responsible to the Minister of Transport. One of these was the British Railways Board, which since then has owned and operated the national railway system. The London Underground system, however, passed to the London Transport Board; when, in 1970, overall responsibility for this passed to the Greater London Council, the name London Transport Executive was revived.

Foreshadowing these alterations, Dr Richard Beeching (now Lord Beeching) had been appointed chairman of the BTC and chairman designate of BRB, in June 1961 for a five-year term. For the full Beeching Report on re-shaping British Railways, however, the nation had to wait until the spring of 1963; in the meantime, modernisation continued. So did the process of closing unremunerative branch lines: the press called it the Beeching Axe. So punch-drunk with closures and rumours of closures did the public become that in July 1962 the BTC found it necessary to deny categorically that Paddington station was to be closed. In Countesthorpe, Leicestershire, it was reported that a new thoroughfare off Station Road was, following closure of the station, to be named, with wry humour, Beeching Close. Entirely serious was the withdrawal from 1 January 1962 of livestock traffic from 2,261 stations, out of 2,493 which dealt with it. Later, the others were to go too.

On the positive side, the first automatically operated barriers at a level crossing were installed in 1961 to replace gates worked from a signal box. More spectacular in the same year was the introduction to East Coast Route Scottish express services of the production batch of Deltic diesel-electric locomotives. They enabled the schedule of the fastest trains between London and Edinburgh to be reduced to six hours. The prototype Deltic, after six years of operation, retired to the Science Museum in 1963. Autumn 1962 saw the end of steam in East Anglia, with all trains in and out of Liverpool Street either diesel or electrically powered. Between Paddington and Birmingham Snow Hill, King class steam locomotives were replaced by the new Western class 2,700 hp diesel locomotives with hydraulic transmission. The first of the second generation of main line diesel locomotives, the 2,750 hp Brush type 4, appeared in 1963: these locomotives remain familiar as class 47.

Widespread improvements were being made in matters of detail. The BR Design Panel had been established in 1956; an advisory body little heeded at first, it was greatly encouraged in its work by Dr Beeching who saw that good industrial design would improve the marketability of rail transport. By 1963 there were few aspects of railways which the panel had not affected, and when an exhibition of new designs of railway equipment was held at the Design Centre, London, that spring, it attracted record attendance. Here was seen for the first time, in mock-up form, a carriage interior of the type which is now in general use in main line trains and has largely superseded traditional types; here too were seen for the first time railway uniforms of the designs which are now familiar. The outward appearance today of many other features of railways—from diesel locomotives to luggage trolleys—results directly or indirectly from the work of the Design Panel at this period.

The Beeching Report

In March 1963 was published the document which has probably had greater effect on the railway system, and on public attitudes towards it, than any other. This was *The Reshaping of British Railways*, commonly known as the Beeching Report or the Beeching Plan.

Dr Beeching, on his appointment as chairman, had initiated a series of investigations into railway traffics, potential traffics and costs. These were deeper and wider-reaching than any other before or since. Some startling conclusions emerged in the report. One third of the route mileage, for instance, carried only one per cent of total passenger-miles, and similarly, one third of the route mileage carried only one per cent of total freight ton/miles. From another viewpoint, it had been found that one third of the total number of passenger stations produced only two per cent of total passenger revenue, and that less than one per cent of stations produced as much as twenty six per cent of that revenue.

In Parliament, such generalities had already been focussed on the particular example of a train between Berwick and Edinburgh which cost £164 a day to run, seldom carried more than eight passengers and on one particular day produced a revenue of ten shillings.

Such services were unlikely ever to pay their way whatever their motive power. The essence of the report was that railways should be used to provide those forms of transport for which they were best suited, and should cease to do things for which they were ill-suited. Steps proposed to achieve these aims included: discontinuation of many stopping passenger trains; closure of many small stations; improvement of inter-city passenger services; dampening down of seasonal traffic peaks (which required many coaches to be maintained for little use); increased block train movements of coal; introduction of the liner train system (that is, freight containers carried by scheduled train services);

2/38 Change at Crewe. In 1960, the year after the first part of the M1 was opened, BR completed electrification of the first section of the London Midland Region main lines to be electrified under the 1955 modernisation plan. This was from Manchester to Crewe. For a few years steam locomotives such as Duchess class Pacific no. 46248 City of Leeds *could be seen alongside 25 kV electric locomotives and trains. This photograph was taken on 7 September 1963.*

and continued replacement of steam power by diesel.

All very worthy; what caused fury were the *details* of closures which were included in the report. Some 2,363 passenger stations (out of a total of 4,709) were named as being proposed for closure. Passenger trains were to be withdrawn entirely from 5,000 miles of route (in 1961 BR had a route mileage of 17,830) and many stopping passenger train services discontinued elsewhere. The earlier vociferousness of those who had proposed closure of railways in general was now drowned by greater howls of rage from those whose stations were actually named for closure.

In the long run not all the proposals for closure were carried out. There are still railways north of Inverness and through central Wales, for instance. Elsewhere, routes which were spared by the Beeching Plan have since been closed—the direct line linking Edinburgh and Perth via Glenfarg was one of them. The plan's greatest defect was probably lack of much apparent concern for the railwaymen affected by it, and lack of awareness of public concern for them. When, for instance, in 1964 closure of wayside stations on the Cambrian Railways main line was announced, the *Cambrian News* of Aberystwyth carried the front page headline 'Forty Minute Speed-up on the Shrewsbury Line'. But it relegated the details to an inner page, and concentrated its front page story on the 126 men who would become redundant.

Bad news is more saleable than good, and Dr Beeching tended to get a bad press. Overall the report, though drastic, was good. As a *Railway Magazine* editorial remarked, it was only six or seven years overdue. Certainly this author's opinion remains that Beeching was the greatest railwayman since Brunel: just about the first since Brunel's time to get down to fundamentals and tackle them with flair. More was the pity that he left British Railways prematurely following a change of government from Conservative to Labour.

Despite that change, withdrawals of passenger services and closure of stations went ahead, though at a slower rate. Economic viability was achieved for a few years in the late sixties and early seventies, only to become elusive again. One need not, here, go into detail of the successive ways contrived to meet continuing deficits. The BR network itself had been reduced to some 11,500 route miles by the early seventies and despite repeated rumours of further drastic pruning has since remained stable with few closures, though one fears for the future in the present harsh economic climate. Passenger stations, reduced to 2,750 by 1967, numbered 2,358 in 1977.

Some lines and stations which had been closed have subsequently been reopened: Kingsnowe and Matlock Bath stations, for instance; and the Ladybank–Bridge of Earn line for passengers, the Thornbury branch relaid for freight. Northern Ireland, where it once seemed railways would become extinct, has seen something of the same process, with the transfer of surviving railways from the road-oriented Ulster Transport Authority to Northern Ireland Railways, the construction of Belfast Central station in 1974 and reopening of the Lisburn–Antrim line to passengers.

Scarcely noticed among the wholesale closures of the Beeching period went the last surviving remnant of the horse-railway era. Although most horse railways were either converted into steam railways during the nineteenth century or abandoned altogether, a few survived into the twentieth. Much of the Nantlle Railway had been converted into steam railway in the 1860s and 1870s, but a stretch of about one and a half miles remained to connect slate quarries with Nantlle station. Horse-worked to the end, it was closed only when the steam-worked line closed in December 1963. In collieries, pit ponies are still used to a limited extent. Even while this book was in production, *The Sunday Times* (11 January 1981) devoted half a page to Pantygaseg privately-owned mine, in Gwent, where ponies still haul trams of coal out of the drift, and referred to another private mine where ponies are used on the surface only, because of the steepness of the tunnels.

Even on steam railways, horses had continued to be used extensively for shunting. The last BR shunting horse was pensioned off about 1966: he had been employed, appropriately, at Newmarket.

British Railways became, for promotional purposes, 'British Rail' in 1965. The blue-and-white livery for passenger coaches and the double-arrow symbol had appeared the previous year. Positive principles enunciated in the Beeching Report have largely been adopted. Rolling stock for inter-city trains has been steadily improved, leading to the diesel High Speed Train, able to reach 125 mph in scheduled service and first put into use in 1976, and the electric Advanced Passenger Train able to reach 150 mph and yet to enter regular service. Speeds of 100 mph had become regarded as commonplace by 1970; a few years later, on roads, the 70 mph speed limit was imposed.

Freightliner trains for containers have become common; so have bulk trains for coal, oil, cement, stone and other commodities; they run from depot to depot and avoid marshalling yards with attendant delays. Coal in particular is much carried between colliery and power station in 'merry-go-round' trains of hopper wagons, loaded and unloaded automatically. The short wheelbase goods wagon without continuous brakes is still with us, however, and so is the semaphore signal, though many routes have been converted to colour lights. The last semaphore on the East Coast Route between London and Edinburgh was replaced in 1978.

Electrification of the West Coast Route southwards from Manchester and Liverpool reached Euston in 1966. It had been preceded by demolition of the old Euston station and construction of the new. The old station was, from the points of view of both operator and passenger, a rabbit warren of a place but it included notable architectural features: the Great Hall and the Euston Arch, or Doric portico, the loss of which has been greatly regretted. Electrification of the loop from Rugby via Birmingham and Wolverhampton to Stafford was completed in 1967. Further north, electrification from Weaver Junction (where London–Liverpool trains diverge from the main line) to Glasgow was authorised in 1970; it was completed in 1974 to provide a main line electrified throughout between London and Glasgow.

The end of steam

Rapid contraction of the railway system in the mid-1960s reduced demand for motive power, and steam locomotives were replaced by BR very much sooner than had originally been expected. By 1964 they were being withdrawn at a rate of between 75 and 100 a week. By the end of 1965 British Rail still had 2,987 steam locomotives in service; by 1967 the total was down to 362. By early 1968 steam working survived only in North West England and on the narrow gauge Vale of Rheidol line from Aberystwyth to Devil's Bridge. This line continues to operate, with its three steam locomotives, as a tourist attraction; otherwise, British Rail ceased to use steam locomotives in the summer of 1968. The last scheduled passenger train to be hauled by a steam locomotive ran on Saturday 3 August: the Liverpool portion of the 17·25 from Glasgow, detached at Preston and worked forward from there at 21·25 behind a class 5 mixed traffic 4-6-0 which achieved a heroic eighty mph on the way to Liverpool. The following day there were several steam farewell specials; the final steam train of all was a farewell special on Sunday 11 August. It ran from Liverpool to Manchester, Blackburn and Carlisle and back, traversing the route of the Liverpool & Manchester Railway and the Settle & Carlisle line. Three class 5 4-6-0s and class 7 4-6-2 *Oliver Cromwell* powered it over various stages of its route.

This was not, however, the final end of steam locomotives in commercial service. London Transport, for instance, continued to use them until 1971 to haul engineer's trains at night when electric power was switched off, and industry—particularly the National Coal Board—continues to use steam locomotives, though to a steadily declining extent.

The railway preservation boom

The rapid disappearance of steam locomotives and branch lines during the 1960s inevitably gave a tremendous boost to railway preservation: to the preservation both of locomotives and rolling stock, static and active, and of entire branch lines as going concerns. The British Transport Commission had an enlightened policy towards preservation of historic relics and in 1961 scheduled twenty seven locomotives of historic importance for preservation on withdrawal, to add to the forty four historic preserved locomotives it already had. The principal home for its collection of historic relics (which included trams and road vehicles) was its Museum of British Transport at Clapham, London, opened for small exhibits in 1961 and large ones in 1963.

With dismemberment of the British Transport Commission however, the exhibits of this popular but loss-making museum had to be dispersed. The fate of the railway exhibits became a cause of acute controversy. The eventual solution was their transfer to the ownership of the Department of Education and Science, and establishment of the National Railway Museum, as an out-station of the Science Museum, at York. York had been the location of a smaller railway museum for many years, and the new museum, unlike Clapham, is rail-connected. The National Railway Museum at York was opened on 27 September 1975, and the quality of exhibits and presentation was such as to dispel immediately any lingering regrets over Clapham. Aided perhaps by the free admission which is the public's right to it as a national museum, it received one million visitors within its first seven months. To provide a focus for voluntary support, the 'Friends of the National Railway Museum' was formed in 1977, and while the government provides the museum's bread and butter, the Friends provides the jam. For instance, it financed restoration to steam in 1980, with great success, of Stanier Pacific *Duchess of Hamilton* (mentioned in chapter five), for the locomotive is on loan to the museum, not owned by the DES, so expenditure from government funds would have been inappropriate. Similarly when Deltic diesel electric locomotive no. 55 022 *The King's Own Yorkshire Light Infantry* received in 1980 what is expected to be its last major overhaul in BR ownership, the Friends arranged for it to be painted in its original green livery of 1961: for the locomotive is reserved for the museum on withdrawal in a year or two's time.

The NRM was the principal, and worthy, contribution of central authority to railway preservation. It is no disparagement to it to write that a far greater contribution has been made by individuals, voluntary societies, and companies which started as voluntary organisations but subsequently became in part commercial. Alan Pegler hit the headlines in 1963 when he purchased the Gresley Pacific locomotive *Flying Scotsman* when she became due for withdrawal. He had

2/39 *The sun did not always shine on steam trains, and rebuilt Patriot class 4–6–0* Southport *is passing through Shap station during a heavy thunderstorm in July 1964, with a relief train from Glasgow to Euston.*

2/40 *The site of Shap station in 1980. The station building is still occupied, but platforms, awning and footbridge have gone; so have bullhead track and pointwork. Long-welded flat bottom rail, and overhead electric wiring and masts, have taken their place: truly a new railway has been built on the site of the old.*

her overhauled and was able to operate her on special trains over BR tracks. His example and those of other pioneers mentioned on page 97 were followed by many individuals and groups who purchased steam locomotives over the next few years.

The example of the Bluebell Railway in preserving and reopening a BR branch line was also widely emulated. Notable among successful schemes are the Worth Valley Railway (Keighley to Oxenhope, reopened 1968), the Dart Valley Railway (Buckfastleigh to Totnes, 1969, and Paignton to Kingswear, 1972), the Severn Valley Railway (Bridgnorth to, almost, Kidderminster; first section reopened 1970), and the North Yorkshire Moors Railway (Grosmont to Pickering, 1973). The Association of Railway Preservation Societies, which coordinates member societies' activities and encourages high standards, was formed in 1965 with nine railway preservation societies as members. Subsequently incorporated as the Association of Railway Preservation Societies Ltd, it now has some seventy societies as full members and as many again as associates. The ARPS does not raise funds: the Transport Trust, formed in 1965, does so; for the benefit of railways among other forms of transport preservation.

The end of steam on British Rail in 1968 was accompanied by a general ban on the operation of special trains hauled by preserved steam locomotives. The reasons for this have never been entirely clear: probably it had something to do with a reluctance by railway management to retain any steam locomotive servicing facilities, coupled with an equal reluctance to provide reminders, for railwaymen and passengers, of supposedly good old days at a time when rapid modernisation was essential. At any rate it was three long years and more before constant gentle persuasion, led by the ARPS, resulted, in October 1971, in a trial excursion over BR by former GWR 4-6-0 no. 6000 *King George V*, (part of the national collection). The results were, evidently, satisfactory and difficulties not insurmountable: since then BR has generally allowed steam specials over selected secondary main lines, using selected locomotives which have passed intensive scrutiny. By 1979 British Rail was sponsoring such trains itself, and in 1980 they appeared in the annual BR timetable.

Shildon and Rainhill

The two greatest and happiest railway occasions in recent years have been the 150th anniversary celebrations of the Stockton & Darlington Railway, in 1975, and those of the Liverpool & Manchester Railway, in 1980. The principal feature of these in each case was a cavalcade of historic locomotives over a section of the original line—between Shildon and Heighington on the S & DR and at Rainhill on the L & M.

Inspiration for the Stockton & Darlington celebrations was probably provided by the earlier events held to mark the fiftieth and one hundredth anniversaries of the S & DR in 1875 and 1925 respectively. Although S & DR *Locomotion* of 1825 survives, by the 1970s it was considered that to make her work again would entail such extensive rebuilding that her authenticity as a museum piece would be destroyed. Instead, a full-size working replica was built, a co-operative effort by engineering training establishments, companies and individuals in North East England, led by M. G. Satow.

On 31 August 1975, the replica *Locomotion* headed the cavalcade and was followed by thirty three historic locomotives, most of them under their own steam, with BR's prototype High Speed Train bringing up the rear. There were nearly 300,000 spectators.

The event was staged by a joint committee comprising, principally, the local authorities, railway preservation groups, and British Rail. Its success led Locomotion Enterprises (which had evolved out of the venture of building the replica locomotive) to consider re-staging the Rainhill Trials with replica locomotives, and it also led British Rail to decide to run the Liverpool & Manchester celebrations itself.

The outcome was the cavalcade at Rainhill staged on three successive days. For this a bank holiday weekend was needed, and as the spring bank holiday offered the best chance of fine weather, the 'Rocket 150' cavalcade, celebrating the 150th anniversaries of both the Rainhill Trials of autumn 1829, and the opening of the Liverpool & Manchester Railway in autumn 1830, was staged on 24, 25 and 26 May 1980. Its principal improvement over Shildon was that many of the locomotives hauled appropriate rolling stock.

The land on either side of the Rainhill level, though not far from Liverpool, has by good fortune not been built over, and stands were erected on either side of the track. The line was closed to normal traffic for the event and at Liverpool Lime Street a notice board of awesome size listed the consequent diversions and re-timings of passenger trains. The crowds that attended were of proportions comparable with Shildon. It was indeed a remarkable experience to be conscious of being present at the precise location where grandstands had been erected and crowds had gathered just over 150 years before, for the trials at which the practicability of steam locomotives, and indeed of mechanical transport on land, had been proved.

As a re-staging of the Rainhill Trials however, the first day of the 1980 event, which I attended, was unfortunately not a success. The replica *Novelty* had earlier shown an unwillingness to perform and was instead displayed, in steam, on a well wagon forming part of an otherwise mostly typical steam-age goods train. Then immediately prior to the cavalcade, the replica *Rocket* became seriously derailed in sidings and in doing so blocked in the replica *Sans Pareil*. Both locomotives took part on the second and third days of the event, but on the opening day. *Sans Pareil* appeared only at the end of the cavalcade, and *Rocket* not at all.

So the honour of leading the cavalcade on the first day fell not to the replica *Rocket* but to the real *Lion*, genuine Liverpool & Manchester Railway locomotive built in 1838 and now the oldest workable steam locomotive. *Lion* led a cavalcade of some thirty-six exhibits in roughly chronological order. Locomotives of the last century were followed by pre-grouping locomotives of the present century, by the finest express locomotives of the big four companies, and eventually, by *Evening Star*. Then came first-generation diesel locomotives, one of them itself withdrawn and preserved, the most modern locomotives, a High Speed Train and an Advanced Passenger Train.

The cavalcade provided an object lesson in the development of motive power. It did more than that: its locomotives and rolling stock, with a multiplicity of styles, colours, whistles, and exhaust sounds, all representative of former owning railways, briefly re-created that variety and contrast which were once—but are no longer—a most attractive part of the railway scene.

2/41 It is October 1971 and British Rail's steam ban, imposed with the end of steam in 1968, has been relaxed after lasting for more than three years. Preserved former GWR 4-6-0 King George V *stands at Kensington Olympia during the course of an experimental tour from Hereford to Birmingham and London, arranged between BRB and H. P. Bulmer Ltd, to establish what difficulties were inherent in running steam excursions. Happily, the experiment was successful and the difficulties not excessive.*

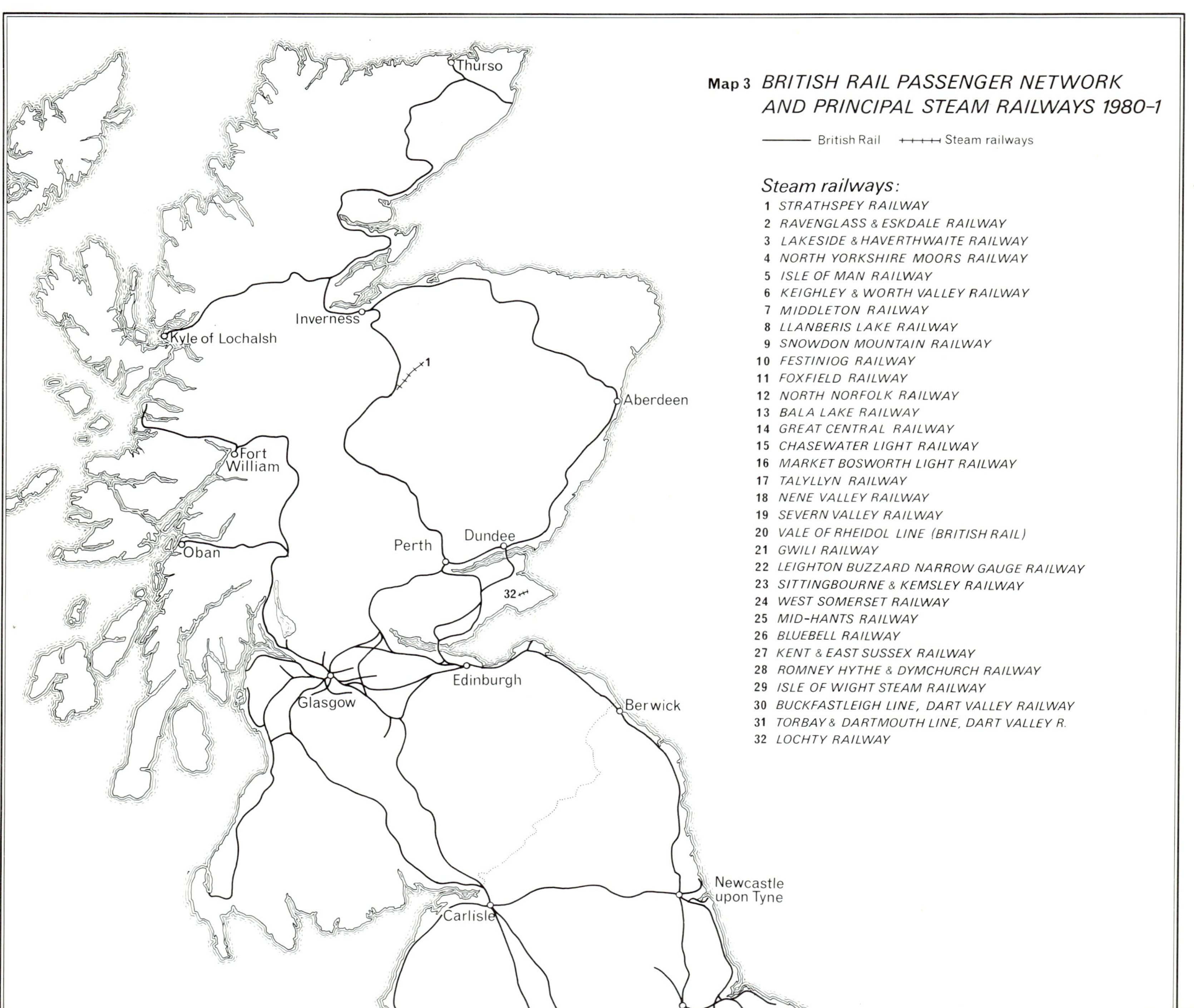
Map 3 BRITISH RAIL PASSENGER NETWORK AND PRINCIPAL STEAM RAILWAYS 1980-1
British Rail
Steam railways
Steam railways:
1 STRATHSPEY RAILWAY
2 RAVENGLASS & ESKDALE RAILWAY
3 LAKESIDE & HAVERTHWAITE RAILWAY
4 NORTH YORKSHIRE MOORS RAILWAY
5 ISLE OF MAN RAILWAY
6 KEIGHLEY & WORTH VALLEY RAILWAY
7 MIDDLETON RAILWAY
8 LLANBERIS LAKE RAILWAY
9 SNOWDON MOUNTAIN RAILWAY
10 FESTINIOG RAILWAY
11 FOXFIELD RAILWAY
12 NORTH NORFOLK RAILWAY
13 BALA LAKE RAILWAY
14 GREAT CENTRAL RAILWAY
15 CHASEWATER LIGHT RAILWAY
16 MARKET BOSWORTH LIGHT RAILWAY
17 TALYLLYN RAILWAY
18 NENE VALLEY RAILWAY
19 SEVERN VALLEY RAILWAY
20 VALE OF RHEIDOL LINE (BRITISH RAIL)
21 GWILI RAILWAY
22 LEIGHTON BUZZARD NARROW GAUGE RAILWAY
23 SITTINGBOURNE & KEMSLEY RAILWAY
24 WEST SOMERSET RAILWAY
25 MID-HANTS RAILWAY
26 BLUEBELL RAILWAY
27 KENT & EAST SUSSEX RAILWAY
28 ROMNEY HYTHE & DYMCHURCH RAILWAY
29 ISLE OF WIGHT STEAM RAILWAY
30 BUCKFASTLEIGH LINE, DART VALLEY RAILWAY
31 TORBAY & DARTMOUTH LINE, DART VALLEY R.
32 LOCHTY RAILWAY
Thurso
Inverness
Kyle of Lochalsh
1
Aberdeen
Fort William
Dundee
Perth
Oban
32
Edinburgh
Glasgow
Berwick
Newcastle upon Tyne
Carlisle

Lancaster
York
Leeds
Manchester
Liverpool
Doncaster
Sheffield
Holyhead
Crewe
Derby
Nottingham
Norwich
Shrewsbury
Leicester
Peterborough
Wolverhampton
Birmingham
Rugby
Cambridge
Fishguard
Hereford
Gloucester
Oxford
Swindon
Didcot
London
Swansea
Cardiff
Bristol
Barnstaple
Dover
Southampton
Exeter
Brighton
Weymouth
Plymouth
Penzance
5
6
7
8
9
10
11
12
13
14
15
16
17
18
19
20
21
22
23
24
25
26
27
28
29
30
31
0 30 miles
0 50 km

CHAPTER 3

WAGGONWAYS, TRAMROADS AND PLATEWAYS

Wooden railways

Of the many periods into which the history of railways divides itself, the longest and least-known is that of the wooden railway. It lasted from just after 1600 to about 1800—from the time, that is, when the first were built, to the time when the iron-railed tramroad took precedence. Even so, the last wooden railways survived long enough to be contemporaries of the first steam-worked main lines.

By later standards, wooden railways were never very extensive. Lewis estimates a maximum mileage of 292 in 1800. However, this total was made up of many short lines, and by the standards of contemporary technology, and by comparison with the poor and unmade state of highways generally, the construction of prepared tracks, over carefully graded routes made possible by bridges, embankments and cuttings, of two, four, five, eight miles or more in length, was a remarkable achievement.

Their greatest memorial, by far, is the Causey or Tanfield Arch, near Stanley, Co. Durham. When built about 1726 it was the greatest work of civil engineering in Britain since Roman times, and it remains impressive yet, an arch of honey-coloured stone, with a span of 105 feet, which crosses a deep, rocky, wooded and, as you approach it, unexpected ravine. It was not, in my experience, easy to find, being reached along the trackbed of the Tanfield Waggonway, which later became a steam-worked branch line. Since the grid reference of the arch has been mis-stated elsewhere, let me state here that the correct grid reference is NZ 201559. But it may become easier to locate, for the arch and its surroundings now belong to Durham County Council, which has renovated the arch and intends it to be the centre piece of a picnic site. Across it there is to be a public footpath. The principal works of renovation were pressure grouting with a resin bonding agent to seal and consolidate the structure, and bolting the rock face at the east abutment to stabilise the foundations. The English Tourist Board and the Department of the Environment contributed towards the cost. The Causey Arch has long been scheduled as an Ancient Monument—since the 1930s at least.

The arch carried a branch of the Tanfield Waggonway but was not used for very long because, probably, the colliery to which the branch led was destroyed by an underground fire. The arch itself was certainly out of use and becoming derelict as early as 1804. Today, apart from a descriptive plaque nearby, there is nothing whatever about the Causey Arch itself to suggest its original purpose. This is the sort of location that demands an instantaneous time machine: only imagination can provide the double track of wooden rails across the arch, the frequent horsedrawn waggons creaking ponderously along them.

The approach to the arch leads along the top of an embankment about 100 feet high. Although the branch of the Tanfield Waggonway which crossed the arch fell early into disuse, its main line did not: having become eventually a branch line of the North Eastern Railway, it closed only about 1963. This embankment therefore, which is part of the earthworks for the main line of the waggonway, carried rail vehicles for some 235 years. It may yet do so again: the non-profit making Tanfield Railway Company which preserves, principally, industrial locomotives and rolling stock, and is based at Marley Hill a mile to the north, hopes to re-lay this section.

In the North East of England, so long industrialised, traces of many early waggonways have been concealed by later developments. But not invariably. In Crawcrook, Co. Durham, for instance, at grid reference NZ 135635, a gravelled footpath curves up and away from the road, opposite the Rising Sun Garage. It passes through a cutting, surmounts a summit, and continues, gradually falling, straight beyond. This is the course of the Ryton Moor Waggonway, opened from staithes near Ryton to Crawcrook by 1663 and later extended westwards to Frenches Close and Mickley.

Across the River Tyne at Wylam, the course of the famous Wylam Waggonway was used for a later North

3/1 The 105-foot span of Causey Arch, built for the Tanfield Waggonway about 1726, is here glimpsed through the trees of the thickly wooded ravine which it crosses, in April 1980. Later in the year abundant foliage renders it almost invisible. See also the colour illustration on page 115.

Eastern branch line, which in turn lasted long enough for its passenger trains to be diesel multiple units. Now its trackbed is 'Wylam Riverside', 'Not', as the notices state, 'a public footpath or bridle path, but the Northumberland County Council invites the public to use it on foot, horseback or bicycle'. Hard beside it at grid reference NZ 127651 stands the cottage in which George Stephenson was born in 1781 and spent his early childhood. Owned now by the National Trust, its external appearance is probably little changed, but the interior has been altered and is not open to the public. At Wylam itself, the bridge carrying the road across the River Tyne was built originally for a late branch of the waggonway, which connected it with the Newcastle & Carlisle Railway at its station on the south bank.

The diligent researcher can find many other similar traces of waggonways in North East England. For instance, the Plessey Waggonway of 1699, four miles long and running to Blyth Harbour, has left substantial traces (Warn's *Waggonways and Early Railways of Northumberland* gives details), and a few days before writing this I observed in the *Railway Magazine* (August 1980) a note to the effect that the last section still in use of the Ravensworth Waggonway—built in 1669 and long since rebuilt as an industrial line—would cease to be used from January 1981.

Elsewhere, too, wooden railways have left their traces. At Newdale, Shropshire, grid reference SJ 676095, a two-arched bridge of brick and stone, probably built in the 1760s, still carries the course of a wooden railway—now a footpath—over a steam which runs in a small dingle below the general level of the land on either side. The situation is reminiscent of the Causey Arch on a smaller scale. The bridge is approached by a stone-built embankment: the footpath runs level (so far as the eye can judge) and un-humped along this and over the bridge to confirm its origin.

From our point of view, however, this part of Shropshire is of greater interest for its relics of the slightly later era of plateways. Similarly the Middleton Railway, Leeds, is of greatest

3/2 This curving footpath and shallow cutting in the centre of Crawcrook, Co. Durham, (grid ref. NZ 135635) indicate the course of the Ryton Moor Waggonway: the cutting dates, probably, from as early as the 1660s. The line was a wooden-railed waggonway connecting collieries with the River Tyne.

interest for its pioneering use of locomotives. The southernmost part of the present-day preserved line does lie on the course of the 1758 waggonway however, although much else of it follows a diversion built in the 1860s to avoid a steeply graded section of the original route. Part of the old alignment has become the street called Old Run Road.

In Scotland, the Tranent-Cockenzie Waggonway has left clear traces, described in chapter seven. Further north, in Alloa, the course of a waggonway built in 1766 survives as a long straight footpath, sunk in a shallow cutting, close to the centre of the town. Short tunnels (or wide overbridges) enable it to pass beneath two of the principal streets, at grid references NS 885926 and NS 886929. The track of this line saw many and successive improvements. It was laid at first with rails of fir, for which in due course were substituted rails in two layers, at first both of fir, later of fir with beech on top. These were followed by wooden rails plated on top with cast iron bars, and subsequently by wooden rails with malleable iron bars. About 1812 these were replaced by cast iron edge rails which lasted about thirty years, after which they were in turn replaced, about 1842, by edge rails of malleable iron which were still, at that late date, carried on stone blocks.

The Alloa waggonway was built to carry coal, not only from pit to harbour but also to a 'glasshouse' near the harbour, where bottles were manufactured—one of the first such in Scotland, I believe. Visiting the site of the line in 1980, I found the harbour end of it mostly submerged beneath the large and apparently modern works of United Glass Ltd. Such is the persistence of local industries.

Wood being perishable, only two surviving examples of wooden track are known to the author. One forms a small and sadly uninspiring exhibit at the National Railway Museum, part of its much larger permanent way exhibit. It comprises two oak rails, about six feet long, mounted on two oak sleepers. Bryan Morgan, in *Railway Relics*, recounts the story of how they were discovered in 1957 in a mine opened in 1816 and abandoned in 1908. The other example, comprising only one rail and one sleeper, is held by the North Western Museum of Science and Industry, Manchester. It too originated in a mine, in Nidderdale, North Yorkshire. An iron bar, of the sort fastened to the top surface of wooden rails, is exhibited in the permanent way collection of Glasgow Museum of Transport. Despite its undoubted historic interest, I must admit that one black iron bar, of rectangular cross-section, looks very much like another.

Canal tramroads

The first line built from the start with iron rails laid on top of wooden ones seems to have been the Trent & Mersey Canal's tramroad by which it extended its Caldon branch from the canal terminus at Froghall, Staffordshire, to limestone quarries at Caldon Low. At least, it was certainly the first public line, possibly there were others in the Coalbrookdale area where the technique first developed. Caldon Low, despite its name, is 1,100 feet above sea level, Froghall 430 feet, and their distance apart about $3\frac{1}{2}$ miles. The line opened in 1778 but had been made too steep; it was, in part, rebuilt and re-aligned in 1785. Even then it was not wholly satisfactory, and it was replaced in 1804 by a plateway on another alignment, on which rope-worked inclined planes alternated with near-level stretches. In 1849 the North Staffordshire Railway, which by then owned both canal and tramroad, replaced the 1804 line by a railway of 3 ft. 6 in. gauge laid out on a more direct route as a continuous inclined plane operated by cable haulage, in three sections. This was used until 1920. The quarries are still busy, and rail-connected, but from a different direction.

The rail/canal interchange wharf at Froghall (grid ref. SK 028477) was long derelict but has recently been made into a picnic site in connection with the restoration to navigable order of the Caldon Canal, as this branch canal is now known. (The eastern part of it became un-navigable in 1961, but was eventually reopened, largely through the efforts of the Caldon Canal Society, in 1974.) It was while sitting at one of the picnic tables in 1980 that I gradually became aware that what I was looking at, almost hidden by turf, was the head of a rail: and closer investigation revealed a length of track surviving from the 3 ft. 6 in. gauge line closed sixty years before.

3/3 George Stephenson's birthplace near Wylam (grid ref. NZ 126651) now belongs to the National Trust, although the interior is not open to the public as it has been much altered. The exterior is probably very much as it was when he was born on 9 June 1781. The Wylam Waggonway passed the door and its course is seen here. Although Stephenson's family moved away in 1789, he later frequently visited Wylam in 1814 to see Hedley's pioneer locomotives at work on the waggonway, by then relaid as a plateway. It was rebuilt again, as an edge railway, in 1830, and used until the 1860s. Then its course was adopted for a branch of the North Eastern Railway, which lasted long enough for passenger services to be worked by DMUs. It was closed in the late 1960s.

Immediately to the east of the canal basin are clear traces of all three rail alignments. Most northerly is an embankment which carried the 1778/1785 lines on a common course here; they appear to have ended at high level beside the basin. A rather boggy cutting, on a gentle upward slope, running in an eastward direction, marks the course of the 1849 line, and the Whiston inclined plane of the 1804 plateway heads sharply upwards in a south-easterly direction. Confusingly, the foot of this incline is concealed behind a later building built on the course of the line and beside the 1849 line. The course of a further short incline is also clear: it appears to have lowered both 1804 and 1849 lines to canal level. The courses of both these lines are signposted as public footpaths.

For those who do not (as I unfortunately did not) have time to follow it on foot, many relics of the 1804 plateway can be seen from the A52 main road eastwards from Froghall: stone embankments, bridge arches, inclined planes, paired stone boundary walls. They are almost more substantial than the remains of the 1849 line which appear at grid reference SK 048479 as a very waterlogged cutting. All courses meet up at Hoften's Cross at the approach to the quarries.

Froghall Basin and its associated tramroad sidings occupied a large area, but Buxworth Basin was greater: its scale amazes even now. Here the Peak Forest Canal met the Peak Forest Tramway, and over a distance of one third of a mile or more (centred on grid ref. SK 023821) there stretches a complex of disused canal arms, basins, stone embankments, bridges, limekilns and pathways which once were tramroad sidings.

The Peak Forest Canal, and with it the Peak Forest Tramway, came under control of the Manchester, Sheffield & Lincolnshire Railway in the 1840s. They were taken over completely in 1883 and so passed to the Great Central and in due course the London & North Eastern. Despite steam-railway competition they remained busy enough for the tramroad to be relaid in the 1860s or 1870s with nine-foot long steel rails, of the same L-section as the old tramplates. However, the last traffic over the tramroad passed in the early 1920s and by 1926 it was disused, though it was not dismantled for another ten years. Buxworth Basin and canal approach lay derelict until 1968, since when they have been the scene of a heroic voluntary restoration scheme by the Inland Waterways Protection Society; the eventual total success of this is now unfortunately prejudiced by proposals for a new road which affect the site.

The most distinctive feature of the Peak Forest Tramway, however, was its tunnel at Chapel Milton: probably the first railway tunnel of any length. One hundred yards long, it was made in 1796 and took the tramway obliquely beneath the highway which is now numbered A624. Its north-western portal has been obliterated by road-widening; the south-eastern portal survives, at grid reference SK 059815, within the grounds of a firm making brake and clutch parts, which I take to be a subsidiary of Ferodo Ltd, whose main factory is across the road and who own part of the trackbed of the tramway.

South east of Chapel-en-le-Frith the tramway gained height by ascending an inclined plane (known here simply as 'the plane' rather than 'the incline'). Its course can be viewed from its foot, where it passed beneath the A624 road at grid reference SK 065808, or better from the same road at Blackbrook where the road runs parallel to the plane. This in its upper part is carried on a stone-built embankment and, along the hillside beyond, a stone retaining wall supports the course of the tramway; at 'Top o' th' Plane' can still be seen the small four-square stone building which, according to P. Clowes writing in the *Railway Magazine* (September 1963), was formerly a stable for tramway horses. A sample of track from the Peak Forest Tramway is preserved by the North Western Museum of Science and Industry; its iron plate rails date from the tramroad's first thirty years. In the National Railway Museum is an example of the tramway's pointwork; the waggon illustrated on page 137 stands upon it.

Both the Peak Forest and Caldon tramroads were laid out to extend the lines of their parent canals, but elsewhere tramroads were built as temporary links in incomplete canal lines. Despite its short working life (1800 to 1805) parts of the course of the temporary tramroad which linked the northern and southern sections of the Grand Junction Canal, pending completion of Blisworth Tunnel, Northants, can still be seen. It now appears as a ledge high on the side of the tunnel's approach cuttings: doubtless in climbing over Blisworth Hill the tramroad ran through shallow cuttings, beside which deeper cuttings for the canal were eventually excavated. At grid reference SP 740503 the tramroad's course can be seen on the east side of the canal, and at grid

3/4 Two centuries of transport history are condensed into this somewhat unprepossessing exhibit at the National Railway Museum. The first railways in Britain were built with rails of wood in the early 1600s, and it was not until the early 1800s that the superiority of iron rails was generally accepted. This pair of six-foot long timber rails, mounted on two wooden sleepers, is probably later even than this, for they were recovered from a mine level opened in 1816 and abandoned in 1908.

reference SP 727530 on the west. Earthworks can also be seen above the tunnel itself.

While searching for steam locomotives in their last haunts around Preston in 1968, I found myself standing upon a long low embankment, of obvious railway origin, but lacking relevance to the contemporary railway network. Investigation showed it to have been older than any locomotive-worked line: the course of the tramroad completed in 1803 to connect the northern and southern sections of the Lancaster Canal. In this instance, although the tramroad was intended as a temporary measure, the canal never was completed and the tramroad remained in use until the 1860s to link its two parts. The bridge over the River Ribble at grid reference SD 541286 has been replaced by a modern one, but the course of the tramroad on either side of the river remains as a footpath. Immediately north of the bridge it ascends the site of an inclined plane; tarmac-surfaced among grottoes and shrubberies, it is incorporated in a municipal park. South of the bridge, by contrast, it runs direct and level along the tree-lined embankment mentioned above. Probably this kept it above flood level across the valley floor: there seems little reason for it otherwise.

Stone block sleepers

Stone sleeper blocks and the L-section plate rails with which, often, they were associated, are the most familiar and characteristic feature surviving from early nineteenth-century tramroads. One tends to forget, therefore, that this form of construction was in fact a deviation from the true path of development of permanent way. The earlier wooden rails were associated with flanged wheels and wooden cross-sleepers and, despite their material, had more in common with later and present-day track. A flanged wheel was awkward in wood, but a flanged rail virtually impossible: it is easy to appreciate that, once cast iron became the usual material for both, the sensible course would have seemed to be to cast-in the flange on the rails and leave the wheels plain. By comparison with wooden rails, cast iron rails, though long-lasting, were short (often about three feet) and inflexible: stone blocks provided a solid base for track which comprised a continuous succession of joints. Or so the author deduces.

At any rate, stone blocks are durable objects and many survive. Detecting them is a satisfying pursuit. In some places they are found re-used in, for instance, boundary walls, buildings and the edges of canal wharves. Elsewhere they remain, even now, in situ. As mentioned in chapter one, the author encountered them on the course of the Penydarren Tramroad. This 4 ft. 2 in. gauge plateway was built by a consortium of ironworks owners to run from Dowlais (Mid Glamorgan) for nine and a half miles southwards to Abercynon, where it terminated at the Glamorganshire Canal basin. This canal ran from Merthyr Tydfil down to Cardiff and the tramroad competed with its upper section. The tramroad was completed in 1802 and two years later gained lasting fame as the site for Richard Trevithick's pioneering steam locomotive trials.

The most convenient access to the section of the tramroad's course where stone blocks remain is not the somewhat complicated route described in chapter one, but by the bridge which

carries a minor road over it at grid reference ST 081977, immediately west of an adjoining bridge over the later Taff Vale line. There are clear traces of two tramroad routes here and it appears to have crossed the road, originally, on the level, a few yards to the west, and later to have been diverted, avoiding a sharp bend round a bluff and passing instead through a cutting and beneath the bridge. From my observation many stone blocks are in place on the course of the line for about a quarter of a mile northwards from this point and also for about three quarters of a mile southwards. (Northwards they may well extend for more than a quarter of a mile as the course of the tramroad is scheduled as an ancient monument between grid references ST 078985 and ST 083968.) In places can be seen vestiges of the surface of small stones that was the made-up horse path between the rails, and at grid reference ST 083971 stone blocks diverge to form a passing loop. The course of the tramroad is a very pleasant walk through leafy woods along a ledge above the River Taff. Whether or not it is a right of way I do not know, but it is certainly used as a footpath, for walking along it I passed three sets of Sunday morning strollers, some bicyclists and an artist at work.

The Penydarren Tramroad was used until about 1880. A plate rail from it is exhibited in the Science Museum, mounted on two of its stone blocks. The shape of the rail makes clear the reason for the B-shaped recess, with central hole, which is to be seen on the top of each stone block and provides a simple and positive means of identification. At each end of the plate, the flange swells into a bulbous projection—its purpose was probably to help spread the load and position the plate—and in the extreme ends of the plate are notches, one at each end. The recess in each stone accommodated the ends of a pair of plates, the hole held a wooden plug into which was driven an iron spike, passing first through the hole formed by adjacent plate-end notches to locate the plates. Recesses and holes of various shapes but similar purpose are typical of all stone block sleepers; where track incorporated edge rails rather than plate rails, cast iron chairs were often mounted on the blocks to hold the rails.

The Penydarren Tramroad crossed the River Taff twice, at grid references ST 091965 and ST 094963, by large and impressive single-span stone-arched bridges which are scheduled as

3/5 When canals were being built, temporary tramroads were used to bypass engineering features such as tunnels and flights of locks which took a long time to construct, and so to link sections of canal already completed. This embankment (grid ref. SP 729528) marks the course of the temporary tramroad laid over Blisworth Hill, Northamptonshire, while Blisworth canal tunnel was being bored. It connected the northern and southern parts of the otherwise complete Grand Junction Canal, the main canal line between London and the Midlands. The tramroad was used between 1800 and 1805, and closely followed the course of the tunnel as eventually completed: towers which top two of its ventilation shafts can be seen in the middle and far distance.

(Above) The Southern Region line from London to Southampton and Bournemouth was the last main line worked by steam in the South of England, and on 10 May 1967 rebuilt West Country class 4–6–2 no. 34104 powers the up Pines Express *(Bournemouth to Manchester) near Brockenhurst. Third rails are already in position for electric trains—the full electric service commenced shortly afterwards, on 10 July. BR blue-and-white was replacing earlier liveries.*

(Below) By the summer of 1968, standard gauge steam on BR survived only in the North West of England, and the end of steam was only two months away when this Stanier 8F 2–8–0 hauled a down freight train northwards out of Preston on 10 June of that year. Like the locomotive, the large gantry of semaphore signals has since disappeared and the line is now signalled by colour lights and electrified on the 25 kV ac system.

Causey Arch is the waggonway era's greatest monument. It was completed as early as 1726, or thereabouts, to carry a branch of the wooden-railed Tanfield Waggonway, but was disused by the beginning of the nineteenth century. Between the wars it was scheduled as an ancient monument, and is seen here in April 1980 while being repaired by Durham County Council. Its location is grid reference NZ 201559.

3/6 (above) The course of the Penydarren Tramroad near Quaker's Yard, at grid reference ST 084966. Along its track through this precise location there came in 1804 Trevithick's locomotive, to demonstrate, for the very first time, that steam could haul a load on rails. From this point northwards for about a mile many stone block sleepers still remain in place. They are seen to best advantage on the most wooded, and so least overgrown, sections: on these, during the author's visit in September 1979, brilliant sunshine with deep shade defeated satisfactory photography.

ancient monuments. Neither dates from the opening of the line, for which bridges of timber were provided: collapse of one of these, with a train on it, in 1815, led to construction of the stone bridges. They are best found by turning west off the A470 road at grid reference ST 097965 and then taking the second turning on the right on to a minor road. This is in fact the course of the tramroad. It leads to and crosses the more northerly of the two bridges and becomes the road referred to in chapter one. It can also be followed in the opposite direction almost to the other bridge which, however, now carries a footpath only. The site of the tramroad's canal basin terminus at Abercynon has been built over, but a plaque commemorating Trevithick and his locomotive has been erected there, beside the A4059 road at grid reference ST 085949.

Survival of the stone blocks along a section of the Penydarren Tramroad is remarkable, but even more remarkable are the remains of the Hirwaun–Abernant Tramroad some fifteen miles north west of Abercynon. They commence in Hirwaun itself: the clue to their location, I found driving into the town from the south east along the A4059, is a side street to the right, succinctly named (according to the plate prominently displayed) *Tramway*. Turning right along this, I found that stone blocks soon started to appear. Then, from grid reference SN 965052 onwards, in an easterly direction, the course of the tramroad becomes, astonishingly, complete except for plates and fastenings, with double row of regularly-spaced stone blocks, made-up horse path between them, passing loops at intervals, culverts over streams, and boundary hedges. It is shown on the 1:50,000 Ordnance Survey map (sheet no. 160) as an un-metalled road along which there is a public footpath. I followed the course of the tramroad on foot as far as grid reference SN 972051 without reaching the end of the blocks, though beyond that point they appear to become less frequent. Baxter states that they run for at least a mile and a half and regards them as the finest stretch of tramroad remaining.

This tramroad was opened in 1805 and closed in 1900. It connected originally with the Neath Canal at Glynneath; later, after the Aberdare Canal was opened in 1812, it connected with that, via the Llwydcoed Tramroad of 1811, and the westward link to the Neath Canal was closed. The chronology of these and other connecting tramroads, the canals with which they were associated, and the ironworks

3/7 (left) The Hirwaun–Abernant tramroad was last used in 1900, but near Hirwaun it remains complete except for plates and fastenings. This is its course at grid reference SN 967051, looking west. The two rows of stone sleeper blocks have a cobbled path between them for horses, and there are boundary hedges on each side. In the foreground is the site of a turnout for a passing loop. The course of the tramroad is used as a rough road by motor cars which straddle the right hand row of blocks.

3/8 (above) The course of the Hirwaun–Abernant tramroad at grid reference SN 967051 looking east. Markings on the stone sleepers suggest that every second block supported a joint, the intermediate blocks supporting the mid-points of the tramplates. Despite its remarkable state of near-completeness, the course of the tramroad apparently lacks statutory protection and artificial preservation alike.

they served, is extraordinarily complicated; Charles Hadfield unravels it in *The Canals of South Wales and the Border*.

The other outstanding tramroad relic in the vicinity is the Llwydcoed Tramroad's bridge over the Afon Cynon at Robertstown, grid reference SN 997036. Between stone abutments, ribs of cast iron span the river, to support a deck of cast iron plates. This is probably the oldest iron railway bridge in the world. The tramroad was used until 1900; immediately east of the river some stone blocks are to be found along its course, which is now a public footpath. The Robertstown bridge is an ancient monument, and the single-arched masonry bridge by which the Hirwaun–Abernant Tramroad also crossed the Afon Cynon, at grid reference SN 990044, is being considered for scheduling at the time of writing.

Study of maps suggests that this area would repay detailed investigation for further remains of these tramroads. But then, tramroads were common throughout much of South Wales, the Welsh Border and the Forest of Dean, and many traces of them remain. One of the most substantial is the very large viaduct of four arches which crosses the valley of the River Afan at Pontrhydyfen (grid ref. SS 795942). It was built in the 1820s for a tramroad serving blast furnaces; later it was used as an aqueduct for water supply, and now it carries a local road. It is scheduled as an ancient monument. As another example, Tram Inn signal box (and former station, closed in 1958) on the GWR Newport–Hereford line are named after the adjacent pub of that name. This in turn is a reminder that when the line was built in the 1850s it followed the course of the earlier Hereford Railway—in fact a horse-worked tramroad—of 1829.

Neither the Surrey Iron Railway, that pioneer railway company, nor its extension the Croydon, Merstham & Godstone Railway, had very long lives: opened in 1803 and 1805, they lasted only until about 1846 and 1838 respectively. Few traces of them remain—though since the district through which they passed has been so extensively developed subsequently, it is perhaps surprising that any remain at all. At Mitcham, for instance, by the station (on the Wimbledon–West Croydon branch) a line of ordinary suburban houses faces the railway across the street. But the street is called 'Tramway Path', and indicates the course of the Surrey Iron Railway. A modern housing development at the end of the road is called 'Jessop Place',

(Above) To carry a wooden railway on the level across a stream and a shallow valley, this stone embankment and brick and stone bridge were built, probably in the 1760s. Their location is Newdale, Telford, Shropshire, at grid reference SJ 676095.

(Right) The course of the Alloa Waggonway, built in 1766, survives as a footpath close to the centre of the town, and passes beneath two of its main streets by short tunnels. This is one of them, at grid reference NS 885926. The track, which was originally entirely of wood, was improved on several occasions: iron bars on top of wooden rails were used, and later on, iron edge rails.

(Above) Sylvan picnic place at Froghall, Staffordshire, was formerly the interchange point between the Caldon branch of the Trent & Mersey Canal, seen in the background, and successive tramroads which, from 1778 onwards, extended the canal's route, to Caldon Low quarries. Rails surviving from the last of these, a 3 ft. 6 in. gauge line, cable-worked and used between 1849 and 1920, can be discerned in the grass to the left of this picture, which was taken in April 1980.

(Left) The track of the Haytor Granite Tramway at grid reference SX 768776 near Haytor Vale, Devon. The functions of plateway rails and stone sleepers were combined in the granite blocks from which the track was made: blocks had an L-shaped recess carved in their top surfaces and were laid end to end. Useless for any other purpose, much of the track survives on uncultivated Dartmoor. The tramway was opened in 1820 and carried granite until the late 1850s.

3/9 This is almost certainly the oldest iron railway bridge. It was built, of locally-produced iron castings, in 1811 and carried the Llwydcoed Tramroad, a plateway, across the Afon Cynon at Robertstown near Aberdare (grid ref. SN 997036). The course of the line, on which stone sleeper blocks can be found, is now a public footpath which curves round to cross a former GWR branch line (now freight only) at the wicket-gated crossing in the background. The tramroad bridge is an ancient monument.

which suggests that the developer—or someone—knew his local history. Tramway Path shows up again, a little to the east and on the opposite side of the later railway, at grid reference TQ 278680. Here it really is a path, with a high hedge on one or both sides, its course typically at variance with other roads in the vicinity.

There are more substantial remains of the Croydon, Merstham & Godstone extension. In the park called Purley Rotary Field (grid ref. TQ 317622) the course appears as a tarmac pathway, north-east to south-west, on a shallow ledge on the gently sloping hillside. And on the course, against one of the park boundaries, there has been reinstated a short length of original track, a pair of plate rails mounted on four stone blocks. A notice describes them and an enclosure of spike-topped railings, reminiscent of the small mammals section at the zoo, protects them from vandalism but unfortunately does not prevent deposit of litter—when I saw them in August 1980 they seemed half-submerged in old beer cans and the like.

The principal engineering work of the Croydon, Merstham & Godstone was a high embankment which carried it across the Chipstead Valley, Coulsdon, and although the northern part of this has been demolished, the southern end remains, at grid reference TQ 296595. Still impressively high and covered by trees, it stands apparently on private ground but can be seen from the car park off Lion Green Road. Further south still, long cuttings between grid references TQ 288550 and TQ 289546 have, I understand, been affected by construction of the M23 motorway, although scheduled as ancient monuments. Heavy rain on the occasion of my visit discouraged close investigation. A detailed map showing the course of both tramroads in relation to later streets and railways appeared in the *Railway Magazine* for February 1950.

Track in situ

Industrial Shropshire, one of the two places where wooden railways first developed, was later the place where iron rails were first made and used. From the late 1780s onwards however, Shropshire edge railways were generally replaced by plateways. A most complex network or series of networks grew up, on several different gauges. Parts of this remained in use well into the present century and at Horsehay Works plateway was still being used as late as the mid-1950s—probably the last instance.

The type of plateway most popular in Shropshire, where it conformed to the traditional use of narrow gauges, was that developed by John Curr of Sheffield in the 1770s, and little used other than in these two areas. Its plate rails were lighter but longer than Outram's more common type: weights were typically 25 lb per yard compared with 40 lb, and length 6 feet compared with 3 feet. Curr originally used wooden sleepers, but in Shropshire cast-iron cross-sleepers were used to carry and locate the plate rails.

Lightweight plateway of this type has been uncovered on its original site in two locations within the Blist's Hill Open Air Museum of the Ironbridge Gorge Museum Trust. At one of these the track runs alongside the Shropshire Canal at the northern end of the restored section—it has, as yet, been only partly excavated and disappears tantalisingly into a bank of earth. The other location is not accessible to the public, but is illustrated in plate 3/10.

Heavier track, including pointwork, from Horsehay is displayed nearby and is set, typically, in brickwork. There is another example in Coalbrookdale Museum of Iron, also part of the Ironbridge museum trust. The vehicles associated with these I refer to later on, but here I must also mention two important plateway structures which survive in the district. Lee Dingle Bridge, adjacent to Blist's Hill museum, is a wrought-iron truss viaduct built as late as 1872, to replace an earlier wooden viaduct, for a plateway which carried coal from Madeley to Blist's Hill ironworks. It is hoped to reinstate track across the bridge eventually, to connect with the former Horsehay track mentioned above.

Buildings which can definitely be associated with plateways or any other type of horse railway are now rare. One such is the Severn Warehouse at Ironbridge, which now contains the Ironbridge Gorge Museum's introductory exhibition. It was built in about 1840, in the form of a Gothic folly, at the wharf which was the interchange point between the Coalbrookdale Company's tramroads and the River Severn. This, in those days, was navigable and much used by the sailing barges called Severn trows. The adjacent quay has been excavated and its brick surface restored; it shows the locations of plateway track of dual gauge. Tracks ran also into the warehouse itself.

3/10 Recent clearance work and excavation at Blist's Hill Open Air Museum, Ironbridge, have revealed this length of lightweight plateway in its original location. It was probably used to take tubs of clay to a tile works and is in a part of the museum not yet open to the public at the time of writing. Plateway of this type was developed by John Curr in the 1770s and much used in industrial Shropshire; the cast iron cross-sleepers are a Shropshire addition to Curr's original concept.

(Above) This small plateway vehicle, recovered in 1968 from the bed of the Shropshire Canal in the background, has here been replaced temporarily on a length of plateway which has been uncovered on its original location, now within Blists Hill Open Air Museum, Ironbridge. Very narrow gauge plateway of this type was popular in Shropshire; the double-flanged plate on the left was probably intended originally for use on a level crossing.

(Right) Locomotive Agenoria *was built in 1829 and is thought to be virtually unaltered since: probably the oldest locomotive of which that can be written. She was built by Foster Rastrick & Co. of Stourbridge and is now the oldest locomotive in the National Railway Museum. The primeval layout of vertical cylinders and overhead beams is very similar to* Wylam Dilly *of c. 1813 (see illustration no. 3/24) but drive is direct from connecting rods to the rear pair of wheels. Furthermore, these wheels have balance weights, the need for which had not, in 1829, occurred to George and Robert Stephenson, however rapidly they were developing the locomotive in other directions, and the front pair of wheels has springs (which with vertical drive are difficult to arrange on the driven pair).*

3/11 (above) Lee Dingle bridge, Blist's Hill, Ironbridge, was built in 1872 for a plateway which carried coal from colliery to ironworks, and replaced an earlier structure of wood. Plateway track and pointwork in the foreground are reconstructions by Blist's Hill museum, using materials from Horsehay. One day, plateway track may be reinstated across the bridge itself.

3/12 The Severn Warehouse at Ironbridge, though given the appearance of a Gothic folly, was built in the 1840s where the Coalbrookdale Company's tramroads met the River Severn (which can be glimpsed to the left). It now houses the introductory exhibition for visitors to the Ironbridge Gorge Museum's many sites. The wharf in the foreground, which had been buried, has been excavated and restored by the museum trust; recesses in the brickwork mark the position of mixed-gauge plateway track. One or two plates survive on the track leading into the warehouse: many more did so at the time of excavation, but were stolen for scrap.

To see track formed from cast-iron edge-rails still in position on its original site, I found it necessary to travel far from the industrial areas in which it originated: to the stately grounds of Belvoir Castle, Leicestershire. This is the home of the Dukes of Rutland and here, in about 1815, a two-mile horse railway was built. It ran from Muston Gorse wharf, on the Grantham Canal, to the castle, where it terminated in a tunnel beneath the building, and its purpose was to carry the castle's coal supply. The scale of the establishment at Belvoir Castle in the nineteenth century is indicated in the castle guide book: a total of 15,550 meals were served there during the period December 1839 to April 1840. The railway was last used in 1918 and most of it went for scrap in 1941; but fortunately track remains in situ in the castle grounds for there is no wish to destroy it.

The rails are fish-bellied, 3 feet long, and mounted on stone sleeper blocks to a gauge of 4 ft. $4\frac{1}{2}$ in. To encounter in actuality, in its original location, a railway of this type, so familiar from written descriptions and old pictures, is an experience akin to that of, say, a military historian who meets, marching up the road, a regiment of soldiers returning from the Battle of Waterloo.

The castle is open to the public, but the railway track is in its private grounds. Permission is generally given, however, to specialists who wish to see it, and may be sought from: The Agent, The Belvoir Estate, Estate Office, Belvoir Castle, Grantham, Lincs, NG32 1PD. It would probably be best to apply for a time when the castle is in any event open to the public, which is Wednesday, Thursday, Saturday and Sunday afternoons during the summer and on certain other days. Waggons also survive and are on view to the public in the castle basement; they are mentioned on page 141.

In general, since iron rails have a much higher scrap value than stone blocks, one can only rely on seeing them in museums. The Science Museum, the National Railway Museum and the Glasgow Museum of Transport all have good collections of early and later permanent way. A substantial length of one other early railway does remain complete however, because of the almost unique nature of its track: the Haytor Granite Tramway, Devon. Its track comprises granite blocks laid end to end having carved in their top surfaces a continuous L-shaped recess analogous to that of iron tramroad plates.

The tramway was opened in 1820 to link Haytor granite quarries with the

Stover Canal at Ventiford, near Teigngrace, which led to the Teign estuary and, in turn, the sea. In their day tramway and canal carried the granite for many of London's important buildings, but the expense of double trans-shipment killed the trade and the tramway was disused by the late 1850s.

The surviving section can best be seen near Haytor Vale where the tramway emerged on to gorsy upland at the edge of Dartmoor. At grid reference SX 769775, at the site of a level crossing, it appears on either side of the road. A few yards to the east, stone 'pointwork' leads to a siding; to the west the line heads away across the moor. It has survived through the accident of its material and, since it is now scheduled as an ancient monument, can be expected to continue to do so; it runs for over a mile to the quarries.

Warden Law and Stratford

George Stephenson's Hetton Colliery Railway of 1822—the first line built with the intention that locomotives and inclined planes, rather than horses, should be used throughout its length—survived until 1959. Its course between Hetton-le-Hole, Co. Durham and the River Wear at Sunderland is now reverting to nature or being obscured by recent developments, but it is still clear at grid reference NZ 366503 where it can be seen as an inclined plane ascending the ridge called Warden Law. The beam engine which powered this incline until closure survives in store at Beamish North of England Open Air Museum. The course of the line at the summit seems to have disappeared into an enormous excavation, but the course of the next, downward, plane is also clear at, for instance, grid reference NZ 369512, where I noticed a wire cable which might (or might not) have been a haulage cable, incorporated into a lineside fence.

The Stockton & Darlington Railway was so remarkable and has left so many traces, that I describe them at some length in chapter seven. Its contemporary, the Stratford & Moreton Railway, has left many traces also. Worked at first solely by horses, it passed eventually into the ownership of the Great Western, which upgraded its southern part and branch to Shipston on Stour sufficiently for steam locomotives to be introduced in 1889. This part of the line survived in this form until 1960. The northern part of

Paddington station has been the London terminus of the Great Western Railway, and after it British Rail's Western Region, since 1854. Its design was due in part to Brunel, and in part to architect Matthew Digby Wyatt; the overall glass roof, of which only part is seen here, owed much to the Crystal Palace of 1851. The principal departure platform has always been no. 1, and the entrance from the road approach leads on to this platform.

(Below) Brunel's Royal Albert Bridge over the Tamar at Saltash (grid reference SX 435587) is overshadowed now by the comparatively recent road suspension bridge alongside, but it still carries the main line into Cornwall. The approach spans were renewed in 1928 and on the main trusses some limited strengthening work was done at the end of the 1960s: but the bulk of the structure is original, completed in 1859 (see illustration no. 4/10). A clearance of 100 feet above high-water level was required in those days of sailing ships by the Admiralty. The inscription I. K. Brunel Engineer 1859 *was made by the Cornwall Rly Co. after Brunel's death, and is correctly absent from the contemporary engraving of the opening.*

Liverpool & Manchester locomotive on the Liverpool & Manchester Railway: 0–4–2 Lion *built in 1838 waits at the start of the Rainhill cavalcade on 24 May 1980.* Lion *is the oldest workable locomotive. After withdrawal in 1859 she was used, under cover, to power a pump in Liverpool Docks until 1928. She was then restored to running order by the LMS for the Liverpool & Manchester Railway centenary celebrations, subsequently appeared in several films—notably* The Titfield Thunderbolt*—and was overhauled again in 1980. Her appearance and design are typical of the period in which she was built.*

(Left) In appearance the compartments of this coach built for the Stockton & Darlington Railway in the 1840s still show derivation from road coaches, but most of the vehicle is pure railway. By that date the S & DR was re-joining the mainstream of railway development and this coach in the NRM is typical of the time. A seat is provided at the end of the roof for the brakesman who, it appears, could in emergency apply the brake with his foot.

3/13 A strong contender for the distinction of being the oldest railway track surviving on its original site must be that of the Belvoir Castle Railway, Leicestershire. The railway was laid in 1815 and there is no reason to suppose that the track was ever renewed: it was last used about 1918. This horse railway carried coal to the castle from a wharf on the Grantham Canal, and the track is here seen within the castle grounds where it crosses the main driveway at grid reference SK 819338. It comprises fishbellied edge rails three feet long carried on stone block sleepers. Track gauge is 4 ft. $4\frac{1}{2}$ in.

the line was never converted and was last used early in the present century; the track was lifted in 1918. It is on this section that most traces of the line in its original form are to be found. Between Newbold on Stour and the approaches to Stratford it ran along the edge of the main road which is now numbered A34—it was because of this feature that steam locomotives were never introduced—and along this section in many places the site of its trackbed, often on low embankment or in shallow cutting, can be seen at the roadside. About a mile short of Stratford the line forsook the road for a long, high, straight embankment; this leads to its finest relic, the handsome viaduct of nine shallow brick arches by which it crossed the River Avon at grid reference SP 205548. Today the viaduct carries a footpath used by Stratford's tourist multitudes; originally it led the line to the canal basin close by. Near it, on the site of the line, a waggon is preserved on a length of track.

Cable haulage and inclined planes

Construction and working of inclined planes by cable haulage (both powered and gravity operated) had been developed to a fine art by the 1820s, although at that period the steam locomotive was still at a rudimentary stage. George Stephenson, who by 1829 and the Rainhill Trials was the champion of the locomotive, had previously had much experience of stationary engines and cable haulage. He had introduced them underground on the tramways of the collieries at Killingworth, and I am inclined to the opinion that his ascent and descent of Warden Law with the Hetton railway was made as much to take advantage of opportunities for mechanical power through cable haulage as from geographical necessity. Certainly inclined planes and the engine houses associated with them (which originally contained stationary steam engines) are very much a feature of railways built during the 1820s and 1830s.

Some of them, particularly those engineered by Stephenson, were laid out like the Hetton railway, with successive inclined planes providing cable haulage over several miles. One such was the six-mile Canterbury & Whitstable Railway (opened in 1830) where locomotive traction was used only over one section of one and a quarter miles. On this line as on some others the planes were not particularly steep: the steepest grade was about 1 in 30. This enabled the line to be locomotive-worked throughout from 1846, and it survived until 1952. Its traces can still be found but I have not had the opportunity to search for them.

The Bolton & Leigh Railway similarly incorporated cable-hauled sections and here again the steepest gradient was 1 in 30 and locomotives started to work over them in due course. Later on, deviation lines, more easily graded, were built. The line is now closed and dismantled; but at Chequerbent (grid ref. SD 673061) for instance, the courses of both the original (1828) and later (1885) lines can still be seen. Both are becoming obliterated however, and the older (the more easterly of the two) is naturally the more so.

The Cromford & High Peak Railway in Derbyshire was completed in 1831 to link the Cromford Canal near Cromford with the Peak Forest Canal at Whaley Bridge; it used inclined planes, concentrated at each end, to ascend onto the Peak District plateau. Much of its 34-mile course lay above the 1,000 feet contour. At first horses hauled trains between the inclines; soon locomotives were introduced and in due course this railway, like the last two described, was incorporated into the main railway system. Part of its western end was closed in the 1890s, but most of the rest survived until the mid-1960s, including Sheep Pasture Incline, 1,320 yards of 1 in 9 and 1 in 8, and Middleton Incline, 708 yards of 1 in 8¼, which were both at the eastern end.

Although the rails on Middleton Incline were lifted in 1964, the engine house at the top survives and with its attendant chimney stands out like a lighthouse above the neighbouring countryside. What is more, Middleton Top Engine House (grid ref. SK 275552) still contains its original machinery installed in 1829 and used until closure: a pair of beam engines which turn a common crankshaft geared to the winding drum. The entire building is an ancient monument and the engines have been renovated by volunteers of the Derbyshire Archaeological Society. The engine house is open to visitors on Sundays, and also on the first Saturday in the month, on which high days the engines are worked, though by compressed air rather than steam since the boilers are no longer serviceable. This author, however, finds it difficult to appreciate Middleton Top Engine House to the full in the absence of railway track: it is like a sail without a ship. Reinstatement of even a short length of track, over the head of the incline, would help to put it back into context.

For seventeen and a half miles, from Cromford to Dowlow near Buxton, the trackbed of the C & HPR has become the High Peak Trail, administered at its eastern end by Derbyshire County Council and at its western end, within the Peak National Park, by the Peak Park Planning Board. This trail is a traffic-free route for walkers, cyclists and riders on horseback. It includes not only the two inclines mentioned but also Hopton Incline (grid ref. SK 253546). Despite a gradient in part of 1 in 14, locomotives replaced cable haulage in 1877, and Hopton Incline was for many years famous, if not notorious, as the steepest steam-worked gradient in Britain operated by adhesion. The countryside ranger's office, with information centre, bicycle

hire point, picnic site and car park, is close by Middleton Top Engine House.

Rail/canal interchange warehouses survive at both of the original termini of the Cromford & High Peak Railway, at Highpeak Junction (grid ref. SK 314558) and at Whaley Bridge (grid ref. SK 012816). The latter is particularly interesting, laid out in three bays with the canal entering it at one end and running along the centre, and railway tracks originally entering at the other end to flank the canal on either side. It has survived a threat of demolition in the early 1970s to become the premises of canal boatbuilders Coles Morton Marine Ltd. Rails remain within the building although immediately outside it they have been removed and their location turned into a road. Close by however, at grid reference SK 012814, the railway's girder bridge over a small river remains, with cobbled horse path between absent rails. This section, closed in 1952, was horse-worked to the end. Whaley Bridge Incline, the foot of which is just beyond the bridge, is now a footpath; it was powered by a horse-worked capstan. Above the incline, beside the site of a level crossing, rails set in cobblestones emerge from the tarmac. It was certainly the practice of the nearby Peak Forest Tramway to set its rails in cobblestones at busy places, and evidently the same obtained here.

The Dundee & Newtyle Railway, also opened in 1831, was another railway which surmounted a range of hills by inclined planes. Like the C & HPR, it at first used horse traction between the inclines but soon replaced it by locomotives; and eventually it too was incorporated into the main railway network built subsequently. Circuitous but comparatively easily graded deviations were built to avoid the inclined planes. Passenger services survived until 1955 and the line later closed entirely and was dismantled. The courses of an original incline and later deviation can clearly be seen in the vicinity of Newtyle, Tayside Region. The incline was Hatton Incline, 1,000 yards of 1 in 13, and there also survive at its foot the original Newtyle station buildings, at grid reference NO 299413. This railway, inclines and

all, had passenger services from the start but the station lost its passenger trains when the deviation line, with new passenger station, was opened. It continued, however, to be used for freight. The main component of the station buildings, which are believed to date from about 1830 and are scheduled as an ancient monument, is the stone built train shed, through which two tracks formerly passed.

A comparable location where a deviation replaces an earlier incline can be seen at Goathland, North Yorkshire; and here are added advantages that the course of the original line has become a public footpath, while the deviation has survived as part of the North Yorkshire Moors Railway, with steam.

The original railway was the Whitby & Pickering, built in the image of the nearby Stockton & Darlington, but remarkable for an Act of incorporation in which section 114 permitted locomotives, while section 134 forbade them. In any event, it was completed in 1836 as a horse railway—by then rather old-fashioned—with a 1 in 15 cable-worked incline about three-quarters of a mile long to raise it onto the moors near Goathland. Newtondale gorge provide an easily graded descent towards Pickering.

As elsewhere the railway later became part of the main railway system and was upgraded for locomotives in the 1840s; the incline, however, survived until 1865 when the deviation, itself having a gradient of 1

3/14 William James's Stratford & Moreton Railway, a contemporary of the Stockton & Darlington, crossed the River Avon at Stratford by this graceful viaduct (grid ref. SP 205548). The line was opened, with horse traction, in 1826, and last used (on this section) in the early years of the present century. Today the viaduct, close by the Shakespeare Memorial Theatre, carries a footpath much used by Stratford's innumerable visitors; its absolutely level deck and parapet, however, betray its railway origin.

in 49, was opened. Today, from Whitby to Grosmont, BR's Esk Valley Line follows the course of the original railway: from Grosmont to Pickering via the deviation, it has become the North Yorkshire Moors Railway.

The new line diverged from the old at Deviation Junction (grid ref. NZ 827047) and rejoined it south of Goathland at grid reference SE 848991. Much of the route of the original line remains clear and the course of the incline is a pleasant walk from Goathland, a grassy downward path between the trees. Its top is at grid reference NZ 833015, its foot, at Beck-Hole, at NZ 822021. A little further on, a North Eastern Railway cast iron notice still warns vainly against trespass, for this is a public footpath. Further details of the walk along the original route from Goathland to Grosmont, and of relics to be seen, are given in the pamphlet *Historical Railway Trail* obtainable from the NYMR.

The other principal relic of the original line is its tunnel at Grosmont. Castellated portals enhance its small-bore, horse railway dimensions. Introduction of steam locomotives required the construction of a second tunnel of larger bore alongside in the

3/15 In the high Derbyshire countryside, Middleton Top winding engine house is a prominent landmark. Formerly the engine powered the Cromford & High Peak Railway's Middleton incline, which is 708 yards long with a gradient of 1 in $8\frac{1}{4}$. The incline top is immediately out of the picture to the left; the railway then ran between engine house and the wall in the foreground. Its trackbed is now the High Peak Trail. The engine house still contains its original beam engines, installed in 1829, which are occasionally operated by compressed air. Grid reference SK 275552.

3/16 The westernmost section of the Cromford & High Peak Railway at Whaley Bridge was worked by horses, latterly as a short branch line from later railways, until closure in 1952. It crossed a small river by this bridge at grid reference SK 012814, and though the rails have been lifted, the cobblestones of the horse path between them are still prominent.

mid-1840s, and it is this tunnel through which the railway passes today. But the original tunnel remains, and through it runs a public footpath much used by visitors to the North Yorkshire Moors Railway's locomotive shed.

The Whitby & Pickering's contemporary, the Festiniog Railway, which in its original form had two inclined planes, is described in detail in chapter seven. Inclined planes—in some cases extremely steep ones—were common on the narrow gauge tramroads serving North Wales slate quarries, and many traces remain. A good example can be seen from the Festiniog Railway's Tanygrisiau station: the course of the incline ascends the mountainside ever more steeply and eventually disappears into a tunnel near the ridge. At Llechwedd Slate Caverns, Blaenau Ffestiniog, the former slate mine which is now a popular tourist attraction, one of the inclines has been adapted to carry passengers, funicular-style.

New construction of horse railways lasted longest in North Wales too because of the time-lag in development of steam locomotives for very narrow gauges. The 2 ft. 3 in. gauge Corris, Machynlleth & River Dovey Tramroad was opened in 1859 for instance, and the 2 ft. gauge Croesor Tramway in 1864. Reference to the latter and its traces is made in chapter seven; the former was adapted for steam traction from Machynlleth (Powys) northwards to Aberllefenni (Gwynedd), as the Corris Railway in 1879. Beyond Aberllefenni however, its northernmost part, the Ratgoed Tramway, continued to be worked by horses until closure in 1952, by which date it had outlived the steam section by four years. And at Aberllefenni itself there still exists, in 1980, a quarter-mile length of former horse-tramroad once connected to the Corris Railway. It links the quarry and mill of Wincilate Ltd (which company produces slate for floors, windowsills, copings and cladding), but it has not been used since 1978, when a fork lift truck was introduced, and for some years previously wagons on it were hauled by a tractor of agricultural type. By contrast, the section west from Machynlleth to the River Dovey at Derwenlas was abandoned after the adjacent standard gauge line opened in 1863. Its rock cuttings remain, close to but at a lower level than the A487 main road (or did when the author last saw them some years ago).

I have digressed from inclined planes. The National Railway Museum exhibits the steam winding engines from two inclined planes and runs them (by electric power) at intervals. Both date from 1833 but are of conspicuously different design. One, from the Leicester & Swannington Railway's Swannington Incline, is a horizontal engine and, since experience of horizontal cylinders at that period was limited, it has the unusual feature of a tail rod and slippers to support the weight of the piston: this was thought necessary to prevent wear in the cylinder. The other engine, from Weatherhill on the Stanhope & Tyne Railroad (sic) has an inverted vertical cylinder with main flywheel shaft above. This drove the winding drums through gears. The railway was opened in 1834 to link quarries near Stanhope, Co. Durham, with the port of South Shields.

Gravity-operated, cable-worked inclined planes remain in use at Seaham, Co. Durham, on the colliery railway which links South Hetton with Seaham Harbour. This was opened in 1833 as the South Hetton Waggonway or Braddyll's Railway. The change-over point between one incline and the next can be seen to advantage from the road bridge at grid reference NZ 427486.

The Bowes Railway

The 1820s-style railway worked by powered inclined planes would have become extinct had it not been for preservation of part of the Bowes Railway. This railway originated with completion in 1826 of the Springwell Waggonway, from Jarrow, Co. Durham, south west for five miles to Springwell and Mount Moor Collieries. It had been designed by George Stephenson for both inclined plane and locomotive haulage. The line was extended westwards and became the fifteen-mile long Pontop & Jarrow Railway, a private colliery line despite its name. In 1932 it was renamed the Bowes Railway.

Successive closures of collieries caused contraction of the line, section by section from the west, and when Kibblesworth Colliery, the last it served, closed in 1974 traffic over the inclines ceased. A short section of the Jarrow end of the line is still worked by the National Coal Board.

A most enlightened local authority, Tyne & Wear County Council, decided to purchase for preservation about one and a quarter miles of the disused line, between grid references NZ 278576 and NZ 285591, and the Tyne & Wear

3/17 Newtyle station (grid ref. NO 299413) was the northern terminus of the Dundee & Newtyle Railway. This was opened, for goods and passengers, in 1831, and used a mixture of horse traction and inclined planes with cable haulage. The foot of one of the latter, which descended the ridge in the background, lay immediately beyond the station. A more-easily graded deviation line was later opened for steam trains, with a station for passengers but the station seen here, left at the end of a spur after the line was extended and the incline closed, was still being used for freight in the 1950s.

3/18 An inclined plane with cable haulage is seen here still in use in 1979 at Seaham, Co. Durham (grid ref. NZ 427486). It is gravity operated, descending laden wagons hauling up the empties. Ascending wagons have to be hauled over the 'kip' on to a slight reverse gradient so that the cable slackens and can be detached, descending wagons have to stand on a slight down gradient, so that they roll as soon as brakes are released. Hence the variations in level of the lines at the incline head.

Industrial Monuments Trust was formed to manage and restore this and other examples of the area's industrial heritage. The purchase was completed in 1976. The section preserved is for the most part on the original Stephenson line, and has been scheduled as an ancient monument. It includes, successively from the west, the top of Black Fell Incline, the sidings above it ('Black Fell bank head'), Blackham's Hill West and East Inclines and the engine house at their common summit, extensive sidings at Springwell Colliery (at the foot of the East Incline), and the top of Springwell Incline. The inclines follow one another consecutively, separated only by sidings for reception and dispatch of sets of wagons up and down. Traffic was formerly worked by cable haulage throughout the section now preserved. Nevertheless, the gradient of one of the two inclines preserved complete, Blackham's Hill East, is only 1 in 70, which has enabled the trust to operate tank-engine-and-brakevan passenger train rides over it. This means that visitors can come to Springwell (grid ref. NZ 285588), the most convenient access, and ride up to the summit to view demonstrations of cable haulage.

It is these that are the particular fascination, the unique feature, of Bowes Railway preservation: the time machine that failed one at Causey Arch here presents a railway operated in the manner of the 1820s at their best, of the immediately pre-Rainhill era, before *Rocket* demonstrated that locomotives, rather than stationary engines and cable haulage, were to be the true course of motive power development.

Yet cable-haulage survived until recently—in principle, the preserved Bowes Railway and its equipment are being restored to 1963 condition. In the North East particularly, cable haulage developed techniques and terms all its own. 'Bank head', for the head of an incline, we have just met, and 'bank foot' is its low-level equivalent. On the Bowes Railway one sees the purpose of the 'kip', the elevated hump at the top of an incline over which ascending wagons are drawn on to a slight reverse gradient, so that the cable slackens and can be detached. In days gone by, sets of wagons drawn over the kip of Springwell Incline and detached from the cable, used to run forward by gravity into the 'dish' or 'hole', a low level track, where the Blackham's Hill East cable was attached for the continued ascent. Wagons about to descend an incline, on the other hand, must stand on a slight down grade at the point where the cable is attached, so that they will roll as soon as brakes are released. The variations in level of one track relative

3/19 Powered, cable haulage, inclined planes are operated in preservation by the Bowes Railway, Tyne & Wear. Here, a set of wagons is beginning the descent of Blackham's Hill West incline. The line originated as the Springwell Waggonway, laid out by George Stephenson and completed in 1826; much of the route was arranged as a succession of inclined planes with cable haulage. This section was last used commercially in 1974.

3/20 A waggon from the Peak Forest Tramway is displayed in the National Railway Museum on appropriate plateway pointwork. The waggon carried limestone, which was unloaded into waiting canal boats by tipping the waggon on end. The narrow treads of plateway wheels are typical, the better to crunch through any gravel or other obstruction lying on the track. The rails are of L-section, carried on saddles on stone block sleepers.

3/21 Chaldron waggons from Seaham Harbour are preserved at Beamish. They date, probably, from the 1880s, but in design they are directly descended from the waggons on the earliest waggonways of North East England. At their head stands the 1975-built working replica of Stephenson's Locomotion *built in 1825 for the opening of the Stockton & Darlington Railway.*

to another that result from these requirements are well demonstrated on the Bowes Railway, particularly at Blackham's Hill beside the engine house.

After all this, it comes as something of an anti-climax to find that power for the inclines is provided by a relatively modern electric haulage engine. One is reminded, irreverently but irresistibly, of that mythical person who, wishing to modernise his water supply, installed an electric winch to haul the bucket up out of the well. . . .

Springwell Incline, of which the head only is included in the preserved section, was formerly about one and three quarter miles long and powered by gravity, the descending laden wagons hauling up the empties. In the absence of mineral traffic to provide loaded wagons, it would in any event scarcely be possible to operate a gravity powered incline in preservation; but Springwell Bank Head, with track layout, large horizontal winding drum, and control cabin reminiscent externally of a signal box, has been preserved static for its historical and technical interest.

Adjacent to Springwell sidings are the engineering workshops. These are housed in the nineteenth century colliery buildings, which are of stone, around a courtyard: themselves a unique relic of a layout once common. The colliery last worked in 1932, and the buildings owe their survival to having been adopted subsequently as the railway's engineering and wagon shops. They retain much of their former equipment and machine tools, now painted green to distinguish them from recent additions, painted blue. Here the 1979 replica of *Rocket* was assembled by Locomotion Enterprises. During 1979 there were guided tours at intervals on railway operating days; these are, usually, about six weekends between April and October (at other weekends the railway is open to the public as a static exhibit).

To work its passenger trains, the trust has been able to obtain on loan 0-4-0 saddle tank locomotive no. 22, built by Andrew Barclay in 1949 and bought originally for the Bowes Railway. Rolling stock acquired with the railway in 1976 included thirty seven ten-ton hopper wagons. Many of them were built either at Springwell, or to Springwell design. Many of them, too, have the curious characteristic that, externally, they appear at first glance to be ordinary open wagons with vertical sides and ends: only closer examination reveals the absence of doors in the sides, a trapdoor in the floor, and additional sloping sides within the wagon body to direct coal to the trapdoor. Wagons of this type survive also at Beamish, and I have yet to find a wholly satisfying explanation of why they were built like this and not with sloping sides like ordinary chaldron waggons and later hopper wagons.

Chaldron and other waggons

In considering the design of the wagons preserved and used on the Bowes Railway I have jumped far ahead, and must now return to consider waggons surviving from the iron tramroad era proper—for no vehicles from wooden railways are known to survive.

The National Railway Museum has a waggon from the Peak Forest Tramway which opened in 1796. It is a four-wheeled plateway vehicle which has wooden frames and an iron body and carried limestone; an open end is closed by an iron grille, hinged at the top. This enabled the waggon to be tilted on end to discharge its contents into canal boats. Its wheels are flangeless, and revolve on fixed axles. Typical of plateway wheels, they have narrow treads, the better to slice through any gravel, earth or mud accumulating on the track. The same feature presumably militated against use of ordinary brake blocks, which in the 1790s had already long been familiar on North of England flanged wheel waggonways. Braking on Peak Forest waggons, which ran downhill by gravity, was primitive: a chain with hooks at each end was used. One end was

3/22 Relics of the first commercially successful type of steam locomotive: two pairs of carrying wheels and a pair of rack wheels, similar to those used in Blenkinsop's and Murray's locomotives for the Middleton Railway. These actual specimens probably originated on a similar line which operated briefly at the Kenton and Coxlodge collieries in Northumberland; they are now exhibited at the National Railway Museum. In 1812, when the locomotives were designed, rails were still of brittle cast-iron and it was necessary to minimise axle-loadings: engineers were uncertain whether a locomotive could work by adhesion alone. See also illustration no 2/6.

3/23 In 1812 William Hedley of Wylam had this model constructed to confirm his theory that if both pairs of wheels of a locomotive were coupled, any tendency for one pair to spin would be overcome by the other. Experiments with it were satisfactory enough for a full-size version to be built, followed by the Wylam locomotives. The model is approximately 21 inches long, 17 inches wide and 5 inches high; the gear wheels, which show a much finer standard of workmanship than the rest of the model, were purchased from a Newcastle clockmaker.

hooked on to the waggon and the other thrown against a wheel, to catch a spoke and make the wheel skid. Alternatively an iron bar was passed through the spokes to jam the wheel, presumably when a 'parking brake' was required.

Since this waggon appears both primitive and primeval compared with later steam railway exhibits which accompany it in the NRM and indeed tend to overwhelm it, it is worth remembering that it represents only a stage in the continuing development of waggon design, which had already been going on for almost two centuries when the Peak Forest Tramway was built; and that its somewhat battered appearance no doubt derives from a long and useful working life, probably over a century.

The frame and wheels of another Peak Forest Tramway waggon are exhibited at Whaley Bridge, in the small museum adjoining Coles Morton's gift shop on the upper storey of the Cromford & High Peak Railway warehouse mentioned above.

Other plateway vehicles survive at Ironbridge. The Coalbrookdale Museum of Iron exhibits one, which stands, like the NRM's Peak Forest waggon, on plateway pointwork. This waggon, partly rebuilt, dates from the early nineteenth century and is displayed carrying a load of wooden patterns for cast iron tramplates. At nearby Blist's Hill, when the author recently visited it, museum staff kindly extracted a small plateway vehicle from store and replaced it, temporarily, on the canalside plateway to be photographed for the benefit of readers of this book. This vehicle, of indeterminate age and purpose, was recovered from the bed of the canal in 1968 and is really no more than the remains of a vehicle, iron wheels and axles still attached to frames of decayed timber.

On the reconstructed plateway at

3/24 William Hedley's experiments led to construction of locomotives Wylam Dilly, *seen here in the Royal Scottish Museum, Edinburgh, and the very similar* Puffing Billy, *now in the Science Museum, London. Return tube boilers, though they provided enough heating surface to generate sufficient steam, meant that furnace door and fireman were at the front of the locomotive, and the tender was propelled ahead of her. The layout of the vertical cylinders and drive through oscillating beams was derived from contemporary stationary engine practice.*

Blist's Hill, close to Lee Dingle bridge, stand several waggons from Horsehay. They were, I understand, in use at Horsehay until moved to Blist's Hill about 1971, though to what extent this was mobile use—rather than static use for storage—is not clear. One of these vehicles is a tank waggon, and their bodies are in part of welded construction, which contrasts sharply with cast iron plateway wheels.

Early edge-railway vehicles which survive include four waggons from the Belvoir Castle Railway. Three of these are displayed in the basement of the castle itself and the other is in the National Railway Museum. None of these waggons is complete, though one of those at the castle appears nearly so. It has wooden frames and wooden sides and the body is set between the wheels: it was apparently loaded and unloaded from the end. The Stratford & Moreton Railway waggon preserved beside the canal basin at Stratford is a larger version of the same basic type. Its wooden frames are extended to form dumb buffers. Surviving horse-railway waggons from the Nantlle and Festiniog Railways and the Croesor Tramway are mentioned in chapter seven.

The typical vehicle of the waggonways of North East England was the sloping-sided chaldron waggon. The name is often abbreviated simply to chaldron, although properly speaking the term chaldron is a measure of coal, standardised at fifty three hundredweight in 1695. No very early chaldron waggons survive—the NRM's oldest dates from 1826—but waggons of this type remained in service until sufficiently recently for many later examples to be preserved and their appearance to be familiar. They were in general use on colliery lines in the North East until the late 1940s and early 1950s, and they were last used, on the lines serving Seaham Harbour, in the 1960s. The author noted three chaldron waggons, out of service, at Seaham Harbour in 1979.

Beamish museum has a total of thirty two chaldron waggons, many of them from Seaham Harbour, of which five have been restored and are workable. Some of these are usually coupled to the replica *Locomotion*, mentioned below. These waggons date probably from the 1880s; the prominent letter L painted in white on their black wooden sides refers to former ownership, along with railway, collieries and harbour, by Lord Londonderry. The NRM also has one of these waggons, exhibited on top of the re-erected Stockton & Darlington iron bridge which originally crossed the River Gaunless.

Tramroad locomotives

Of Trevithick's earliest locomotives nothing remains, but it was announced in 1979 that the Welsh Industrial and Maritime Museum, Cardiff, was to construct a full-size working replica of the Penydarren locomotive, and a stretch of plateway on which it would operate. Of Blenkinshop's 1812 rack locomotives, the first locomotives to work both successfully and commercially, there is however a tangible relic in the form of a pair of rack wheels, with a pair of carrying wheels either side, mounted on a short length of original track at the National Railway Museum.

Blenkinsop's first locomotive went into service in the summer of 1812. The same autumn William Hedley at Wylam was asked to construct a locomotive, and it occurred to him that if all the wheels, though smooth, were coupled together, any tendency of one pair to spin would be overcome by the remainder. To investigate this theory he had a small test carriage built, a wooden frame about twenty one inches long, with two pairs of wheels connected by gears which were driven by handles. This model was presented to the Patent Office Museum in 1862 and is now held by the Science Museum, not usually on public view due to lack of space; it is illustrated

here in plate 3/23. Experiments with it gave results which were satisfactory enough for a full size version to be built.

As mentioned in chapter two, the full size test carriage was converted into a locomotive which did not prove satisfactory, but provided the basis for an improved design to which, probably, three locomotives were built, Two of them, known as *Puffing Billy* and *Wylam Dilly*, are preserved, in the Science Museum, London, and in the Royal Scottish Museum, Edinburgh, respectively. Black and sombre, they are still impressive. Cylinders are vertical and a complex motion of beams and rods, derived from contemporary stationary engine practice, drives the gears which in turn drive and couple the wheels. Originally they were four-wheeled plateway locomotives, but in about 1815 they were put onto eight wheels to spread the load on the plates. They reverted to four wheels in 1830 when the Wylam Waggonway was converted from plateway to edge railway, and the locomotives were fitted with flanged wheels.

For all their fame, the circumstances surrounding these locomotives remain tantalisingly vague. In recent years research among Blackett (Wylam) papers in Northumberland Record Office has cast doubt on their authenticity, for these papers suggest, but do not apparently confirm, replacement of the original locomotives during the period 1828 to 1832. *Yearly Valuations of Stock* indicate, for example, 'old', 'spare' and 'new' locomotive engines in 1829, and there are similar entries for other years, but engines are not individually identified. On the other hand the locomotives as they now exist correspond generally to the illustration of them in Wood's *Practical Treatise on Railroads* of 1825, apart from being on four wheels instead of eight, and Dendy Marshall, in *A History of Railway Locomotives down to the end of the year 1831*, quotes a letter written by Hedley himself in 1836 in which he says 'Several of the engines constructed at first . . . may be seen on four wheels at this day'. I suspect that the 'new' valuation entries refer to what we would now call substantial rebuilding rather than wholly new construction.

There is uncertainty, too, about the names of these locomotives. Probably

3/25 This long-lived locomotive built by George Stephenson for the Hetton Colliery Railway in 1822 was rebuilt several times and is seen here, probably, shortly before withdrawal about 1912. By that date she had gained smokebox, coupling rods and brakes, none of which was present originally. Neither was the curious little cab which gave limited shelter to the driver. This was removed after the locomotive was preserved. Now part of the national collection, she is housed at Beamish.

they were originally nicknames: no known contemporary illustration shows nameplates. Waggons on the Wylam Waggonway are said to have been called 'dillies' by the workmen: hence *Puffing Dilly*, soon corrupted to *Puffing Billy*, and *Wylam Dilly*. A third locomotive of the same type was apparently called *Lady Mary*.

The Wylam engines worked until the 1860s. Two of them at least were at that period certainly considered to be originals. The one now called *Puffing Billy* was loaned to the Patent Office Museum in 1862. The owner, by then a Captain Blackett, was prepared to sell her to the museum for £1,200, which was probably the cost of a replacement locomotive; the museum offered £200. Captain Blackett then asked for her to be repaired so that she could be returned to work. The price of £200 was, however, eventually agreed towards the end of 1864 and Blackett was paid the following January.

William Hedley's sons appear to have purchased in 1869 from Wylam a locomotive described as *Puffing Billy* for a mere £16 10s 0d. This they preserved at Craghead Colliery, Co. Durham, and one wonders if it might not have been at this stage that she became known as 'the Wylam dilly'. At any rate, this was the locomotive that was acquired in 1882 by the Royal Scottish Museum.

Vagueness almost as great surrounds the history of the next oldest surviving locomotive, one of those which Stephenson built for the Hetton Colliery Railway in 1822. Part of the national collection, she is exhibited on loan at Beamish. It is known that she was rebuilt about 1859 and again about 1883 and withdrawn as recently as about 1912, after which she was preserved by the North Eastern Railway Co. At some stage in her career she acquired a smokebox and coupling rods, neither of which were present originally. She also acquired a miniscule driver's cab, alongside the boiler, which after preservation was removed. Original features still present are the single large-diameter furnace tube and the two vertical cylinders set into the boiler along its centre line, and long, more or less vertical connecting rods which drive the wheels directly without intermediate gearing.

The extraordinary lolloping gait of a locomotive fitted with similar above-boiler motion can be observed at Beamish, for the 1975 replica of Stephenson's *Locomotion* (Stockton & Darlington Railway) is now exhibited there and regularly steamed. Indeed, on *Locomotion* the effect is probably heightened by the parallel link motion which the Stephensons used to keep her piston rods vertical, instead of the guide bars used on both earlier and later locomotives. The notoriously poor steaming qualities of the original were simply cured on the replica by fitting cross-tubes into the front of the main flue tube to increase the heating surface. Preservation of the original *Locomotion* of 1825 at Darlington North Road Station Museum is mentioned in chapter eight.

Another early Stephenson locomotive of similar type is preserved, at Newcastle-upon-Tyne Museum of Science and Engineering; she is known as *Billy*. Once again, vagueness descends about her early history—her building date being, according to the source one chooses, sometime between 1826 and 1832. The earlier date seems the more likely, for this locomotive too has the vertical, within-the-boiler cylinders characteristic of the locomotives just described. She was built for the Killingworth Colliery Railway, rebuilt in 1867, and worked until 1880. The following year she was presented to the mayor and corporation of Newcastle upon Tyne to mark the centenary of the birth of George Stephenson.

J. U. Rastrick, engineer of the Stratford & Moreton Railway (1822) and in due course one of the judges at the Rainhill Trials, was a partner in Foster, Rastrick & Co. of Stourbridge. In 1828–9 this firm built four locomotives, three of them for export to the USA, and one, *Agenoria*, for use much nearer home on the Kingswinford or Shutt End Railway. This line connected coal mines at what is now

3/26 Apart from Trevithick's and Hedley's early locomotives, there were few other attempts to build steam locomotives for plateways. This neat little 0–4–0 saddle tank was one of them: she was photographed on plateway track at the Coalbrookdale Company's Horsehay works, probably about 1880. Nothing else appears to be known about her.

called Shut End, north of Stourbridge, with a wharf on the Staffs & Worcs Canal, and was completed in 1829. According to J. Ian Langford's *A Towpath Guide to the Staffordshire & Worcestershire Canal*, it was financed by Lord Dudley and John Foster of Stourbridge, the latter presumably being the Foster part of the Foster, Rastrick partnership.

Agenoria, with beam-engine transmission and enormous chimney, worked the line for many years and was eventually acquired by the Science Museum in 1884; today she is the oldest locomotive in the National Railway Museum. The design retains Hedley's inverted vertical cylinders on either side of the boiler, but drive from the beams is direct to the rear pair of wheels, and these are coupled to the front pair by rods.

Cylinders, though still steeply inclined, reached the front of a locomotive for the first time on *Invicta*, built in 1830 by Robert Stephenson & Co. for the Canterbury & Whitstable Railway. *Invicta* also has the distinction of being the first steam locomotive to have operated a regular service of passenger trains, for the Canterbury & Whitstable opened for passengers more than four months before the Liverpool & Manchester. *Invicta* hauled passenger trains over one and a quarter level miles near the northern end of the line, and it would be pleasant to record that she had done so successfully. Unfortunately this was not the case: the locomotive was underpowered, and was replaced by horses in 1839. But she was not scrapped: after the Canterbury & Whitstable was absorbed by the South Eastern Railway, *Invicta* was preserved at the latter's Ashford Works. In 1906 she was presented to the City of Canterbury and exhibited on an outdoor plinth.

There *Invicta* stayed, corroding gradually, until 1977. In that year the Transport Trust purchased her, and took her to the National Railway Museum to be restored by volunteers. *Invicta* returned to Canterbury in 1980 in time to take part in the 150th anniversary celebrations of locomotive and railway, and the intention is that she should be put on public display there, under cover.

CHAPTER 4

THE FIRST GREAT MAIN LINES

Liverpool & Manchester

Some early waggonways and tramroads were incorporated eventually into the later steam railway system, but many were not. Of the Liverpool & Manchester Railway however, and the trunk lines which followed, the main characteristic is that even now, to a large extent, they form the backbone of that system.

Their routes are as direct as the lie of the land permits, without sharp curves and easily graded, so their earthworks and civil engineering features are extensive and large. Their engineers, particularly the Stephensons, had little confidence in the powers of steam locomotives over lines with more than minimal gradients.

Their continuing use as main lines is not invariable, however. In some instances later and even more direct or more convenient routes became the main lines and wholly or partially superseded the originals.

The Liverpool & Manchester Railway is a case in point, for while most of its line is still the principal rail route between those two cities, at each end passenger trains diverge from it to reach later stations which superseded the original termini. Let us commence at the Manchester end, where the original terminus, Liverpool Road, was used by the passengers for only fourteen years, until 1844. Subsequently it was used as a goods station only and for a long time it was a very busy one, closed only in 1975. Remarkably, among many later additions the original buildings, not only goods but also passenger, survived. Equally remarkably, it was people concerned with building conservation rather than railway preservation who then expressed concern over their fate. These formed in 1977 the Liverpool Road Station Society, a pressure group at first, which has been largely (but not entirely) successful in its aims. The historic buildings, some of the others, and the land between them have been acquired from British Rail by the Greater Manchester Council. Track has been reinstated and here was held, for six weeks during the summer of 1980, the Great Railway Exposition marking the station's 150th anniversary. Eventually Liverpool Road is to become the home of the North Western Museum of Science and Industry.

Seen from its road approach, Liverpool Road station has little in common with later railway stations—when it was built, there were no preconceived notions of how a station should look. Its passenger building, with ornate entrance for first class passengers and less ornate one for second class, forms part of a long low range of buildings and was entered off the pavement: it has at first glance more in common with the coaching inns of the period. Within, however, it was quite different, with booking offices on the ground floor and staircases (the first class one alone survives) leading to waiting rooms above at the same level as the railway. This approaches by a bridge over the River Irwell and is at a higher level than its surroundings. There is no platform. Opposite, beyond several tracks, stands the goods warehouse of 1830, a red brick building of many bays and entrances, at right angles to existing tracks and formerly approached by turntables.

Passenger trains for Liverpool now leave from Manchester Victoria and traverse a winding viaduct to gain the original route after about a mile. This is, by contrast, remarkably straight and direct. At Patricroft it crosses over its old rival, the Bridgewater Canal; then the houses end and with surprising suddenness give way to the expanse of Chat Moss. Part of this has been reclaimed, having fields of black and peaty soil, but part is still wild with woods of silver birch. Further on, a large memorial on the south side of the line commemorates Huskisson and marks the spot where opening day events changed suddenly from delight to tragedy.

Earlestown station was the junction for the Grand Junction Railway. Nine-arched Sankey Viaduct, which follows at grid reference SJ 569947, is, when seen from below, imposing in view of its early date, though eclipsed in grandeur by many later viaducts for which it was the prototype. The St Helens Canal, which passed beneath it and features in many early pictures, has sadly been filled in recently. The sidings on the south side of the line at Bold Colliery (grid ref. SJ 543934) were the collecting point for locomotives and rolling stock taking part in the 150th anniversary cavalcade in 1980; the Rainhill level, site of both the cavalcade and the original Rainhill Trials, stretches over about a mile leading to Rainhill station. Here there survives, still carrying a main road, the skew bridge of which the Liverpool & Manchester company was so proud.

4/1 *On the left, the Liverpool & Manchester Railway; on the right, the Grand Junction, originally at this point the Warrington & Newton and now reduced to single track. This is Earlestown station, once called Newton Junction, and the Tudor-style station building probably dates from the early 1830s. It was renovated for the celebrations of the 150th anniversary of the Liverpool & Manchester Railway, and used to house an exhibition about railways in the vicinity.*

The outer suburbs of Liverpool follow; then, suddenly, the train is running through the depths of vertical, rock-sided Olive Mount cutting, the scale of which, despite its later widening, astonishes even today, particularly by contrast with flat lands to the east. Then, at Edge Hill, present-day trains diverge from the original 1830 route on to one which replaced it, for passenger trains, in 1836. They descend through long and grimy cuttings, which once were a tunnel, with cable haulage, to Liverpool Lime Street. This must have been one of the earliest instances in which a railway was diverted in this manner, for Lime Street was far more conveniently situated for central Liverpool than was Crown Street. Edge Hill itself is so remarkable a place that I describe it in chapter seven.

The Grand Junction

Successful operation of the Liverpool & Manchester Railway demonstrated that the steam-worked main line between centres of population was not only practicable but desirable. Nevertheless, it took time for this lesson to be fully learned, and for the L & M's immediate successors, the Grand Junction and London & Birmingham Railways, to obtain their Acts of Parliament and build their lines. So it was not until 1837, seven years after the opening of the Liverpool & Manchester, that the next trunk line was opened: the Grand Junction. It was intended not only to link Birmingham with

4/2 The Grand Junction Railway crossed the River Mersey south of Warrington by the stone viaduct in the foreground, which was designed by Joseph Locke. It is still used to give access to sidings, but the West Coast Main Line runs at a higher level in the background: it was diverted in order to cross the Manchester Ship Canal at a level high enough to give headroom for ships. Grid reference SJ 599866.

Liverpool and Manchester, but also to be the first link in a chain of railways connecting London with both Scotland and a port for the crossing to Ireland, and its line continues to a large extent to do just that. But since its name was not explicit about the places served, and in any case the company lost its identity before many years had passed, by absorption into the London & North Western Railway, the precise role of the pioneer Grand Junction company is often overlooked.

The Grand Junction's line commences at Earlestown (formerly Newton Junction) by a triangular junction with the Liverpool & Manchester. This junction antedates the GJR, for the Warrington & Newton Railway, which the GJR eventually absorbed, was opened in 1831, and it may well have been at that time that the attractive Tudor-style station building was constructed. This stands in the angle between the northern and south western sides of the triangle; it was cleaned and renovated for the 1980 Liverpool & Manchester 150th anniversary celebrations, during which it housed an exhibition showing the part played by the locality in the development of railways over one and a half centuries. Both the southern sides of the triangle remain, although trains from Liverpool and Manchester to the South have long since found more direct routes. The south east curve is now used by trains between Manchester

and North Wales, the south west curve by regular passenger trains not at all, so far as I am aware; it has been reduced to single track.

Only one and a quarter miles south of Earlestown, however, is Winwick Junction, and here the West Coast main line, which has burrowed beneath the Liverpool & Manchester on its way south, trails into the Grand Junction line. From this point southwards for over fifty miles, through Warrington and Crewe to Stafford, West Coast main line expresses follow the course of the Grand Junction Railway; and if they are heading for Birmingham rather than direct for London via the Trent Valley line, they continue along it as far as Bushbury, which is only a mile and a half short of Wolverhampton.

Of actual Grand Junction structures, however, circumstances changed by the passage of time mean that they are few, particularly since electrification necessitated increasing overhead clearances. Of survivors, the most interesting are the viaduct over the River Mersey at Warrington (grid ref. SJ 599866) and Dutton Viaduct over the valley of the River Weaver (grid ref. SJ 582764). Passengers in West Coast expresses get a good view of the former, for it is now used only for access to sidings. The main line was diverted about 1890 so as to climb and cross over the Manchester Ship Canal (three quarters of a mile to the south) at high level with headroom for ships; it crosses the Mersey on a newer, higher bridge alongside the old. This is a stone viaduct with two wide arches over the river, several smaller ones over land on either side and, towards its south end, a further arch, larger than the other land arches, which formerly crossed the Mersey & Irwell Navigation. This was superseded by the ship canal, and at this point is now dry.

Dutton Viaduct, completed in 1836, is much bigger, with twenty arches carrying the line above the River Weaver. Yet it is not easy to view, for today's electric expresses are so fast that they are across, I suspect, before many passengers begin to notice, and no roads pass beneath the viaduct or in its immediate vicinity; it does stand out well, though, when seen from a boat on the river. Further south, the very obvious presence of Crewe Works on the west side of the line is a reminder that they were established there by the Grand Junction in 1843.

At the southern end of its line, the Grand Junction passed north of Wolverhampton and followed the valley of the River Tame, passing north of Birmingham too and then curving round through almost a semi-circle to enter it from the east, terminating at its own station at Curzon Street alongside the London & Birmingham Railway's terminus. This part of the Grand Junction is no longer a through route for passenger trains, but the final nine miles, approximately, are traversed by suburban electric trains between Birmingham and Walsall. These depart from Birmingham New Street; within a few minutes there can be seen, below and to the left, the sidings and goods station which mark the site of the two companies' original termini (grid ref. SP 078871). Trains then traverse a high viaduct which (as can clearly be seen from other trains approaching New Street from the Coventry direction) is in two stories: the lower part being the original Grand Junction structure, the upper a later addition, made when the line was extended.

To travel farther on this line, as the author did recently, is to see how its easy grades and gently curving track (it is on a continuous curve to the left for some four miles from Curzon Street to Perry Barr) confirm its origin as part of an early main line. They enable an electric multiple unit to gallop along between stations at a respectable speed. And once past Aston, this is a main line for freight, for it serves Bescot's immense marshalling yards—one gets the impression that passenger trains here are something of an unimportant side line. Indeed, at Bescot the Walsall trains diverge from the main Grand Junction line, which continues for freight only as far as Bushbury, where it is joined by the passenger trains from Birmingham via Wolverhampton.

London & Birmingham

The London & Birmingham Railway's station at Curzon Street, Birmingham, was opened in 1838. The company's architect Philip Hardwick embellished it, as the terminus of the first trunk line serving London, with an imposing entrance building consisting, principally, of a large Ionic portico. The comparable Doric arch at Euston has gone, but the Curzon Street building happily remains, and has outlived the rest of the original station which was closed to regular passenger trains as long ago as 1854. It in fact faces on to New Canal Street; it is now owned by the local authority and, as a listed building grade II, it is being restored, and will house community organisations.

Once past Curzon Street, Birmingham New Street-to-London expresses are on the original London & Birmingham route, and stay on or close to it all the way to Euston. Up West Coast main line trains join it at Rugby. The L & B's civil engineering works were of necessity greater than those of the Grand Junction, and remain more conspicuous as reminders of the line's origin. Greatest of all is Kilsby Tunnel (grid refs. SP 565715 to SP 578697). The epic of its construction through unexpected quicksands has often been told, and need not be repeated here, but the length of the tunnel (1 mile 666 yards) is so great that it can scarcely go un-noticed by the least observant of passengers in the fastest of present-day expresses. As they roar onward through the blackness, sudden brilliant daylight from the very wide ventilation shafts gives, at intervals, the false impression of having reached the far end.

There are several lesser tunnels on the London & Birmingham, and long and deep cuttings, notably those of Roade (grid ref. SP 750525) and Tring (grid ref. SP 937140) both of which have been widened to take four tracks instead of two. There are other, more curious, reminders of the line's origin

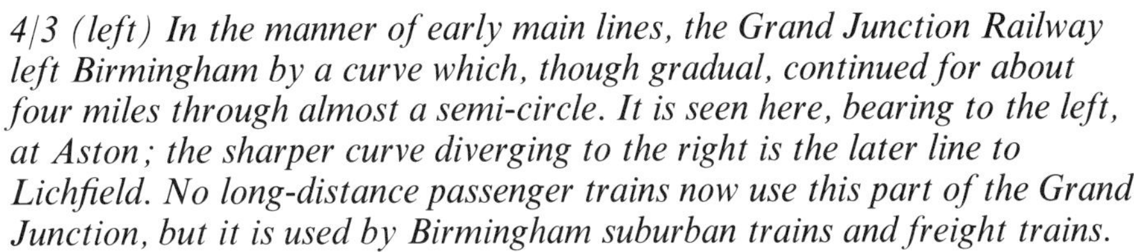

4/3 (left) In the manner of early main lines, the Grand Junction Railway left Birmingham by a curve which, though gradual, continued for about four miles through almost a semi-circle. It is seen here, bearing to the left, at Aston; the sharper curve diverging to the right is the later line to Lichfield. No long-distance passenger trains now use this part of the Grand Junction, but it is used by Birmingham suburban trains and freight trains.

4/4 (below) The London & Birmingham Railway embellished termini in its name cities in the classical manner. The Doric arch at Euston has gone, but the entrance building to Birmingham Curzon Street station, with its Ionic portico, survives. The station was last used by regular passenger trains in 1854, but is still used for freight. This building, however, is now owned by the local authority and was being restored in 1980.

4/5 (left) The London & Birmingham Railway crosses the Towcester–Northampton turnpike, c. 1838. The locomotive is one of Bury's with polished dome over the firebox.

4/6 (above) British Rail, London Midland Region, crosses the A43, 1980. It appears that the level of the road has at some time been raised. Grid reference SP 728542.

too. The former Blisworth station (grid ref. SP 723545) was the junction for the long branch to Northampton and Peterborough built by the London & Birmingham before amalgamation formed the London & North Western. The branch is closed, the junction is plain line and the station demolished, but across the road from its site there still stands the Blisworth Hotel, a mile distant from the village of its name. Wolverton carriage works is a reminder that the London & Birmingham sited its works for both locomotives and carriages here at its midpoint, and that the LNWR subsequently concentrated the locomotive side at Crewe. Wolverton might otherwise have become a nineteenth-century industrial town comparable to Crewe or Swindon; in fact it remained small and had to wait until the second half of the twentieth century before being incorporated into the new town of Milton Keynes.

At Camden Town, London, the L & BR locomotive shed of 1846, a 'round house' in which tracks for locomotives radiated from a central turntable, has become the Round House arts centre. The final descent from Camden Town to Euston is noticeably steep, for this is Camden bank, which was worked originally by cable haulage, like the Liverpool & Manchester's approaches to its Wapping, Crown Street and Lime Street termini in Liverpool.

City termini

Of the London & Birmingham Railway's Euston station, only the site remains the same, since the station, much extended and altered, was rebuilt entirely in the early 1960s for electrification. Elsewhere, terminus buildings from the early trunk lines do remain in use. It was the original practice at them that departures were all made from a single platform at the extreme left side (looking down the line) and arrivals at a single platform on the right: the train sheds, and the grandiose all-over roofs which developed from them, and are characteristic of such stations, originally sheltered mostly a grid of carriage sidings between arrival and departure roads. Only as traffic increased were carriage sidings gradually replaced by additional platforms. King's Cross, which with its two great arched roofs over the tracks was completed in 1852 for the Great Northern Railway, was originally of this pattern, and the main passenger entrance and booking office remained adjacent to platform no. 10, the original departure platform, until the new concourse was opened in 1973. Behind it the old station remains, though its original roof arches of wood were replaced by iron in Victorian times.

Heuston Station, Dublin (formerly Kingsbridge), was opened by the Great Southern & Western Railway in 1846 with the usual arrangement of arrival and departure platforms separated by carriage sidings, all within the train sheds. It retained this layout, supplemented only by one external platform outside the train sheds, until as recently as 1973 when an additional platform was inserted. The stark interior layout was in great contrast to the flamboyant baroque of the exterior of the station buildings, a contrast typical of other large stations of similar date.

The present Paddington Station dates from 1854, when it replaced the Great Western Railway's earlier temporary terminus. Paddington's original layout was a development of what was then usual, for as well as the two main platforms it had an additional island platform for departures and another for arrivals; these were, in turn, separated by carriage sidings. The island platforms really were island platforms, for at the terminal end of the station turntables and cross-tracks connected all the principal tracks through it. The two departure platforms were connected by a section of removable platform across the tracks between them which, when necessary, was lowered hydraulically and rolled out of the way beneath the main platform. Additional platforms have long since been inserted, replacing the carriage sidings, and they are connected by a circulating area adjacent to the buffer stops which has replaced the early cross-tracks and turntables; but the road approach still delivers passengers to platform no. 1, the original main departure platform, and the booking office is still adjacent to it. The original great overall roof at Paddington remains a period glory.

Brunel's broad gauge

Between London and Bristol, the route of Brunel's original Great Western Railway remains in use as the main line. From its broad gauge origins, the GWR retained, after narrowing, a loading gauge more ample than that of other lines; and while locomotives built to it are now seen only in preservation, a clear reminder of the broad gauge is to be found on the quadruple track sections near London. Here the two fast lines occupy the locations of the broad gauge tracks and are noticeably farther apart (so that they may come alongside station platforms without swerving) than the later slow lines which have always been standard gauge.

The Wharncliffe viaduct (grid ref. TQ 150804), the long shallow-arched two-span brick bridge over the Thames at Maidenhead (grid ref. SU 902810) and the long deep cutting at Sonning (grid ref. SU 760743) are all original GW features subsequently widened for quadruple track. Swindon works is still prominent (its origin was mentioned in chapter two). The greatest engineering feature of Brunel's original line, however, was and is Box

Tunnel, nearly two miles long on a gradient of 1 in 100. A persistent story is that the sun shines through it in the early morning on Brunel's birthday, 9 April. An observer in 1965 saw it do so not on that date but on 16 April: the date seems too close to be wholly coincidental. The western portal of the tunnel (grid ref. ST 829688) is heavily ornamented and its opening wide (for broad gauge) and high (for appearance's sake); it is in full view of travellers on the Bath Road and here there does indeed seem to be present an element of Brunelian bravado. The east portal of the short Middle Hill Tunnel, equally in view but down the line rather than up, is similarly ornamented.

At Bristol the original Bristol & Exeter Railway passenger station was at right angles to the Great Western

4/7 Paddington station, opened in 1854, is seen here in the 1890s, with mixed gauge track. It has changed little subsequently (see the colour illustration on page 126), apart from removal of the outer rail; and in the absence of steam locomotives it is now possible to keep the roof clean.

one, with a connecting curve between them. Inevitably, in due course, a station grew up on the curve; hence the sharply curved station which is Bristol Temple Meads today. But the original 1841 Great Western train shed and station building survive, although the train shed, after the early 1960s, spanned not railway tracks but a car park. It has an impressive pseudo-hammerbeam roof of oak; the station building too is in neo-Gothic style. The whole is a most important example of terminal buildings of the earliest main lines in Britain and is listed grade I. It has recently been leased by British Rail to the Brunel Engineering Centre Trust which aims to convert it into an exhibition centre featuring the great engineer's works.

From Bristol to Penzance the route originally built by the Bristol & Exeter, South Devon, Cornwall and West Cornwall Railways remains in use. As far as Cogload Junction, short of Taunton, it carries principally trains from the Midlands and the North; at that point, trains direct from Paddington, which have diverged to a shorter route at Reading, re-join the original main line. Between Newton Abbot and Plymouth steep gradients are a reminder that it was intended to work this section as an atmospheric railway. On the Exeter-to-Newton Abbot section that was, very briefly, actually worked by atmospheric trains, one of the air pumping stations survives at Starcross. It is a listed building and an application for permission to demolish it was refused in 1979.

The atmospheric railway was a flop, but Brunel's other great engineering feature on the line to the South West was an outstanding success: the Royal Albert Bridge over the Tamar at Saltash (grid ref. SX 435587). It was completed in 1859 (shortly before his death), it still carries the main line into Cornwall, and the most important components are original. Its appearance is striking and unusual. A normal suspension bridge would, in railway use, have undulated excessively when a train attempted to cross. Brunel developed the suspension bridge concept to incorporate, in each of two spans, an immense arched tubular wrought-iron strut, positioned between the tower-top anchorages of the suspension chains. Vertical iron pillars were fastened between tube and chains and extended downwards to support the deck: and so each span became a self-contained truss, rigid enough for trains.

Of lesser buildings, perhaps the most typical of Brunel's lines were the timber train sheds which spanned the tracks at stations. Many have gone in recent years, but one survives in use at Frome. The station dates from about 1850 and the offices and train shed are both of timber. They are listed grade II and in 1980 work commenced on refurbishing them, only to come to a standstill after a few months, pending financial review, as their general condition proved unfortunately much worse than expected.

Brunel designed the Great Western's broad gauge track with rails of bridge section laid on longitudinal baulks connected by cross ties. The rail remains familiar, for redundant lengths were used throughout the GWR as fence posts and supports for notices. They were also put to a more unusual use on the GWR-owned Kennet Navigation. This early river navigation had primitive locks with sloping sides of turf: to prevent boats settling on these slopes as the water level fell, the locks were equipped with frameworks of bridge rail which kept boats towards the middle. One such lock is Sheffield Lock (grid ref. SU 649706) which is illustrated in my book *The Archaeology of Canals*.

Another use to which redundant broad gauge bridge rail was put, in about 1898, was to construct sidings for the standard gauge Westleigh Mineral Railway at Burlescombe, between Taunton and Exeter. Eighty years later, and some twenty years after the mineral railway ceased to be used, what was left of these sidings was extracted from the overgrowth by members of the Great Western Society. And what was left amounted to over seventeen tons of rail, including four complete sets of points.

Some of this was destined for the National Railway Museum, but most of it has been moved to the society's depot at Didcot, Oxfordshire, to which more extended reference is made in a later chapter. The society already owned Didcot transfer shed; this had been built sometime after 1863, in a period when standard gauge trains could run both north and east of Didcot but only broad gauge to the west, and in it goods were transferred between standard and broad gauge vehicles. After Didcot had ceased to be an interchange point between the gauges, it was used as an ordinary goods shed but retained, in one end, wide and narrow entrances for broad and narrow gauge sidings. The shed was dismantled and moved to the GWS depot in 1977; and when the author visited Didcot in 1980, it was being re-erected. The broad gauge track materials were stored nearby, pending reconstruction as mixed gauge trackwork. In the meantime, the full effect of broad gauge width can be

4/8 (left) On the former GWR main line out of Paddington, the two fast lines are unusually far apart, for they occupy the site of the original broad gauge double track. This feature can be seen clearly here at Southall, by comparison with the slow lines on the left which have always been standard gauge; see also illustration no. 2/29. The former steam locomotive shed in the background is still used by diesel trains, though it has lost the smoke cowls which were once prominent, and the accompanying water tank still stands.

4/9 (below) Box tunnel, two miles long with a gradient of 1 in 100, took five years to bore and was completed in 1841, the principal engineering work on the GWR's original main line from London to Bristol. When finished it was the longest tunnel in Britain and a source of trepidation to intending passengers. Brunel made the west portal particularly imposing: this is the view of it seen by travellers and coachmen on the Bath Road. Grid reference ST 829688.

appreciated in the Great Western Railway Museum, Swindon, where the replica locomotive *North Star*, mentioned on page 170, is displayed on a short length of mixed gauge track.

South West to North East

North east from Bristol ran the successive lines of the Bristol & Gloucester, Birmingham & Gloucester, Birmingham & Derby Junction, North Midland and York & North Midland Railways. As mentioned in chapter two, the first four of these were in due course amalgamated into the Midland Railway, and the Y & NM into the North Eastern. Together these lines still form the basis of Britain's most important cross-country main line, from Bristol to York, although there are several places where through trains deviate from it for some distance—on the outskirts of Bristol, through Birmingham and through Sheffield, for instance. But they still have to contend with the Birmingham & Gloucester's most famous feature, the Lickey Incline, two straight miles of 1 in 37 which commence at Bromsgrove station (grid ref. SO 968693) and lift the line up onto the Birmingham plateau. The incline was opened in 1840 and, despite its apparent suitability for cable haulage, was worked from the start by locomotives. The coming of diesel traction has made the ascent less of a feat than it was, though one can still see the hump at the top and, as a passenger in a fast south bound train going over it, feel it too.

From Birmingham, trains for Derby depart in an easterly direction, a reminder that originally this was a branch of the Birmingham & Derby Junction, joining at Whitacre its main line running northwards from Hampton in Arden on the London & Birmingham. A later avoiding line means that trains for the North East no longer have to go through Whitacre itself, but

4/10 The Royal Albert Bridge, Saltash, was officially opened by the Prince Consort on 2 May 1859, and the royal train is seen here at Saltash station. Railways had markedly reduced journey times during the previous twenty years, and the prince was able to undertake this engagement as a day out from Windsor, even though this meant leaving Windsor station at 6.00 am and returning at 12.50 am the following day. The bridge still carries the main line into Cornwall—see the colour illustration on page 126.

nevertheless between Water Orton and Kingsbury they turn through nearly ninety degrees to take up the northerly direction of the Hampton-to-Derby line. From Whitacre south to Hampton has long been abandoned.

Between Derby and Chesterfield the line of the North Midland Railway is conspicuously easily graded and skilfully engineered through the broken country east of the Pennines. This railway's original stations were a series of architectural treasures, each one different, designed by architect Francis Thompson. The little classical station building at Wingfield (grid ref. SK 385557) survives, although the station is closed. Stone built, having a central block and projecting wings, shallow pitched roofs and overhanging eaves, it is probably best seen from a passing down train. (Being on the east side of the line, a glimpse from an up train would be too fleeting).

The station most evocative of hopes unfulfilled, however, is Normanton (grid ref. SE 381227). South of the station the Manchester & Leeds Railway joined the North Midland, its trains running forward to Leeds over the track of the latter. North of it the York & North Midland diverged, leading to York and points further north. At the time of its construction, the North Midland was not only the route from Birmingham and the South West, it was the route from London also, for passengers at first travelled north over the London & Birmingham to Rugby, and thence by the Midland Counties Railway to Derby. Normanton was to be a great railway crossroads, as important to the east side of England as Crewe was to the west. It had two large island platforms, and 'neat offices, commodious refreshment rooms and a splendid hotel', according to the descriptive text accompanying A. F. Tait's lithographed *Views on the Manchester & Leeds Railway* (1845). Normanton had become 'one of the centres from which a railway conveyance to almost every part of the kingdom can be secured several times a day'.

Then gradually Normanton was bypassed. The Great Northern Railway completed its main line, the direct route from King's Cross to York and the North, in 1852. Expresses of the

Lancashire & Yorkshire Railway, which had absorbed the Manchester & Leeds, were diverted onto a more direct route to Leeds about 1854. Between Rotherham and York, through trains from the Midlands and the South West were re-routed onto the more direct Swinton & Knottingley Joint Line opened in 1879.

Normanton station was rebuilt as a single island platform, with bays at both ends, in 1871. It saw a brief resurgence of importance in 1876 when the new Midland Scottish expresses started to call there for a half-hour refreshment stop: passengers got a six-course dinner for half a crown. But soon the introduction of dining cars reduced the importance of its refreshment rooms, and eventually they were closed. Today, Normanton is a wayside station at which local trains between Leeds and Sheffield call. No trace survives of one of the original island platforms. The remaining platform still carries part of a once-extensive range of buildings, now little used; part of it has already been demolished, the rubble filling in the sites of former tracks between the bay platforms. The island platform is still very extensive, and wild flowers grow up and bloom between its flagstones.

Further north

The train shed evolved into the all-over roof at Newcastle upon Tyne. There, for the first time, in 1850–1, architect John Dobson supported the train shed roofs by wrought-iron girders rolled to a curve, the girders themselves being carried on iron columns. There were three bays each spanning sixty five feet; they were the precursors of wider roofs of the same type soon to come, notably at Paddington. Dobson's roof at Newcastle Central still shelters passengers waiting for East Coast expresses; less ornate than many of its successors, its appearance is strikingly enhanced by construction on a sharp curve. Nearby is Robert Stephenson's great High Level Bridge of 1849 across the Tyne gorge (grid ref. NZ 252637). With upper deck for rail and lower deck for road, it represents a successful early attempt to co-ordinate plans for rail and road which, unlike the station roof, has had regrettably few imitators. The bridge has six bow string spans of 125 feet, with cast iron arches and wrought iron ties.

George Hudson's York, Newcastle & Berwick Railway had a branch to Monkwearmouth, on the north bank of the River Wear, where the station served Sunderland, which lies principally on the south bank. Hudson was elected Member of Parliament for Sunderland in 1845 and so Monkwearmouth got a particularly imposing station, with its main building of stone in the classical style, opened in 1848 to replace an earlier and inadequate station. The station building was, unusually for a terminus, located on the arrival side of the station. This suggests that the possibility of extending the line over the river was considered, but that did not in fact happen until 1879, when a new station at Sunderland Central was opened. The importance of Monkwearmouth station then declined rapidly, although it remained open to passengers until 1967. All railway use of the station building ceased in 1970.

Dirty and neglected, it might have been demolished had it not been purchased by Sunderland Corporation in 1971 for use as a museum. Today, Monkwearmouth Station Museum (grid ref. NZ 396577) houses the land transport collection of Tyne & Wear County Museums Service, and a good collection it is too, for the area is rich in material. The façade of the building has been cleaned and restored, and would be entirely recognisable to passengers of 1848.

Diesel pay trains still pass the station's disused platforms and, since

4/11 Redundant bridge rail from broad gauge lines was used all over the GWR for fence posts and similar purposes. It survives here in a boundary hedge of the dismantled Wellington–Much Wenlock branch, far from the location of any regularly-used broad gauge line, and is seen from the site of the track at grid reference SJ 677096. The footpath which passed between the posts is the site of an earlier waggonway, which ran across the bridge in the colour illustration on page 118.

the museum would provide a built-in source of traffic, I venture to express the hope that British Rail might consider re-opening it as an unstaffed halt comparable to North Road, Darlington, which is mentioned in chapter seven.

Official opening of the York, Newcastle & Berwick Railway's Royal Border Bridge over the River Tweed at Berwick in 1850 was considered to close the last gap in rail communication between England and Scotland by the East Coast Route. In fact a temporary wooden bridge had been in use for almost two years and the Great Northern main line was not then complete. Nor does the bridge lie on the border between England and Scotland, for this is some three miles to the north; but it is certainly royal, for Queen Victoria herself requested the name at the opening ceremony. Quibbles apart however, it is a grand structure, designed by Robert Stephenson, a masonry and brick viaduct of twenty eight arches which still carries the East Coast main line and, since it has a curved approach from the south, offers a fine spectacle to passengers.

From York through Newcastle and Berwick to Edinburgh the East Coast Route still follows (except for its southern approach to Newcastle) the routes of the original trunk railways built at this period. North of Edinburgh however, for forty years the Firth of Forth presented an insuperable obstacle, crossed by ferry rather than bridge. The Edinburgh Leith & Granton Railway, to which I have earlier referred, originated as the Edinburgh, Leith & Newhaven Railway which obtained its Act of Parliament in 1836, so its choice of location for a southern terminus at Canal Street, which lay somewhere about the middle of the present-day Waverley Station, must have been fortuitous: the next railway laid out to serve this point, the North British from Berwick, was not incorporated until 1844. By the time the EL & G's Scotland Street Tunnel, mentioned on page 14, had been completed in 1847 however, the 'General Station' was already served by the North British, opened in 1846 and the Edinburgh & Glasgow, extended from Haymarket later the same year.

4/12 (above) Broad gauge bridge rail recovered from the Westleigh Mineral Railway is stored at Didcot by the Great Western Society. Since this photograph was taken in August 1980, some of it has been used to lay mixed gauge track into Didcot transfer shed in the background. This was being re-erected after removal from another site at Didcot; originally, parallel broad and standard gauge tracks entered it for goods to be transferred between vehicles of each gauge.

4/13 (opposite) A vast expanse of island platform, little used, and the faded grandeur retained by the station buildings despite partial demolition, are reminders that Normanton was once an important crossroads of the railway system: here the North Midland Railway from Derby and the South to Leeds was joined by the York & North Midland and the Manchester & Leeds. Later direct routes bypassed Normanton, though the station saw a brief resurgence of importance in the 1870s when the new Midland Scottish expresses made half-hour refreshment stops here. Now it is served by local trains between Sheffield and Leeds.

The Canal Street terminus must have been extremely cramped, for even allowing for the fact that the adjoining general station was notoriously cramped also, there is little room for a station at right angles to it. (Present-day Waverley dates from reconstruction in the 1890s.) However, the EL & G station would not have had to allow space for locomotives to run round, for Scotland Street Tunnel falls towards the north at 1 in 27 for most of its 1,052 yards length, and trains came up by cable haulage.

The course of the railway was aligned on Trinity chain pier and ran direct with only one very slight bend; the first section from Scotland Street station, at the north end of the tunnel, to Trinity was opened in 1842. Then Granton Harbour was developed, and the line extended there with altered name. There was also the branch to Leith. This railway was eventually absorbed by the expanding North British company which in due course opened the more circuitous but more

easily graded connection from the main line near Abbeyhill, which joins the EL & G at grid reference NT 251764. From this point to Granton Harbour the line is still in use for freight; southwards from the junction to Scotland Street survived for freight until 1967. And Scotland Street Tunnel, is still there, though used for 21 years and disused for 122; the elaborately rusticated stonework of the substantial northern portal looks as if it were meant to last for a thousand years. Its grid reference is NT 254748. The former Scotland Street goods yard has become an adventure playground called Scotland Yard (!) and further north the course of the line crosses the Water of Leith and an adjoining street by a three arched viaduct (grid ref. NT 253754) on a sharp skew, symptomatic of the extreme lengths to which railway engineers of the 1830s and 40s were prepared to go to maintain a direct course.

On the far side of the Firth of Forth there stands another reminder of this early route in the form of the original Edinburgh & Northern Railway station building at Burntisland, built about 1848 (grid ref. NT 232856). A stone building of classical design with a portico, it appears at the time of writing dilapidated and apparently disused, except that an entrance passage to the existing station passes through it. The remainder of the station is now at high level and dates from the opening of the Forth Bridge Railway in 1890; this line rejoins the original route north of the station. Almost the whole station is, however, scheduled as an ancient monument and will presumably survive. It is adjacent to the docks and the passenger slip is nearby; but I have been unable to find any certain traces of the train ferry berth. A plaque on a

4/14 Monkwearmouth station was built in 1848 as the Sunderland terminus of the York, Newcastle & Berwick Railway's line from Gateshead and Newcastle. That railway was part of George Hudson's kingdom, and to mark Hudson's election as MP for Sunderland the station was given an imposing façade. Later extension of the line into Sunderland proper reduced its importance and in the 1970s, with the station closed, the buildings might have been demolished had they not been purchased by Sunderland Corporation. The façade was restored and Monkwearmouth Station Museum now houses the land transport collection of Tyne and Wear County Museums.

building adjoining the station does however commemorate it: 'The first rail ferry sailed from this port on 1 March 1850'.

The first trunk line to enter Edinburgh, the Edinburgh & Glasgow Railway, was opened in 1842 to its terminus at Haymarket. The original station building is still in use, though in 1980 it appears to be in poor condition, with weeds growing out of the stonework. It stands at a slight angle to both existing and original lines, to face directly its principal road approach from which it is prominent. Immediately behind it there survives, remarkably, the original train shed (or possibly part only of it). Since nothing now terminates at Haymarket, it shelters not rails but part of the station car park.

The existing railway passes immediately to the south, and its tracks make distinct S-bends through the platforms to leave the original alignment, pass south of the station building and enter the tunnels which lead towards Waverley.

The Edinburgh & Glasgow is still the principal route between the two cities. It is very much a railway of its period: such curves as there are are very gentle, and for forty three miles from Haymarket to Cowlairs, at the edge of Glasgow, there is no gradient steeper than 1 in 600. Much of the line, despite its location in what is generally considered a mountainous country, is level. This achievement was only made possible, however, by use of high viaducts and steep-sided rock cuttings. At Cowlairs the line commences the descent of the one and a quarter miles of Cowlairs Bank to reach Glasgow Queen Street. Its gradients range from 1 in 41 to 1 in 51 and much of the bank is in tunnel. It was worked by cable haulage originally; an attempt to replace this by locomotives in the late 1840s was unsuccessful. After that, locomotive-hauled trains were assisted by cable up the incline, until as recently as 1908. Even today, travelling in the front seat of a westbound DMU, one gets at Cowlairs (particularly if one has recently been investigating the cable-hauled lines of North East England) a definite sensation of approaching Bank Head. The line disappears over the hump, eventually to be revealed descending steeply through the cutting and vanishing into the distant tunnel, just discernable through diesel fumes.

Woodhead and Menai

This tour of early trunk lines has of necessity been selective. Elsewhere the lines of both the London & Southampton and the London & Brighton Railways, for instance, still form the greatest parts of the main present-day routes between those places. The London & Brighton line—engineered by J. U. Rastrick—still incorporates the original and very fine Balcombe Viaduct, thirty seven brick-and-stone arches which carry it across the Sussex River Ouse. The Manchester-to-

Sheffield cross-Pennine line of the Manchester Sheffield & Lincolnshire Railway, on the other hand, after a brief renaissance following electrification at 1,500 volts dc in the 1950s, is now, for the most part, used only for freight and is threatened with closure. It includes the new Woodhead Tunnel, opened in 1954. One of the old tunnels alongside, closed at that time after a century of use, has been re-used since 1966 to carry a high voltage electric power line beneath the Pennines.

Architecturally, probably the grandest provincial station building of this period is that of Huddersfield. Local enterprise determined to put Huddersfield on the railway map by forming the Huddersfield & Manchester Railway & Canal Co., which got its Act of Parliament in 1845, and York architect James Pigott Pritchett provided it with a station building with a classical frontage 410 feet long: a central block with a large portico is linked by colonnades to lesser buildings, with smaller porticos, on either side. Originally these were booking offices, one for the LNWR, which had absorbed the local company, and the other for the L & YR which also ran into the station. About 1970 the station building was purchased from BR, and leased back, by Huddersfield Corporation, which then thoroughly cleaned and renovated it; it is listed grade I.

Two other important engineering works of this era must be mentioned: Robert Stephenson's bridges at Conwy and across the Menai Strait, at grid references SH 785775 and SH 542710 respectively. They were built some years before Brunel's Saltash bridge, being completed in 1849 and 1850 for the Chester & Holyhead Railway.

To cross the Menai Strait, Stephenson originally proposed a bridge with two main cast-iron arched spans of 350 feet, with 100 feet headroom, but the Admiralty considered these dimensions inadequate, and demanded main spans of 460 feet, with a minimum headroom of 100 feet for a distance of 370 feet. To achieve this Stephenson, aided by William Fairbairn, designed spans which were vast wrought-iron tubes, of rectangular cross-section, through which the railway passed.

The bridge at Conwy, where the line had to cross the estuary of the river of the same name, was treated as a trial run, and comprised two tubes side by side, each of 400 feet. The Britannia Bridge across the Menai Strait had three intermediate towers between the abutments and four spans, each of two tubes side by side, the two central spans each being 460 feet long. The towers were built high enough to anchor suspension chains which, it was eventually decided, were not needed.

To protect them from the weather, the iron tubes were given a roof of timber and tarred hessian, and were themselves coated with tar from time to time. On 23 May 1970, on a dry evening with a strong wind, the tarred roof caught fire and before long the tar over the whole length of the bridge was blazing. It continued to do so for nine hours: the heat damaged the tubes beyond repair.

The bridge was rebuilt over the next five years: Admiralty requirements evidently having been relaxed, it then appeared much as Stephenson first proposed, with main spans which are lattice steel arches. In 1979 an upper deck was added to provide additional road access to Anglesea, the only road access previously being by Telford's suspension bridge of 1826. Of Stephenson's Britannia Tubular Bridge, only towers and abutments remain; but the former are still extra-high for the suspension chains which have never been needed. Those who wish to see what the original tubes were like however, can still visit Conwy, where the tubular bridge remains in use.

The Rainhill locomotives

Locomotives and rolling stock which survive from the period of early trunk railways are few but famous. Survivors include the most famous of all, *Rocket*, one of her would-be rivals at Rainhill, *Sans Pareil*, and parts of the third, *Novelty*. All these belong to the Science Museum.

Since the appearance of *Rocket* is so well known and her fame so great, it is perhaps unfortunate that her design represents only an intermediate stage reached during a period of very rapid development. During three years of concentrated experiment and improvement following his return from America in 1827, Robert Stephenson developed his father's primitive colliery tramroad locomotives, able to work only at low speeds over limited distances, by stages into railway locomotives able to travel fast and far. The process started with the construction of *Lancashire Witch* in 1828 and culminated with the construction of *Planet* in 1830, in which the steam locomotive reached its definitive form. *Rocket*, built in 1829, was the stage which had been reached by the time of the Rainhill Trials and which was, fortunately, far enough advanced to prove the superiority of the locomotive over cable-haulage.

Nevertheless *Rocket* even then was a machine of ungainly appearance and swaying motion and it is not surprising that at the start of the trials *Novelty* was the favourite. *Rocket* herself was modified soon afterwards: in 1830 a smokebox, newly developed, was fitted, and the chimney shortened, and in 1831 the inclination of the cylinders was reduced from 35 degrees to 8

4/15 (next page) Typically of their period, the builders of the Edinburgh, Leith & Newhaven Railway in 1841 laid out their viaduct over the Water of Leith on a sharp skew so that their railway need not deviate from a direct course. This part of the line survived for goods traffic until 1967, but has since been dismantled. Grid reference NT 253754.

4/16 Edinburgh Haymarket station was the original terminus of the Edinburgh & Glasgow Railway opened in 1842 and, remarkably, part of the original train shed survives, for when the line was extended to Edinburgh Waverley four years later it was diverted slightly to the south. Since this photograph was taken in 1967, railway tracks have been removed, and the car park extended in their place.

degrees, which must have made the locomotive ride much more steadily. *Rocket* worked on the Liverpool & Manchester Railway until the late 1830s, after which she was sold and worked near Carlisle for a few years. Partially dismantled, she eventually reached South Kensington in 1862.

The fame of *Rocket* has led to the construction of several replicas of her in 1829 condition. Four were built in 1929 by Robert Stephenson & Co., of which one is in the Science Museum, the other three having been made for USA customers. Construction of the latest and steaming replica, for the 1980 celebrations of the Liverpool & Manchester's 150th anniversary, was undertaken by Locomotion Enterprises, led by M. G. Satow, at the request of Dame Margaret Weston, Director of the Science Museum. This replica incorporated metal parts of a largely wooden replica made by the LNWR in 1881 for the centenary of George Stephenson's birth, and a welded boiler with 90 standard 1⅝ inch diameter steel tubes in place of the original's 25 copper tubes of 3 inches diameter; in this the replica is however close to the design of *Meteor*, one of *Rocket*'s immediate successors delivered in 1830, which had 88 tubes of 2 inches diameter.

From all the publicity that the replica has received, her general appearance must be well known: but the opportunity to ride behind her, that occurs from time to time as at, for instance, the Great Railway Exposition at Manchester, Liverpool Road, during 1980, is not to be missed. Only like this can one begin to appreciate the intense impression the original made on our forefathers of 1829. They were accustomed to coach travel: impatient, restless horses pawing at the ground, followed by the jerk, snatch and clatter of a coach setting off across a cobbled inn-yard. Replica *Rocket* waits motionless and almost silent; and then moves off with smooth, urgent acceleration (and much less puff than later, high pressure locomotives). She will no doubt, given sufficient length of run, reach a speed like that of the original, twice that of the fastest horse.

Close beside *Rocket* in the Science Museum stands Timothy Hackworth's *Sans Pareil*. Though her performance at Rainhill was much inferior to that of *Rocket*, and she did not conform properly to the conditions, being both unsprung and overweight, she was nevertheless purchased by the Liverpool & Manchester company. In 1831, however, she was sold to John Hargreaves of Bolton. John Hargreaves & Son were carriers by canal and railway—the principle that railways, like canals and turnpike roads, should be available to all comers was still current—and they carried on the Liverpool & Manchester. They also leased the Bolton & Leigh Railway, and it was here that *Sans Pareil* was set to work, hauling goods and passengers. She was rebuilt with larger cylinders in 1837, and lasted until 1844, by

of wheels, purchased by the museum in 1914. In 1929 they were incorporated into a full-size reproduction of the locomotive; during 1980 this was exhibited at Liverpool Road Station, Manchester, by the North Western Museum of Science & Industry, with which it was hoped it would remain for some years. The workable replica of 1980 was built by Locomotion Enterprises. As things turned out, she was completed only immediately before the Rainhill event (just like the original) and it was not possible to iron out teething problems: hence the locomotive was carried on a wagon in the cavalcades. Construction of this replica was sponsored by Mr W. H. McAlpine and she is owned and operated by Flying Scotsman Enterprises; it is anticipated that her permanent home will be Steamtown Carnforth.

which time loads had grown to the extent that she was considered to be underpowered. Hargreaves then used her as a stationary engine at a colliery until 1863; the following year he gave the engine to John Hick of Soho Iron Works, Bolton, on the understanding that he would restore her and present her to the South Kensington Museum. This was accomplished the following year.

The working replica of *Sans Pareil* made for the 1980 celebrations was built, like the original, at Shildon by, in this case, British Rail Engineering, Ltd and the Hackworth Trust. It has to be admitted that this replica demonstrates that, while *Rocket* was an ungainly machine, *Sans Pareil* was even more so. The driver perches high up on a ledge at one end, accompanied by reciprocating eccentric rods which pass round this end of the boiler, and the fireman is at the other, endeavouring to stoke a furnace which has its door beside a very hot chimney. Like the replica *Rocket*, she is painted in the colours born by the original at Rainhill: yellow, green and black. Replica *Rocket* is yellow and black with a white chimney: the garish colour schemes adopted for entrants at the original Rainhill Trials seem to have been regarded, in the race meeting atmosphere of the event, as analogous to the identifying colours worn by the jockeys of race horses.

The parts of *Novelty* which survived to reach the Science Museum are one of the cylinders, with crosshead, guide bars and associated parts, presented to the museum in 1904, and the two pairs

Lion and other early main-line locomotives

So far all the locomotives mentioned in this chapter and the last have either been preserved static, their condition far removed from working order, or else have been relatively modern replicas. The next to be described is the oldest workable locomotive in Britain and indeed, so far as I am aware, anywhere else: *Lion* (see page 127).

Lion was built in 1838 for the Liverpool & Manchester Railway by Todd, Kitson & Laird of Leeds. She is a 0-4-2 of Stephenson's Patentee type: that is to say, derived from *Planet* but with two pairs of driving wheels coupled and with an additional pair of carrying wheels to the rear of the firebox. This is of the 'haystack' type, projecting well above the level of the boiler to collect dry steam, a function performed elsewhere by a steam dome. *Lion* ran on the L & MR, and then on the LNWR, until 1859. She was then sold to the Mersey Docks & Harbour Board, which had her set up on blocks, under cover, to work as a stationary engine driving a pump: and this mundane task she continued to perform until 1928.

By then interest was developing in the approaching centenary of the Liverpool & Manchester Railway and, at the instance of Liverpool Engineering Society, the harbour board decided to electrify its pumping arrangements and presented the locomotive to the society; she was taken to Crewe Works for overhaul and restoration by the LMS.

In 1930 *Lion* ran under her own steam at the centenary celebrations of the L & MR. She was then preserved on a plinth at Liverpool Lime Street station until the Second World War, when she was removed to Crewe Works. She emerged from time to time to appear in films, of which the most notable was *The Titfield Thunderbolt* (made in 1952). In this, with due respect to the human performers, she was undoubtably the star. She returned from Crewe to Liverpool in 1967 for display in the City of Liverpool Museum Land Transport Gallery, which was opened in 1970.

In 1979, so that she could take part in the 150th anniversary celebrations of the Liverpool & Manchester, she was overhauled by Ruston Diesels Ltd of Vulcan Works, Newton-le-Willows: the company is successor to the Vulcan Foundry, established on the same site 150 years ago and for long a famous builder of locomotives. On the opening day of the Rocket 150 cavalcade at Rainhill (24 May 1980), in the absence of replica *Rocket*, derailed, it was *Lion* that led the cavalcade of historic locomotives and rolling stock. She is owned by Merseyside County Museums and will eventually return to Liverpool.

Remarkably, there appears to be a lot of original work left in *Lion*. That the frames and motion are original is not entirely surprising, for she worked as a locomotive for only twenty one years. The frames are particularly interesting, being of composite construction, with wooden beams sandwiched between wrought iron plates. This was typical of the period. What is more remarkable is that the boiler shell, though not original, appears to date from no later than the 1840s and is in good condition. The wheels, too, are thought to date from a major overhaul during her working life as a locomotive. Other features are not original: the chimney and wheel splashers, for instance, were supplied by the LMS, and so was the tender which is at least in part of Furness Railway origin. The boiler tubes, some of the boiler stays and the regulator valve body are new, fitted during the recent overhaul. The green and black paintwork may or may not represent the original colour scheme—records are uncertain. What is certain is that *Lion* in steam is a most interesting and fascinating sight.

It is not my intention here to describe models of locomotives and rolling stock in general, but there are exceptions which are justified. One of them is *Wildfire*. The original *Wildfire* hauled the Grand Junction Railway's first public train from Birmingham to Liverpool on 4 July 1837. She was no. 8 of that railway, a 2-2-2 built by Robert Stephenson & Co., and proved so reliable that, according to Norman W. Webster in *Britain's First Trunk Line*, in the 89 days following the opening she ran no less than 11,865 miles. Her appearance is shown by a delightful model, made as early as

4/17 The Stephensons' Rocket, *displayed in the Science Museum. She was modified considerably after Rainhill, to take advantage of later developments in locomotive design. At some date much of the firebox has been removed, revealing the plate forming the rear of the boiler with its many holes for the firetubes, the secret of* Rocket*'s success.*

1839, which has survived and is exhibited in the National Railway Museum. Originally a working model, it may be slightly out of proportion, but not, I judge, very much. Flangeless driving wheels are fitted, which might have been a feature of the original: the GJR certainly had problems with its locomotives on the sharp curves of Newton Junction.

The greatest of the problems was breakage of crank axles; since they broke while a train was in motion, bad accidents sometimes resulted, quite apart from the expense of replacements. The solution, adopted from 1840 onwards, was to build, or rebuild, locomotives with plain driving axles and cylinders once again outside the wheels, but now positioned adjacent to the smokebox, slightly inclined and rigidly supported by double frames. Locomotives of this 'Crewe type' were built at Crewe works, and elsewhere, for many years. The National Railway Museum's 2-2-2 *Columbine* is one such, built by the Grand Junction Railway at Crewe in 1845. She lasted in service on the LNWR until 1902, having latterly been used to haul engineers' inspection saloons.

Robert Stephenson was the London & Birmingham Railway's engineer for constructing the line, and its first locomotive was built by Robert Stephenson & Co. Then, from motives in which correctness appears to have been tinged with jealousy, the company decided to order no more from Stephenson's company; it appointed Edward Bury as locomotive superintendent and obtained its locomotives from his firm, Bury, Curtis & Kennedy of Liverpool. Bury was a rival of the Stephensons: he provided the Liverpool & Manchester Railway in 1830 with the 0-4-0 *Liverpool*, a contemporary of *Planet* in which, also, the cylinders were placed horizontally beneath the smokebox. Characteristic features of this and later Bury locomotives were inside frames made up from iron bar, and a large firebox, D-shaped in plan, rising to a dome well above the level of the boiler barrel. In the latter feature one wonders whether he was influenced by the ideas of Braithwaite and Ericsson, for these two endeavoured to follow *Novelty* with two larger locomotives (*King William IV* and *Queen Adelaide*) in which the horizontal component of the boiler was very much larger than *Novelty*'s and the vertical part not unlike Bury's firebox. They did not, however, use steam blast to draw the fire but relied on totally inadequate extractor fans, largely in consequence of which the two locomotives were complete failures.

History has tended to treat Bury's locomotives harshly too, on the grounds of the London & Birmingham Railway's experience with them. As traffic grew they were rapidly outclassed, but the superintendent's principle seems to have been not to build larger and larger locomotives, but to provide more and more small ones, per train (as many as seven, on one occasion!). But Bury's locomotives must have been soundly built, for though no London & Birmingham examples survive, two others do, from railways where traffic remained within their capacities. The best known is the NRM's Furness Railway 0-4-0 *Old Coppernob*: the name was originally a nickname, derived from the domed cladding of polished copper over her firebox. This locomotive was one of four built by Bury, Curtis & Kennedy in 1846 for the opening of the railway, and delivered to Barrow-in-Furness by sea. She worked until about 1900, latterly as a shunting locomotive at Barrow, and was then preserved. The other surviving Bury locomotive, also built in 1846, is a 2-2-2 version built for the Great Southern & Western Railway (Ireland) which had twenty of them. She is said to have run 500,000 miles before withdrawal in 1875, and is displayed static at Cork (Kent) station.

As larger locomotives became essential, a pre-occupation of designers at this period was to keep the centre of gravity low. To this end was designed the Crampton locomotive, with large diameter driving wheels behind the firebox and boiler placed low down over the axles of the small carrying wheels. None survives in Britain, although French Railways have one which has been steamed in recent years. For comparison with the Crampton type, Francis Trevithick, son of pioneer Richard Trevithick and LNWR locomotive superintendent at Crewe, built there in 1847 a 2-2-2 with driving wheels so large, at 8 ft. 6 in. diameter, that the boiler could be placed beneath their axle. This was *Cornwall*. In this scarcely credible form the locomotive lasted eleven years; she was then rebuilt with a normal boiler above the driving axle, and rebuilt again in 1897. She ran in normal service until 1905, and then from 1907 to 1922 hauled the LNWR chief mechanical engineer's saloon. After this she was preserved; having eventually become part of the national collection, she was loaned by the NRM to the Severn Valley Railway in 1979 with the intention that she should be restored to working order. As a working express locomotive of early Victorian type she will be of great interest: but how much of her actually dates from 1847 is another matter.

So *Cornwall* is wholly untypical, and if anything the two extant representatives of broad gauge motive power are even more so. *North Star*, in the Great Western Railway Museum, Swindon, is in any event a replica built

4/18 Timothy Hackworth's 1829 Rainhill locomotive Sans Pareil *is preserved in the Science Museum, London. Wheels and cylinders, however, are not originals but replacements fitted in 1837, at which date the locomotive was working on the Bolton & Leigh Railway. She ran there until 1844, after which she was used as a stationary engine until shortly before she was presented to the museum in 1864.*

for the railway centenary celebrations of 1925, though it incorporates many parts of the original locomotive. This, a 2-2-2, was built by Robert Stephenson & Co. for the 5 ft. 6 in. gauge New Orleans Railway but, left on the builder's hands, was purchased by the Great Western. The gauge was widened and she was delivered in 1837, to become the GWR's first reliable locomotive and the prototype for many which followed. The original *North Star* and the later broad gauge 4-2-2 *Lord of the Isles* were eventually preserved at Swindon, only to be broken up in 1906.

The only actual 7 ft. 0¼ in. gauge locomotive, then, is *Tiny*. Extremely small for the gauge, this is a 0-4-0 tank locomotive with vertical boiler and cylinders, built in 1868 by Sara & Co. for the South Devon Railway. She was used for shunting at Newton Abbot and then, in 1883, she was taken into the workshops to be used as a stationary engine working pumps in the boiler house. In this way she escaped the holocaust of broad gauge locomotives which followed gauge conversion, for she remained in the boiler house until 1927. In that year she was overhauled and placed on public view on one of the platforms of Newton Abbot station. Here she stayed until 1980; by then a part of the national collection, she was moved to Buckfastleigh, Dart Valley Railway, to be exhibited in a new railway museum being established there. This offers the opportunity of wholly-enclosed storage, while still being close to Newton Abbot. While at Newton Abbot she was exhibited on a short length of broad gauge track, with bridge rail on longitudinal sleepers; whatever one knew about broad gauge academically, to see its width in fact was to find it almost unbelievable. No advantage was taken of available width in *Tiny*'s case, for all four wheels are outside the frames and are the widest part of the locomotive.

At least two pairs of actual broad gauge locomotive driving wheels survive, apart from those on the above two locomotives: an 8 ft. diameter pair from an Iron Duke class locomotive is in the Swindon museum, and a flangeless 8 ft. 10 in. diameter pair at the National Railway Museum, which originated on a locomotive of the Bristol & Exeter Railway.

4/19 Parts of Braithwaite and Ericsson's Rainhill entrant Novelty *survived to reach the Science Museum early in the present century. They are the wheels, and one cylinder with associated parts, including the pedestal and the cross head, guide bars and side rods. In 1929 they were incorporated into a full size replica which is seen here exhibited in 1980 at the Great Railway Exposition, Manchester, by the North Western Museum of Science and Industry.*

4/20 The apparent flimsinesss of bar frames did not prevent the Furness Railway's 0–4–0 no. 3, built by Bury Curtis & Kennedy for the opening of the line in 1846, from working until 1900. Bar frames were typical of Edward Bury's locomotives; so was the prominent 'haystack' firebox with its polished cladding which gained for no. 3 the nickname Old Coppernob. *She is seen here in the National Railway Museum.*

Coaches and carriages

While locomotives of this period are scarce, coaches are scarcer still. Replicas of early Liverpool & Manchester coaches were built for the centenary of 1930, three-compartment, four-wheeled vehicles in which first class passengers had closed accommodation and third class were exposed to the elements. Lately some of them have found homes at the NRM, others at Liverpool with *Lion*, but during the 1980 Liverpool & Manchester celebrations they were frequently seen elsewhere coupled to the replicas of *Rocket* and *Sans Pareil* and to *Lion*. The National Railway Museum however does have carriages which date, at least in part, from the 1830s, when they were built for the Bodmin & Wadebridge Railway. Here too third class passengers travelled in the open air, superior classes had better accommodation, though all had to suffer the jolts derived from dumb, rather than sprung, buffers.

Very much better accommodation was provided by the London & Birmingham Railway in 1842 in the coach built for Queen Adelaide, which is now in the NRM. The frames generally follow normal early railway practice (which, in four-wheeled vehicles, has since altered little), but the body, with two full compartments and a coupé end, was built and luxuriously upholstered by coachbuilder Hooper. This coach is the earliest example surviving of a succession of better-than-general coaches provided for royalty. Two ordinary coaches of the 1840s are those of the Stockton & Darlington Railway, of which one is in the NRM and the other in North Road Station Museum, Darlington. By the mid-1840s S & D had re-entered the main stream of railway development, and the appearance of these coaches is typical of the period. The NRM example is illustrated in the colour plate on page 127; the North Road example is generally similar. Its central first class compartment is upholstered, the second class ones on either side are not; luggage went on the roof.

The National Railway Museum has a section of a broad gauge coach of about 1860 from the Cornwall Railway, which was found as a lineside hut and is, in 1980, being restored. Wheel arches about seven feet apart are conspicuous.

Since relics of the 7 ft. 0¼ in. gauge are so few, it is worth mentioning that a railway of this gauge, with British-built locomotives, was still in use in the Azores in the 1960s. Railways of this gauge suited builders of harbours who needed to move large pieces of rock, and one was built for this purpose at Holyhead. One of the locomotives from Holyhead was subsequently used on the line in the Azores: the function of this was to assist in maintenance of the mole at Ponta Delgada harbour on the island of São Miguel. This line went unnoticed for many years, for anyone encountering broad gauge tracks on a quayside naturally associates them with cranes. It is quite possible that relics survive, or even that this railway is still in use. It would be interesting to find out: an enquiry sent to the Portuguese Embassy in London while this book was being prepared has, perhaps understandably, gone without reply, so any readers visiting the Azores are invited to let me know, via the publisher, what they can find.

4/21 North Star, *built in 1837 and the GWR's first successful locomotive, was preserved at Swindon works until 1906, but then broken up. Less then twenty years later this replica was built at Swindon for the Stockton & Darlington Railway centenary celebrations of 1925, and consists to a large extent of original parts re-assembled. She is now in the Great Western Railway Museum, Swindon. The extent to which the original locomotive was widened can be seen, for she was first built to the 5 ft. 6 in. gauge, left on builder Robert Stephenson & Co.'s hands, and widened to 7 ft. 0¼ in. gauge for the GWR. Extreme width enabled a railed walkway to be provided along each side.*

MOTIVE
(REPLICA)

CHAPTER 5

SURVIVORS FROM THE AGE OF STEAM

Steam still in service

Despite the apparent awful finality of the end of steam on British Rail in 1968, steam is with us yet. What that event really meant was the abolition of the steam locomotive as everyday motive power throughout the national railway system. Steam locomotives continue to be used in specialised circumstances and in industry, although their numbers steadily dwindle. In preservation, on the other hand, their numbers steadily increase as more and more, once sold for scrap, are restored to working order.

The obvious and famous exception to the 1968 end of steam was and is British Rail's Vale of Rheidol line. This $11\frac{3}{4}$-mile light railway of 1 ft. $11\frac{1}{2}$ in. gauge runs inland from Aberystwyth through spectacular scenery to Devil's Bridge. Since the 1930s it has been operated only for summer tourist traffic, and at the present day that means continuing to use steam locomotives. It has three, all 2-6-2 tank locomotives, two of them built in 1923 at Swindon by the GWR, the then owners of the line, and the other built in 1902 for its original opening and subsequently rebuilt by the GW to conform with those it had built itself. The coaches they haul have the lesser distinction of being the only pre-nationalisation locomotive-hauled coaches still carrying BR passengers.

Even more specialised is the Snowdon Mountain Railway, the rack railway which ascends from Llanberis to Snowdon summit. Its gauge, 80 cm, is the usual one for Swiss rack railways, and it was Swiss technology that was used in constructing the Snowdon line, which was opened in 1896. Almost all such Swiss lines are now electrified, but the Snowdon railway remains faithful to its seven Swiss-built steam locomotives, which came in two batches, four of them in 1895–6 and three more in 1922–3. Paradoxically, when the Snowdon line was built, steam was said to be only a temporary expedient, pending its electrification.

Though everyday use of steam has gone from the main lines of Britain, its atmosphere lives on in 1980 in the miniaturised form of the 15 in. gauge Romney Hythe & Dymchurch Railway. From Hythe's impressive terminus with its all-over roof, double track stretches away across Romney Marsh, gently curved and almost level. Along it speed expresses of eight or nine bogie coaches, hauled by locomotives which, as likely as not, are contemporary miniatures of Gresley's LNER Pacifics. Truly the spirit of the main line of the 1930s survives here.

The Industrial Railway Society's publication *Industrial Locomotives 1979 (including Preserved and Minor Railway Locomotives)* recorded 81 steam locomotives at work in industry, with a further 87 lying out of service. Three years earlier the figures had been 151 and 116. The National Coal Board—as might be expected—is the biggest user, with 48 working steam locomotives in 1979. Even so, its use of steam locomotives is gradually declining. Regular use of steam locomotives at collieries in Northumberland, for instance, which began in 1814, ceased in 1975.

When I visited Comrie Colliery, near Saline, Fife, by permission of the NCB in 1980, I found the use of steam going out gently. The colliery is linked to BR by a coal board line about one and three quarter miles long, and the motive power situation was very much what might have happened, eventually, on BR branches had the 1955 modernisation plan not been overtaken by economic events. Since 1978 the line had been worked regularly by a diesel shunting locomotive (in this instance hired from BR), and there was another diesel, NCB-owned and low-powered, for shunting only. There were also three steam locomotives. One of them was coaled and watered, ready to be lit up and used in the event of unavailability or perhaps failure of the BR diesel. Another was in the locomotive shed, prepared for a hydraulic test of the boiler to establish whether or not any further life lay before it. The third, its boiler worn out and its fittings removed for re-use, was shunted out onto a siding for sale as scrap. For the benefit of those who keep records, they were respectively no. 19 (built by Hunslet in 1954, builder's number 3818), no. 7 (built Bagnall 1945, no. 2777) and no. 5 (Hunslet 1955, no. 3837), all of them 0-6-0 saddle tank locomotives of the highly successful 'Austerity' type developed by Hunslet Engine Co. during the Second World War. Clearly, steam locomotives were still part of everyday life at Comrie Colliery: no. 19, though clean, was not polished to excess, and the legend chalked on her bunker was not 'steam for ever', or anything like that, but the more human information: 'Janet loves Willie'.

5/1 (above) Steam still survives in specialised situations on British Rail: many of its breakdown cranes are still steam-operated.

5/2 (below) The Snowdon Mountain Railway has used steam locomotives since it was opened in 1896. Here no. 5, Moel Siabod, *built the same year by Swiss Locomotive Works, is approaching the valley terminus at Llanberis with a descending train. Since the locomotive's boiler is inclined relative to its frames, it is kept more or less level on the steep gradients made possible by construction of the line as a rack railway.*

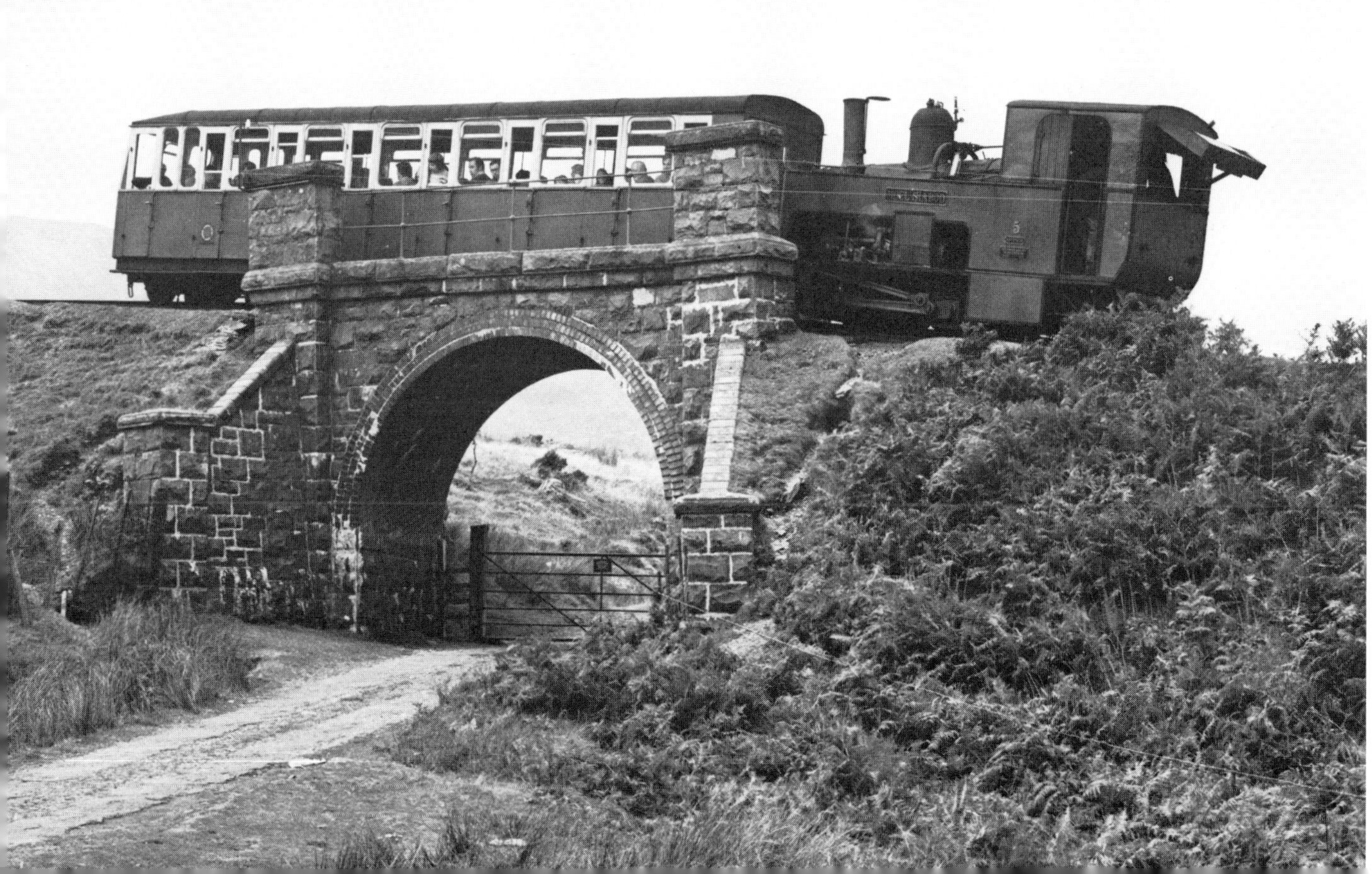

The 1 ft. 11½ in. gauge Vale of Rheidol line is well known as British Rail's sole steam-worked section. Here, a train hauled by 2–6–2T no. 9 Prince of Wales *is approaching Nantyronen in 1977. The conventional crossing-no-gates sign is for once wholly appropriate! Absence of gates from the crossing results from construction of the line as a light railway. The locomotive was originally built in 1902 for the opening of the line, and substantially rebuilt by the GWR in 1924.*

(Below) An early postcard shows a Vale of Rheidol Light Railway train with locomotive Prince of Wales *(then no. 2 of the VoRLR) as built in 1902.*

Steam locomotives are still used commercially in 1980, to a limited extent. Here is the National Coal Board's 0–6–0 saddle tank no. 19 at Comrie Colliery, Fife, on 16 April 1980. With water in her boiler and coal in her bunker, she is ready to be lit up (or kindled, as they said) in the event of failure or unavailability of the diesel shunting locomotive in the background. No. 19 was built by Hunslet Engine Co. in 1954.

GWR lightweight Manor class 4–6–0 no. 7819 Hinton Manor *is prepared at Bewdley for the day's work on the Severn Valley Railway, 9 August 1980. This class was built for secondary main lines and* Hinton Manor, *built in 1939, spent most of her life on the Cambrian and associated lines, principally those from Shrewsbury and Whitchurch to Aberystwyth. After an interlude of several years in Barry scrapyard, she came to the SVR in 1973, and four years later re-entered service. It is difficult to realise that this gleaming locomotive was once a heap of rusting scrap; even more so to appreciate the amount of dedicated effort put into restoring her and others like her. Pages 202–4 give some idea of what is involved.*

Throughout most of the steam era, the 0–6–0 was the typical goods locomotive of British and Irish railways. This particular example is the North British Railway's no. 673 Maude, *built in 1891 and named after her return from service in France during the First World War. She ran until 1966 and is now preserved by the Scottish Railway Preservation Society; she is seen here at Rainhill on 24 May 1980, attached to one of the society's Caledonian Railway coaches.*

5/3 The atmosphere of the steam-worked main line of the 1930s has lived on in recent years on the Romney, Hythe & Dymchurch Railway, with Pacific locomotives hauling expresses over double track. In the picture only close comparison of track and train with lineside fences and electricity poles confirms that this is a miniature railway—in fact, the track is 15 in. gauge and the locomotive approximately one-third scale.

Steam locomotives in preservation

Austerity 0-6-0 saddle tanks being steam locomotives of a modern, simple, easily-maintained design (the last two were built for the coal board as late as 1964, four years after *Evening Star*), they are popular with preserved railways needing motive power for their passenger trains. Within a month of visiting Comrie Colliery I was watching two more of them, immaculate, double heading a train of the Lakeside & Haverthwaite Railway, and they are also to be found on the Kent & East Sussex Railway and elsewhere.

There are probably about 270 former BR steam locomotives now preserved in Great Britain. It is surprisingly difficult to obtain an accurate figure for the total: estimates vary according to whether, for instance, they include the three Vale of Rheidol locomotives, or a locomotive such as *City of Truro* which, though preserved long before nationalisation, did run under her own steam during BR ownership.

The chief variable, however, is in ascertaining how many locomotives sold for scrap to Woodham Brothers of Barry, South Wales, have, at any particular moment, been re-sold to preservation groups. The total constantly increases: in 1979 it topped one hundred, and there are eight on Severn Valley Railway alone. Yet when BR originally sold these locomotives for scrap it was on condition that they should not be re-sold. It took a great deal of careful negotiation, by the Association of Railway Preservation

5/4 (above) No. 43924, seen here at Haworth, Worth Valley Railway, in 1977 restored to early British Railways livery, was the first locomotive to be re-purchased for preservation (in her case, by the Midland 4F Preservation Society) after sale to Woodham Bros., Barry, for scrap. This 0–6–0 goods locomotive was built by the Midland Railway in 1920, one of a large class to which many more locomotives were later added by the LMS. One of the Worth Valley's four-wheeled railbuses, built in Germany in 1958 for BR, is seen on the right.

The Isle of Man Railway's 3 ft. gauge 2–4–0T Pender, *built by Beyer Peacock in Manchester in 1873, is now a sectioned exhibit of Manchester's North Western Museum of Science and Industry. Normally hidden locomotive features which are clearly visible include regulator valve in the dome, copper inner firebox and brass boiler tubes. Wheels and motion are now driven electrically; the drive components were donated by Renold Ltd, to whom I am grateful for the use of this photograph.*

(Right) LMS Pacific Duchess of Hamilton *was being restored to working order in the National Railway Museum's reserve collection building during 1979. The work was completed in time for her to haul special trains and take part in the Rainhill cavalcade in 1980; she had not steamed previously since withdrawal from service in 1964. She was built in 1938 with a streamlined casing, which was removed ten years later to improve accessibility for maintenance, and hauled West Coast Route expresses.*

Mechanical coaling plants were a well-known feature of large motive power depots in steam days, and after dieselisation their demolition by explosives produced some spectacular pictures. Now the coaling plant at Steamtown Carnforth is unique, and is still used to coal locomotives based there for working steam specials. Loaded coal wagons are hoisted up the right-hand side of the tower and tipped for their contents to fall into it: coal is then released to locomotives below as required. The water columns on the left are fed by a large water tank out of the picture, and the running shed is seen in the background. BR based steam locomotives here right up to the end of steam in 1968.

(Below left) Steam on BR: Midland Compound 4–4–0 no. 1000 and LMS Jubilee class 4–6–0 no. 5690 Leander *double head a special up the grade west of Ulverston on 5 May 1980. The train, called* The Royal Wessex, *was chartered by the Merchant Navy Locomotive Preservation Society Ltd, and originated from Southampton; it was steam-hauled from Carnforth to Sellafield and back. No. 1000 was built in 1902 but now appears as rebuilt in 1914; she was withdrawn and preserved in 1951 but restored to working order by BR for specials in 1959. Of several other historic locomotives similarly restored to steam at that period, she is the only one now operating.* Leander *was built in 1936 and withdrawn in 1964; in 1972 she was purchased privately from Barry scrapyard and restored to working order by British Rail Engineering Ltd's Derby works.*

G W
3717
PASSENGER LOCOMOTIVE 'CITY OF TRURO'

Societies and the Midland 4F Preservation Society, to extract the first of them, Midland-built 0-6-0 no. 43924, in 1968.

Just why Woodham Bros bought a great many steam locomotives but have not, as yet, cut many of them up, I do not suppose we shall ever really know; but Mr Dai Woodham did give a strong hint when he addressed the railway preservation symposium at Manchester in September 1980. At the time when steam locomotives were about to be withdrawn in large quantities, Woodhams were invited to tender for them. Dai Woodham then spent some days at Swindon to study the construction of steam locomotives, so as to judge how best to cut them up: and in view of the difficulties of doing so, he decided against tendering. Only a chance meeting with a friend in the ship-repairing business, who at that date had equipment available that could be used to scrap the fireboxes, made him reverse his decision and purchase locomotives. He also purchased a great many redundant wagons, and it is these for the most part, rather than locomotives, that have been cut up.

Jack Simons, writing *The Railways of Britain* (published in 1961), was able to include a list of preserved locomotives which occupied only a three-page appendix, and Bryan Morgan in *Railway Relics* (1969) managed a comprehensive review, although it occupied two chapters. Today, no such thing is possible, and for a detailed list of preserved locomotives and rolling stock the reader is referred to annual publications such as Roger Crombleholme's and Terry Kirtland's *Steam* yearbook. *Steam '80* is a centimetre thick and lists 511 locations in the British Isles where there are preserved or miniature locomotives etc—which gives some idea of the present day scale of the subject.

Preserved locomotives can, however, usefully be categorised by type, and it is most convenient to do so under a series of headings.

Primeval Steam Locomotives. These, and those of the earliest great main lines, are covered in detail in chapters three and four.

Pre-grouping Passenger Tender Locomotives. These are few in number, but include three splendid 4-2-2 'single driver' express locomotives, Great Northern Railway no. 1 of 1870 at the National Railway Museum, Caledonian Railway no. 123 of 1886 at Glasgow Museum of Transport, and Midland Railway no. 673 of 1897 at the Midland Railway Trust. Contemporary coupled-wheel passenger locomotives include LNWR 2-4-0 no. 790 *Hardwicke* and LBSCR 0-4-2 no. 214 *Gladstone*, both at the NRM. Later and larger locomotives date from the period at the turn of the century when expresses were getting heavier: such as the GNR's Ivatt Atlantics nos. 990 and 251, built in 1898 and 1902, Midland Compound 4-4-0 no. 1000 also of 1902 (these three being at the NRM) and the GWR's record breaking 4-4-0 *City of Truro*, built in 1903 and now in the Great Western Railway Museum, Swindon.

5/5 On 9 May 1904, GWR 4-4-0 City of Truro *took a Plymouth Ocean Mails special from Exeter to Bristol at an average speed of over 70 mph, and is claimed to have reached 102·3 mph in doing so: this was unbroken as a world record until 1935. She had been built to G. J. Churchward's design in 1903; she was eventually withdrawn in 1931 and preserved in York Railway Museum. In 1957 she was restored to working order to haul special trains (and, when not required for these, some ordinary ones), and withdrawn again in 1961. She is now displayed in the Great Western Railway Museum, Swindon.*

(Right) Just like the days before yesterday, a GWR-style steam train of the Dart Valley Railway's Torbay & Dartmouth line approaches Churston at Easter 1980, with Torbay in the background. The locomotive is 2-6-2T no. 4588 (built in 1927), of a type once common on GW branch lines, and the coaches include some of early BR construction: such coaches are useful to preserved railways for shifting holiday crowds without causing wear and tear to more historic vehicles. These have been repainted in GW chocolate and cream, as indeed some BR coaches were at one time to work the Western Region's principal expresses.

(Below right) This was Birmingham, Snow Hill: the principal station in Birmingham of the Great Western Railway. Until 1967 it was served by expresses between Paddington and Birkenhead, which were withdrawn when the Euston-to-Birmingham New Street route was electrified. The station closed completely in 1972. The site has now mostly been levelled for use as a car park, by filling in between the platforms. So to walk about it is to find that the dirt surface alternates with the paving stones of the platforms and the mosaic floor of what was once, I suspect, a refreshment room. Within the fenced-off areas former subways can be glimpsed through wire-netting covers, and the linings of the tunnels, at the London end of the station, are still encrusted with soot from the smoke of locomotives.

(Below) The ornate, and now sadly disused, little station building on the up platform at Cromford probably originated from the Midland Railway's desire to encourage tourist traffic to this attractive area. The line was formerly the Midland's main line from London via Derby to Manchester; today, reduced to single track and truncated, it terminates at Matlock. The far end of the line, in the neighbourhood of Peak Forest, is still in use for freight, and the Peak Railway Society Ltd has ambitious plans to reinstate the intervening twenty miles of line, which were closed in 1968 and subsequently dismantled.

5/6 Small but hard-working, William Stroudley's 0–6–0 tank locomotives built in the 1870s for the London Brighton & South Coast Railway gained the nickname Terriers. *They were intended for London suburban services but later became popular motive power for standard gauge light railways. This example, built in 1876, is now preserved appropriately on the Kent & East Sussex Railway.*

Pre-grouping Passenger Tank Locomotives. Several examples of the LBSCR's famous 'Terrier' 0-6-0 tank locomotives, built between 1872 and 1880, are preserved, on the Bluebell and Kent & East Sussex Railways, at the NRM and elsewhere. The Bluebell Railway, early in the field, was able to secure passenger tank locomotives of several other pre-grouping companies. Further examples include the Metropolitan Railway 4-4-0T dating from as early as 1866, in the London Transport Museum, Covent Garden, the Caledonian Railway 0-4-4T no. 419 of 1907 of the Scottish Railway Preservation Society, and London & South Western Railway 0-4-4T no. 245 of 1897 at the NRM.

Passenger Tender Locomotives of the big four grouped companies. These include examples of the most famous express locomotive classes. There are several survivors of the GWR Castle class 4-6-0, such as no. 4073 *Caerphilly Castle* of 1923 in the Science Museum and no. 5051 *Drysllwyn Castle* at the Great Western Society, Didcot; and the most famous GWR locomotive of all, no. 6000 *King George V* of 1927, is based at the Bulmer Railway Centre, Hereford. The LNER is represented by Gresley Pacific no. 4472 *Flying Scotsman* of 1923 at Steamtown, Carnforth, and by several examples of the streamlined A4 class, including no. 4498 *Sir Nigel Gresley* also at Steamtown, and unbeaten record holder no. 4468 *Mallard* of 1938 at the NRM. From the LMS survive 4-6-0 no. 6100 *Royal Scot* of 1927 at Bressingham Steam Museum and Stanier 4-6-2 no. 6229 *Duchess of Hamilton* (1938) at the NRM, among others. Preserved Southern Railway express locomotives include 4-6-0 no. 850 *Lord Nelson* (1926) at Carnforth and the Merchant Navy Locomotive Preservation Society Ltd's 4-6-2 no. 35028 *Clan Line* of 1948. The latter, like other contemporary locomotives, was completed after nationalisation to pre-nationalisation design. Lesser passenger locomotives include several examples of the LMS Railway's Jubilee class 4-6-0s, introduced in 1934 for second-rank expresses and now found at, for instance, Dinting Railway Centre and Steamtown Carnforth; and several examples also of the GWR's Manor class lightweight 4-6-0s introduced in 1938 for secondary routes (Didcot, Severn Valley etc.).

5/7 In the locomotive fleet of the Bluebell Railway in Sussex are several passenger tank locomotives from pre-grouping railways in the South of England. This one is South Eastern & Chatham Railway 0–4–4T no. 263 built at Ashford works in 1905. The SE & CR was grouped into the Southern Railway which, intent on electrifying its suburban lines, had little money to spare for new steam locomotives for un-electrified lines. So locomotives of this type were still being used in the early 1960s, and this particular example was not withdrawn until 1964. She is now owned by the H Class Trust.

Passenger Tank Locomotives of the big four. Several examples of the GWR's 2-6-2 tank locomotives of various classes, large and small, can be found: at the GWS, Didcot, on the Dart Valley Railway and elsewhere; and so can examples of the GWR's little 1400 class 0-4-2Ts introduced in 1932 for branch lines. The Lakeside & Haverthwaite Railway has two 2-6-4 tank locomotives built after nationalisation to LMS design, and the Railway Preservation Society of Ireland has LMS (Northern Counties Committee) 2-6-4T no. 4 of 1947 of similar design.

Goods Locomotives. Throughout almost the whole of the steam era, the 0-6-0 tender goods locomotive was ubiquitous. The first was built in 1833 for the Leicester & Swannington Railway, the last to be built was 2251 class no. 3219 completed to GWR design for British Railways in 1948. No. 3205 of this class, built in 1946, is preserved on the Severn Valley Railway. Earlier extant examples of the type include GWR 'Dean Goods' no. 2516 of 1897 in the GWR Museum, Swindon, North Eastern Railway no. 876 of 1889 at Beamish, Great Eastern Railway no. 564 of 1912 (North Norfolk Railway) and Great Southern & Western Railway J15 class, nos. 184 and 186 of 1899 and 1879 respectively (Railway Preservation Society of Ireland). Although 0-6-0 goods locomotives continued to be used until the end of steam, increasingly heavy loads from late Victorian times onwards led to the development of more powerful goods locomotives. Among those which survive are famous Highland Railway no. 103 of 1894, of the 'Jones Goods' class which were the first 4-6-0s built for service in Britain, and now in Glasgow Museum of Transport; GWR 2-8-0 no. 2857 of 1918 on the Severn Valley Railway, and LMS 2-8-0 no. 8233 (1940) of Stanier's highly successful 8F class, which is owned by the Stanier 8F Locomotive Society Ltd and runs on the Severn Valley Railway.

Mixed Traffic Locomotives. In the search for flexibility and intensive use,

The ornamental cast-iron brackets supporting the platform awnings at Hellifield incorporate not only a monogram of the Midland Railway's initials but also a representation of the wyvern, the mythical beast which formed the crest on the company's coat of arms and appeared elsewhere on cap badges and the like. Hellifield, when built, was an important junction: here, passengers brought by the Lancashire & Yorkshire Railway from the Manchester area joined the Midland Route to Scotland. Today it is no longer a passenger junction and has become an unstaffed halt. Its buildings, now very much more extensive than traffic warrants, are in poor condition and would probably have been demolishd had they not been listed. In the circumstances a compromise solution envisages demolition of much of the buildings and awnings, but retention of enough to reflect the history of the station.

Midland elegance: development of steam sanding gear and a liking for short light trains enabled the Midland Railway to build some 'single driver' locomotives remarkably late, although many of its lines were by no means level. This is 4–2–2 no. 673 (originally no. 118) which was built in 1897. Sister engine no. 117 was timed on one occasion at 90 mph; the type gained the nickname 'Spinner'. Restored to steam by the Midland Railway Trust Ltd, no. 673 is part of the national collection and is seen here at Rainhill in 1980.

Midland Railway six-wheeled coach no. 901 was built at Derby works in 1885 and owes its survival to having been used from 1922 until 1959 by CWS Soap Works Ltd for a one-and-a-half mile private train service between the works and a platform near the Cheshire Lines Committee station at Irlam. There, the central luggage compartment had been converted for use by the guard; it has since been reinstated. The coach was restored for exhibition at the National Railway Museum by British Rail Engineering Ltd, Wolverton.

(Below) In some places the old railway companies equipped their stations with tiled wall maps of their systems. This gigantic example was provided by the Lancashire & Yorkshire Railway in the booking hall at Manchester Victoria, where it was photographed in September 1980. The L & YR was merged into the London & North Western in 1922, a year before the grouping took the combined L & Y/LNW system into the LMS. Below the map is the L & Y Railway's war memorial.

5/8 Seen here at Rainhill on 24 May 1980, Bulleid Merchant Navy class 4–6–2 no. 35028 Clan Line *was completed in 1948, after nationalisation, to Southern Railway design. She was rebuilt to her present form in 1959, and is now owned by the Merchant Navy Locomotive Preservation Society Ltd; she has gained an enviable reputation for reliability as motive power for steam specials, most of which have been based on Hereford, Carnforth or York, far from the homes of members of the owning society in the South of England. Locomotives of this class hauled the* Golden Arrow *express between London and the Channel Ports, and were decorated for it, as here, with headboard and British and French flags. The* Golden Arrow *Pullman service between London and Paris ran from 1929 to 1939 and again from 1946 until 1972.*

all four big pre-nationalisation companies developed designs of locomotives suitable for both passenger and freight work. Stanier's class 5 4-6-0s for the LMS are probably most famous, and examples are preserved on the Worth valley and North Yorkshire Moors Railways, at Steamtown Carnforth, and elsewhere. The GWR's equivalent was the Hall class 4-6-0, and there are preserved examples at Didcot and on the Severn Valley Railway. More-powerful mixed traffic types were Gresley's LNER V2 class 2-6-2s, of which *Green Arrow* is preserved by the NRM, and Bulleid's Southern Railway West Country class 4-6-2s, of which examples in original condition are to be found on the Bluebell and Worth Valley Railways and in rebuilt form on the Mid-Hants Railway.

Small Shunting Tank Locomotives. These were used not only for shunting but also for local freight trains and, to a lesser extent, for local passenger trains. The Midland Railway Trust has three of the well-known LMS class 3F 0-6-0Ts and there are other examples elsewhere; the GWR built 0-6-0 pannier tank locomotives of many classes, several examples of which survive, for instance at Didcot and on the Dart Valley Railway. The Great Western Railway Museum, Swindon, has no. 9400: built in 1947, it represents one of the last developments in a long line of similar locomotives. Gradual introduction of modern techniques is evinced by welded construction of water tanks and wheel splashers, although the cab is still rivetted. Also in this category comes the little 0-6-0T no. 69023 (named, in preservation, *Joem*) which is now at the National Railway Museum: she was built by British Railways in 1951 to a design introduced by the North Eastern Railway as long before as 1898.

British Railways Standard Locomotives. Preserved examples of many of the classes are fittingly widespread, from the Bluebell and East Somerset Railways in the South to the SRPS at Falkirk in the North, from Bressingham in the East to the Severn Valley in the West. Notable individual locomotives are 4-6-2 no. 70000 *Britannia*,

5/9 North Eastern Railway C class 0–6–0 no. 876 is preserved on the 'new' branch of the NER being built within Beamish North of England Open Air Museum, with original materials, equipment and buildings brought from other sites. Designed by T. W. Worsdell, the locomotive has a large cab based on American practice and was built as a two-cylinder compound in 1889. She was rebuilt with simple expansion by the LNER and survived to become British Railways no. 65033: she was withdrawn in 1962. Intended for preservation, she was later sent for scrap, but fortunately she was recovered. The coach is a Stockton & Darlington Railway second class four-wheeler of c. 1850, and the locomotive partly visible behind no. 876 is Lambton Hetton & Joicey collieries 0–6–0T Twizell *built by Robert Stephenson & Co. in 1891.*

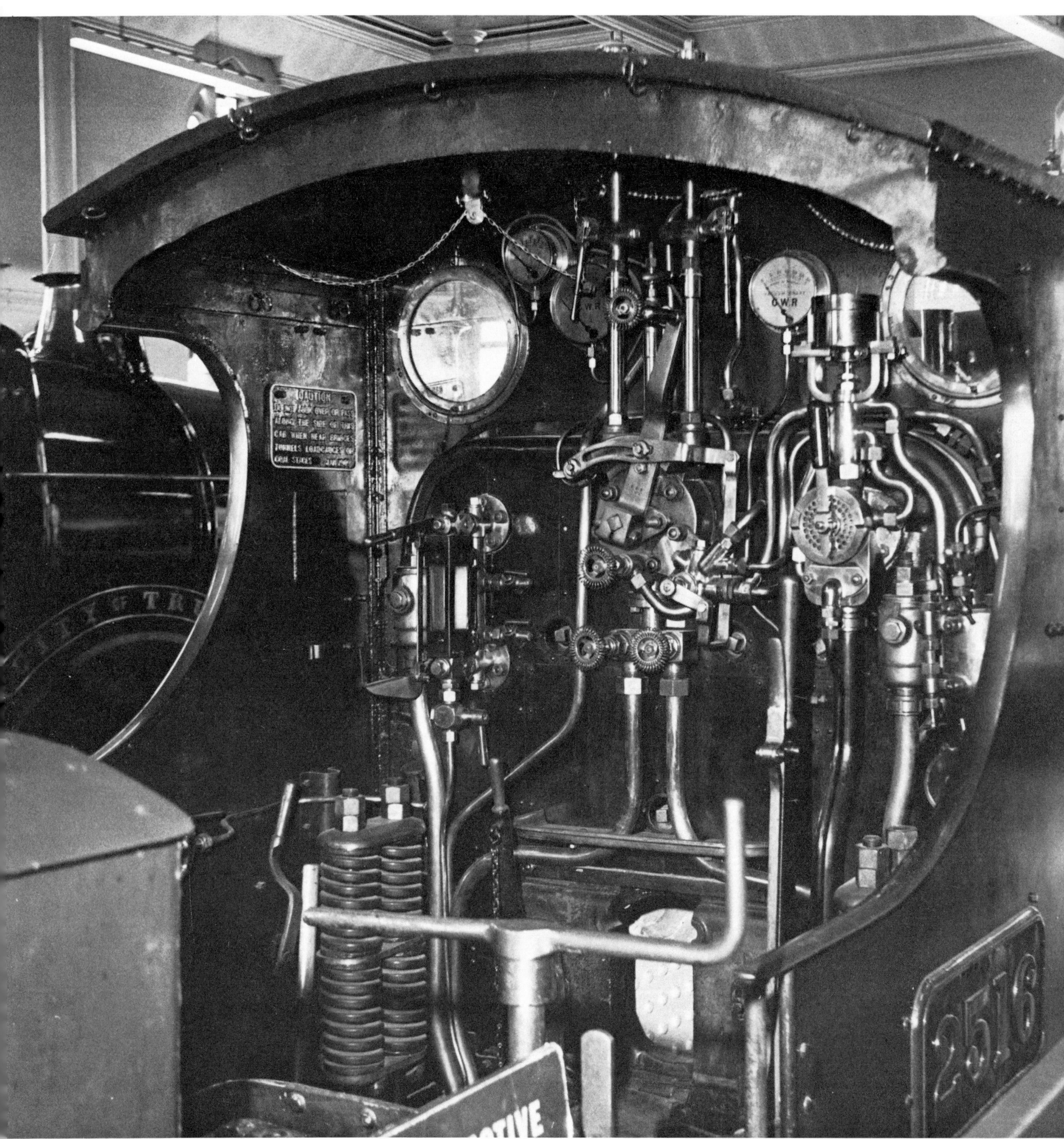
CAUTION
G.W.R
2516

first of its class and now on the Nene Valley Railway, 2-10-0 *Evening Star* of the NRM, and prototype class 8P 4-6-2 *Duke of Gloucester* which is being restored from scrapyard condition by the Duke of Gloucester Steam Locomotive Trust Ltd at Loughborough. Other classes of which representatives are preserved include: the class 5 4-6-0 (Midland Railway Trust, Nene Valley Railway), class 4 4-6-0 (Bluebell, East Somerset, Severn Valley, Worth Valley), class 4 2-6-4T (North Yorkshire Moors, Worth Valley etc.), and class 2 2-6-0 (Worth Valley, Severn Valley).

Narrow Gauge Locomotives. Surviving locomotives from public narrow gauge railways are few, for the railways they ran on were never very numerous, and closed early. Several preserved narrow gauge railways do however still continue to operate locomotives of great interest, which were originally built for them. The Talyllyn Railway has its 0-4-2T *Talyllyn* of 1865 and 0-4-0T *Dologoch* of 1866, which alone worked the line throughout its commercial existence from 1866 to 1950; the Festiniog Railway operates the many-times rebuilt 0-4-0T *Prince* of 1863 and 0-4-4-0 double Fairlie *Merddin Emrys* of 1879; the Welshpool & Llanfair Light Railway still has the two 0-6-0 tank locomotives *The Earl* and *Countess* which were built for the line in 1903 (though the former is on loan to the NRM); and the Isle of Man Railway is still operated by survivors from the fleet of elegant 2-4-0Ts built for it between 1873 and 1926. Far more narrow gauge locomotives, however, come into the next category.

Industrial Locomotives. The range of types of preserved industrial locomotives is very wide, the extremes perhaps being the extraordinary long-wheelbase 0-4-0 *Fire Queen* built for the Padarn Railway in 1848 and now displayed at the Industrial Railway Museum, Penrhyn Castle, and the 0-4-4-0 Beyer Garratt articulated locomotive *William Francis* built for a colliery line in 1937 and now preserved at Bressingham. The great majority of them, however, are small tank locomotives, usually with saddle tanks, and some of them of standard gauge, some of narrow. Their popularity for preservation, so far as standard gauge examples are concerned, derives from the fact that they have continued to be available successively in limited quantities since 1968; while small narrow gauge industrial locomotives were a convenient size for individuals to purchase to preserve in a shed at the bottom of the garden (although even the smallest of locomotives is large by the standards of domestic equipment). Particular favourites among the latter

5/10 The spartan, functional, austere and satisfying layout of the footplate of a Victorian locomotive is exemplified by Dean Goods 0–6–0 no. 2516 of the GWR, in the Great Western Railway Museum, Swindon. As many as 260 of these locomotives were built between 1883 and 1899; in the 1950s a few of the class outlived the rest in order to work the thrice-weekly goods train over the branch from Abermule to Kerry as an interlude in working a goods train from Oswestry to Newtown. In March 1956 a friendly train crew allowed the author to join them on the branch, which had long since lost its passenger trains, to travel unofficially up to Kerry in the brake van and down to Abermule on the footplate of no. 2538, in just such surroundings as these (though they were not, in my recollection, quite so immaculate!). Railwaymen who thus turned a blind eye to regulations must surely have been the railways' best P.R.Os. Within a few weeks the branch had closed, and not long afterwards the last Dean Goods locomotives were withdrawn.

5/11 (above) Most successful of all heavy freight locomotives were Stanier's 8F class 2–8–0s designed for the LMS in 1935. No. 8233 of this class was built in 1940, and spent the period from 1941 to 1952 in the Middle East as the property of the War Department, followed by five years on the Longmoor Military Railway. In 1957 she was bought by British Railways. She and other 8Fs lasted until the end of steam in 1968, at which time no. 48773, as she had become, was considered to be in excellent all-round condition, and so was purchased for £3,000 for preservation by the group which in due course became the Stanier 8F Locomotive Society Ltd. She was taken to the Severn Valley Railway and has since been a familiar sight hauling its passenger trains: here she is approaching Bewdley in 1980.

5/12 (opposite) The mixed traffic 4–6–0 is typified by Stanier's class 5 for the LMS, introduced in 1934. No less than 842 locomotives of this class were built. They included a batch of experimental locomotives fitted with various types of valve gear and other differences, to enable relative maintenance costs to be assessed. No. 4767, built in 1947, was unique among them in being fitted with Stephenson's valve gear, unusual on a main line locomotive built at so late a date. She was eventually withdrawn in 1967 and purchased privately for preservation. At Shildon in 1975 she was named George Stephenson, *and is seen here at work on the North Yorkshire Moors Railway.*

have been the numerous little open-cab 0-4-0 saddle tanks built by Hunslet for the slate quarries of North Wales. Some former industrial railway locomotives have been put into service on preserved lines to haul passenger trains, notable examples being the Festiniog Railway's 2-4-0s *Linda* and *Blanche*, which had a previous existence on the Penrhyn Quarry Railway, for which they were built in 1893, and two handsome 0-6-2 tank locomotives of 1904 and 1909 formerly of the Lambton (colliery) Railway and now on the North Yorkshire Moors Railway.

Imports. The end of steam on British Rail caused enthusiasts for main line steam locomotives to look abroad—as enthusiasts for light and narrow gauge railways had been doing for a decade or more previously—to places where such things could still be found. The consequence has been importation of an increasing number of locomotives from the Continent and further afield. The author was one of the first people to import for preservation, by the purchase in France in 1965 of the locomotive which is now the Festiniog Railway's *Mountaineer*: a 60 cm gauge 2-6-2T, built in 1917 by the American Locomotive Co. for the British War Department's light railways in France, and latterly used by the Tramway de Pithiviers à Toury. The Nene Valley Railway operates locomotives obtained from Sweden, Denmark, France and Germany; other locations having Continental locomotives include Steamtown Carnforth and Bressingham. In some instances locomotives originally built in Britain and then exported have been brought home for preservation. The Welshpool & Llanfair Railway has British-built 2 ft. 6 in. gauge locomotives from Antigua and Sierra Leone; the Worth Valley Railway has recovered a WD Austerity 2-8-0 of 1945 from Sweden.

Case histories

Having considered preserved locomotives in general, it is instructive now to consider a selection of them in detail.

Gladstone. This locomotive's principal claim to fame is that she was, in 1927, the first locomotive purchased for preservation on withdrawal from service, by an enthusiasts' society. She was built in 1882 by the London, Brighton & South Coast Railway at its Brighton works: a 0-4-2 of class B, designed by William Stroudley whose engines were standardised, small and hard working (see colour illustration on page 59), and painted that curious shade of yellow which he called 'improved engine green' because, it is supposed, he was colour blind.

Gladstone cost £2,655 to build, and was given the number 214. For many years she hauled the principal daily expresses between Brighton and London Bridge: the 8·45 am up and the 5 pm down, which were first class only. She was a popular and well-known locomotive.

She was given a new boiler in 1907 and new cylinders in 1896 and again in 1913; she was re-numbered 618 in 1920 and, under the Southern Railway, became no. B 618. When she was eventually withdrawn in 1927, she had run 1,346,918 miles.

After her purchase by the Stephenson Locomotive Society, the Southern Railway restored her, at the society's expense, to LBSCR condition. Her boiler was replaced by one of her original type, dating from about 1901. In other words, *Gladstone*'s present boiler, although it is of the type with which she was originally built, was never carried by her in service. She was placed on display in the Railway Museum, York, then recently opened.

2686
47383

70000

In 1959 the society, as part of its Golden Jubilee celebrations, presented the locomotive to the British Transport Commission. So she became in due course part of the national collection, and is exhibited in the National Railway Museum.

Hardwicke. *Hardwicke* was built by the London & North Western Railway at Crewe in 1892, a 2-4-0 of the Precedent class designed by F. W. Webb for express passenger trains between Euston and Carlisle. Nominally she was a rebuild of an earlier locomotive of the same name built in 1873: in fact, probably little more than the nameplate remained. Railway companies were inclined to do this sort of thing for obscure reasons of accountancy. In her 1892 manifestation *Hardwicke* had 6 ft. 9 in. diameter driving wheels, 17 in. by 24 in. cylinders, and Allan straight link valve motion, and weighed in total 35 tons 12 cwt. Her number was 790.

Locomotives of this class gained the nickname 'Jumbo' because of their capacity for hard work. *Hardwicke* certainly lived up to this, becoming famous when on 22 August 1895 during the course of the 'races' to Aberdeen, as mentioned in chapter two, she ran the 141 miles from Crewe to Carlisle at an *average* speed of 67·2 mph including the ascent of Shap. Probably speed reached the nineties on the descent.

Hardwicke continued to run until 1932, by which date she had become LMS no. 5031. She was then withdrawn, having reached a total mileage of 1,326,470 miles. Because of her historic interest she was not scrapped but was preserved at Crewe until 1962, after which she went to the British Transport Museum at Clapham; on examination in 1973 she was found to be in remarkably good condition. In the following year she was restored to working order by Steamtown Carnforth at the expense of the NRM; she was ready in time to take part in the Shildon cavalcade in 1975. She has since worked several special excursions, and took part in the Rainhill cavalcade in 1980 (see page 207).

For the author, at Rainhill she made the day. She also vindicates a policy of restoring certain historic locomotives to steam, even at the risk of wear and tear or possible damage. *Hardwicke* as a cold and static museum exhibit looks plain and primitive: tales of high

5/13 (opposite above) No. 47383, seen here in British Railways livery, was one of the very large class of 0–6–0 tank locomotives built by or for the LMS—in this instance, by Vulcan Foundry in 1926. She now operates on the Severn Valley Railway, and at Arley on an 'enthusiast's day' in September 1978 she is hauling a convincing steam-age freight train of preserved wagons and vans.

5/14 (opposite below) No. 70000 Britannia *was the first British Railways standard steam locomotive to be completed, early in 1951, and the first standard class 7 4–6–2. The type met a mixed reception: very popular and successful on the Eastern Region, less so on the Western where it was at variance with GWR traditions.* Britannia *was eventually withdrawn in 1965 and after her intended place in the national collection had been taken by no. 70013, the last standard gauge steam locomotive to be overhauled by BR for its own use, she was acquired by the Britannia Locomotive Society and restored to working order on the Severn Valley Railway. She is seen here at Bewdley South on 13 April 1980. Too heavy to work north of Bewdley, however, she was shortly afterwards transferred to the Nene Valley Railway and has entered service there.*

speeds through the night seem fanciful. But to see *Hardwicke* in steam and alive, with three royal coaches full of VIPs on her tail, and then to hear her accelerate purposefully away up the bank, is to understand that this is an engine that means business.

The Ivatt Atlantics. To meet the growing demand for locomotives able to haul heavy passenger trains fast, the Great Northern Railway built the first British tender locomotives of 'Atlantic' or 4-4-2 type at its Doncaster works in 1898. The designer was GNR locomotive superintendent H. A. Ivatt. The first of the class, no. 990, cost £2,522 and was named *Henry Oakley*. Oakley himself had recently been made a director of the Great Northern after twenty seven years as general manager.

Four years later, Ivatt designed an improved version of the type with a very much larger boiler and a wide firebox over the trailing axle. Ninety one locomotives of this type were built, compared with only twenty one of the small-boiler version. No. 251, which survives in the national collection along with no. 990, was one of the later type and was built at Doncaster in 1902. Locomotives of the earlier type were successful enough to be fitted, in due course, like the later ones, with superheaters and piston valves. In no. 990's case, both were fitted in 1922; no. 251 was fitted with a superheater in 1918 and piston valves in 1923. The large-boilered locomotives were the usual motive power for East Coast Route expresses until the coming of Gresley's Pacifics.

No. 990 became no. 3990 of the LNER and was given a replacement boiler in 1932, but was withdrawn in 1937 having run 1,296,000 miles. No. 251 lasted longer, becoming under the LNER first no. 3251 and then, in 1946, no. 2800; she was withdrawn the following year. In 1953 however, both locomotives came temporarily out of retirement: they were used to double head two successive special excursions called the *Plant Centenarian* which were arranged to mark the centenary of the opening of Doncaster works. No. 990 was steamed again in 1975 for the Shildon cavalcade, and during 1977 and 1978 ran in service on the Keighley & Worth Valley Railway.

Mallard. With the possible exception of the Stephensons' *Rocket*, *Mallard* must surely be the most famous steam locomotive. Whereas the Science Museum has only the remains of *Rocket*, small, black and sadly uninspiring, the National Railway Museum however has *Mallard* in all her glory. This locomotive, LNER no. 4468, is restored to the external appearance and garter blue livery in which she achieved her speed record on 3 July 1938, as illustrated on page 210.

Mallard had been built at Doncaster earlier the same year to the design of Sir Nigel Gresley. Gresley had been chief mechanical engineer of the Great Northern Railway, and subsequently of the LNER, since 1911, and had been knighted in 1936 for his achievements. The streamlined A4 class, to which *Mallard* belonged, was a direct descendant of his first Pacific built for the GNR in 1922: the product of thirteen years' development, the A4s, introduced in 1935, had been successful from the start. A further development of the design was the fitting of Kylchap double blastpipes to four A4s built in 1938; of these, *Mallard* was the first.

The circumstances of the run which broke the speed record, made during a series of tests of a new type of brake intended for exceptionally fast trains, are mentioned in chapter two. The train comprised the LNER's dynamometer car and a set of six coaches,

5/15 Old train, new station. The 2 ft. 3 in. gauge Talyllyn Railway's 0–4–2 saddle tank Talyllyn, *built in 1865, hauls the railway's original passenger coaches which were built a year or two later. This occasion was the first public passenger train over the TR's extension to Nant Gwernol, on 23 May 1976. The line occupies the site of the railway's former mineral extension; the new station building on the right follows the style of old ones elsewhere on the railway.*

in three articulated pairs, normally used for the *Coronation* express. Coaches weighed 236½ tons, weight of engine and tender was 167 tons 18 cwt. The record was achieved during the descent of Stoke bank, between Grantham and Peterborough. The dynamometer car chart recorded 125 mph, and it was considered that a momentary peak of 126 mph had been reached at a point a little over 90 miles from London.

Mallard continued in service until 1963, by which date she was no. 60022 of British Railways. She was withdrawn in that year, restored, and exhibited at the Clapham museum; and so, in due course, she was moved to the NRM. There are thoughts of restoring her to steaming condition. I personally am not convinced that this is wholly desirable—with three other A4s preserved as workable locomotives (*Union of South Africa, Bittern*, and *Sir Nigel Gresley*), might it not be better to keep *Mallard* in her record-breaking state so far as possible, and employ scarce restoration-to-steam resources elsewhere? On the other hand, if *Mallard*, restored to steam for the fiftieth anniversary of her record, should do the ton down Stoke bank in 1988, I suppose I would cheer as loudly as anyone.

Duchess of Hamilton. Gresley's A4s on the LNER had their rivals in the form of Stanier's Duchess Pacifics on the LMS. No. 6229 *Duchess of Hamilton* which, like *Mallard*, is now usually exhibited at the National Railway Museum, was built at Crewe works in 1938 at a cost of £10,136 (for the engine) and £1,601 (for the tender). In 1939 she was given the number 6220 and name *Coronation*, to form part of the *Coronation Scot* train which was sent on a publicity tour of the USA. Outbreak of war marooned her there temporarily, but she was eventually shipped back to the UK to be returned to traffic on the LMS in March 1942; it was 1943 before she regained her original number, during repairs completed that April. Her streamlined casing was removed (to improve accessibility for maintenance) at the beginning of 1948 and in July of that year she was re-numbered 46229, of British Railways.

In the 1950s, Duchess Pacifics were still in the front rank of express locomotives. When, for instance, in 1957 Cecil J. Allen timed the down *Caledonian* crack Euston-to-Glasgow express at a maximum of 86 mph at Wamphray, between Lockerbie and Beattock, the locomotive was no. 46229 *Duchess of Hamilton*. The comprehensive maintenance techniques developed by the LMS meant that, as mentioned in chapter one, the boiler she now bears is her ninth, fitted in 1959, and had previously been fitted to six other locomotives. She was last overhauled in 1961 and eventually, in February 1964, having run over one and a half million miles, she was withdrawn.

She was not scrapped, however, but instead was placed on display at Butlins' holiday camp at Minehead, Somerset, Butlins having at that time the pleasant policy of purchasing steam locomotives for this purpose at several of their camps. *Duchess of Hamilton* remained at Minehead until 1975; early that year, Butlins offered her on extended loan to the NRM. En route to York she went into Swindon works where she was repainted.

By the late 1970s, no Duchess Pacifics had been seen in steam on BR since they were withdrawn in the mid-1960s. In these circumstances *Duchess of Hamilton* was restored to working order in 1979 with the aid of funds raised by the Friends of the National Railway Museum. She was returned to steam in time to take part in the Rainhill calvalcade in May 1980, and has become regular motive power for steam specials over BR.

GWR *Hagley Hall* and LMS class 5 no. 5000. It is convenient to take these two 4-6-0s together because they represent two classes of locomotive built by different companies for similar mixed traffic work, and because furthermore both were restored to working order in 1979 on the Severn Valley Railway.

No. 4930 *Hagley Hall* is the older of the two, having been built at Swindon works in 1929. Like other mixed traffic locomotives, her subsequent work was

5/16 The smallest industrial locomotives—once used in quarries, on construction sites and so on—became popular objects for private preservation. This is 0–4–0 saddle tank Peter Pan, *built by Kerr Stuart in 1922 and one of their Wren class, in steam on the 1 ft. 11½ in. gauge line of the Dowty Railway Preservation Society, Ashchurch, Gloucestershire, in September 1979.*

prosaic but essential; she hauled both passenger and freight trains throughout much of the GWR system—though mostly in the West Country—until 1963 when, having run 1,259,000 miles in 34 years, she was withdrawn. She was sold to Woodham Bros and arrived at Barry in 1964.

Class 5 no. 5000 was the first of the class built by the LMS, at Crewe in 1935. (Others of the class, built by Vulcan Foundry, were delivered earlier, in 1934.) She cost £7,062. She was typical of Stanier's designs, with Belpaire taper boiler, piston valves and Walschaerts valve gear. She spent most of her working life in the former LNWR section of the LMS, and much of it shedded at Crewe North or South. In accordance with LMS practice, her boiler was changed in 1939, 1943, 1944, 1949, 1953 and 1957, and each time a repaired boiler from another locomotive was fitted. She became BR no. 45000 and eventually, having run over 961,000 miles, she was withdrawn in 1967, a year before the final end of steam. She was not sold for scrap: she had been selected for preservation as part of the national collection and was therefore stored, latterly at Preston Park, Brighton.

The Department of Education and Science makes a practice of loaning items from the national collection to responsible preservation groups, and so no. 5000 was loaned to the Severn Valley Railway, arriving in 1977. Examination showed that the locomotive, although fairly complete, was in run-down condition; furthermore, the grate, ashpan and smokebox still contained the ashes of the last fire of ten years previously, with all their corrosive effect. Fortunately, apart from a great deal of scale, boiler and firebox were found to be basically sound. In October 1978 the locomotive was requested for a main line run the following May, and a group of five volunteers set about restoration work in earnest. This meant, first, removing cab and boiler, and then repairing pistons and valves (the right hand valve heads had seized in their bore) and refurbishing all the motion. In the boiler, at the request of the BR boiler inspector, about 350 stays had to be changed, all stay nuts renewed and all stays and seams caulked. After much midnight oil had been burned, the boiler was lifted back onto the frames in mid-April, and during Easter week the volunteer team replaced fittings which had been removed for repair during the winter. The locomotive moved under her own steam on 28 April 1979 for the first time in nearly eleven years; she was successfully completed in time for the railtour (postponed by BR) on 2 June.

In the meantime, no. 4930 *Hagley Hall* had been purchased by the SVR Company from Woodham Bros and moved to the Severn Valley line in 1973; she had been at Barry for over eight years. Limited essential restoration work was done then, but it was early in 1978 that restoration work really began. She received one of the most extensive overhauls of any preserved locomotive, which can be itemised as follows:

Wheels and frames
- Wheels reprofiled and journals skimmed and polished
- Axleboxes remetalled and refitted
- Main frames straightened
- Horn blocks ground to true and parallel
- Bogie stripped and overhauled
- Brake system and rigging overhauled and repaired

Valves, pistons and motion
- Valves and pistons removed, steam chest liners rebored, valves and pistons reringed
- All motion parts remetalled, rebushed etc, and refitted
- Valves reset
- Cylinder drain cocks made and fitted

Boiler
- Stripped out for internal examination
- All staynuts renewed
- New superheater elements made
- Retubed
- All seams and stays caulked
- Header refurbished
- New ashpan made
- New cleating sheets made

Boiler Mountings

All boiler mountings were missing, as is usual on locomotives from Barry. A few parts were obtained secondhand, but many were made new, including:
- Manifold
- Whistle valves
- Hydrostatic lubricator
- Injector steam valves
- Blower valve
- Safety valve and clack valves
- All copper pipework.

In addition to this an available tender from a Castle class locomotive was overhauled and repaired, and the work was completed in time—just—for no. 4930 *Hagley Hall* to double head with class 5 no. 5000 on the *Inter-City* railtour between Hereford and Chester on 22 September 1979. When the author visited the Severn Valley Railway during the summer of 1980, *Hagley Hall* was working one of the ordinary service trains, and she now appears here in illustration no. 1/10. No. 5000 appears in illustration 6/37, page 265.

For completing, during 1979, the restoration to working order not only of these two locomotives, but also of three others out of Barry, the Association of Railway Preservation Societies made to the Severn Valley Railway its annual award for an outstanding contribution to railway preservation.

Evening Star. Standard class 9F 2-10-0 no. 92220 *Evening Star* was completed at Swindon works in 1960, the last steam locomotive to be built for British Railways. She cost £33,497 which, if nothing else, indicates how prices had risen since the 1930s. Her working life

was not destined to be a long one; for part of it, she worked over the steeply-graded Somerset & Dorset joint line with passenger trains. Although intended for heavy freight, class 9F 2-10-0s had shown themselves capable of hauling passenger trains when the need arose, with a remarkable turn of speed. Then, in 1965 when she was shedded at Cardiff Canton, she was damaged in a collision: her main frames forward of the cylinders were bent, footplating buckled, and part of her pony truck distorted. This was not serious damage, and in normal times would quickly have been repaired; but by 1965, when the tide of dieselisation was in full flood, it was enough to precipitate withdrawal of a steam locomotive. *Evening Star* was withdrawn in March 1965, five years after she had been built; she still carried her original boiler, and had received no major overhaul.

She was, of course, listed for preservation as part of the national collection, and so became the subject of a fairly intense internal wrangle within BR between those who wished to ensure that she was in fact preserved (headed by the late John Scholes, curator of historical relics) and those who were unwilling to bear the cost of repairs and would have preferred to substitute another 9F, possibly changing over the nameplates etc. It was found that the latter course of action had been pre-empted, however, when it was learned that the nameplates had already been stolen from the locomotive, before she had gone to be shedded at Cardiff. Eventually, in 1967, four British Railways loco-men pleaded guilty in court to the theft. Meanwhile, the curator of historical relics had ordered replacement plates entirely identical to the originals.

Meanwhile, too, the locomotive was standing out of doors. Towards the end of 1966 it appeared that the impasse over repairs might be overcome by selling the locomotive to a private purchaser who would pay for repairs, overhaul and repainting. Crewe was by then the only BR works still repairing steam locomotives, and so *Evening Star* was hustled into Crewe just before the final date at which steam locomotives were to be accepted for repair. The overhaul was finished in 1967, but no sale was completed and *Evening Star* was stored at Preston Park, Brighton along with other preserved stock.

From there, at the instance of that noted railway enthusiast the late

5/17 Shortage of former BR passenger locomotives since 1968 has caused many preserved railways to turn to industrial locomotives to haul their passenger trains. Two such locomotives which look the part better than most are a pair of 0–6–2Ts which now operate on the North Yorkshire Moors Railway but were originally built for Lambton, Hetton & Joicey Collieries Ltd. No. 29, built by Kitson in 1904, is seen here with a train at Goathland. The signal is one of the NER's slotted-post type—the arm is mounted within a slot in the post. On the right is a four-wheeled railbus, one of several introduced in the late 1950s by British Railways in a belated and in the long run ineffectual attempt to stem loss of passengers from branch lines.

5/18 The London Brighton & South Coast Railway 0–4–2 no. 214 Gladstone, *built in 1882, ran over one and a quarter million miles before withdrawal in 1927. She then became the first locomotive purchased for preservation by an enthusiast society, the pioneer group being the Stephenson Locomotive Society. Since 1959 she has been part of the national collection.*

Bishop of Wakefield, she was transferred on loan to the Keighley & Worth Valley Railway in 1973. For two years she worked passenger trains, culminating with a ten-coach special—and the Worth Valley line, nearly five miles long, has a continuous up gradient, with long stretches of 1 in 56 and 1 in 68. In 1975 she was transferred to the then new National Railway Museum, and continues to form part of its collection though leading a fairly mobile existence—while preparing this book I encountered her successively at York, Rainhill and Didcot. She appears in illustrations 5/22 and 7/7.

Running sheds, preservation centres

From up West Coast electric expresses, racing southwards after the descent from Shap, the tower of the coaling plant at Carnforth is a prominent landmark, visible from afar. When steam was commonplace, such things were a familiar part of the lineside scene and excited little comment—they were installed at all large modern motive power depots. Now, Steamtown's coaling plant is unique.

The sudden disappearance of steam locomotives was the obvious aspect of the end of steam on BR. Less obvious and more gradual was the consequent disappearance of the facilities they needed. Even now, examples can occasionally be seen on BR. During 1979 I noticed a water tower, still complete with 'bag', or large capacity hose for filling locomotive tenders and tanks, at Nantwich, and a water column, with bag, at Cudworth. Some former steam locomotive sheds are still used for diesel power, such as the shed prominent beside the GWR main line at Southall. This even retains an adjacent turntable, another rarity since modern forms of motive power, unlike most steam locomotives, are usually double ended and can work equally well in either direction.

The steam locomotive shed and its appurtenances can now be seen best at the depots of those few preservation groups which have based themselves at former running sheds. Foremost in this respect are Steamtown Carnforth and the Great Western Society's Didcot Railway Centre.

There were once three locomotive sheds at Carnforth, one for each of the three companies which ran into or through the station—LNWR, Furness and Midland. The present shed, which replaced them, was built during the Second World War by Italian prisoners; in its heyday 80 locomotives were based here, and as many as 200 more would visit it for servicing. It survived to be one of the last sheds used for steam locomotives, and turned out three of the four locomotives used for BR's farewell special between Liverpool and Carlisle on 11 August 1968. The shed closed completely the following year. Even before closure a section of track had been rented from BR for storage of preserved locomotives, and in due course the entire shed and its surroundings were established as a depot for preserved locomotives and rolling stock, modelled on the concept of Steamtown USA at Bellows Falls, Vermont.

Since 1972 Steamtown Carnforth has become important as a base for locomotives used on steam specials over BR. Even so it is unusual for more than three locomotives to be in steam simultaneously: far more of the shed is given over to storage and overhauls than was previously the case. Formerly, this was a running shed: locomotives requiring more than minor repairs were sent away to works. Nevertheless, some useful original maintenance equipment survives—there is in the shed a hydraulic wheel drop, for removing pairs of wheels needing attention, and the machine shop alongside still includes a wheel lathe able to turn large-diameter steam locomotive wheels to correct profile. By contrast, the stores nearby has become a book and souvenir shop.

The shed itself is of the 'straight through' type with six roads, and the layout of the whole depot is typical of a large motive power depot built in the latter days of steam. Turntable and

5/19 Few locomotives look impressive cold and static as museum exhibits, and LNWR 2-4-0 Hardwicke *of 1892, small and archaic, looks less so than most. In steam, it's a different matter, and tales of her high-speed run in 1895 from Crewe to Carlisle at an* average *speed of 67·2 mph become more plausible. She stands here at the starting point of the Rainhill cavalcade of 24 May 1980, attached to three preserved coaches from the London & North Western's royal train. Locomotive and coaches all came from the National Railway Museum.*

water tank, the latter supplying strategically placed water columns, are still used for their intended purposes. The most interesting features, however, are the mechanical coal and ash plants, superficially similar concrete towers straddling one of the tracks outside the shed. At the coaling plant, wagons of coal were hoisted bodily up the outside to the top, and tipped for their contents to pour into the tower (capacity 150 tons). Coal was then released as required to locomotives beneath. The plant continues to be used, with the difference that since the colliery from which the coal comes is no longer rail-connected, coal is delivered by road to Steamtown and there tipped into wagons.

It was the usual practice to coal locomotives when they came on shed, while still in steam, so that wherever they might be placed dead in the shed, they would have plenty of coal available for lighting up. The ash plant therefore serves the same road as the coaling plant: here locomotives coming on shed dumped ashes, from ashpan and smokebox, and clinker

5/20 Great Northern Railway Ivatt Atlantic no. 990 Henry Oakley *and BR standard class 4 4–6–0 no. 75078 are prepared for the day's work at Haworth, Worth Valley Railway, in 1978. No. 990 was withdrawn by the LNER in 1937, but preserved and steamed on various occasions; she is now part of the national collection and ran on the Worth Valley Railway during 1977 and 1978. Fifty years of development separate the designs of these two locomotives: the elegance of no. 990, built in 1898, is as typical of her period as is the austere practicality of no. 75078, designed about 1950.*

75078
10
G
SC
SKIPTON

5/21 (below) Unbeaten record holder: Mallard, *LNER A4 class 4–6–2 built in 1938, still holds the world record for speed by a steam locomotive, of 126 mph. The small plaque on the side of her boiler was placed there by the LNER to record her achievement. After withdrawal by British Railways in 1963, she became part of the national collection, and was restored to her 1938 appearance. Streamlined casings applied to express passenger locomotives in the late 1930s were valuable both for reducing air resistance and for publicity.*

5/22 (left) Didcot locomotive shed is the hub of the Great Western Society's Didcot Railway Centre, though when it was completed, in 1932, it would have been inconceivable that by 1980 it would be, as here, an attraction for holiday visitors. Locomotives facing the camera are, left to right, no. 6697, a GWR 0–6–2T of 1928 designed to haul coal trains in the South Wales valleys; no. 92220 Evening Star, *completed at the former GWR works at Swindon in 1960 as the last steam locomotive built for British Railways, and now part of the national collection; and no. 5900* Hinderton Hall, *GWR Hall class 4–6–0 built in 1931 and restored at Didcot from scrapyard condition.*

from their fires. The ash plant is similar to the coaling plant in reverse: ash was dumped into small narrow gauge wagons which were then run into the elevator, raised up and tipped. The ash was then delivered into ordinary wagons for disposal.

Didcot depot, the main component of Didcot Railway Centre which is the home of the Great Western Society, is both smaller and slightly older than Carnforth shed. Didcot shed was completed by the GWR in 1932, using funds available for relief of unemployment. Changed circumstances eventually made the depot redundant and it was last used by BR in 1969; the Great Western Society had been allowed to use part of it since 1967 to store its acquisitions, and was then able to use the whole depot.

The shed proper has four roads, accessible from one end only. Coaling arrangements are simpler than at Carnforth: wagons are propelled up an incline to the coaling stage where coal is shovelled from them into small skips, from which in turn it is tipped into the bunkers and tenders of waiting locomotives. Above the stage is the large water tank which supplies the depot. Ashes are simply dumped into pits between the rails from which they are removed by shovelling. Behind the shed is the single road lifting shop for locomotive repairs. Beyond again is the turntable: the former turntable was removed by BR in 1965 and the present turntable was obtained from Southampton Docks and installed by the GWS.

The layout of a typical large modern steam locomotive shed laid out as a roundhouse can be seen at the National Railway Museum. The main building, before transformation into a museum, was part of York North motive power depot, and was built only in the early 1950s. It retains its basic layout, with two turntables, one of 70 feet diameter, the other of 60 feet, and tracks radiating from them. Outside the shed at the north end, there stands beside the track a water column installed by the North Eastern Railway in 1920. A water column of more ornate design which has been installed at the south end of the museum was in use at Coventry from as early as 1847 until 1962.

Other preservation groups based on former locomotive sheds include the Dinting Railway Centre, with a small shed which once belonged to the Great Central Railway, and Steamport Southport with a much larger shed built by the Lancashire & Yorkshire Railway and extended by the LMS. Original locomotive sheds re-used by preserved railways are few, though the Talyllyn Railway continues to use its original 1865 shed, and the Strathspey Railway has been able to obtain the four-road shed at Aviemore, which was built in 1897 by the Highland Railway in connection with the then-new direct route to Inverness via Carr Bridge. Most preserved railways have not been so fortunate, being based on branch lines which did not have a locomotive shed on the section preserved; which in turn has meant converting goods sheds or building anew. In the latter case, a need to reserve scarce finance for restoration of locomotives and rolling stock, and to provide as large as possible an area of undercover storage for them, has led to construction of modern and undistinguished concrete-and-asbestos buildings. A shining exception is the new two-road shed at Cranmore on David Shepherd's East Somerset Railway, designed by architect Robin Butterell in the manner of a traditional Victorian locomotive shed.

Steam on the main line

Wait with the crowd at a bridge over, say, the Furness line near Ulverston. A DMU or two trundle by. Then there comes a distant whistle, which might be a steam locomotive or might be a small boy. It is followed by a far-off roar, that might be steam locomotives working hard, or might be the wind in the trees. It disappears for a moment or two, then comes louder and clearer, no mistaking it now. Further whistles, gradually increasing roar, sound and fury approach round the bend. The train passes beneath you and heads onwards, beyond the bridge—all at a pace which, though by no means excessive compared with the speeds at which steam trains used to run, is still much faster than is to be found on preserved railways operated under speed-restricting light railway orders. Only the main line steam special, allowed by BR to reach sixty miles per hour or more, wholly re-creates the authentic sound and movement of the pre-1968 steam train.

5/23 Maespoeth shed (grid ref. SH 753068) was the 2 ft. 3 in. gauge Corris Railway's locomotive shed and works from the introduction of steam traction in 1878 until closure of the line in 1948; locomotive no. 3, shown in later use on the Talyllyn Railway in illustration no. 2/34, was based here throughout that time. Latterly used by the Forestry Commission, the shed is being sold to the Corris Railway Society at the time of writing. The trackbed of the railway's main line is seen to the right of the shed.

On other points it is not quite so true to life—surely the locomotives were never quite so immaculate as they are now! Certainly they never hauled blue-and-white coaches, except for a very few during the last four years or so of steam traction. A still photograph of a steam special does not convey a great deal of what steam trains were like in the past—from that point of view it is unfortunate that this is a book rather than a ciné film or recording.

D. H. Ward, passenger marketing manager of British Rail, London Midland Region, addressed the Railway Preservation Symposium held at the Institution of Civil Engineers, London, on 28 November 1978, on the subject of privately owned steam on BR. He said that BR's overall policy was that provided good public relations could be stimulated and a profit made, after taking into account the additional management effort required, then private steam locomotives may run on BR main lines under strictly limited conditions. The principal conditions cover routes, types of locomotives, and the physical state of individual locomotives.

Diversion of management effort, out of proportion to the return, was great when steam trains were reintroduced as specials in 1972, but has since been much mitigated by establishment of SLOA, the Steam Locomotive Operators' Association. This was set up in 1975 with the aim of promoting continued operation of steam locomotives on British Railways lines, by ensuring maximum co-operation between locomotive owners,

5/24 Broad gauge of 5 ft. 3 in., light flat bottom rails, an elderly 0–6–0 climbing hard between barren hills: the classic Irish railway scene is epitomised by a Railway Preservation Society of Ireland special climbing Barnagh bank, between Tralee and Limerick, in 1972. It is hauled by J 15 class 0–6–0 no. 186 built for the Great Southern & Western Railway in 1879. The RPSI has been organising steam excursions continuously since 1965, with the close co-operation of both Coras Iompair Eireann and Northern Ireland Railways, and by 1981, it is expected, they will have covered the entire surviving Irish railway system.

operators, and BRB. SLOA has become the official contact with BR for co-ordinating and agreeing the annual steam excursion programme, and for consultation on all matters of policy. It also markets many of the steam specials itself. The net effect of this at the beginning of 1980 was that regular steam excursions were allowed over a total of about 1,080 route miles of British Rail, with 17 steam locomotives certified for use and a further 19 provisionally listed. These figures exclude both the Liverpool & Manchester line and locomotives certified temporarily for the Rocket 150 celebrations.

The criteria for selecting routes are five: that they are near locations where suitable locomotives are based, have fine scenery or other interesting features, are lightly used main lines where steam trains are unlikely to impede Inter-City services, are convenient for providing qualified locomotive crews, and have turntables or triangles at each end. Routes which have become notable for steam specials include Newport–Hereford–Chester, Carnforth–Leeds, Leeds to York (circular, by two routes) and the Settle & Carlisle line. Omitted from the routes are any within the Southern Region: steam trains regrettably encourage trespass on railways by those whose enthusiasm has got the better of their good sense, and the risks inherent in trespass on lines electrified on the third rail system are regarded as excessive.

Because total costs of individual excursions are high, they have to carry as many passengers as possible to keep fares at a reasonable level. This means that the most powerful steam locomotives are preferred as motive power; besides, they have the most popular appeal. Some much older locomotives, of greater historic interest, are also sometimes used.

Certificates for steam locomotives to run on BR are issued by Regional Chief Mechanical and Electrical Engineers, and last about six months. Before one is issued the locomotive concerned gets a complete boiler and

5/25 (above) The Portrush Flyer *leaves Belfast York Road in 1976. This is a regular steam excursion run on several Saturdays each summer from Belfast to the seaside at Portrush and back. The locomotive is the RPSI's 2–6–4T no. 4 built for the LMS (Northern Counties Committee) in 1947 and purchased by the society in 1971 when NIR ceased to use steam locomotives. The train too is composed of coaches owned by the RPSI, and originating from the Great Northern, Great Southern, and Great Southern & Western Railways.*

5/26 (right) No. 6201 Princess Elizabeth *was one of Stanier's first Pacifics, built by the LMS in 1933. She is now owned by the* Princess Elizabeth *Locomotive Society, and in this photograph is leaving Skipton with a steam special in 1980. The signal cabin in the background is of typical Midland Railway design.*

mechanical inspection and a steam test. Immediately before it goes out to work a train the locomotive is inspected again; it has been prepared by the staff or volunteers of the depot at which it is shedded—Carnforth, Didcot, Bulmers, NRM or wherever—and is then handed over to a BR crew. En route there are on the footplate driver, fireman and inspector, all from BR, and a representative of the owner. After the day's run, the BR men hand the locomotive back to depot staff for disposal. Every five years comcs a major boiler inspection: the boiler is removed from the frames and the tubes removed for an internal inspection of the boiler, which, when in use, is subject to steam pressures as high as 250 lb per sq. in. according to class of locomotive. The expense of this inspection is considerable, and frustrating for the owner if no repairs are found to have been needed: but it is not unusual for the boiler tubes to need replacement after five years in any event.

In the short term, BR proposes to allow steam excursions at least until 1985; this decision, taken about 1978, allowed owners of steam locomotives to justify big and expensive repairs. In thc longcr tcrm, the future of steam specials is not yet clear. It is unlikely that revenue derived from fares is sufficient to cover long term costs of maintaining and overhauling the steam locomotives concerned; and no owners of standard gauge locomotives have yet had to meet the expense of a complete new boiler (although many narrow gauge preserved locomotives have been reboilered). When heavy repairs are needed, it seems likely that owners will have to continue to rely on private and public benevolence. A minor problem is that for every fare-paying passenger on a steam special there are a great many more lineside photographers and spectators who photograph and watch the train for nothing. They can usefully contribute by purchasing timing sheets (which give the times a train is due at places on its route) for individual specials from tour organisers at £2 each (1980 price) plus stamped addressed envelope. It is

not very much to pay for so fine a spectacle as a steam train going by.

The spectacle is better than ever when the train comprises not only a preserved locomotive but preserved coaches also. The Scottish Railway Preservation Society has been a pioneer here, promoting widely travelled specials of its own historic coaches from Scottish companies, with diesel haulage. A complete train of preserved locomotives and rolling stock from a single company ran over BR for the first time in 1975 when the Great Western Society was able to run a train comprising seven restored GWR coaches double headed by no. 7808 *Cookham Manor* and no. 6998 *Burton Agnes Hall.*

Subsequently the Severn Valley Railway has promoted specials over BR using GW coaches from everyday service on its own line; and the SRPS has arranged specials of its own coaches including one from Falkirk through to Oxenhope, changing over from diesel to steam haulage at Keighley with the change from BR to Worth Valley Railway. A preserved-coaches special of different nature was the *Centenary Express*, a train of historic catering vehicles which toured British Rail (with, in places, steam haulage) in September 1979 to celebrate one hundred years of dining cars. About the same time, however, it seemed that the Great Western Society vintage train, which had made many journeys over the previous four years, had reached the end of the line: new regulations introduced by BR had the effect that certain necessary maintenance to the coaches should be carried out in British Rail Engineering Ltd Workshops. This implied a cost to the GWS of some £50,000 to overhaul the train for the following season, a cost which was excessive.

Apart from the Vale of Rheidol coaches, no pre-nationalisation locomotive-hauled passenger coaches survive in public use on British Rail. Among the last to go were some of Gresley's buffet cars for the LNER, which lasted until 1977, their teak panelled bodies disguised beneath blue-and-white paint. Coaches of pre-nationalisation design are still to be seen in engineers' use on BR, and contemporary bogie brake vans in full use are still common.

BR coaching stock does include a strong reminder of the steam age in the form of the large (but declining) number of BR Mark I coaches still in use—their construction was contemporary with that of the BR standard steam locomotives. These coaches tend to be kept together in sets to work specific services—while preparing this book I noticed them much in evidence in trains between Crewe and Cardiff, Nottingham and Glasgow, and Glasgow and Dundee. They are also very popular with preserved railways as vehicles to carry holiday crowds, and so relieve rolling stock which is more historic from excessive wear and tear. The Severn Valley Railway has a set of Mark I coaches restored to their original scarlet and cream livery; GW and LMS coaches, likewise restored to original liveries, are similarly kept together in sets with convincing results. Such reminders of the old companies belong properly, however, to the next chapter.

5/27 (left) To celebrate the hundredth anniversary of dining cars, British Rail operated the Centenary Express *in September 1979. Comprised mostly of preserved dining, Pullman and buffet cars, it toured BR, going on exhibition, and running public excursions with meals served in the historic vehicles. Here the train approaches Hereford in the evening of 15 September, hauled by GWR 4–6–0 no. 6000* King George V. *The train comprises: LNWR first class corridor brake coach of 1905; LNWR first class dining saloon of 1900; Midland Railway third class dining carriage of 1914; modern buffet car for preparation of meals; two Pullman cars of 1960; Pullman car* Topaz *of 1913; Gresley LNER buffet car of 1937; BR mark one griddle car of 1960; LNWR first class corridor brake coach of 1905.*

5/28 (below) Locomotive-hauled passenger coaches of pre-nationalisation origin are no longer in use on British Rail (except on the Vale of Rheidol line), but many bogie brake vans from the former companies are still in service. Here at Crewe in 1979 is no. M 31034, built by the LMS at Wolverton in 1939. That was the year Duchess of Hamilton, *disguised as no. 6220* Coronation, *was touring the USA with the* Coronation Scot.

CHAPTER 6

THE OLD COMPANIES AND THEIR RAILWAYS

Great Western

In 1922, immediately prior to the grouping, the nine largest British railways were the Great Western (3,005 miles), the London & North Western (2,667 miles), the Midland (2,170 miles), the North Eastern (1,757 miles), the North British (1,377 miles), the Great Eastern (1,191 miles), the Caledonian (1,114 miles), the Great Northern (1,051 miles), and the London & South Western (1,020 miles). The London & North Western had been swollen the previous year by absorption of the Lancashire & Yorkshire Railway (601 miles): the LNWR proper extended to 2,066 miles.

So the two most extensive pre-grouping railways were in effect the Great Western and the Midland. The subsequent histories of their two systems, since the grouping, have been totally dissimilar, yet each company has left its mark.

The Great Western kept its identity at the grouping; its lines radiated, fan-like, from Paddington to Wales and the West of England, and even today they form the nucleus of British Rail's Western Region. To the Midland, by contrast, the grouping brought an unhappy merger with the LNWR. It served no single area: its lines extended continuously (if one includes joint lines and the Heysham–Belfast steamer service) from near Bournemouth to near Carlisle, and from Lowestoft to Killybegs. What is left of them today is split up between the Eastern, London Midland and Western Regions and Northern Ireland Railways.

Let us consider the Great Western first. The GWR had about it an air of spaciousness. This may originally have had something to do with standard gauge tracks laid to broad gauge clearances, but it was also a feature of its station architecture. With its air of spacious confidence, the GWR was a country gentleman of a line: appropriate to its clientele. Not without reason did P. G. Wodehouse set Blandings Castle in country served by the Great Western. Where GWR lines still run, so does this atmosphere survive. Yet one of the GWR's most familiar features is quite different. The Western Region, alone on BR, still has a preference for lower-quadrant semaphore signals, and these are of GWR pattern. They are now to be found even on lines not, or not wholly, of Great Western origin, which the aftermath of nationalisation has brought into the Western Region. I noted one recently on the West London Extension Railway's approach to that hub of the Southern Electric system, Clapham Junction.

Most of the Great Western's main lines are still the principal routes to the places they serve. The main route to Devon and Cornwall is the Great Western's, from Paddington via Reading, Newbury and Taunton to Exeter, Plymouth and Penzance. The original main line to Bristol still performs its function. The main line to South Wales still diverges from it at Wootton Basset and passes through the GWR's greatest engineering feature, the Severn Tunnel. From Didcot, another main line still runs north west to Oxford, Worcester and Hereford. Only on the GWR main line to Birmingham and beyond is the situation totally different, but before considering this, let us first look at two of the branches.

A great many GWR branches have of course gone but some, of surprisingly wayward and bucolic character, survive. The branch from Liskeard to Looe, Cornwall, is an example. But for the Second World War it would probably have closed in the early 1940s, for the Great Western had started work on a more direct line to Looe which would almost have halved the journey time from Plymouth: work which was subsequently abandoned. Goods trains to Looe eventually ceased in 1963 and complete closure was proposed in 1965 and 1966, but the Minister of Transport did not consent to withdrawal of passenger trains because of the difficulty of providing a satisfactory substitute bus service.

So passenger trains still run on the Liskeard to Looe branch. Its layout is extraordinary, understandable only in terms of history and is worth further consideration. Looe trains have their own small station at Liskeard, at right angles to the main station on the Plymouth–Penzance line, and although their destination is to the south, they depart in a north-easterly direction. They then describe, clockwise, three-quarters of a circle, descending steeply all the time, passing beneath a main-line viaduct, and eventually at Coombe Junction trailing into another line. Onto this they reverse, to continue in straightforward fashion down the valley of the Looe River to Looe terminus.

Beside the line, and particularly in the vicinity of Causeland and Sandplace halts, can be seen clear traces of the Liskeard & Looe Union Canal,

completed in 1828—the canal era lasted longer in the South West than elsewhere—which provide the key to the layout of subsequent railways in the vicinity. The canal ran from the tideway of the East Looe River up to Moorswater, in the valley west of Liskeard. After copper mines had been opened up around Caradon Hill to the north, the Liskeard & Caradon Railway, a standard gauge line worked at first by horse and gravity, was opened in 1844 to connect them to the canal at Moorswater; and in 1860 the canal company replaced its canal by the present railway line down the valley to Looe. It was built, like the L & C, to standard gauge. Meanwhile, in 1859, the broad gauge Cornwall Railway main line had been opened, passing over a viaduct high above the L & L canal/railway at Moorswater without connecting with it. It was not until after the main line had been converted to standard gauge more than thirty years later that a connecting link was built: the present steeply graded and circuitous line from Liskeard to Coombe Junction, which was opened in 1901. Later, the GWR took over the local railways.

From Coombe Junction (grid ref. SX 239635), which is still complete with Great Western signal box and GW style signals, the L & L Railway line still extends northwards for half a mile to Moorswater for china clay traffic. North of this point, however, the Liskeard & Caradon line was closed as early as 1917 after mines were

6/1 The glazed all-over roof was a notable feature of the Victorian city station. This example is at Glasgow Queen Street; the western terminus of the Edinburgh & Glasgow Railway was opened on this site in 1842, but the present all-over roof was provided by the North British Railway about 1880. Fortunately a proposal in 1960 to replace it by separate awnings for individual platforms was not put into effect.

6/2 The Great Western look: large taper-boilered 4–6–0, copper capped chimney, polished brass safety valve cover. Were it not for the local train lamp code (and BR-type flat-bottom rails), Drysllwyn Castle *might be heading for Paddington with the* Bristolian. *In fact, on 10 August 1980, she is trundling up and down the demonstration line at Didcot Railway Centre, rather after the manner of a caged tiger.*

worked out. Its traces are still remarkably clear; there is a fine overbridge at grid reference SX 245660 for instance. South of Coombe Junction the Looe branch has become a basic railway, without sidings or signals, finishing at the buffer stops at the platform end at Looe station. Goods yard and quayside sidings beyond have been lifted. When I travelled on the branch in April 1980, there was no lack of passengers.

Another archetypal country branch line of the Great Western was that from Princes Risborough to Watlington. It too was built by a local company, with minimal earthworks in the manner of later light railways, and opened in 1872; after the local company got into financial difficulties, the GWR took the line over. Passenger trains did not survive into the diesel era, though they did last until 1957. Their survival, as long as that, cannot have been helped by the method of working, which latterly was to use a locomotive shedded at Slough: this entailed a light engine journey from Slough to Watlington of about one and a half hours outward every morning, and home again in the evening. To me, travelling on the line in the spring of 1957, it looked as though the final straw came when, as a result of relaying the track, the maximum speed allowed over much of the branch was (as I noted at the time) no more than ten mph. It would have been quicker by bike.

Probably these were symptoms of lack of management attention, understandable if unjustifiable. In any event

6/3 (left) 6/4 (above) Platform ornaments: railway companies in their affluent days ornamented small stations as well as large, and did so particularly in tourist areas. In illustration 6/3 a painted stork atop a pedestal of local granite, which was probably once a fountain, now forms the centre piece of a garden on the platform at Dalmally, Callander & Oban line. Elsewhere many companies incorporated a monogram of their initials into the cast iron uprights of their station seats, but the Furness Railway went one better with a squirrel eating a bunch of grapes. The example in illustration 6/4 is now on the platform of the Ravenglass & Eskdale Railway's station at Ravenglass.

it is unlikely that passenger traffic would have lasted much longer, for although the principal demand for transport from Watlington must have been in a south-easterly direction towards High Wycombe and London, the town lies beneath the Chiltern escarpment, which runs in a line south west to north east. The railway followed this, so any railway journey commenced with nine miles of branch line, probably at right angles to the intended direction of travel, to join the main railway system at Princes Risborough.

That same geographical feature which was such a hindrance to passenger traffic has, however, ensured survival of part of the line for freight. The Chilterns are chalk hills, and at Chinnor, three and three quarter miles down the branch from Princes Risborough, there was founded in 1908 the Chinnor Works to quarry the chalk and produce lime and, later, cement. These works have since expanded greatly and, although freight beyond Chinnor ceased in 1961, the branch as far as that place is still used to deliver large amounts of coal and gypsum to the works. These require two trains, five days a week.

Mention of Princes Risborough brings us to its main line, the Great Western and Great Central Joint Line. This formed part of the GWR route from Paddington to Birmingham and Birkenhead: this is the only one of the GWR's principal main lines to have become totally distintegrated as a consequence of modernisation elsewhere. Until the 1960s King class locomotives used to steam out of Paddington hauling expresses with carriage roof boards inscribed (if memory serves correctly) 'Paddington Birmingham Shrewsbury Chester and Birkenhead'. Their route diverged from the main line to the West at Old Oak Common, three miles from Paddington, and took in also High Wycombe, Princes Risborough, Banbury, Leamington Spa and Wolverhampton Low Level. The fastest trains from Paddington to Birmingham Snow Hill generally took two hours, the same journey time as the fastest from Euston to Birmingham New Street.

Electrification in 1967 of the line from Euston to New Street and Wolverhampton High Level meant concentration of passenger traffic on to that route, and withdrawal of through trains from Paddington over the GW route: and in anticipation of this, the Great Western route had already been transferred, from Banbury northwards, from the Western Region to the London Midland. The present state of the former GWR route is as follows. From Old Oak Common as far as Northolt Junction, about six and a half miles, it sees but one regular passenger train in each direction daily, between Paddington and Birmingham New Street. At Northolt Junction, however, suburban services now based on Marylebone join it, to run as far as Banbury. From Princes Risborough for twenty six miles to Aynho the line has been reduced to single track; at Aynho the older and longer route via Oxford joins it, bringing Paddington-to-Birmingham trains which, with the exception mentioned, have reverted to it. Short of Birmingham, these are diverted into New Street; some Birmingham suburban services continue along the old main line to terminate at Moor Street, the GW's suburban terminus laid out beside the vacant trackbed of the former line to Snow Hill.

Passenger trains rejoin the Great Western route beyond Wolverhampton: but they no longer originate from Paddington. Nowadays they are mostly only local trains from Wolverhampton High Level to Chester, and the few through trains from Euston to Shrewsbury. What Shrewsbury got out of London Midland electrification was to find that its service of seven through trains a day from London (Paddington) had been cut suddenly to only one from London (Euston): their number has since recovered slightly, to three. North of Shrewsbury there are now only the local train services to Chester, and from Chester to Rock Ferry. From Rock Ferry, electric trains run to Birkenhead Central and Liverpool; the final one and a half miles of the old route from Rock Ferry to Birkenhead Woodside are closed and dismantled.

The story of the decline and fall of Birmingham Snow Hill station, which was re-signalled during the period 1956–60, when it was very busy, is particularly poignant. Having lost its main line services in 1967, it became an 'unstaffed halt' for the few surviving local services; and then in 1972 it was closed completely. The buildings were demolished in 1977, and the site, levelled, is now 'Snow Hill Car Park'. A BR notice board still gives details of train services (from New Street), presumably for the benefit of any intending passengers just returned from fifteen years or so in Patagonia or some similar spot to which news travels slowly. The station site in its present form appears in the colour illustration on page 186; visiting it in 1980 for the first time since pre-1967, the author found it redolent with memories—of early journeys to boarding school, made tolerable by the presence of Star class *Knight of the Grand Cross* and suchlike; of trains which called there on later journeys returning from leave to National Service; of the last journey behind a King and the first behind a Western diesel hydraulic.

Enough of this. Now let us consider

6/5 Restored Great Western goods vehicles at Didcot. Left to right: guard's brake van (code named Toad*) of 1924; covered van (code named* Mink A*) built 1924; fruit van, built 1892; five-plank open wagon for china clay, built 1913. On the extreme right is 'private owner'* Royal Daylight *oil tank wagon of 1912, and on the extreme left 0–6–0 pannier tank locomotive no. 3738 (5700 class) built 1937.*

6/6 (*above*) 6/7 (*right*)

'Yes. I remember Adlestrop—
The name, because one afternoon
Of heat the express-train drew up there
Unwontedly. It was late June.

The steam hiss'd. Some one clear'd his throat.
No one left and no one came
On the bare platform. What I saw
Was Adlestrop—only the name . . . .'

wrote Edward Thomas at the turn of the century. The express halted by signals might well have been one of those non-stop Paddington–Worcester trains mentioned in chapter one. Although most GWR main lines remain open, they have lost many of their wayside stations; this is the site of Adlestrop station (grid ref. SP 236264). Platforms have been demolished, although some lengths of platform fencing remain on the left; the small station building was on the right where the new fence now runs, and the base of a platform formerly within a large goods shed can be seen. A few overgrown ornamental trees, and their shadows, are reminders that the station once had attractive gardens. It was closed in January 1966; a

nameboard and a station seat were subsequently incorporated into a wooden bus shelter, shown in illustration 6/7. This is located three-quarters of a mile away, in the village itself, which is not large: circumstances which perhaps symbolise one of the reasons for closure of this and many other small stations.

where more tangible reminders of GWR trains can be found. The Great Western image was strongest in the appearance of its expresses—long trains of chocolate-and-cream coloured coaches hauled by dark green taper-boilered 4-6-0s with copper-capped chimneys and polished brass safety valve covers. A strong family resemblance between locomotives large and small resulted from the work of G. J. Churchward, who was locomotive, carriage and wagon superintendent, later re-titled chief mechanical engineer, from 1902 until 1922. As a result of a long period of detailed experiment (which included importing locomotives from France for comparison with his own) he provided the GWR with a series of locomotives of advanced design which provided the basis for all subsequent classes. GWR locomotives powered principal Western Region expresses until the end of steam (even though their design was by then beginning to seem slightly archaic).

The minimal effect which the grouping had on the GWR greatly assisted this continuity of locomotive design, as it did another aspect of the GWR: the esprit de corps of its employees. (Mildly jealous men of other lines were wont to remark with sarcasm that Great Western men thought GWR meant God's Wonderful Railway). With an industrious publicity department too, the GW probably had a greater fan-following than any other railway.

The combination of these influences is reflected in the extent to which GWR locomotives, rolling stock and other equipment have been preserved, and in many cases continue to operate. Most of the principal locations devoted to preservation of the GWR and its equipment have already been mentioned individually in earlier chapters, but may usefully be summarised here.

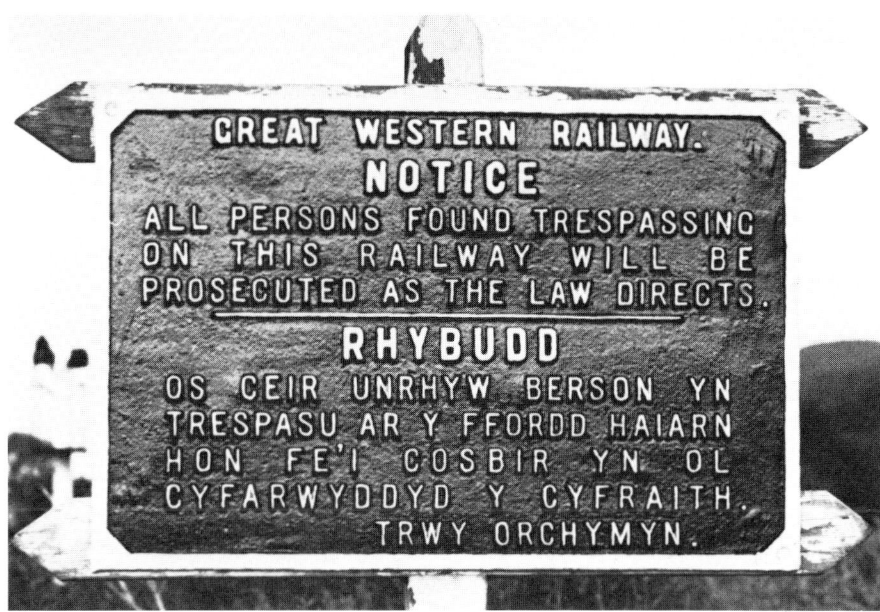

6/8 (above) The Great Western, like other lines in Wales, used warning notices which were bi-lingual in English and Welsh. This one is at Llanuwchllyn, on the Bala Lake Railway, which is laid on the trackbed of part of the former GWR line from Ruabon to Dolgellau.

6/9 (left) There was a time, in the 1930s and 1940s, when closed railways lingered on for years, becoming ever rustier and more thickly overgrown; then, as closures became more common, skills in quick removal for scrap of the remains seemed to improve. A line which recently lingered on for a surprisingly long time was that from Honeybourne to Cheltenham, opened in 1906 to form part of the GWR route from Birmingham to Gloucester. It is seen here at Toddington in September 1979; the station had closed to passengers in 1960 and the line had been disused since 1976, although closure was not confirmed until July 1979. By the time the photograph was taken, track was being lifted elsewhere on the line, despite proposals for preservation. The signal is typical Great Western pattern.

The Great Western Railway Museum, Swindon, operated by Borough of Thamesdown Museums and Art Galleries, has four representative standard gauge GW locomotives as static exhibits: Dean Goods no. 2516 (built 1887), *City of Truro* (built 1903), 4-6-0 no. 4003 *Lode Star* built 1907 to Churchward's famous Star class, and 0-6-0 pannier tank no. 9400 built 1947.

Birmingham Railway Museum, Tyseley, has eight GWR locomotives including no. 7027 *Thornbury Castle* and no. 7029 *Clun Castle*, and, with well-equipped workshops, acts as a base for steam runs over BR.

Bulmer Railway Centre, Hereford, is the home of no. 6000 *King George V*.

Didcot Railway Centre is the home of the Great Western Society, which originated when a group of schoolboys formed a society which was successful, in 1964, in purchasing one of the 0-4-2 tank locomotives and one of the auto-coaches with which the GWR formed push-pull trains to work its smallest branch lines. Its stock now includes 18 locomotives from the GWR (and five others) many of them in working order, and 44 GWR coaches.

The Dart Valley Railway has two lines—the Torbay & Dartmouth and the Buckfastleigh—both of them former GWR branches which are now operated with GWR steam locomotives and according to GWR practices.

The Severn Valley Railway operates passenger trains over the former GWR line between Bewdley and Bridgnorth. Many Great Western locomotives and coaches, restored to their original colours, are included in its stock.

The West Somerset Railway operates over the former GWR Minehead branch and has several Great Western tank locomotives.

6/10 Midland locomotive, Midland station. On 3 May 1980 former Midland Railway three-cylinder compound 4–4–0 no. 1000 double-heads The Mancunian *charter steam special through Skipton on the Midland Railway's Leeds-to-Carlisle main line. The Midland's use of compound expansion of steam, first in a high pressure cylinder, then in two low pressure ones, was the most successful of any British railway, and no. 1000 was the first of 45 such locomotives built by the Midland: the LMS built 195 more. The second locomotive is no. 4771* Green Arrow, *the prototype V2 class 2–6–2 designed by Gresley for the LNER in 1936. An expanse of glazed platform awning is a typical feature of a Midland station.*

The Midland

If the character of the Great Western was that of a country gentleman, then the Midland was surely a *nouveau riche* industrialist, all plush and pretension. As such persons are, it was wealthy and influential, and had become so by competing with, and to a large extent beating, its rivals. I am not sure whether I should have appreciated it in the full glory of its brash prosperity: but today it has the fascination of a fallen giant, and excites the same sort of sympathy. With the exception of its south-west to north-east route, which remains one of the principal arteries of the railway system, all its main lines have declined in importance, in some cases to the point of total closure.

While preparing this book I had occasion to travel from Bristol to Stirling, to arrive in the late evening. The quickest and most direct route, and the usual one today, would have been the Midland line to Birmingham, and the electrified West Coast Route thence to Carlisle, from which place there is an evening train through to Stirling and Perth. How much more interesting, I thought, to take the route familiar to our grandparents, and travel as far as possible by the Midland: for the Midland, like all of the old companies, naturally arranged its timetables and connections so that passengers travelled as far as possible on its own system. Study of the current timetable showed that I could indeed do this: by catching a Paignton to Leeds train at Bristol at 1308 and continuing on it over the Midland line beyond Birmingham as far as Sheffield, I could there connect with another Midland line train from Nottingham which would take me to Carlisle over the Settle & Carlisle route. It was slower than going via the West Coast Route, but there were fewer changes of train.

Throughout the journey from Bristol to Carlisle, which entailed crossing from Western Region to London Midland, then from London Midland to Eastern, and eventually from Eastern back to London Midland again, there were reminders that the whole route had once belonged to the Midland alone (apart from short sections at each end). The Midland, for instance, had its own terminology—such as 'switch' where other companies used the term 'catch points': and a 'switch' sign survived beside the line at King's

Norton, south of Birmingham and another at the approach to Sheffield. The Midland, too, used platform fencing with diagonal rails (see illustration 7/6) to such an extent that it was almost a trademark: and there it was, at Dore (between Chesterfield and Sheffield), at Settle, and again at Appleby. From the outskirts of Leeds to the approach to Carlisle, semaphore signals have not yet been replaced by colour lights, and distinctive Midland signal boxes (illustration 6/21) came at frequent intervals.

Another idiosyncracy of the Midland was to name a signal box 'So-and-so Junction' even when it controlled merely, say, a crossover between different lines of quadruple track, rather than a divergence of routes. So at Keighley the little Midland box controlling the connections between the tracks serving platforms one and two, and those serving platforms three and four, bears the name board 'Keighley Station Junction'. With the passage of time this has become more appropriate in conventional terms, for platforms three and four are now used by the Keighley & Worth Valley Railway. This is itself a former Midland branch line, though generally cosmopolitan in outlook. However, when it put in a half-way passing loop at Damems, it installed Midland signals, and a Midland signal box, recovered from Frizinghall near Bradford; and this box, which controls the loop, was named by the Worth Valley 'Damems Junction'.

The Midland's Settle & Carlisle line I describe separately, in chapter seven. It was of course the route of the Midland Railway's London-to-Scotland trains which originated from St Pancras. The line from St Pancras to Carlisle is still there, but through passenger trains are not. Very few trains from St Pancras now travel farther north than Sheffield. London to Leeds and Edinburgh traffic is now concentrated on King's Cross, London to Carlisle and Glasgow on Euston. By way of compensation however, traffic from London to Leicester, Nottingham and Sheffield is concentrated on the Midland route from St Pancras, at the expense of the former Great Central route from Marylebone and, to the last two places, the Great Northern route from King's Cross. So St Pancras, with its noted Victorian Gothic station building—formerly a hotel, closed in 1935, and now offices—and vast all-over roof of 1868 with its single span covering seven platforms and ten tracks, remains a

London terminus of importance even though the variety of likely destinations is much less than formerly. Distinctive station architecture was a feature of the Midland, not only at its London terminus, but also at many lesser stations.

The Midland identity was scattered much earlier than the Great Western, and so interest in preservation of its relics is more limited, though no less intense. The various elements—static museum, steam depot, preserved line, voluntary society, local authority involvement—which are exemplified by separate GW-orientated organisations are, in the case of the Midland, concentrated into one: the Midland Railway Trust Ltd. This originated in 1969 with a proposal by the then curator of Derby Museum (Derby was the headquarters of the Midland Railway) that a living, working museum of the Midland should be established. And that is what the trust, a volunteer organisation with local authority support, is creating, under the name of the Midland Railway Centre, on the former Midland branch line between Pye Bridge and Ambergate. Eventually, it is planned, it will include a working line some three and a half miles long (the western end of the branch could not be obtained) with four stations, and a complementary museum to be established on an adjacent sixty-five acre site. Stations are being built using original MR buildings dismantled from other locations and re-erected; at least twelve MR signal boxes and their equipment have been recovered and stored pending re-erection; locomotives and rolling stock have been acquired and workshops and storage sheds constructed. At present, access to the Midland Railway Centre is at Butterley station, Derbyshire (grid ref. SK 402519).

Most striking among preserved Midland motive power are three passenger locomotives restored to Midland red livery. Outside-framed 2-4-0 no. 158A dates from as early as 1866 and is a static exhibit at the Midland Railway Centre, though there are hopes that she may steam again. The elegant 4-2-2 no. 673 which is illustrated on page 190 was built at Derby works at the late date (for a 'single-driver' locomotive) of 1897, and has been restored to working order at Butterley. Compound 4-4-0 no. 1000 was built in 1902 and became the prototype of a class of which a great many examples were built by the Midland, and subsequently by the LMS: she is familiar power on steam specials. All these are part of the national collection: the first two are on loan to the Midland Railway Trust, and no. 1000 is based at the NRM.

Other Midland locomotives preserved are 0-6-0T no. 1708, built in 1880, with partly open cab, at Butterley, and 4F class 0-6-0 no. 43924, built in 1920 and now on the Worth Valley Railway. The latter type, like the compound 4-4-0, was later built in quantity by the LMS, and no. 4027, built by the LMS in 1924, is preserved at the Midland Railway Centre. This also has three LMS 0-6-0Ts, built in the 1920s to a design which is basically Midland, which are intended as motive power for the passenger trains on the eventual operating line.

Two finely restored Midland coaches are exhibited at the National Railway Museum: a six-wheeled composite coach of 1885 (first and third class only, the Midland had already abolished second class ten years before

6/11 LMS class 2 2–6–2T no. 41241 (with BR number and livery) arrives at Keighley, Worth Valley Railway; the leading coach of the train is of BR standard design. Only the photographers to the right suggest that the date of this scene may not be c. 1955; in fact the photograph was taken in 1980.

2
41241
1350

it was built) and a third class dining carriage of 1914 which was included in the *Centenary Express*. The Midland Railway Centre has been able to acquire a selection of Midland coaches all of which, on acquisition, required restoration to a greater or lesser extent. A quite astonishing survival, which it has also been able to obtain, is the body of the Midland's first Pullman sleeping car of 1873. This had not yet, in 1980, been moved to Butterley, but the bodies of two other very early Midland Pullman cars were already there. One appears in illustration 6/15.

North Eastern, North Western

The headquarters of British Rail's Eastern Region is an ornate Victorian baroque building of stone and red brick, just within the city walls of York. As the initials NER picked out in gold among the wrought iron of its balconies suggest, it was formerly the head office of the North Eastern Railway. A BR flag floats above the North Eastern coat-of-arms, which is carved in stone and painted. In 1980 the building appeared recently cleaned, and well up to the standard of a city which has no lack of historic and well maintained buildings. This is encouraging, for it suggests management confidence in the undertaking, which sometimes has appeared to be lacking.

York station, with its extensive overall roofs, was built during the years 1873–7, and is clean and cared-for too. Here again the North Eastern badge appears, cast into the iron spandrels of the roof supports, and in some instances painted in correct heraldic colours. A wall map of tiles indicates the extent of the North Eastern system; and though any modern railway map of the area would look sadly uncrowded by comparison,

6/12 (left) The Midland paid attention to the architecture of its stations, witness the cottage ornée *station buildings with patterned barge boards at Appleby on the Settle & Carlisle line. Small stations as well kept as this are becoming regrettably rare in the present era of paytrains and staff-less, vandalised halts.*

6/13 (next page) Supreme monument of the railway age: the Forth Bridge crosses the Firth of Forth between North and South Queensferry. It was completed in 1890 by a consortium of the four companies involved in the East Coast and Midland Routes between England and Scotland (Great Northern, North Eastern, North British and Midland). It now carries the East Coast Main Line between Edinburgh and Aberdeen. The total length of the bridge including the approach spans (which alone would elsewhere be substantial engineering works) is 1 mile 23 yards.

it would also show that the backbone of that system survives in today's rail network.

The greatest deliberate concentration of relics of the NER however is to be found nowhere on that map, but within the grounds of Beamish North of England Open Air Museum. Here, where formerly there was no railway at all, what amounts to a new branch of the North Eastern Railway is being built with authentic buildings and equipment transferred from other sites. The station building came from Rowley, near Consett, and gives its name to the reconstructed station; the signal box, with equipment by that noted firm of signal engineers McKenzie & Holland, came from Carrhouse East, the goods shed from Alnwick, the covered coal and lime cells from West Boldon, the footbridges from Dunston and Witton le Wear. The period in which the railway is set is about 1910: concern for reproduction of period authenticity in the total railway scene is at its greatest at Beamish, illustrated on pages 238–9.

The railway will eventually extend for about three-quarters of a mile, to connect with a colliery line already constructed. Although the North Eastern Railway had a virtual monopoly of public rail transport in its area this was, naturally enough, resented by the coal owners. Canny men who inherited many early waggonways, they provided North East England with a most extensive network of private industrial lines, such as the Lambton, Hetton & Joicey Railway which had twenty five miles of route—including Stephenson's Hetton Railway—and over one hundred locomotives. This and other industrial lines exercised running powers over parts of the NER. So at Beamish, at the colliery end of the railway, the station (yet to be collected) will represent the miners' halt; and while some of the trains running on the line will be North Eastern, others will represent a colliery railway exercising running powers. Locomotives and rolling stock for

both have been collected, notably North Eastern 0-6-0 no. 876 mentioned in the previous chapter. Elsewhere, North Eastern locomotives are to be seen at the National Railway Museum and on the North Yorkshire Moors Railway, itself a former North Eastern branch.

Even on a railway such as the London & North Western, much of which has been extensively modernised in connection with electrification, it is not difficult to find reminders of the past. At Wigan, for instance, its station, though modernised, is still called Wigan North Western, both on the nameboards and in the timetable. A visit to platform five at Crewe reveals that the footbridge, according to the plate it bears, is bridge no. 78B of the L & NWR Co. Further south, although many principal stations—Stafford, Birmingham, Coventry, Northampton, for instance—have been entirely rebuilt, there remains among them Rugby, little altered. It has still its single immensely long island platform with bays at each end, a range of buildings down the centre and, over platform and tracks alongside, roofs supported by a trelliswork of iron and steel. It is cleaner than it used to be, however.

London & North Western signal boxes were typically tall and with roofs of shallow pitch. An impressive surviving example is Severn Bridge Junction at the south end of Shrewsbury station (formerly LNW/GW joint): with its frame of as many as 180 levers it must be one of the largest manual signal boxes still extant.

No twentieth-century LNWR passenger locomotives survive, the last of them having regrettably been cut up after the Second World War. Nineteenth-century ones still exist however; among lesser locomotives, Coal Tank 0-6-2T no. 1054 built in 1888 made a brave showing at Rainhill in 1980 as seen in plate 6/22. LNWR passenger carriages are better represented in preservation, thanks largely to that company's privilege of providing the Royal Train.

Old companies and survival of their initials

Traces of many former companies and their railways are scattered, and it is simplest to consider them by type rather than company. The initials and even the names of old companies still appear on their buildings, particularly stations. Waterloo still has upon its façade the initials LSWR and SR. The ironwork of gates and fences at Marylebone still incorporates the letters GCR. LMS appears in mosaic over a former entrance to Preston station, and the station building at Stirling is signed and dated in stone CR 1913 by the Caledonian Railway. Manchester is particularly rich in this sort of thing: the inscription Lancashire & Yorkshire Railway appears not once but three times (at least) on the façade of Manchester Victoria, and on the stonework of Deansgate station there appear intertwined on a carved shield the initials MSJ & AR, for Manchester South Junction and Altrincham Railway.

Not far away the Great Northern Railway's goods warehouse still announces its former owner and function in enormous letters of white brick between fifth floor and roof; a warehouse lettered 'London Midland & Scottish Railway' in similar manner overlooks Bolton station.

A few—a very few—of the old companies survive. The Festiniog

6/14 A particularly Midland touch was use of 'saw-tooth' platform awnings, with successive ridges at right angles to the track, and partially cantilevered by ornamental brackets from cast-iron columns. Many have gone, but proposed replacement of those at Kettering, seen here, by flat roofs has been avoided by the expedient of replacing glass panes, which slip and cause problems, with sheets of lightweight translucent plastic. The work was in progress when this picture was taken in August 1980, and is an example of the enlightened attitude which BR now often adopts towards its old buildings.

and Talyllyn Railway Companies were incorporated by Act of Parliament in 1832 and 1865 respectively. The Derwent Valley Railway Company was incorporated under a Light Railway Order of 1907. Since it is still operating, unpreserved, it deserves more than passing mention.

When opened in 1913, the Derwent Valley Railway, standard gauge, extended from York (Layerthorpe) for sixteen miles in a direction first east and then south to Cliff Common: at each terminus it connected with the North Eastern Railway. Regular passenger traffic ceased as early as 1926, and between 1965 and 1973 the length of line remaining open for freight was cut back by stages from the southern end. Even now however, the Derwent Valley Railway continues to operate rather more than four miles of line between Layerthorpe and Dunnington.

It is a unique survivor of those independent light railways built to serve agricultural areas (in Britain: such lines are still to be found on the Continent, where they were always more common). That it has survived as such is due in part to the inflexibility of bureaucracy—the railway did not come under government control during the Second World War (although it was in practice very busy) and so it was not nationalised—and in part to the commercial acumen of its management. Land at stations has been leased for industrial and other developments in order to bring traffic to the railway.

From 1977 to 1979 the Derwent Valley Railway ran a steam train service for tourists, using the 0-6-0 tank locomotive *Joem*. In the summer of 1979 trains ran once a day, four days a week, with a free connecting bus from the NRM. Despite this the service was unprofitable and was withdrawn at the end of the season.

Unprofitable is the key word: for as a freight carrier the Derwent Valley Railway is profitable, and has been increasing its dividend. Among the shareholders is the British Railways Board, as successor to the North Eastern Railway Company which put up some of the money for construction of the DVR. So the little railway's profits contribute, in a small way, to alleviating the big one's losses. There must be a moral somewhere.

Closures and downgradings

Closure of railways, sometimes total, sometimes not, had some curious effects. In some places individual lines survive, downgraded in status, as remnants of former networks in what a cynic might otherwise describe as a rail-free zone. Consider the London & South Western Railway's lines in Devon and Cornwall. Once, this company's main line extended beyond Exeter, round the north side of Dartmoor, to Plymouth; north and west, far flung branches extended from it to Ilfracombe, Bude and Padstow. In summer they bustled with holiday traffic; winter was not so good. So far as passengers are concerned, all that are now left of this network are the lines from Exeter to Barnstaple and, a most curious remnant, Plymouth to Gunnislake.

The latter survives because, by force of geographical circumstance, it provides a very much more direct route into Plymouth from the villages it serves than does any alternative road. This is particularly so from the intermediate stations of Bere Alston and Bere Ferrers: these lie on the spit of

6/15 (right above) Wholly American in outline, this is one of two bodies of early Pullman cars, which operated on the Midland Railway, now preserved at Butterley. They date from about 1880 and were among the earliest bogie vehicles to run in Britain; they were built in America, shipped to England in parts, and re-erected at Derby works. After withdrawal, both bodies were used as mess huts at Bradford. The Midland Railway Trust also has the body of the original Midland Railway Pullman car of 1873 but had not, at the time this photograph was taken, moved it to Butterley.

6/16 (right below) Midland Railway enterprise built this van in 1916, to be used for delivery of motor vehicles; they were loaded through the end doors. It is now preserved at the Midland Railway Centre.

land between the Rivers Tavy and Tamar; the railway crosses the former near its confluence with the latter, but main road bridges are very much higher upstream. The route is not, historically, any sort of self-contained branch. Its trains commence from the former GWR station at Plymouth, run west along the GW main line, and cross on to what was once the LSWR main line by a connecting link installed during the Second World War for emergency use. Northwards they follow the LSWR line, now reduced to a single track. At Bere Alston, formerly a junction (the main line beyond is now lifted), they reverse onto a circuitous and steeply graded line built as a light railway, which nevertheless crosses the Tamar at Calstock by a viaduct which is both high and long. For the last half mile or so into Gunnislake (which was once a through station but is now the terminus) they take up the alignment of the one-time East Cornwall Mineral Railway, opened in 1872 with the narrow gauge of 3 ft. 6 in. to link mines near Gunnislake and Callington with a quay on the Tamar at Calstock. The light railway from Bere Alston was built to link this to the main railway system when narrow gauge was widened to standard in 1908; its engineer was Col. H. F. Stephens, who was to become well-known as a promoter and operator of light railways; light railway origin of the line is still evidenced by an ungated level crossing at grid reference SX 429694.

The line to Gunnislake remains open exclusively for passengers; elsewhere, downgraded remnants of former main lines remain in use for freight only. The British Rail system map, published in three sheets by Geographia Ltd (63 Fleet Street, London EC4Y 1PE), makes in this respect a revealing comparison with the Passenger Network maps included with the annual BR timetable.

Notable in this category is part of

6/17 Coal drops or cells, into which coal was delivered by hopper wagons, were a characteristic of North Eastern Railway goods yards, and originated from the presence on the waggonways of the area of chaldron waggons with bottom discharge for delivering coal into ships. A coal drop still in use is seen here at Shildon in 1979.

6/18 Re-use of original buildings and equipment gives authentic appearance to the new railway being constructed within Beamish North of England Open Air Museum. As yet incomplete, it represents the North Eastern Railway about 1910. Rowley station building was originally built in 1867; it was re-erected at Beamish in 1974. Booking office period detail is complete down to NER ledgers and NER labels for eggs and livestock. Visitors may enter the signal box and, it is intended, they will continue to be able to do so when it has been made operable: actual operation of the line by one-engine-in-steam principle will enable the signalling to be, principally, a demonstration for the public. The 'birdcage' brake van at the rear of the train on the left enables the guard to look out over the roofs of vehicles, and dates from 1895.

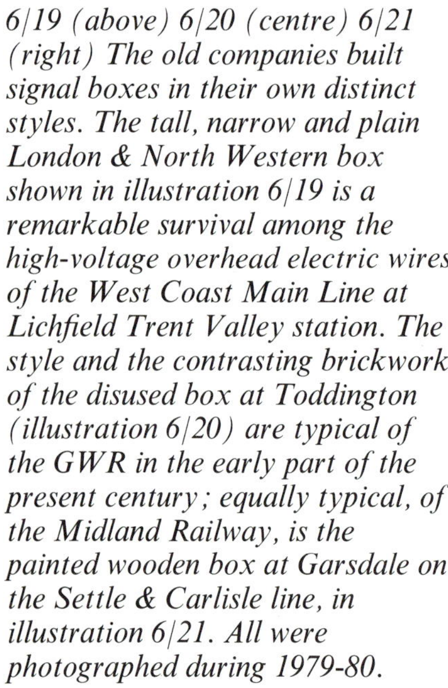

6/19 (above) 6/20 (centre) 6/21 (right) The old companies built signal boxes in their own distinct styles. The tall, narrow and plain London & North Western box shown in illustration 6/19 is a remarkable survival among the high-voltage overhead electric wires of the West Coast Main Line at Lichfield Trent Valley station. The style and the contrasting brickwork of the disused box at Toddington (illustration 6/20) are typical of the GWR in the early part of the present century; equally typical, of the Midland Railway, is the painted wooden box at Garsdale on the Settle & Carlisle line, in illustration 6/21. All were photographed during 1979-80.

the original West Coast Route to Aberdeen. Beyond Perth, it ran inland by Coupar Angus and Forfar to Kinnaber Junction, where the East Coast Route joined it; and although traffic from the South to Aberdeen had long been concentrated on the East Coast Route, it remained the principal route from Glasgow to Aberdeen until 1967, when passenger trains were diverted over the parallel route via Dundee. Only a short segment of it however, from Forfar to Bridge of Dun, was closed to all traffic and dismantled. From Stanley Junction where the Highland Railway diverges north of Perth, the old main line along which Caledonian trains raced through the dawn in the 1890s, and A4 Pacifics sped on their last passenger turns in the 1960s, still survives, but only as twenty five miles of straggling single-track goods-only branch line, to Coupar Angus and Forfar.

Other examples of segments of former main lines which survive as freight only branches include: part of the north west end of the Midland line to Manchester, the line from Grimsby to Louth, which formerly extended onwards to Boston and Peterborough as the main line to London, the line from Claydon Junction (on the LNWR Bletchley–Oxford line, itself now goods only) south to Aylesbury, which is a segment of the Great Central's London Extension, and the line from Kettering to Manton Junction, formerly part of the Midland Main line to Nottingham via Melton Mowbray, which was used by expresses between St Pancras and the North.

The circumstances of the one-time Callander & Oban line of the Caledonian Railway are different again. From Oban eastwards it remains in use for both passenger and freight trains. Some of the intermediate stations have been closed, however: among them Loch Awe station is particularly interesting. It adjoins a pier on the loch of its name; this is the longest inland

loch or lake in Great Britain and down it plied steamers for passengers and goods. Here as on other Scottish lochs, steamers provided the same sort of service that was provided elsewhere by branch line railways. On Loch Awe the last of them (strictly speaking, a motor vessel) was withdrawn in 1953. The imposing Scottish baronial Loch Awe Hotel—now a guest house of The Holiday Fellowship Ltd—stands on a rocky knoll above station and pier, to which it was once connected by lift. The hotel was built in 1881, a year after the railway opened, and it offered railborne Victorian tourists a panorama—of mountain, loch, wooded islands and ruined castle—which must have equated with their ideal of the Highlands. By the early 1900s however it was already advertising sinisterly 'Motor Garage with Pit'.

As they approach Crianlarich, trains from Oban diverge from the C & O line to enter Crianlarich Upper, the station of the West Highland line, on which they continue their journey: for it offers a shorter route to Glasgow than the old C & O (although a longer one, I suspect, to most other places). Crianlarich Lower, the C & O station, remained in use until 1980 as a railhead for loading timber to be carried over the West Highland line to the pulp mill at Corpach near Fort William but, following closure of the mill, its future is in doubt. From Crianlarich to Callander, and indeed to the main line junction at Dunblane, the course of the former line is now rail-less trackbed. The closure date of the railway was 30 October 1965; in fact, trains between Crianlarich and Callander ceased on 28 September when a landslip blocked the line, to the closure of which the Minister of Transport had already consented. Bridges and viaducts remain, where they were built of stone or concrete, rather than iron or steel with their scrap value. So do the platforms at Glenoglehead (grid ref. NN 558282) where for a time in the 1870s the railway from Callander terminated, at the top of a pass 941 feet above sea level, while finance was raised for its extension.

Down Glen Ogle itself, where the line was carried on a mountainside shelf, its course has become part of the Glen Ogle Trail, a waymarked country walk which also incorporates the course of an eighteenth century military road. At Balquidder station (grid ref. NN 576212) the main road has been straightened to occupy in part the site of the track, but the station's entrance subway can still be seen; some three miles short of Callander, a notice 'Prize Length' beside the vacant trackbed still indicates the location of past triumphs by the permanent way gang. The local authority plans that the entire route from Crianlarich to Dunblane should become a long-distance footpath.

(Above) One of the few surviving remnants of the once-extensive network of lines operated by the LSWR, and latterly by the Southern, in North Devon and Cornwall is the Exeter to Barnstaple line, seen here at Lapford. The second track from the right leads to an island platform, behind the photographer; evidently increasing traffic once necessitated provision of a passing loop which, with the eventual decline of traffic, is no longer needed. Station buildings were unoccupied when this photograph was taken in April 1980, and presence of a 'bus-shelter' on the platform suggests that their demolition was contemplated.

(Opposite above) A procession of many-armed telegraph poles, a signal box in decay, space for double track and gently sweeping curve combine to suggest that the line through Burrelton station (grid reference NO 198378) was once more important than the rusting single-track, goods-only branch that it is today. It was indeed for over a century part of the Caledonian and then the LMS Railways' main line from Aberdeen to Glasgow and the South. Visualise Duchess of Hamilton *(see illustration on page 182) sweeping through in 1950 with the up 'Postal' at a speed—remarkable for the period—in the high seventies, as recorded by C. J. Allen in the January 1951* Railway Magazine. *With diversion of Aberdeen trains via Dundee in 1967, the line was closed to passengers, though retained from Stanley Junction to Forfar for freight. Burrelton, however, had closed to passengers earlier, along with other wayside stations on the line, in 1956.*

(Left) Except for the diesel locomotive, and the upper quadrant signals, the scene at Dalmally on the Callander & Oban line can have changed little over a century. This train, however, the 12.20 from Oban to Glasgow on 18 June 1979, will diverge from the C & O line at Crianlarich, to complete its journey to Glasgow over the West Highland line. From Crianlarich to Callander, and on to the main line junction at Dunblane, the former route of Oban to Glasgow trains is now rail-less trackbed.

Traces of closed lines

The picture presented by the course of the railway between Crianlarich and Dunblane, of the trackbed's gradually reverting to nature or being obscured by later developments, is repeated in many, many other places. Let us consider two closed lines, both notable, but otherwise quite dissimilar: the Waverley Route, and the Lynton & Barnstaple Railway.

The Waverley Route was probably the most important, and certainly one of the most contentious, lines to be closed under the Beeching Plan: for although there are alternative routes from Edinburgh to the South, the Waverley Route on its way to Carlisle passed through the substantial towns of Galashiels and Hawick. These had no alternative rail service and closure left industrial Hawick some forty miles from the nearest station. But apart from these and a few small towns, the line passed through the empty hill country of the Borders, and in doing so it had severe gradients and sharp curves to contend with. It was closed to passengers on 6 January 1969; goods trains between Edinburgh and Hawick lasted only a little longer. Reopening the line independently of BR was unsuccessfully proposed, and indeed proposals for reopening are still made from time to time.

The most remarkable station on the Waverley Route was Riccarton Junction, a dot on the map (grid ref. NY 539978; illustration no. 6/30) at which there diverged the Border Counties line to Hexham on the Newcastle & Carlisle Railway. A small village of railwaymen and their families grew up but throughout its existence, Riccarton Junction had no access by public road. Visited in 1980 (with permission) the site of Riccarton Junction proved to be an eerie, amazing place of enormous extent, laid out in a hollow in the hills, rail-less and deserted but for the barking of a dog at an inhabited house nearby. An extensive island platform with a bay at the south end had modern edgings of concrete; on it a long low row of derelict station buildings (which once included a railwaymens' co-op shop) culminated in an empty telephone kiosk still prominent in Post Office red. The derelict signal box in the fork of the diverging routes still contained its lever frame, and on the platform there still grew one ornamental tree.

The Waverley Route has left many other traces. Its trackbed is everywhere conspicuous from its double-track width, and a surprisingly large number of its bridges remain intact apart from the track. Highlights are the many-arched viaduct at Newtongrange (grid reference NT 327648), and the platelayer's eye view of overbridge and trackbed vouchsafed to motorists on the A74 main road, where it crosses the course of the line on the level just before the start of the M6. At the site of Newcastleton station, however, little remains except trackbed and platforms as a reminder of how in the middle of that snowy January night in 1969 a crowd of villagers, reluctant to see their railway closed, for an hour kept the level crossing gates shut against the last train. John Thomas recounts the story in *Forgotten Railways: Scotland.* During the course of this incident the minister of the parish (occupying a similar position to the vicar of an English parish) was arrested: to be released eventually, and the train allowed to proceed, through the

6/22 The London & North Western Railway had a devoted following, the rationale of which, in view of its locomotives' austere and even primitive appearance, was always lost on the author. However, latter-day liveries, dirty or clean, did not suit them. At Rainhill in 1980, Hardwicke *(illustration 5/19) and Coal Tank no. 1054, seen here, took part, and to see them restored to their original livery of shiny black, and to hear the purposeful beat of their exhausts, and the imperious note (no other cliché will do) of their whistles, was to begin to understand what the LNWR mystique was all about. Coal Tank 0–6–2s were intended for freight, but were free-running, could reach 60 mph, and were often used on passenger turns. No. 1054 was restored to working order at Dinting Railway Centre.*

6/23 Such is the durability of railways and their equipment that one does not need to look far, even now, to find obvious evidence of former ownership by railway companies. This photograph was taken in 1980: the initials of the London Midland & Scottish Railway still appear in mosaic at Preston station, thirty-two years after nationalisation.

6/24 Manchester Victoria station still bears the name of its former owner, the Lancashire & Yorkshire Railway Co., both in the position seen in this photograph, and in several other places. The façade, until recently black with grime, has been cleaned following a meeting between Sir Peter Parker, chairman of BRB, and Arnold Fieldhouse, Leader of Greater Manchester Council, at which they agreed that BRB and GMC should share the cost. The main building was constructed in 1909; the lower storey of the building at right angles to it, on the left of the picture, dates from the opening of the station in 1844.

(Above) The viaducts of the Callander & Oban line still stand in Glen Ogle (grid reference NN 571264): this section was opened in 1870 and closed in 1965. Part of the trackbed, including these viaducts, is now incorporated into the Glen Ogle Trail, a waymarked footpath.

(Below) The trackbeds of many other closed railways are now footpaths. This is the course of the North British Railway's branch to Aberfoyle, at grid reference NN 525007 near its terminus. The line was opened in 1882 and closed to passengers in 1951; it was closed completely in 1959.

(Opposite above) When photographed in 1980, coach no. 6992 from the 1 ft. 11½ in. gauge Lynton & Barnstaple Railway (Southern Railway numbering) had been stationary in a Devon garden for almost forty-five years: considering its exposure to the elements for so long, its condition is good. Its active life on the L & B was shorter, lasting only thirty-seven years, even though it was built for the line's opening in 1898. The near end of the coach was arranged as an observation car for first class passengers to view North Devon's attractive scenery; some blue padded upholstery remains. A third class compartment has wooden slatted seats, and luggage and guard's brake compartments occupy the far end of the coach.

(Opposite below) The principal civil engineering work of the Lynton & Barnstaple Railway was Chelfham viaduct, about seventy feet high with eight arches (grid reference SS 609356). It was built in 1896–7, has been disused since 1935, and was photographed in 1980. Although it is a substantial work, the sharp curve at the far end is a reminder that the line was laid to a very narrow gauge.

6/25 The Tay Bridge, seen from the south. As is well known, the centre spans of the first bridge completed in 1878 were blown down, with a train, by a gale in December 1879, in the most horrific of British railway disasters. The present bridge, completed in 1887, was built alongside the earlier one, and the latter's piers, demolished down to water level, can still be seen. The near spans of the present bridge are those of the original, re-used: it was the columns of the original bridge that were inadequate. Construction of the bridge encouraged commuter traffic to Dundee, in the distance on the north shore of the estuary, from towns and villages on the south shore. One of these is Wormit, the station of which appears in the foreground. It was closed in 1969, commuters having taken to the then new Tay Road Bridge. Since this photograph was taken, the station building has been acquired by the Scottish Railway Preservation Society for re-erection on its line under construction at Bo'ness.

Wolferton station, on the Great Eastern line from King's Lynn to Hunstanton, was more ornate than most branch line stations: for this was the station for Sandringham, and so a frequent terminus for royal train journeys. The line was closed in 1969 and the down-side station buildings of 1898 seen here (grid reference TF 661286) are now Wolferton Station Museum. Visitors enter the retiring rooms provided for King Edward VII and Queen Alexandra, and the main hall which led from the royal train to carriages waiting for the final stage of the journey to Sandringham. Many relics of royal journeys are exhibited.

The Fighting Cocks Inn (grid reference NZ 342142) was a point of call, coaching-inn style, for the horsedrawn coaches which offered the first passenger service over the Stockton & Darlington Railway. It gave its name to the station subsequently built nearby. The track across the level crossing marks the original course of the railway, although in this locality it has long been reduced in status to a freight-only spur.

Station buildings at Edge Hill, Liverpool, were built by the Liverpool & Manchester Railway in 1836: British Rail has recently cleaned and renovated them, and removed later additions, to remarkably good effect. BR facilities are now concentrated in the building on the right; that on the left houses the Edge Hill Railway Trust Ltd's visitor centre. The bridge in the distance was originally the mouth of a tunnel, later opened out, and the tracks, which lead down to Lime Street station, were originally worked by cable haulage beyond this point.

6/26 The Great Northern Railway reached Manchester only by running over other companies' tracks for long distances, which is perhaps why it felt impelled to announce its presence so boldly. Its warehouse by Deansgate was built in the late 1890s and incorporated hoists down to the Manchester & Salford Junction Canal which passed beneath it in a tunnel. These enabled goods to be exchanged, by boat, with the docks of the recently built ship canal. The bridges carrying the approach tracks to the warehouse have been demolished, but the building itself was listed grade II in 1979.

mediation of Mr David Steel MP, who was travelling as a passenger.

Should the Waverley Route have been closed? It is hard to say. It was always a difficult and expensive route to operate: an express hauled on the Waverley Route by a Gresley A3 Pacific was usually handed over at Carlisle, for onward haulage over the Settle & Carlisle line (itself no sinecure), to a much less powerful Jubilee 4-6-0. The route's misfortune was that at the grouping its owning company, the North British, became part of the LNER, while the Midland, which carried Waverley Route traffic south beyond Carlisle, became part of the LMS. Both LNER and LMS owned other complete routes between Edinburgh and London: neither had any incentive to develop through traffic via the Waverley Route. Even after nationalisation, Waverley Route trains remained linked, apparently indissolubly, to the dilatory Midland route to St Pancras, though there was little apparent reason why they should not have taken the much faster route to Euston. The real tragedy of the Waverley Route, however, was that it so narrowly missed benefiting from electrification between Carlisle and Euston, and the accelerations that resulted. When, in 1968, closure was approved by the Minister of Transport, electrification of the West Coast Route north of Weaver Junction, where the Liverpool line diverges, was still a dream; by the time the Waverley Route track was eventually lifted, most of it during the winter of 1970–1, the masts for overhead electrification from Weaver Junction to Carlisle and Glasgow were already going up.

Both the Waverley Route and the Lynton & Barnstaple passed through rugged, sparsely populated areas and brought little financial joy to their owners. There, however, similarities largely end, for the Waverley Route, a double track main line, closed late, but the Lynton & Barnstaple, a 1 ft. 11½ in. gauge rural byway, closed early. The local company was merged with the

Southern in 1923; but although the line's diminutive trains remained as attractive as ever, winding their way along its $19\frac{1}{2}$ miles of route and in doing so ascending from (in effect) sea level to a summit almost 1,000 feet higher, that was not sufficent to enable the railway to survive once motor road competition became serious. The Southern closed it at the end of the summer season of 1935.

It was to be many years before such closures brought about formation of railway preservation societies as an instant reaction: but the L & B had its friends and among them was Mr R. C. Copleston, churchwarden of Clannaborough, near Crediton, Devon, where he lived at the rectory with the rector and his wife. He determined to preserve something of the L & B and when, after closure, the railway was put up for sale in lots by auction, he purchased coach no. 6992 for £13 10s 0d. This was then conveyed, on a trailer hauled by a steam road locomotive, to the rectory, where it was with difficulty installed in the garden on a short length of track to act as a summer house and venue for deanery meetings. The tobacco smoke generated by ecclesiastical pipes at these functions had apparently become too much in the house for the rector's wife! The coach was joined by a home signal from the L & B's Chelfham station, and some lesser relics.

There, forty five years on, in 1980, coach and signal still stand. Considering the length of time the coach has been in the open, it is in remarkably good condition, and also remarkably complete. It has been stationary at Clannaborough now for much longer

6/27 The Derwent Valley Railway is noted for its attractive station buildings—yet, half-timbered at the front and corrugated iron at the sides and back, they cannot have been expensive to build. The line was opened in 1913 and the type of construction is typical of light railways of the period.

This is Chatsworth Street Cutting, Liverpool & Manchester Railway, looking from the mouth of the tunnel up from Wapping. The trench in the foreground, recently re-excavated, originally contained the tensioning gear for the haulage cables for the tracks through the tunnel. The three large arched openings in the cutting side contained boiler houses and the location of the Moorish Arch, which housed the haulage engines, is immediately beyond the third of them where the cutting narrows. The bridge in the middle distance marks the approximate viewpoint of the print in illustration no. 2/14, looking in the reverse direction.

For over sixteen miles the Midland Railway's Settle & Carlisle line, which was completed in 1876, threads its way among the Pennines at altitudes more than 1,000 feet above sea level. On this section is Dent Head viaduct (grid reference SD 778844); beyond it, the line is carried high along the hillside above Dentdale.

(Right) This handsome viaduct near Low Gill (grid reference SD 616965) is a reminder of the inter-company competition that brought the Settle & Carlisle line into being. It carried the LNWR Low Gill-to-Ingleton branch, which joined a Midland branch end on at that place and could have—indeed, should have—been used for the traffic that went by the Settle & Carlisle. But competition prevented that, and today the viaduct carries only a trackbed without tracks.

than the thirty seven years during which it was mobile on the Lynton & Barnstaple Railway. It gets a steady trickle of interested visitors, who are not unwelcome provided they make appointments. The coach's present owner—its third since arrival at Clannaborough—is Mr W. S. Mitchell, The Old Rectory, Clannaborough, Bow, Crediton, Devon.

Another former Lynton & Barnstaple Railway coach, its body rebuilt but its frames and running gear little altered, survives in use on the Festiniog Railway as buffet car no. 14.

The course of the Lynton & Barnstaple Railway can still be clearly traced: its narrow trackbed and sharp curves are reminders of the 1 ft. 11½ in. gauge, but its civil engineering works were none the less substantial. To explore its route, as it winds and climbs among the wooded coombs and breezy uplands of the edge of Exmoor, is to see clearly how very attractive a railway it must have been—and also, sadly, how hopeless as a means of transport. Many bridges and earthworks remain; the most substantial engineering work is Chelfham viaduct (grid ref. SS 609356); and Blackmoor Gate station is now the Old Station Inn.

New uses for old railways

Interest in walking along the courses of old railways is growing at the present time and some instances of their conversion into public footpaths and bridleways have already been mentioned. Christopher Somerville's *Walking Old Railways* lists a great many more, to a total of 151, actual or proposed. One of the earliest instances of conversion of a railway into a footpath followed the closure of the Leek & Manifold Valley Light Railway. This line, of 2 ft. 6 in. gauge, had an even shorter life than the Lynton & Barnstaple: built by a local company

6/29 One might wistfully suppose that this train, standing at the east end of Crianlarich Lower station with snow-covered Ben More beyond, is ready to leave for Callander and Stirling. In fact, this is the spring of 1979 and the track ceases at buffer stops a few hundred yards ahead; the line beyond was closed in 1965. The locomotive is shunting wagons of pulpwood for papermaking, which will leave in the opposite direction, bound for the pulp mill at Corpach on the West Highland line. Even this scene may now be historic: the mill was an early casualty of the 1980 recession, and at the time of writing pulpwood wagons stand idle at Crianlarich.

6/28 (left) Substantial engineering for a light railway, Calstock viaduct over the Tamar (grid ref. SX 434687) was completed about 1908 for the Plymouth, Devonport & South Western Junction Railway, a satellite of the LSWR. To Calstock, however, there had first come in 1872 the narrow gauge East Cornwall Mineral Railway, descending an inclined plane to a quay on the left bank of the river as seen here. The light railway project included widening the narrow gauge line to standard gauge and constructing a link, including the viaduct, to the main railway system. The inclined plane was abandoned, but for some years a lift beside the second arch from the left enabled wagons to be lowered to the quay. The viaduct remains in use.

6/30 This is the expansive site of Riccarton Junction (grid ref. NY 539978) eleven years after closure; the station never had public road access, and the nearest public road is one and a half miles away, as the crow flies. When the North British-backed Waverley Route was built southwards from Hawick to Carlisle in the early 1860s, this remote spot in the Border hills was chosen for the junction with a branch line to Hexham. The signal box, which retains its lever frame, stands in the Y of diverging routes. The Waverley Route was maintained as a main line to the end: a farewell special which called here two days before closure was composed of the most up-to-date stock—a Deltic locomotive and eleven air-braked coaches.

6/31 In their days of affluence, railways could equip even branch lines with striking and expensive engineering works. Connel Ferry bridge (grid ref. NM 911345) now carries the A828 trunk road across Loch Etive, but it was built for the Ballachulish branch of the Caledonian Railway, opened in 1903. Its span is 500 feet; at low tide, a series of cataracts called the Falls of Lora appears beneath the bridge. For many years, the bridge was used by road and rail; since closure of the branch in 1966 it has been road only.

6/32 Part of the trackbed of the Leek & Manifold Valley Light Railway has been converted into a minor road, and here, at grid reference SK 091576, it passes through Swainsley tunnel. The bore of the tunnel is exceptionally large for a 2 ft. 6 in. gauge line, and is a reminder that the tunnel was made large enough to take standard gauge vehicles carried on narrow gauge transporter wagons. The L & MVLR was the only British line to use transporter wagons, though they are still in use in some Continental countries.

but operated by the North Staffordshire, it was opened in 1904, passed to the LMS at the grouping, and was closed in 1934. One of its trains appears in the colour illustration on page 63.

The line, eight and a quarter miles long, ran along the highly scenic valleys of the Rivers Hamps and Manifold in Staffordshire, and after closure the site of the track was presented by the LMS to the county council for use as a public footpath. The council then asphalted it from end to end—possibly the first and last time this has been done, at any rate in the country! It certainly makes it hard walking. About 1953 some two miles of path were converted into a narrow road, between grid references SK 098556 and SK 091577; driving on to it at the southern end one exchanges the extremely steep hills of narrow local roads for the almost level but equally narrow and sharply curved route of the L & MVLR. The climax however, comes at the northern end where one follows the road through Swainsley tunnel. At the railway's northern terminus, Hulme End (grid ref. SK 103593) the station buildings and locomotive shed still stand as part of a council depot.

Despite the agitation in the late fifties, it has been unusual for closed railways to be converted into roads, the characteristics of the trackbed of a railway being usually too far removed from those of a road for simple conversion. Where they were converted, there were usually special circumstances. A case in point—and a spectacular one at that—is Connel Ferry bridge. This very large bridge of 500 feet span (grid ref. NM 911345) was built for the Caledonian Railway's branch from Connel Ferry to Ballachulish, which was opened in 1903. It crosses the tidal Falls of Lora at the foot of Loch Etive. Without the bridge, to travel by road from one shore to the other at this point would be a journey of nearly ninety miles. Initially the bridge was rail only. Private cars were ferried over by rail; then in due course a very narrow road was positioned to one side of the railway track, usable by road vehicles when no trains were due, on payment of a toll. When the railway closed in 1966, a condition of consent by the Minister of Transport to closure was that the bridge should be devoted entirely to road traffic and should become toll free. It remains so today: although its narrowness, by road standards, means that traffic flows in each direction alternately, controlled by traffic lights.

By contrast, a motorist pausing to examine Cross Keys swing bridge, by which the A17 crosses the River Nene at Sutton Bridge (grid ref. TF 483210), and finding a plate which states that it was made and erected by A. Handyside & Co. of Derby and London in 1897, might well wonder what they were doing at that date in providing a dual carriageway. Of the Midland & Great Northern Joint Railway, for which the bridge was built, there is no apparent trace. In fact the bridge formerly carried both road and rail: road on the northern side, single-track rail on the southern. The M & GN was closed in 1959; the bridge was taken over by the Ministry of Transport in 1963, and the carriageway for westbound road vehicles uses the site of the railway across the bridge. Other examples of former railway bridges adapted to carry road traffic cross the Trent at Nottingham, and the Medway at Rochester.

The buildings of many stations on closed railways have survived, after adaptation to other uses. Some examples have already been given. As well as these, the conversion of these stations into dwelling houses—particularly where they already included a house for the station master—has become commonplace; they are also used for light industry and as caravan sites and cafés. More unusual conversions include Lochearnhead as a scout station, Strathpeffer as a visitor centre with an

6/33 Lochearnhead station on 16 April 1979 presented a scene probably more animated than at any time since its original opening in 1904. The occasion was an open day to celebrate its purchase from BR by Hertfordshire Scouts, who had been leasing it since 1962 and use it as a base for sailing and mountaineering. The station was closed in 1951 and lay derelict until leased by the scouts. Despite the absence of tracks, at Lochearnhead scout station a railway atmosphere is maintained.

VEHICLES
DRIVE SLOWLY
BRIDGE
TO SUCTION
14'-3"
HEADROOM

audio visual presentation *All Change for the Highlands*, Walsingham (Norfolk) as a Russian Orthodox church, Lord's Bridge (near Cambridge) as an observatory, and Wolferton, formerly the station for Sandringham, as a museum with the emphasis on royal travel.

Revivals

Personally, I find that closed railways and their stations, whether derelict and returning to nature or well maintained in a second existence are, although fascinating, above all a melancholy subject. It is pleasanter to consider some lines which, after closure to passengers, have subsequently reopened. This is by no means as rare as might be supposed. Early 1978 for instance, saw the reopening, as part of the electrified Merseyrail network, of the line of the Cheshire Lines Committee between Liverpool Central and Garston. This had been closed in 1972. Reopening included sympathetic restoration of Cressington station, of which the building dates from 1871 and is listed. In London in 1979, the link between the North London line at Dalston Junction and the Great Eastern at Stratford was reopened.

In Scotland, the line between Barassie (on the Glasgow–Stranraer line) and Kilmarnock (on the GSWR Glasgow–Carlisle line) was closed to

6/34 There is little now to suggest that Cross Keys swing bridge, Sutton Bridge, was built for the Midland & Great Northern Joint Railway. In fact, although the left span was always road, M & GN trains used the right hand span until closure of the line in 1959. When it was photographed in 1979 the bridge was being re-painted. Grid reference TF 483210.

6/35 'You'ld think it was a village station, with all these trees' remarked a fellow passenger to the author while photographing Cressington station in 1980. In fact, it is on the Northern line of Liverpool's electrified Merseyrail network. It was built originally by the Cheshire Lines Committee on what was then its Liverpool-to-Manchester route. Reduced in status, the line was eventually closed in 1972. The station was listed grade II in 1975 and is within a conservation area: for re-opening of the line, between Liverpool Central and Garston. early in 1978, it was restored by BR with the assistance of grants from the Historic Buildings Council (£8,000) and Liverpool Heritage Bureau (£1,000). The work included curing wet and dry rot, cleaning brickwork, and replacing the footbridge, which was unsafe, with a modern one of identical design.

passengers in 1969. It has come quietly and gradually back into passenger use again: at first by diversion of the overnight Stranraer–Euston train along it, more recently by the addition of daytime trains also. The line concerned originated as the Kilmarnock & Troon plateway, opened as early as 1812.

The branch line from Ladybank, Fife (on the East Coast main line) to Bridge of Earn was closed to passengers in 1955, but today it forms part of British Rail's Inter-City network. It was opened first in 1848 as part of the Edinburgh & Northern Railway's original route from Edinburgh, via ferry to Burntisland, to Perth. The building of the Forth Bridge, however, was accompanied not only by construction of a link between its northern

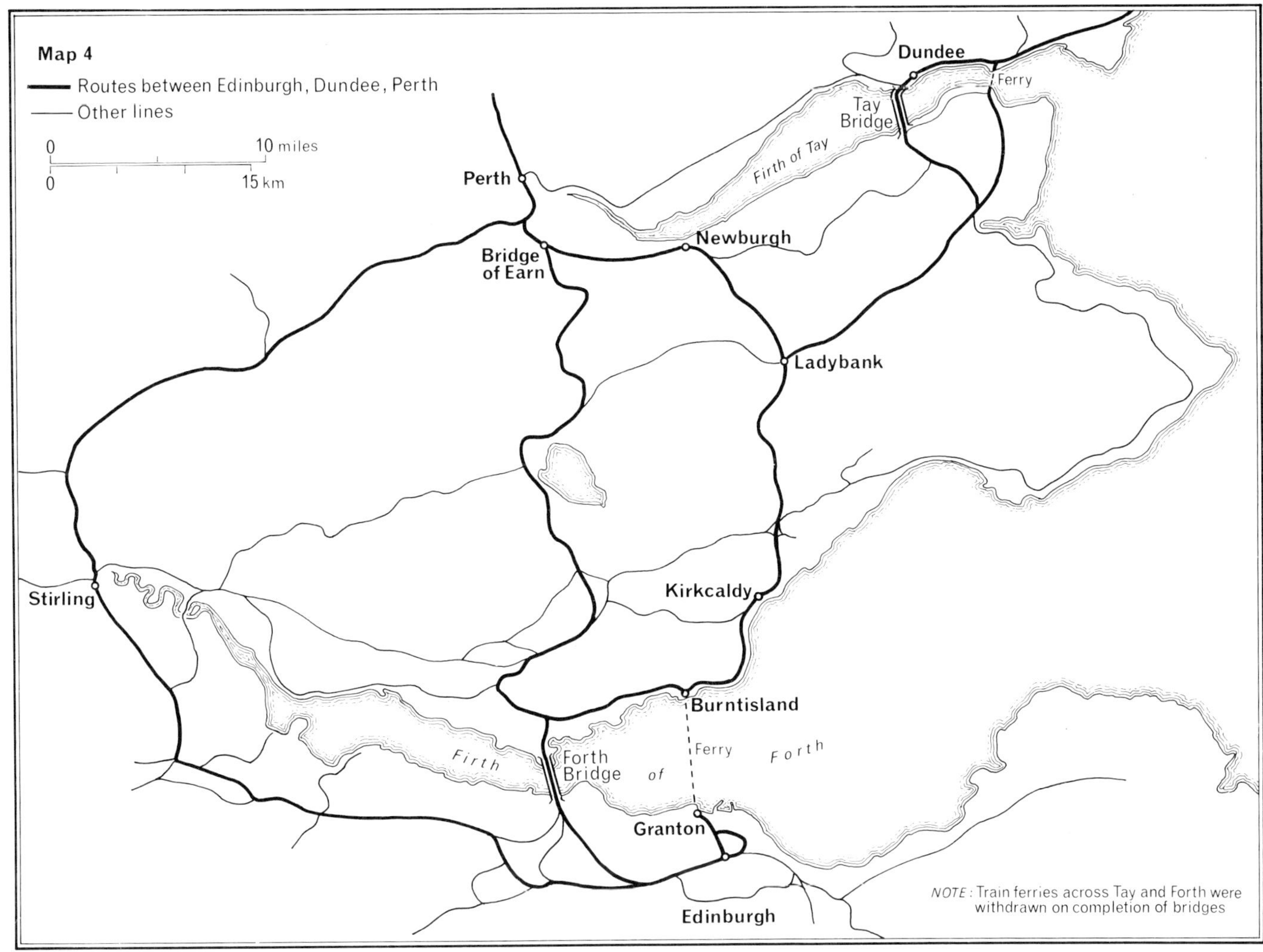

end and Burntisland, to complete the East Coast Route to Dundee and Aberdeen, but also of a direct route from the bridge to Perth, made by improving old lines and constructing new links between them. This joined the original route at Bridge of Earn, a few miles south of Perth; thereafter, Edinburgh to Perth and Inverness trains took the direct line and Ladybank to Bridge of Earn became an unimportant branch which, as mentioned, was closed to passengers in 1955.

In 1970 however, the direct line from the Forth Bridge to Perth was itself closed as a through route, and part of it was closed completely. In places its course has subsequently been used for the Edinburgh–Perth motorway. Although some goods trains and the Inverness to York car-carrier service were diverted to run via Ladybank, regular passenger trains between Edinburgh, Perth and Inverness were diverted to run via Stirling. This diversion increased the distance travelled between Edinburgh and Perth from 48 miles to 69½ miles. Eventually, twenty years after closure to passengers, the Ladybank to Bridge of Earn line was reopened in 1975, and Edinburgh to Perth and Inverness trains diverted onto it. Curiously, the motive for reopening was publicised as being to give the Fife towns of Inverkeithing and Kirkcaldy a direct link with Perth. In any event, it brought the Edinburgh to Perth distance down again, to 57 miles. It also meant that between Burntisland and Perth trains had reverted to the original route of 1848.

On 7 September 1963 I travelled down the Severn Valley line from Shrewsbury by a diesel railcar which, having called at Bridgnorth, deposited me at Bewdley to await a train for Birmingham. I had been to Bewdley the previous summer, at which time there was pinned up by the ticket window a cartoon cut from the *Daily Mail*. It showed an old fashioned station with the booking clerk addressing a passenger: 'I wouldn't take a return if I were you—we may not be here when you come back'.

Then, the Severn Valley line had been under the shadow of the axe; and 7 September 1963 was the day of closure. Other services from Bewdley seemed unlikely to last long. If, as I waited on the island platform, someone had told me that seventeen years

6/36 Newburgh station (grid ref. NO 228180) was closed to passengers in 1955 along with the rest of the Ladybank to Bridge of Earn branch. This line, part of the original Edinburgh & Northern Railway line from Burntisland to Perth opened in 1848, was by that date an insignificant branch, having been superseded as a main line by a more direct route. In 1970 this itself was closed, and after a five-year period during which Edinburgh-to-Perth trains took the roundabout route via Stirling, the Ladybank to Bridge of Earn line came back into use in 1975 as the main line for trains from Edinburgh to Perth and Inverness. Newburgh station, however, remains open only for freight.

later I should be standing on the same platform with, on one side, a train of coaches in the red-and-cream livery lately discarded by BR, bound for Bridgnorth behind a steam locomotive, and on the other side a DMU in an unknown blue and white livery ready to depart from Birmingham, I would have regarded him with the mixture of disbelief and scorn which one reserves for crystal gazers and similar charlatans.

Of course, he would have been right. As is well known, Bewdley has for some years now been the southern terminus of the Severn Valley Railway's steam trains to and from Bridgnorth. Almost more remarkable in the present immediate context is the train service in the opposite direction, to Kidderminster. Formerly, a BR branch linked Bewdley with Kidderminster and the main line to Birmingham. Only part of this was disposed of to the Severn Valley Railway however, for BR operated a freight service over it from Kidderminster as far as Foley Park. At that place, BR and SVR make an end-on connection. So reliable, however, does BR now consider the SVR, and so useful as a potential source of revenue that, on certain days each year, a British Rail diesel train service is reinstated between Birmingham, Kidderminister and Bewdley, running for the final part of its route over the track now belonging to the SVR.

This was the first location where BR ran passenger trains regularly onto the track of a preserved railway. In general terms, however, the greater achievement of the Severn Valley Railway is its own regular steam train service: like other railways which have followed the lead of the Talyllyn, Festiniog and Bluebell Railways, it successfully perpetuates the ambience of the steam train era in a way which no amount of special steam runs over BR can ever do. Only on a preserved line can a total railway—coaches, signals, buildings and the rest—be maintained in a manner contemporary with steam locomotives.

Many preserved lines achieve this and at the same time perpetuate the use of a railway which would otherwise have become a deserted trackbed. The North Norfolk Railway, for instance, continues to operate a short section, between Sheringham and Weybourne, of the Midland & Great Northern Joint Line, and the Main Line Steam

6/37 The ambience of the steam railway: trains pass at Arley, Severn Valley Railway, in 1980. Class 5 4–6–0 no. 5000, part of the national collection, was restored to working order on the SVR. Sandbags on the platform were left over from filming wartime scenes for television.

Trust Ltd does the same for a segment of the Great Central's London Extension from Loughborough to Rothley. The Kent & East Sussex and the Welshpool & Llanfair both operate original light railways, of standard and 2 ft. 6 in. gauge respectively. The railways and tramways of the Isle of Man retain a Victorian air. The Lakeside & Haverthwaite's trains connect at Lakeside with the motor vessels which BR still operate on Windermere as successors to the Furness Railway's steamers. The Bala Lake Railway, 1 ft. 11½ in. gauge, is laid on the trackbed of part of the former GWR Ruabon-to-Dolgellau line; and the Ravenglass & Eskdale Railway, 15 in. gauge since 1915, occupies the site of the earlier 3 ft. gauge line built in 1875 from which it inherits, among other things, some conveniently outsize overbridges. A little of the original rail remains in use in a siding at Irton Road Station. Without these railways, and others like them, the small puffing train would have become a thing of the past.

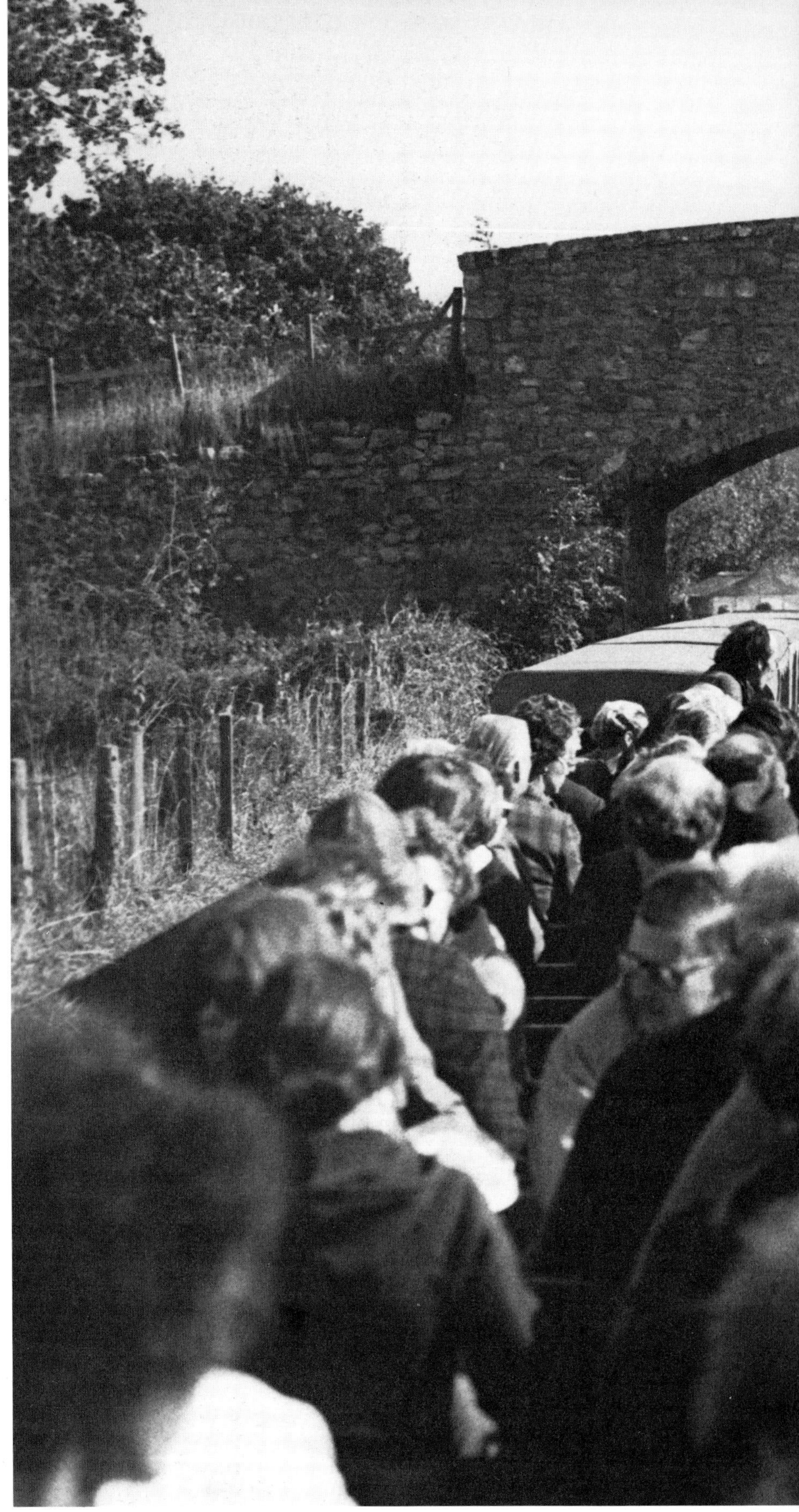

6/38 Outsize overbridge at Irton Road station is a reminder that the 15 in. gauge Ravenglass & Eskdale Railway was originally built, in the early 1870s, as a 3 ft. gauge line. The locomotive on the right is 0–8–2 River Irt. *She was built as a small (rather than miniature) 0–8–0T* Muriel *in 1894 by Sir Arthur Heywood, Victorian protagonist of minimum-gauge railways, for his own line at Duffield Bank, Derbyshire. She was purchased by the R & ER in 1917 and rebuilt in 1927 as a 0–8–2 with a new boiler, and with short chimney, small boiler mountings and 'scale model' cab, to make her appear a miniature locomotive; present-day R & E management has recently restored her to 'narrow gauge' appearance.*

CHAPTER 7

SOME LOCALITIES OF SPECIAL INTEREST

The Tranent - Cockenzie Waggonway

Cockenzie harbour, with stone breakwaters protecting a narrow entrance, is by today's standards very small, though it is still used by fishing boats and a small boatbuilding establishment. But in its early heyday 250 years ago this harbour, and an associated two-mile waggonway, and a coal mine with a fire engine, must have represented a very large undertaking. To tour their sites is to appreciate just how great an achievement an eighteenth-century waggonway was in relation to the resources and skills of the period.

The Tranent–Cockenzie Waggonway was opened in 1722 having wooden rails, the first railway in Scotland. It originated indirectly from the Jacobite rising of 1715 and played a tactical part in the rising of 1745; it was later converted into an iron tramroad and later still, in part, into a mineral railway which is now closed and dismantled. Traces of its route are still remarkably clear.

After the 1715 rising, nobles and gentry who had taken part were obliged to forfeit their property to the Crown. Among them was the Earl of Winton, whose property included a coal mine at Tranent, east of Edinburgh in Lothian Region. This mine and much other forfeited property were eventually purchased from the Crown by the York Buildings Company, which was itself a remarkable institution. It had been incorporated in 1675 to pump water from the Thames in London and distribute it through wooden pipes to houses around St James's and Piccadilly. This task it carried out for many years without apparent incident until, at the time of the South Sea Bubble, it fell into the hands of speculators who managed to use the company and its royal charter as a vehicle to purchase forfeited estates.

They evidently considered the coal mine to be a fairly juicy plum, for the company then invested some £3,500 in improvements. At the mine it installed a 'fire engine' (presumably a Newcomen-type pump, also the first in Scotland), it built the waggonway to link the mine with the harbour and saltpans at Cockenzie a couple of miles to the north, and it renovated and enlarged the harbour itself. Financially, the company seems to have overreached itself, being unable to get an adequate return, and letting the mine etc. to tenants from time to time. Nevertheless, the mine was to have a long life.

It is indicative both of how long ago this took place, and of how peaceful a country Britain has been for the last couple of centuries compared with other parts of the world, that the part played by this waggonway in the Battle of Prestonpans, 1745, is the only occasion on which a railway in Britain has been directly involved in land warfare. In that year the Young Pretender, Prince Charles Edward Stuart, having taken Edinburgh on his way south, was opposed by government General Sir John Cope. Cope positioned his troops and cannon along the waggonway where it traversed a low straight embankment, but Stuart forces attacked in the early morning and the government troops, still half asleep, were quickly defeated.

'Cope sent a challenge frae Dunbar
Charlie meet me an ye daur
And I'll learn you the art of war
If you'll meet me in the morning.

Hey Johnnie Cope are ye wauking yet?
Or are your drums a-beating yet?
If ye were wauking I would wait
To gang with the coals i' the morning'

became the derisive Jacobite chant. The last line, in the present context, is significant.

The wooden waggonway was relaid as a tramroad with cast iron rails on stone blocks in 1815. When the main line from Berwick to Edinburgh was built, it passed beneath the tramroad at Meadowmill, about half way along the latter's course. By the 1880s ships had outgrown Cockenzie harbour; the tramroad was closed and, north of the main line, dismantled. South of this its course was used for a mineral railway to link the mine with the main railway system.

The site of the coal mine was, approximately, at grid reference NT 413731. When I visited the area in autumn 1979 it might or might not have been represented by a depression in the ground beyond a field of gone-to-seed cauliflowers. The course of the former mineral line/tramroad/waggonway is however clearly marked by a pathway between the same field and a housing estate, though I could find no trace of stone sleeper blocks reported here in the 1960s. From this point the course of the line lay in a north-easterly direction, on a down gradient, and has largely been re-incorporated into farmland so that little can be seen of it, apart from rails still embedded in the road surface of the former level crossing with the B6371 road (grid ref. NT 406736). At grid reference NT 403738 the original line turned sharply, to run almost due north; the later mineral line entered sidings at Meadowmill washery, the site of which has now become waste ground with no obvious rail significance.

The course of the waggonway then becomes a rough road leading to the point at which it crossed over the East Coast main line at grid reference NT 403742. The abutments of the bridge remain (see illustration 1/1) though its deck has gone, and the southern abutment forms a continuous structure with a road overbridge. The main road A198 runs parallel to and immediately to the north of the main railway line; beyond it, the course of the waggonway runs straight and clear across the battlefield of Prestonpans. The low embankment is bounded by stone walls, and is a footpath easily walked—fortuitously this is the best-preserved section of the

7/1 The course of the Tranent-Cockenzie Waggonway, opened in 1722, heads for Cockenzie and the sea. This is the site of the Battle of Prestonpans, 1745: Government troops and cannon were positioned along the waggonway embankment, but Stuart forces attacked them in the mists of early morning and quickly routed them. Sidings for Cockenzie power station, the first to be served by Merry-go-Round coal trains, are seen on the extreme left. Grid reference is NT 403743.

route. Here in the misty dawn of 21 September 1745, Jacobite forces approached from the east and attacked Cope's army stationed along the waggonway—and, in the short space of eight minutes, routed them. In those eight minutes, forty Jacobites were killed, and hundreds of government soldiers.

It was an eerie experience to reflect on this carnage when walking through the site of the battle along the course of the waggonway on a bright and breezy autumn day 234 years later. Sunshine illuminated broad fields of stubble on either side of the line; nearby, beside the main road, a monument, a stone cairn, is inscribed simply *1745*.

From a viewpoint near it, that is the site of the tramroad bridge across the main railway line, almost the entire layout of the waggonway can be seen, and with it the reason for its abrupt change of direction at Meadowmill: for the mine lay on comparatively high ground to the south, and from it the route can be seen descending the slopes slantwise to produce a gradient down which waggons could run safely by gravity. At Meadowmill the ground becomes sufficiently flat for it to run northwards and, passing the viewpoint, head direct for Cockenzie in the distance, and the Forth beyond.

Exploration to the north showed that, after the battlefield, the course of the waggonway becomes incorporated into the B6371 road leading to Cockenzie. The old harbour itself is approached by a dirt road on the site of the waggonway, but here again I could find no trace of the stone sleeper blocks at this location which were illustrated in Baxter's *Stone Blocks and Iron Rails*; possibly they have been buried. The harbour today is overshadowed by Cockenzie's colossal power station, which is prominently in view from most parts of the waggonway route. It is not inappropriate that, in the curious way that history has of repeating itself, this locality became once again the scene of innovation in coal-transport-by-rail when, in 1965, the power station became the destination of the first merry-go-round coal trains. The reception sidings were placed close to the course of the waggonway across the battlefield.

Stockton & Darlington

Stockton & Darlington, George Stephenson, first railway (or something of the sort), 1825 (if you are good at dates): these are history-lesson facts absorbed into one's consciousness at a fairly early age. They lie there, hackneyed and unadorned, along with William the Conqueror 1066, the Spanish Armada, the Battle of Waterloo. One has always known of them, it seems, while forgetting the details, if indeed one ever knew them; and because of this, they tend to be disregarded.

So the historic significance of the Stockton & Darlington Railway overshadows its intrinsic interest. Fortunately the 150th anniversary celebrations, in 1975, had the side-effect of promoting interest in surviving traces of the original line. These are many and fascinating.

As built, the Stockton & Darlington was, as I remarked in chapter two, at one and the same time the horse-and-inclined-plane colliery waggonway at the peak of its development, and the first of the new generation of public railways designed for locomotives. It developed in its own individualistic way for some years—notably in the form of Hackworth's locomotives for heavy coal trains—but it eventually became merged into the mainstream of railway development in the 1860s, following amalgamation with the North Eastern Railway. Today, some sections of the original line form part of the main railway system of the area and are busy, but others are long-disused trackbeds.

First to go were the sections west of Shildon worked by horse and inclined plane. When the line was built in the early 1820s, rope-haulage was as convenient as other means of traction. But the countryside here, though broken, is not exceptionally rugged, and rapid development of the steam locomotive led to construction of other routes, suitable for locomotives, to replace the original. Most of its course can still be traced however, and in 1975 the Shildon Rail Trail was established, a signposted footpath route of about six miles which follows for most of its course the original railway route, and elsewhere runs as closely as possible to it. A leaflet guide to this was available in 1979 from the Hackworth Museum at Shildon, mentioned below.

To walk the full length of the rail trail remains for the author an unfulfilled ambition, available time being too short: but from what I have seen from car-borne visits to points of interest, it would be an attractive and interesting walk and I hope to return. The precise location of the western end of the line at Witton Park Colliery seems to have been forgotten or obliterated by subsequent mining or both. The rail trail starts near Phoenix Row at grid reference NZ 167296; or, rather, finishes at that point, for one is recommended to start at Shildon. Here, however, I will describe the railway from west to east. The gentle slopes of Etherley North and South Inclines are crossed by roads at grid references NZ 168288

7/2 Stone block sleepers remain in situ on Brusselton west incline, part of the original course of the Stockton & Darlington Railway (grid ref. NZ 212256). Buildings in the distance mark the incline top, whence waggons were lowered by the east incline to Shildon, from which point locomotives could take over as motive power. The S & D trackbed here forms part of the Shildon Rail Trail.

7/3 Daniel Adamson's coach house, Shildon, (grid ref. NZ 224264) was built c. 1830 to house the horsedrawn passenger coach he operated over the Surtees and Stockton & Darlington Railways. Almost certainly the oldest surviving building intended to house a railway passenger vehicle, it deserves preservation; but in 1980 it was threatened with demolition, though a fund to save it had been opened.

and NZ 176277 respectively. This section of the railway was closed as early as the 1850s, but traces of the engine house at the summit between the inclines remain and are being scheduled as an ancient monument. So too are much of the trackbed and the abutments of the bridge by which the line crossed the River Gaunless near West Auckland. The bridge itself, a cast iron structure of nevertheless flimsy appearance (for it was designed to carry nothing heavier than horses and loaded chaldron waggons), is now a prominent outdoor exhibit at the National Railway Museum. Disused after 1856, it remained in situ until dismantled in 1900.

A minor road crosses the course of Brusselton West Incline at grid reference NZ 212256. The incline is on an embankment; the bridge under which the road passed has been demolished in the interest of road improvement. But beside its site another little stone arched bridge remains in good condition, an accommodation bridge built to reconnect two parts of a farm separated by construction of the railway. Bridge and incline are now ancient monuments. The bridge is on the west side of the road; on the east side, by climbing up onto the embankment, two good rows of stone sleeper blocks can be found on their original locations. It is a pleasant walk to follow them, along the rail trail, upwards to the incline top. A row of railway houses on the south side of the level section of line at the summit includes one which was originally part of the winding engine house from which both inclines were operated. Immediately beyond, the East Incline commences, falling through a shallow cutting. The immaculately mown grass and ornamental trees surrounding the incline top give way quickly to industrialisation. Part of the way down the incline on its north side is a private coal mine, the last of innumerable coal mines which have been worked in this area, and at its foot spread out the Shildon Works of British Rail Engineering Ltd.

Today, these works are one of BREL's principal wagon-building works, but they descend directly from the Stockton & Darlington's original works established at the foot of this fourth and last inclined plane. Thus far, the Stockton & Darlington as built was a typical horse-and-inclined-plane railway of the 1820s, but from here to Stockton it was made suitable all the way not only for horses but also for steam locomotives. So it is now at Shildon Works that the course of the railway becomes a railway in fact, and the first point at which a public road impinges on it is Mason's Arms level crossing (grid ref. NZ 228256), where on that historic opening day in long-ago 1825 *Locomotion* was first coupled to her train, and at that more recent commemoration in 1975 steam locomotives in their greatest gathering for years lined up at the start of the cavalcade.

Just under half a mile further on the line from Bishop Auckland trails in from the north (it was formerly a Stockton & Darlington branch, and more extensive) and on this branch, immediately before the junction, is Shildon passenger station. Passengers in early Stockton & Darlington days were more conveniently served: bisecting the Y of the junction was the Surtees Railway, opened in 1831 to the centre of Old (i.e., pre-railway) Shildon and coal mines nearby. Daniel Adamson had operated a horsedrawn passenger coach over the S & DR from Shildon to Stockton, starting from Mason's Arms, from 1827; when the Surtees Railway was opened he diverted the coach to run over that and constructed a stone building to serve as coach house and ticket office. A curious structure of weathered stone, the arches in its walls filled-in, it still stands at grid reference NZ 224264 with appropriate plaque. Or did, when this book was being prepared: plans to bulldoze it, according to the *Railway Magazine* April 1980, had been met by an appeal for funds for preservation. It is much to be hoped that the appeal will be successful, for the building is listed grade II and must surely be the oldest surviving building constructed to house a railway passenger vehicle.

The Surtees Railway was dismantled in the 1930s but its course is now a footpath leading back to the junction. Here can be found the Timothy Hackworth Museum, in Soho House, once the home of Hackworth himself. It forms the starting point of the rail trail. Inside, part of it displays material relating to Hackworth and railways in the area, and part is re-furnished and equipped in style contemporary with Hackworth himself, including workshop and kitchen.

The house, at the end of a row, faces on to the Stockton & Darlington Railway. Nearby is another building, the Soho engine shed, the only surviving building to have formed part of Hackworth's own Soho locomotive works (a contemporary plan in the house shows that these works, which extended to six acres, occupied much of the immediate vicinity). The shed was being restored (almost complete in 1979) to form part of the museum complex, and to be the permanent home of the replica *Sans Pareil.*

From Shildon onwards the pace of exploration of the Stockton & Darlington Railway can be increased, to the speed of a British Rail DMU to be precise, for much of the line is in use for passenger traffic and can be seen well from the front seat of trains from Bishop Auckland to Darlington and from Darlington to Stockton.

7/4 Soho House, Shildon, has been renovated to house the Timothy Hackworth Musuem. Hackworth, whose home this was, was in effect manager and engineer of the Stockton & Darlington Railway, and a talented locomotive designer and builder on his own and the railway's account. The house faces the railway.

Leaving Shildon, wide and empty spaces between track and boundary fences mark the sites of the former Shildon Sidings, described on old postcards as 'the most extensive in the Kingdom' or, alternatively, the 'largest in the world'. These spaces serve as a reminder that this part of the line saw not only pioneering use of steam power, but also of electric traction. With coal mines booming during the period before the First World War, the North Eastern company electrified its line from Shildon to Newport, Teesside, using overhead wires at 1,500 volts dc. The work was completed in 1915, the first instance in Britain of main-line electrification for freight. It was not the route of the S & DR that was electrified, however, but the shorter route of its former rival the Clarence Railway which diverged from the S & D two miles east of Shildon. This pioneering electrification scheme was successful: successful enough for the North Eastern to propose electrification of the East Coast main line between York and Newcastle. Unfortunately this proposal did not survive the grouping; had it been put into effect the subsequent history of railways might have been very different. On the Shildon–Newport route itself, declining coal production and a need for expensive repairs to electric equipment led to a reversion to steam in 1935; much of the route was closed in 1963. In the vicinity of the former junction, however, trains on the Stockton & Darlington call at one of the newest stations in Britain, Newton Aycliffe, opened in 1978 to serve the new town of that name.

7/5 This is the site of St John's level crossing, Stockton-on-Tees, early in 1980 (NZ 447184). Here, in 1822, the first rail of the Stockton & Darlington Railway was laid, and later, from the cottage on the left, passenger tickets for its horsedrawn coaches were sold. Hopper wagons in the distance are standing over coal drops.

In due course trains arrive at North Road station, Darlington. This, which from present-day maps or timetables one might in ignorance suppose to be a mere suburban station on the outskirts of Darlington, was formerly the Stockton & Darlington Railway's principal station there. It dates in part from 1842, which makes it very early among the stations still in use; by that date the S & DR had for some years operated its own steam passenger trains in place of earlier contract horsedrawn coaches, and needed improved accommodation for passengers. It became in course of time the hub of S & DR passenger trains which reached not only Stockton and Shildon but also, over its own lines or those of associated companies, Middlesbrough, Penrith and Tebay. So the station was enlarged both lengthways and across the tracks, where it incorporated a carriage shed built on its north side. After amalgamation of the S & DR with the NER, the importance of North Road declined in favour of Bank Top station on the main line. Between 1939 and 1964 passenger train services calling at North Road were successively withdrawn to leave only today's Darling–Bishop Auckland service. This is operated as a paytrain service, which means that North Road is an unstaffed halt; trains call at the outermost platform in what was once the carriage shed.

But far from being demolished, the usual fate of the buildings of large stations in such reduced circumstances, the late-Georgian style original buildings of North Road remain, with extensions and the train shed (walled in at the ends) imaginatively converted into North Road Station Railway Museum. This was opened in 1975.

The most important exhibit is *Locomotion*. From 1857 onwards this locomotive was preserved in the open air outside North Road station; in 1892 it was removed to Darlington Bank Top station for display under cover, and became a familiar sight to generations of travellers on the East Coast main line. Finally in 1975 it was moved back to North Road to be within fully-enclosed accommodation. Here, it stands upon, or very close to, the site of the line on which it originally ran in 1825. As always, of course, just how much of the original 1825 locomotive is present is an open question—the boiler is said to be the locomotive's fourth—but the layout and working principles of the locomotive appear to be original. Near *Locomotion* stands *Derwent*, a 0-6-0 built in 1845 and representative of the type of locomotive designed by Hackworth for the S & DR's coal traffic. With tenders fore and aft, its direct descent from the Wylam locomotives of more than thirty years before is apparent, although drive is direct to the wheels from inclined outside cylinders. Other exhibits include a Stockton & Darlington four-wheeled, three-compartment coach of the 1840s and a North Eastern Railway twenty-ton hopper wagon for coal, a type which provides the link between early chaldron waggons and modern all-steel hopper wagons. There are many more exhibits, large and small.

The whole station was renovated for the opening of the museum, but while the museum side of it remains spick and span, the railway side had, in sad contrast, become dilapidated by 1979 when I saw it: broken window panes, peeling paint, litter and graffiti. An unfortunate introduction for those who, one hopes, arrive by rail to view the world-famous exhibits within the museum.

Leaving North Road, trains cross Skerne bridge over the river of that name. Part of it dates from the opening of the line, on which it was the largest masonry bridge, but the sylvan surroundings depicted in contemporary pictures have long since given way to an industrial area. The existing railway then curves sharply to the south to meet the main line, passing a region of absent tracks marked by an expanse (in summer) of purple willowherb and vacant ballast. The original S & D line ran straight ahead, to be crossed on the level at right angles by the main line constructed in the early 1840s; this crossing remained for many years, but the S & D line through it had been removed by the early 1970s. In curving southwards, however, as far as Darlington Bank Top station, trains are still on or very close to an original S & D route, that of its Croft branch opened in 1829 and later incorporated, in part, into the East Coast main line.

Passenger trains for Stockton leave from the south end of Darlington station and branch off onto a line opened in 1887. They gain the original line, by a speed-restricted S-curve, at Oak Tree Junction (grid ref. NZ 353137). Part of the original S & DR line back towards Darlington remains in use for freight trains to serve various works. Close beside it still stands the Fighting Cocks Inn (grid ref. NZ 342142), one of the inns at which the original horsedrawn railway passenger coaches called, stagecoach style. It gave its name to the later station nearby. Traces of the passenger station remain, though it was closed when the 1887 line was opened, and the goods sidings are still called Fighting Cocks.

Beyond Oak Tree Junction the original line, used by frequent clattering diesel trains, runs direct and level to Eaglescliffe. Here it joins the direct line from the South, via Northallerton, to Tees-side. When this line was built by the Leeds Northern Railway in the early 1850s, the S & DR diverted its line to run to Stockton alongside the newer line and abandoned about two miles of its original route which lay to the east of the road now numbered A19. Within Stockton however, the final part of the original line remained in use to serve the quay on the River Tees, passing on the way St John's level crossing (grid ref. NZ 447184). Here the first rail was laid, in 1822, and here still stands a cottage which, although at the end of a roadside row, faces the railway at right angles to it: from it, it is said, railway passenger tickets were first sold—the first railway booking office.

The quay was closed during the 1960s and track lifted, so that the existing railway terminates just short of the crossing site. Visiting this on a gloomy, foggy February day in 1980 I parked on the trackbed and found the cottage, and indeed the whole row, empty and with windows boarded up. They have however, according to Dr W. J. R. Tyerman, writing in the *Railway Magazine* (March 1980) been leased by British Rail to a local charity for use as a hostel for homeless people, so their short-term future seems assured. Although the crossing itself has lost its metals, the railway as far as this point remains in use to serve sidings. Dimly discerned through the murk was a row of hopper wagons: a sudden roar announced that one was being emptied into a coal drop below—an activity as old as the railway itself.

Edge Hill, Liverpool

As seen in 1980, the passenger station at Edge Hill (grid ref. SJ 371899) is something of a triumph for British Rail's current practice of respecting and renovating its historic buildings. Two classical pavilions of rosy sandstone, freshly cleaned, flank the line, with doors, window frames and station clock newly picked out in green and cream paint. Walls of the same stone separate the railway from upward-sloping cobbled carriage driveways which lead to Tunnel Road, and frame the bridge, once a tunnel-mouth, which carries this street over the railway. See illustration on page 251.

These buildings and their approaches date from 1836, when the Liverpool & Manchester Railway opened the Edge Hill-to-Lime Street line beside which they stand. This date must put the building on the north side of the line high on any list of contestants for the title of oldest station building still in use for its original purpose.

Their appearance now is closer to the original than it has been for many years. During the Victorian era, as traffic increased, so they were extended, and added to, many times over. One most conspicuous difference from early days is that the buildings now stand on island platforms, an additional track having been laid behind each of them during the 1880s. Then, in recent years, traffic declined to the extent that only a small part of the resultant complex was in use and the rest was deteriorating. But, quite apart from any historic interest, BR needed to maintain some facilities here, for in the event of any emergency or accident closing Lime Street, trains can be terminated at and started from Edge Hill. The result, encouraged by the listing of these historic buildings at the instance of the North Western Society for Industrial Archaeology and History, has been an imaginative scheme, commencing in 1976, for the restoration of the buildings and removal of later accretions—wooden luggage bridge, platform awnings and so on. Restoration included those buildings on the north platform provided in the 1840s for the stationary engine which worked the branch from Edge Hill to Waterloo Dock. This, like the earlier lines to Wapping and Lime Street, burrowed downwards beneath Liverpool through a long tunnel. The line down to Lime Street was originally worked by cable haulage, and the engines were housed in classical buildings similar to and immediately east of the passenger buildings. After locomotives had replaced cable haulage by about 1870, the engine rooms were rebuilt as waiting rooms and a tunnel between them for cable machinery became a passenger subway.

The effect of the restoration scheme has been to provide BR with a building on the north platform, of about the size it needed for the facilities to be maintained, with a subway to the south platform. Most of the building here it has made available to the Edge Hill Railway Trust Ltd (which was established in 1978) to use as a visitor centre. This was opened in 1980 and contains a display which informs visitors about the Liverpool & Manchester Railway generally and its remains in the vicinity of Edge Hill in particular; it acts as an introduction to the trust's Edge Hill Rail Trail.

This leads visitors into sheer rock-sided Chatsworth Street Cutting, as it is now called: the point on the original line famous from contemporary engravings as the 'Entrance to the Railway' or something to that effect. In some prints the cutting is seen to terminate, apparently, in three tunnels—the right hand one, single track, led up an incline to Crown Street passenger terminus, the centre one, double track, led down away and under the city to Wapping by the docks, and the left hand one was in fact a blind entrance, inserted to balance the architectural composition and used for storage. The location is illustrated on pages 57 and 254.

The significance of the place was that, since the inclines through the tunnels were worked by cable haulage, it was the changeover point between this and the locomotives which worked the rest of the line. The Moorish Arch, which spanned the railway and appears in so many early pictures, was in fact elaborate architectural camouflage for the stationary engines which powered both inclines, one up and the other down. It is noteworthy that George and Robert Stephenson, while championing locomotive haulage at the Rainhill Trials, nevertheless provided the Liverpool & Manchester Railway at Edge Hill with a highly developed cable haulage installation.

Today the Moorish Arch is no more, for it was demolished, probably in the 1860s when the cutting was widened on its south side and the original blind southern tunnel entrance was enlarged into a real tunnel to give additional access to Crown Street, then still used for goods although long superseded by Lime Street for passengers. Now there are no tracks through any of the tunnels, though one track still enters the cutting to run along its south side and stop short of them; this track is required by British Rail for some inscrutable purpose connected with shunting freightliner trains and is fenced off from the trail.

Since 1974 the site, which was then strewn with rubbish and part-submerged by rubble, has been surveyed and partially excavated by members of the NWSIAH, the Edge Hill trust, and others, and the rail trail has been established. The work has not been without its problems, for this is an inner city area and local youths, to whom a ten-feet high fence erected round the site presented only a challenge, have from the cutting top bombarded diggers with missiles as large as supermarket trolleys, and continue to replace during the week much of the rubbish extracted at weekends.

Nevertheless, clear traces of many of the features seen in those early prints have emerged. The foundations of the Moorish Arch, for a start, were uncovered where expected and the interior wall of the engine house forming the northern side of the arch can be discerned on the rock of the cutting. Fixing points for machinery remain. Further excavations have revealed large pits for the horizontal pulley wheels and tensioning devices for the Wapping tunnel cable. The engine house chimneys did not rise directly above the boiler rooms (which were excavated in the rock next to the Moorish Arch) but were curiously sited one on either side of the tunnel entrances. The southern one has been demolished, presumably when the cutting was widened, but the stump of the northern chimney can still be seen. So can the castellations of the wall which ran between them above the tunnel entrances, although it has been heightened since it was originally built. Steps descending the north side of the cutting, depicted in early prints, are still to be seen. They are carved in the sandstone of the cutting side which, for all that it lends itself to vertically-sided cuttings of the impressive appearance, is I understand fairly easily worked. This is confirmed by the many large recesses excavated in the rock of the cutting sides at track level, which can still be seen and which originally provided accommodation for locomotives, horses and railway staff as well as for the boilers which supplied steam to the stationary engines. One of

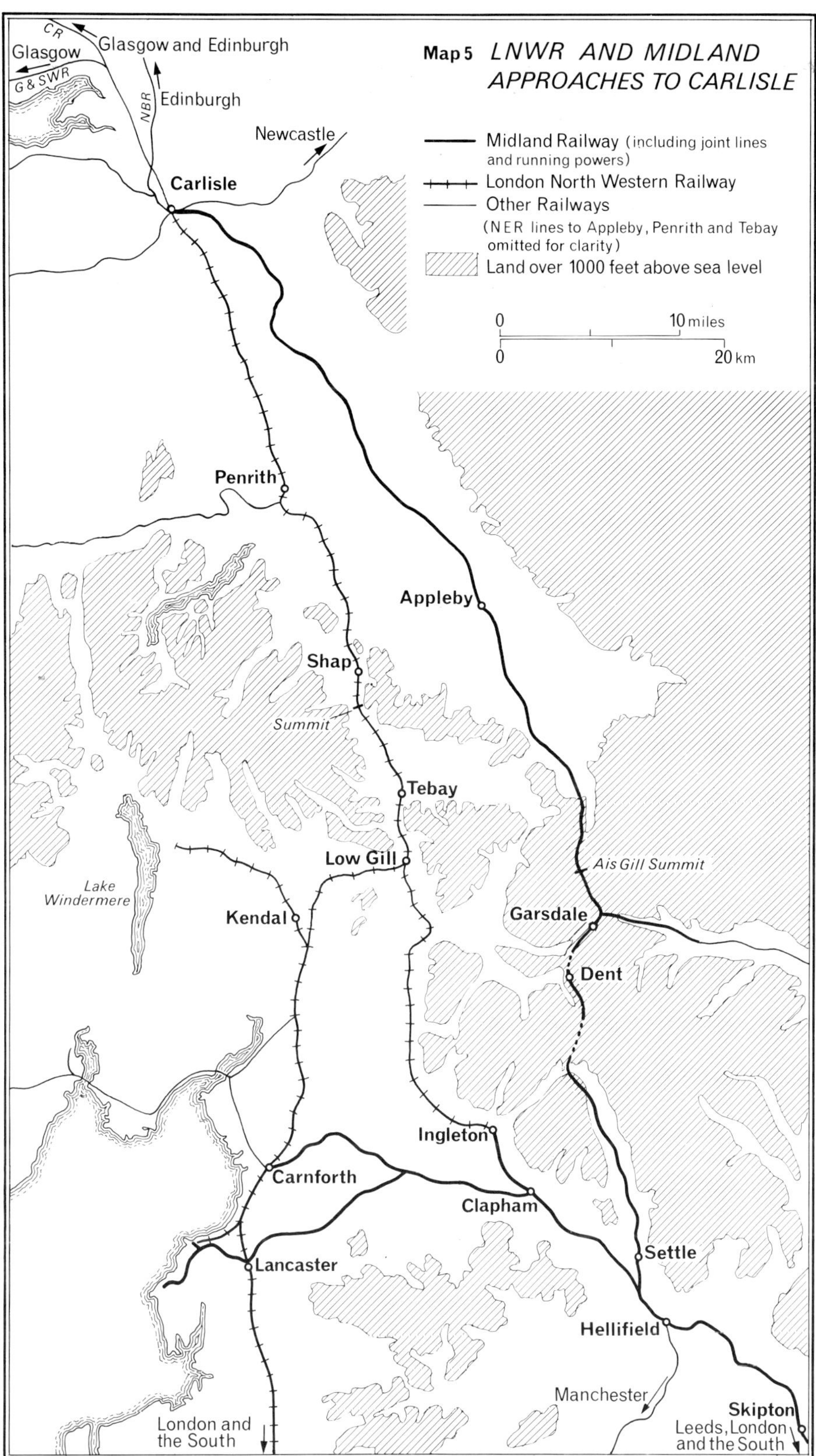

these boilers, made in 1836, supplied steam through a tunnel to the engines at Edge Hill station, some 450 yards away, which worked the incline from Lime Street. It is scarcely surprising that the boiler was soon replaced by a boiler house at the station itself, but the entrance to the steam tunnel can still be seen, high up on the side of the cutting next to the steps.

Visitor centre and rail trail were open during 1980 on Wednesdays and at weekends, and access to both is from Tunnel Road. Visitors arriving at Edge Hill by train have to leave the station by the north carriage road and re-enter by the south, for there is no direct access from platform to visitor centre.

Settle & Carlisle and the Ingleton branches

During the summer of 1975 I caught the down *Thames–Clyde Express* at Kettering. The *Thames–Clyde* was then one of the last surviving remnants of the Midland Railway's London-to-Scotland service: the only daytime train from St Pancras to Glasgow, and I acted more wisely than I knew, for within a year it had been withdrawn. For much of the southern part of its route it was, sadly, an express only in name; indeed reference to contemporary timetables suggests that it had in fact lost its name the previous May. Named or not, the train found its way into Nottingham, reversed, and trundled northwards across the coalfield of Nottinghamshire and Derbyshire with its speed restrictions resulting from colliery subsidence. Eventually it reached Leeds, having been allowed four hours nineteen minutes from London. King's Cross to Leeds expresses at that time took about two and a half hours.

Then, after Leeds, the train changed its character. From being a distinctly second rate, unimportant affair, it had become The Principal Train of the Day. There was a new urgency about it as it hummed along the Aire Valley. At Skipton, passengers joining it laughed and joked with friends on the platform to see them off. At Settle, accelerating away upgrade from the station, the train growled over a viaduct high above the main road; and passers-by turned, looked up, and stared. After all, they did not see many passenger trains—at that time, northbound, only two a day left Settle during daylight. I sat back to enjoy lunch in the restaurant car as the train gathered speed, climbing steadily up Ribblesdale between the pale limestone hills, through ever-wilder scenery. At speed, it pierced the mile-and-a-half of Blea Moor tunnel, traversed the high hillsides above the head of Dentdale, reached the summit at Ais Gill and rushed onwards down the Eden Valley to Appleby and Carlisle.

Settle & Carlisle scenery is not very mountainous, compared with, say, parts of Scotland or even North Wales; but the line (and this is its peculiar fascination) certainly does penetrate the most rugged country of any line in Britain laid out as a trunk route for fast running. To this day its trains still run fast.

The line has no sharp curves, and its ruling gradient is 1 in 100. From its start at Settle Junction, however, it rises almost continuously at that gradient for 15 miles. About 11½ miles up it crosses the 1,000 feet contour, and stays above it for the next 16 miles or so as it threads its way among far higher hills. Ais Gill summit is 1,166 feet above sea level (according to the British Rail system map—other authorities give 1,167 and 1,169 feet). Whatever it may be, it is an impressive altitude. From the north the summit is approached by another 15-mile climb at 1 in 100.

In its length of a little over 72 miles the Settle & Carlisle line has 17 viaducts and 12 tunnels. Four of the

viaducts—Smardale, Arten Gill, Dent Head and Ribblehead (grid refs. NY 733083, SD 776859, SD 778844 and SD 759794 respectively)—have been scheduled as ancient monuments. Curving Ribblehead viaduct with 24 arches and a maximum height of 165 feet is the greatest. That long high-level section is subject to all the extremes of weather to be expected of it: deep snow and hard frost in winter, still hot days in summer, drizzle, rain, mist and gales at any time of year. To build the line, armies of Victorian navvies toiled in these conditions for nearly six years.

The Settle & Carlisle is indeed heroic, a monument to Victorian engineering. But it is also a monument to the competitive excesses of Victorian *laissez-faire* capitalism. There was no physical need for this main line to be built through such inhospitable country: an alternative route at lower level already existed. The Settle & Carlisle originated out of inter-company rivalry.

Back in the 1840s the North Western Railway (a local concern, not the

7/6 Dent station on the Settle & Carlisle line is 1,150 feet above sea level, the highest station in England on a main line. The train speeding through is a West Coast Route express diverted for Sunday engineering works; the station is normally closed, but is re-opened from time to time for Dales Rail specials. Snow fences to the left help to prevent drifts across the railway in winter, but on this day hot weather haze has obscured the hills in the distance. The platform fencing with its diagonal rails is typical Midland, and so is the signal box.

London & North Western) was authorised to build from Skipton up the Lune Valley to a junction at Low Gill with the Lancaster & Carlisle Railway, with a branch from Clapham, Yorkshire, to Lancaster. It managed to complete its main line from Skipton past Clapham to Ingleton, and the branch from Clapham to Lancaster. The line from Low Gill south to Ingleton was eventually built instead by the Lancaster & Carlisle, and opened in 1861. Physically a through route, Clapham to Low Gill was never developed as such, for the little North Western Railway became part of the Midland Railway, and the Lancaster & Carlisle part of the London & North Western. The LNWR had no interest in encouraging the Midland to compete for Anglo-Scottish traffic by taking that traffic forward from Ingleton.

The consequence was promotion of the Settle & Carlisle line by the Midland, for which it obtained an Act of Parliament in 1865. Had Victorian Britain been a country where state direction of transport was less abhorrent—as were France, say, and Belgium—the Settle & Carlisle would doubtless not have been authorised. The LNWR would have been directed to work Midland traffic forward from Ingleton to Carlisle, and to quadruple over Shap if necessary. In fact, soon after the Settle & Carlisle had been authorised, the Midland did succeed in obtaining acceptable terms from the LNWR to convey its traffic, and then sought powers from Parliament to abandon the Settle & Carlisle proposal. But there were other companies which wanted the Settle & Carlisle built: the Lancashire & Yorkshire, which needed a route to Scotland independent of the LNWR, and the North British and the Glasgow & South Western which needed an alternative route southwards. Their opposition caused the abandonment bill to be lost, and the Midland had to build as planned.

For a few years prior to the First World War, relations between the LNWR and the Midland improved sufficiently for one Midland Anglo-Scottish express daily to be routed via Ingleton instead of over the Settle &

Carlisle. This was the only instance when the Ingleton branches were used regularly for through long distance trains. Otherwise, each company ran its own branch line service on its own section; after the grouping, which brought the whole line into the LMS, these services were combined into a through local service between Clapham, Low Gill and Tebay, which survived until 1954 when the line was closed to passengers. Subsequently it was closed also to freight (in 1966) and dismantled.

Many traces remain: the most impressive are two large viaducts. One of them, handsome but rail-less, curves away from the existing West Coast Route at Low Gill (grid ref. SD 616965) and is still a landmark for main line passengers (and, indeed, motorists on the M6). The other, further south at grid reference SD 631930, crosses the River Lune with six spans of stone and a fine central span, of 124 feet, made of cast iron. Massive bridges elsewhere, and double-track width of earthworks, confirm the former presence of a railway built to be a main line, whatever limited branch line services its operators actually saw fit to provide.

As the third Anglo-Scottish main line, the Settle & Carlisle saw many years of intensive use, but after the grouping and the coming of road competition Anglo-Scottish traffic was concentrated on the lines of older

7/7 The last steam locomotive built for British Railways, Evening Star, *hauls a 1978 steam excursion over Ribblehead viaduct, largest and longest of the many viaducts on the Settle & Carlisle line. It took five years to build and is now an ancient monument. In the background is Pen-y-ghent Hill, 2,276 feet high above sea level; the railway itself is more than 1,000 feet high. Effects of long exposure to Pennine weather cause concern for the viaduct's long-term future.*

rivals. In recent years survival of the Settle & Carlisle line has often been in doubt. In 1959 the BTC considered that, by introducing diesel traction between Crewe and Carlisle, it would be able to divert traffic from the Settle & Carlisle line and close much of it. Withdrawal of passenger trains was proposed by the Beeching Plan in 1963, but consent was withheld by the Minister of Transport in 1965 because of the hardship it would have caused. By 1967, BR's long term plans again included withdrawal of passenger trains and complete closure between Horton-in-Ribblesdale and Appleby. Happily these plans seem since to have been revised. It appears that electrification over Shap, far from enabling the Settle & Carlisle line to be closed, has resulted in so much intensive high speed traffic that the Settle & Carlisle continues to be useful for slower goods trains, and for diversions of passenger trains during weekend maintenance.

In 1970, however, local passenger trains were withdrawn, and fourteen wayside stations closed, leaving only Settle and Appleby open, to be served by long-distance trains. These then totalled three each way daily: daytime and overnight trains between London and Glasgow, and a shorter working between Leeds and Glasgow. Through trains to and from Edinburgh had vanished with closure of the Waverley Route in 1969, despite existence of the alternative route between Carlisle and Edinburgh via Carstairs.

By this date in any event, through passengers from London to Glasgow by the Midland route had dwindled to virtual non-existence because of the very much longer time taken for the journey than by the West Coast Route. Instead, through trains were being used mostly by passengers from London to the North Midlands and Yorkshire, and by other passengers from the North Midlands and Yorkshire to Glasgow. Each group differed in its demands, in terms of class of accommodation and refreshments. So in 1976 the London-to-Glasgow day train was split into London-to-Nottingham and Nottingham-to-Glasgow trains; the overnight train was withdrawn in 1977. The daytime service, however, has been improved: there are now three trains daily in each direction between Nottingham and Glasgow, all of them with buffet cars. Traffic is encouraged: British Rail publish a free leaflet *Highlights of the Settle & Carlisle Line* which describes the route and the sights to be seen on either side.

Much of the most scenic part of the Settle & Carlisle line lies within the Yorkshire Dales National Park. A basic national park objective is to provide access to the countryside in a way which does not conflict with its conservation. To this end, since 1975, the national park committee has sponsored 'Dales Rail': an imaginative and successful venture. Several times a year, many of the closed wayside stations are reopened for special trains from West Yorkshire and Lancashire. Special bus services connect with trains at some of the stations, and guided walks are arranged for visitors. And as visitors get off the trains, so local people replace them, to visit Leeds or Carlisle for a day's shopping.

The line's scenic and historic attractions have also made it a prime favourite for steam excursions, using locomotives based at Steamtown Carnforth which is within convenient reach. On one noted occasion (21 August 1980), gleeful in retrospect though possibly not so for delayed passengers at the time, Jubilee class 4-6-0 *Leander* had to abandon its train to go to the rescue of a freight train ahead, the diesel locomotive of which had failed. The steam locomotive then hauled both diesel and lengthy freight train to a convenient siding before she could return for her own excursion. The steam excursions run during the summer and also, for those who want the full benefit, during the winter too, as the *Cumbrian Mountain Express*. So the Settle & Carlisle line is not only well worth visiting but also easier than it was to visit.

Nantlle, Festiniog, North Wales narrow gauge and Welsh Highland

Both the Nantlle Railway and the Festiniog Railway were built as horse railways. The Nantlle Railway Company was incorporated in 1825, and the line was opened in 1828; it ran from slate quarries near Nantlle to the harbour of Caernarfon, $9\frac{1}{4}$ miles, with edge rails laid on stone sleeper blocks to a gauge of 3 ft. 6 in. It was the first public railway in North Wales, although there were a few earlier privately owned ones, and in South Wales the horse railway or plateway was already common.

Proposals for the Festiniog Railway, to link slate quarries near Blaenau Ffestiniog with the harbour of Porthmadog, had been in the air since William Madocks created the habour as a by-product of his reclamation of the Afon Glaslyn estuary. To do so he had built across its mouth the embankment called the Cob, over three quarters of a mile long and finally completed in 1814. Iron railways were used in the work, and where the diverted river entered the sea at the west end of the embankment, the harbour and town of Porthmadog eventually grew up.

Madocks and others had already proposed a railway to the Ffestiniog quarries, but it was not until after his death in 1828 that the successful proposal arose out of a chance meeting between Ffestiniog quarry proprietor Samuel Holland and wealthy Irishman Henry Archer. Holland, travelling to Caernarfon, called at the inn at Pen-y-groes, close to the Nantlle Railway, before catching its horsedrawn coach. Here he met Archer, who was thinking of leasing the Nantlle Railway;

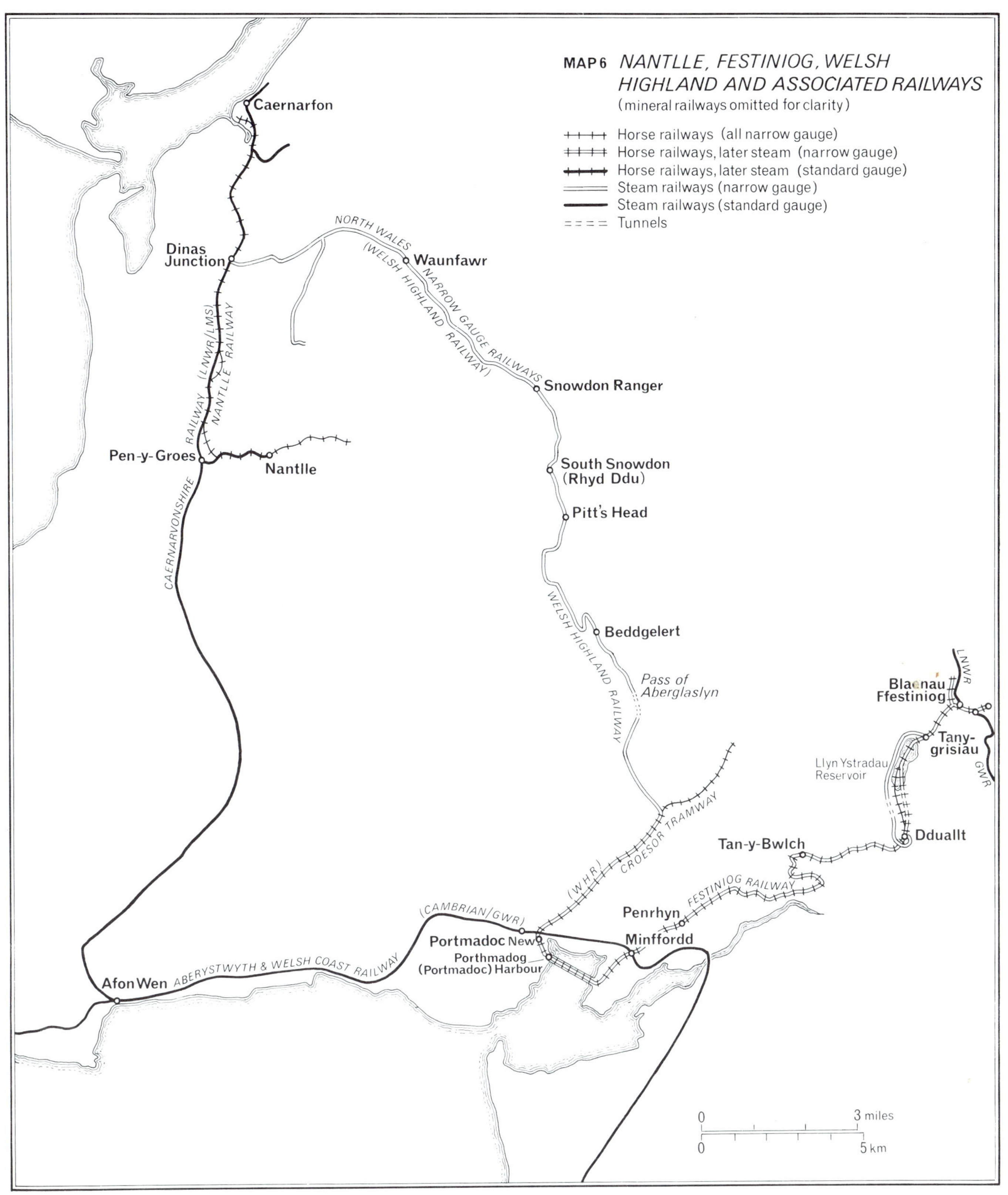
MAP 6 NANTLLE, FESTINIOG, WELSH HIGHLAND AND ASSOCIATED RAILWAYS
(mineral railways omitted for clarity)
Horse railways (all narrow gauge)
Horse railways, later steam (narrow gauge)
Horse railways, later steam (standard gauge)
Steam railways (narrow gauge)
Steam railways (standard gauge)
Tunnels
Caernarfon
Dinas Junction
Waunfawr
NORTH WALES NARROW GAUGE RAILWAYS
(WELSH HIGHLAND RAILWAY)
(LNWR/LMS) RAILWAY
NANTLLE RAILWAY
CAERNARVONSHIRE RAILWAY
Snowdon Ranger
Pen-y-Groes
Nantlle
South Snowdon (Rhyd Ddu)
Pitt's Head
WELSH HIGHLAND RAILWAY
Beddgelert
Pass of Aberglaslyn
LNWR
Blaenau Ffestiniog
Tany-grisiau
GWR
Llyn Ystradau Reservoir
Dduallt
Tan-y-Bwlch
CROESOR TRAMWAY
(WHR)
FESTINIOG RAILWAY
Penrhyn
(CAMBRIAN/GWR)
Portmadoc New
Minffordd
Porthmadog (Portmadoc) Harbour
Afon Wen
ABERYSTWYTH & WELSH COAST RAILWAY
0
3 miles
0
5 km

Holland persuaded him instead to promote the Festiniog. Its Act of Parliament was passed in 1832 and the line, thirteen and a quarter miles long, was opened in 1836. The surveys had been done by James Spooner assisted by Thomas Prichard, who had worked on the surveys for the Chester & Holyhead. The track of the Festiniog was similar to that of the Nantlle but, for economy, the gauge had been made very narrow, less than 2 ft. In that feature it resembled the earlier Penrhyn Railway.

With a fall of 700 feet between Blaenau Ffestiniog and the east end of the Cob, the line was laid out on a continuous down gradient so that gravity might, as on many earlier lines, power laden trains. Exceptionally, where a ridge lay across the course of the railway south of Tanygrisiau, the line was at first carried over it by a pair of inclined planes; the 730 yard Moelwyn tunnel beneath the ridge was completed in 1842 and thenceforward gravity trains could run down without interruption.

The railway was managed by James Spooner until his death in 1856, after which his son Charles E. Spooner succeeded him. It was under the latter's management that the Festiniog saw its great days, and steam locomotives were introduced in 1863. There does not seem to have been any proposal to upgrade the Festiniog into a standard gauge steam line, the usual course of development for horse railways with much traffic. Probably the amount of engineering work that would have been necessary prevented it—for the width of the Festiniog's right of way had been kept to the minimum, and curves were very sharp.

The Nantlle Railway was upgraded at this period, however, or rather, most of it was. In 1862 the Caernarvonshire Railway (engineer, Charles E. Spooner) was incorporated to build a standard gauge line from Caernarfon to Porthmadog. The Nantlle Railway ran in a southerly direction as far as Pen-y-groes (at which point it turned due east), and so that section was rebuilt as the standard gauge steam railway, which meant building in part on a new alignment, where the old was unsuitable. South of Pen-y-groes the Caernarvonshire built onward to Afon Wen, where it made a junction with the Aberystwyth & Welsh Coast, which had been building northwards through Porthmadog. The Caernarvonshire Railway was opened in 1867 and became part of the LNWR; the Aberystwyth & Welsh Coast, however, became part of the Cambrian. A further mile-and-a-half stretch of the old Nantlle line was converted to standard gauge in 1872, as far as Nantlle station; this then became the interchange point for the remainder, which continued in its old form to the quarries over a distance of about a mile and a half or so.

Successful introduction of steam locomotives on the Festiniog was followed by passenger trains in 1865, as mentioned in chapter two; and rapidly increasing traffic was met by introduction of double-ended locomotives carried on bogies to the patent of Robert Fairlie. They combined power with flexibility over sharp curves, and the FR's first was built in 1869. It was followed by the first bogie passenger coaches in Britain in 1872. The Festiniog became the narrow gauge prototype to be copied world-wide.

The consequence nearest home was formation of the North Wales Narrow Gauge Railways Company in 1873. Spooner was closely associated with it. It proposed eight lines, not all of them connected, in the region between Corwen and the Lleyn Peninsula, but it succeeded in building, in effect, only one: a 1 ft. $11\frac{1}{2}$ in. gauge line opened in stages between 1877 and 1881. It ran from Dinas Junction, on that part of the Caernarfon–Afon Wen line which had been constructed a few years before by upgrading the Nantlle Railway, south east to Rhyd-ddu (South

7/8 Vehicles from the Festiniog Railway's horse-railway period are exhibited in the railway's museum at Harbour Station, Porthmadog. The horse dandy ran at the back of gravity trains; this one probably survived through use as a coal wagon after steam locomotives took over from horses. Waggon no. 79 is typical of wooden slate waggons of the period. Festiniog cuttings and tunnels were made for vehicles of these dimensions, so later steam locomotives and coaches were both restricted in size and a tight fit.

Snowdon) with a branch to Bryngwyn. This railway was never very successful. Rhyd-ddu, though a convenient starting point for walking up Snowdon, was no more than a hamlet. Beyond lay Beddgelert, and beyond that Porthmadog, with the Croesor Tramway running north east from it. The Croesor Tramway had been opened as a two-foot gauge horse railway as late as 1864. Its upgrading for steam, and a link between the two lines, were perpetual dreams of successive proprietors of both the Croesor Tramway and the NWNGR.

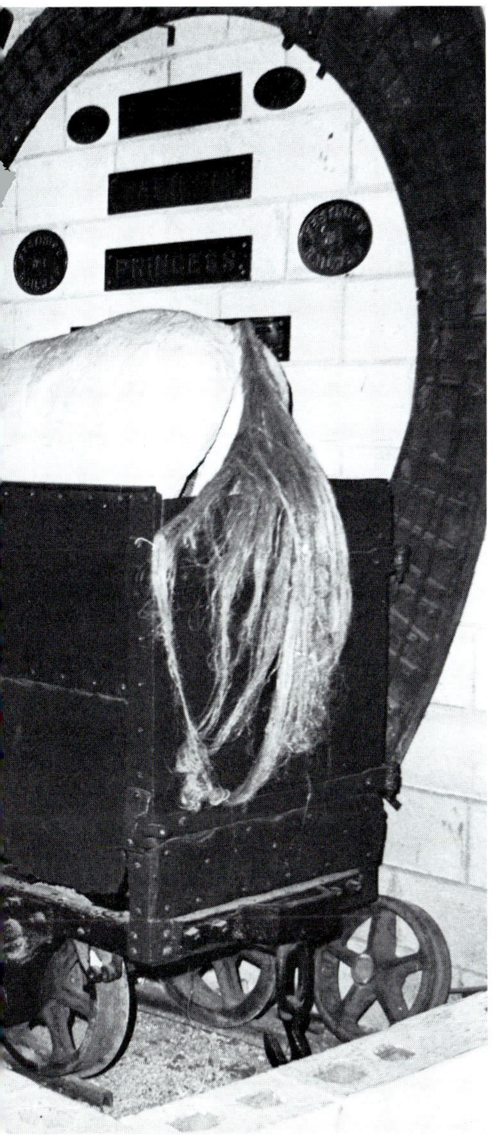

To link them, successive companies were formed and disbanded, successive powers were granted and lapsed or were passed on. In 1906 the Portmadoc, Beddgelert & South Snowdon Railway (which by then owned the Croesor Tramway) obtained a light railway order; it built most of the civil engineering works needed for the link, laid some track, and then ran out of money. Attempts to revive the scheme went into abeyance during the First World War. The company which was eventually to complete the link, and absorb both PBSSR and NWNGR, was incorporated by light railway order in 1922: the Welsh Highland Railway (Light Railway) Co. The WHR was completed throughout between Dinas Junction and Porthmadog in 1923. It included only the southernmost three and a half miles of the Croesor Tramway—the rest continued to be worked by horses and inclined planes. At Porthmadog, the Festiniog Railway built a new connecting link between the two railways.

The Welsh Highland Railway was completed too late. Not only was motor road transport by then in the ascendant, and a $21\frac{3}{4}$-mile 1 ft. $11\frac{1}{2}$ in. gauge light railway with a 15 mph speed limit was ill-equipped to compete, but the great days of the Festiniog itself were long past. C. E. Spooner had died in 1889 and subsequently the railway had gradually declined. Standard gauge railways direct to Blaenau Ffestiniog took much of its traffic. By 1923, both the FR and WHR companies were under common control.

Attempts to provide a full, year-round passenger service over the Welsh Highland Railway lasted only about eighteen months, for the financial results were disastrous. At the end of 1933 the railway closed, but the following June the Festiniog leased it: although by then full year-round passenger services had ceased on the FR also, its summer tourist traffic was improving. The FR worked the WHR for passengers for the short summer seasons of 1934, 5 and 6; goods were carried intermittently and, with losses mounting, the WHR was closed again in 1937. Most of the track was lifted during the Second World War. That same war ended the Festiniog's passenger traffic in 1939, and it was closed for freight also in 1946.

The revival of the Festiniog Railway since 1954 is one of the great success stories of railway preservation; it is also too well-known to need more than an outline here. Control of the company was purchased by Alan Pegler and passed by him to a charitable trust set up for the purpose; the Festiniog Railway Society Ltd provided voluntary support, both financial and practical. Track was cleared of overgrowth and re-laid, locomotives and rolling stock were rebuilt, buildings were repaired. The line was reopened by stages from Porthmadog starting in 1955. Tourist passengers in rapidly increasing numbers necessitated acquisition of further locomotives, and construction of new coaches. Reopening throughout to Blaenau Ffestiniog has been delayed by construction of a reservoir for Tanygrisiau hydro-electric power station, under powers granted while the line was closed. This reservoir submerged part of the course of the railway, and necessitated construction of the Llyn Ystradau Deviation between 1965 and 1978. Since 1978 trains have run as far as Tanygrisiau, and at the time of writing work is going ahead on reconstruction of the Festiniog Railway into Blaenau Ffestiniog.

There is scarcely anything about the Festiniog Railway which is not of historic interest in one context or another. Here, however, I propose to look at traces of the Spooner era—or rather, of the two Spooner eras, horse-drawn and locomotive-powered—followed by traces of the NWNGR, PBSSR and WHR; and preceded by traces of the Nantlle.

Nantlle station was located at the village of Tal-y-sarn, and there the course of the line which lasted as a horse railway until as recently as 1963 remains as a tarmac footpath beside

7/9 (above) Horse-railway waggons from the Croesor Tramway are still in occasional use on the Festiniog Railway. Rings to which horses' traces were attached can be seen.

7/10 (left) Track materials dating from c. 1870 are in use in several places on the FR—in this instance, a siding at Porthmadog. Double-headed rails and chairs with S-shaped bases are comparable to standard gauge practice at that date; fishplates which clamp the lower heads of the rails as well as their webs are to a patent taken out by C. E. Spooner and G. A. Huddart in 1869. Originally, chairs were spiked to specially-sawn sleepers; here, they are screwed to second-hand standard gauge sleepers cut in half.

the road at grid reference SH 489530. The site of the extensive exchange sidings at Nantlle station is marked by a new playing field, though the buildings of the passenger station still stand. At least two small four-wheeled open waggons from the horse railway survive, one in the Industrial Railway Museum at Penrhyn Castle and the other in the Narrow Gauge Railway Museum, Tywyn.

In places where they were not used for the Caernarvonshire Railway, some of the original earthworks and structures of the Nantlle Railway survive. There is a good example at Bont-newydd (grid ref. SH 480599) where the large stone arch of a bridge still spans the Afon Gwyrfai. Its narrow, steep-sided approach embankments can be seen, although one has been pierced in several places where a new housing estate has been built around it, and indeed its side has become a mountainous rock-garden for one of the new houses. The bridge of the Caernarvonshire Railway, now equally disused, stands a little way downstream on an easier curve than that of the original line.

From Porthmadog to Dduallt the route of the Festiniog Railway is that of the original horse railway, with only a very few deviations made in the steam-locomotive era to ease curves. The extreme narrowness of the right of way, where for much of its length the line passes through rock cuttings or along embankments, and the correspondingly restricted clearances between vehicles and cutting sides or lineside walls, are all consequences of the line's origin. So too is the limited height of Spooner-era locomotives and coaches: it was restricted by the horse-railway dimensions of the bore of Moelwyn tunnel. Since the tunnel was blocked so that its northern end might be submerged by Llyn Ystradau reservoir, and the Deviation avoids it, the height restriction has been eased and newly-introduced vehicles are taller than the originals.

The location of the railway's Porthmadog terminus beside the harbour is itself an indication of the early origin of the line, as a local quarry-to-

7/11 Festiniog Railway passenger trains last used its Duffws terminus at Blaenau Ffestiniog in 1931. Site of tracks is now a car park and in the middle of this still stands the station building, long since converted into a public convenience (!) The ticket window, blocked up can still be seen, the brick surface of what was once the platform is similar to the platform at Porthmadog Harbour, and the FR's badge, the Prince of Wales's feathers, still appears, carved in slate.

shipping-point railway typical of the period before construction of the main railway system. On leaving Porthmadog the railway runs along Madocks's Cob; at the far end the railway's Boston Lodge works, which originated during the horse-railway era, occupy the site of a quarry from which stone for the embankment was obtained. Further up the line Rhiw Goch passing loop, installed in 1974, occupies the site of a loop used during horse railway days but dismantled after steam took over. The widened formation survived to be adopted for the new loop. Further on still, the iron bridge by which the railway crosses the B4410 road, at the approach to Tan-y-bwlch, has its date, 1854, cast in.

Beyond Dduallt trains enter the Llyn Ystradau Deviation. They traverse a spiral, unique in Britain, to gain height, and then run parallel to, but higher than, the original line. So at grid reference SH 679427 there can be seen below the train not only the south portal of the Moelwyn tunnel of 1842 but also the course of the earlier 1836 line with one of its inclined planes. This line has become a public footpath, and along it stone sleeper blocks can be found in situ. Elsewhere they are common alongside the FR in walls, buildings and even chimneys.

The Llyn Ystradau Deviation passes through a new tunnel and then runs along the bed of a former reservoir, which originally provided water power to work the inclines and survived until it was drained for the Deviation to be built. The new line passes through a gap made in its dam. It then runs along above Llyn Ystradau, and from trains there can be seen both the north incline of the original line, and the flooded northern approach cutting to the 1842 tunnel. At Tanygrisiau the Deviation re-joins thc original course of the line, and from there to the outskirts of Blaenau Ffestiniog the railway is being renovated on its original site.

Two vehicles from the FR's horse railway period survive in the Festiniog Railway Museum at Porthmadog Harbour station. One is a wooden bodied, slat sided, typical slate waggon built about 1857, the other a horse dandy, complete with full-size imitation horse. Horses used on the FR rode in such vehicles at the tail of downhill trains; this example, with iron sides, probably survived through use as a coal wagon after horse haulage ceased. The museum also contains a specimen of the original track, fish-bellied rail on stone blocks. Other horse railway vehicles which survive on the FR, in occasional use, are three small iron-framed, iron-sided waggons from the Croesor Tramway. They retain the rings to which traces were once attached.

7/12 Festiniog Railway 0–4–0 Prince, *built originally in 1863, is seen here at Boston Lodge in 1980 after completion of her latest rebuild. Just how much of the original locomotive is still present after at least four rebuilds is anybody's guess, but the essence of* Prince *is still the same. Original appearance was similar to that of* The Princess, *shown in illustration no. 2/24.*

Of the Charles Spooner steam locomotive era of the FR, many relics survive among its buildings, tracks, locomotives, carriages and wagons. At Porthmadog Harbour station the main part of the station building dates from this period, and so does the museum building which was formerly the goods shed; the building linking the two is a recent addition. Festiniog Railway track in the Charles Spooner period was comparable to the best contemporary main line practice, and incorporated double headed rail in chairs with S-shaped bases; sidings laid with this material (recovered from the main line) can be seen at Porthmadog and elsewhere. At Boston Lodge works many of the buildings are Spooner-period, notably the erecting shop; on the opposite side of the line is the former locomotive shed, now used for carriage storage.

From a train approaching Minffordd, there can be seen to the north the site of former exchange sidings with the Cambrian Railways. These were opened in 1872 and were intended, to some extent, as a showpiece for visitors who came to examine the narrow gauge. Adjoining standard and narrow gauge tracks were laid out at various levels to minimise the effort needed to transfer goods between them, and cranes and a wagon tippler were installed. Narrow gauge tracks remain in use; standard gauge survived until 1973. Minffordd and Penrhyn station buildings are both Spooner-period; that at Penrhyn, partly of timber, was renovated between 1966 and 1972 to form part of a hostel for Festiniog Railway Society volunteers. At Tan-y-bwlch, the present booking office and café is the former goods shed converted; the original small wooden station building survives on the same side of the line further along the station.

In Blaenau Ffestiniog, the principal terminus of the FR, last used for passenger trains in 1931 (after which they terminated at the joint station with the GWR), was called Duffws. Its site is now a car park but islanded in the tarmac there survives the station building. Internally it has long since been adapted as a public convenience (!); externally it is little altered: an attractive little stone building roofed with ornamental slates and with, at the front, two small wings which still bear, above doorways, slate tablets on which are carved the FR's crest: the Prince of Wales's feathers. There is still a ticket window (blocked up) and above it a circular opening, probably for a clock; and in front the former platform is still paved with blue bricks as is the platform at Porthmadog.

Spooner and Fairlie equipped the FR well with locomotives and after 1886 the FR acquired no other steam locomotives (apart from one from the Welsh Highland on closure of that line) until 1962. When locomotives, or parts of them, wore out they were dismantled and, if required, rebuilt. New components were incorporated, according to need and finance available. Since 1955 the new management has acted similarly and, for good measure, has added modifications to improve performance.

The first locomotives on the FR

were 0-4-0 tank locomotives with separate tenders for coal. They were not wholly superseded by Fairlie locomotives, for they were used for shunting and, in due course, hauling trains on the Welsh Highland. Four survive, of which *Prince* is a working locomotive. Originally built in 1863, this locomotive has been rebuilt at least four times, emerging most recently from Boston Lodge in 1980. *Princess* (1863) and *Welsh Pony* (1867) are stored against future rebuilding, and *Palmerston* (1864) which was in by far the worst condition, was disposed of for private restoration in 1974. These locomotives all have saddle tanks but the 1863–4 locomotives at first had side tanks only; their original appearance is indicated by the remarkable $3\frac{1}{8}$ in. gauge miniature locomotive *Topsy*, which was built for C. E. Spooner at Boston Lodge in 1869 and is now exhibited in the FR Museum.

Two double Fairlies, much rebuilt, survived in 1955: *Taliesin* of 1886 and *Merddin Emrys* of 1879. Both were in due course repaired and put back into service, and both, after a few years, required new boilers. Two new double boilers of modified design were delivered by Hunslet Engine Co. in 1969. One of them was used to rebuild *Merddin Emrys*. The other was used not to rebuild an old locomotive with new parts, but rather to build a new one incorporating a few old parts. This locomotive entered service in 1979 (see illustration no. 1/9) bearing the name *Earl of Merioneth*, a name latterly carried by *Taliesin*. The old boiler (built 1905), tanks and other parts of that locomotive have been retained for eventual display.

The Festiniog's earliest passenger carriages for steam trains were diminutive four-wheelers with back-to-back longitudinal seats over the wheels, dating from 1863–4. Four of these survive in occasional use, and a fifth is a museum piece. Remarkable survivals though these are, they are eclipsed in interest by the two original bogie coaches of 1872, numbers 15 and 16, which are both in regular service. Long and rectangular, their wooden bodies conceal massive wrought iron frames: they carry their years well. They are accompanied by a further four carriages (nos. 17, 18, 19 and 20), with bowed sides giving a markedly more advanced appearance, which

7/13 Bogie coach no. 16 is one of the Festiniog Railway's first two bogie coaches, built in 1872—the first bogie coaches to go into service in Britain. Adjacent bow-sided coaches date from later in the 1870s. The height restriction imposed on these coaches by the horse-railway dimensions of Moelwyn tunnel is emphasised by comparison with the roof of a recently-built vehicle behind no. 16. The two classes of passenger accommodation on the Festiniog Railway are still described as first and third, as they were on most British railways prior to 1956.

date from 1876 and 1879. Many goods wagons from the Spooner period also survive and now carry materials for reconstruction and maintenance of the railway. They include slate wagons large and small, with iron slatted sides, of a design developed from the earlier wooden example mentioned above. There are also wooden bodied coal wagons rebuilt in recent years, and a large iron-bodied six-wheeled open wagon with flexible wheelbase to Cleminson's patent which enjoyed brief popularity during the last century.

Revival of the Festiniog prompted attempts to restore the Welsh Highland, or one or other section of it. These commenced in 1961 but have met with only limited success so far. However, in 1980 the Welsh Highland Light Railway (1964) Ltd was able to open a short narrow gauge line on the site of the former standard gauge connecting link to exchange sidings at Porthmadog, with a view to extension on to the trackbed of the Welsh Highland proper. Long before this, the new company had obtained the former WHR 2-6-2T *Russell*, and had her reboilered by Hunslet Engine Co. who built her originally in 1906.

Two passenger coaches built for the NWNGR and used subsequently on the WHR are in use on the Festiniog, where they are numbered 23 and 26: the former was taken over by the FR on closure of the WHR in 1937; the body of the latter, which had remained on the WHR and eventually been sold, was purchased in 1958 from a farm where it had served as a hen house, and mounted on FR bogies.

There are still many traces to be seen of the buildings, structures and course of the WHR and its constituents. The site of Dinas Junction is now the Dinas Depot of Gwynedd County Council Highways Department. All railways are but memories here, since the Caernarfon to Afon Wen line was closed in 1964 under the Beeching Plan. The twin overbridges by which a road crossed over first the NWNG and then the LNW Railways are still there, at grid reference SH 477587, and from them can be seen the NWNGR passenger station building and its large goods shed for transfer of goods between narrow and standard gauge vehicles.

7/14 (below) Attempting to link the North Wales Narrow Gauge Railways with the Croesor Tramway, the Portmadoc, Beddgelert & South Snowdon Railway built this bridge over the Beddgelert–Porthmadog road, at grid reference SH 588478, about 1908. It was never used, for this part of its line was never completed: the incomplete embankment, now overgrown with trees, finishes to the right of the bridge. When the Welsh Highland Railway was eventually built in 1922–3, it took a different course. The photograph was taken in October 1979.

17/15 (opposite) This is the course of the Welsh Highland Railway, on one of the sections built in 1922–3 to complete it, at grid reference SH 592474 where it crosses the Afon Glaslyn. The embankment in the background was built at the same time and carries the Beddgelert–Porthmadog road, which crosses over the course of the line behind the trees, left. The sharpness of the curve is indicative of the line's very narrow gauge.

The NWNGR built small four-square station buildings of stone and yellow brick, and they remain elsewhere too. At Waenfawr (grid ref. SH 527588) the walls of the station building still stand in a field, and at Snowdon Ranger the station building has become a bungalow. The site of Rhyd-ddu station (grid ref. SH 572525) is now a car park.

At Pitt's Head, three quarters of a mile south of Rhyd-ddu, the trackbed passes beneath the A4085 road by a stone-arched bridge. This is Portmadoc, Beddgelert & South Snowdon work, for this section was completed, with track laid, in about 1908. The PBSS was laid out for electric traction—the period was the heyday of the electric tramway—and was intended to have gradients in some places as steep as 1 in 28. The eventual Welsh Highland was intended for steam, and so the steepest PBSS sections, some of which had been built, were not used, and a less severely graded route was constructed. The most remarkable relic of this change of plan is the substantial PBSS overbridge which still crosses the A498 road south of Beddgelert at grid reference SH 588478. It has never been used: the incomplete embankment to the east of it peters out after a few yards.

The NWNG and the PBSS made their buildings and structures of brick and stone; the WHR used concrete, steel and corrugated iron. The site of Beddgelert station (grid ref. SH 587480) is an open space with concrete bases for vanished corrugated iron buildings, and concrete pillars for a locomotive water tank. South of the abandoned PBSS bridge the A498 road passes over the course of the WHR, on its amended route, by an overbridge of steel girders and concrete at grid reference SH 591474. Close by is the Bryn-y-felin girder bridge by which the WHR crossed the Afon Glaslyn. The bridge has been converted to a footbridge; immediately beyond, the trackbed rejoins the formation built for the PBSS. To the left is an embankment, never used; to the right, the PBSS works were used to carry the WHR through the Pass of Aberglaslyn.

There are many other traces. The site of Portmadoc New station is the most evocative. Built for the WHR, it was used also by the Festiniog, even for a short time to the exclusion of the Harbour station. It lay at grid reference SH 571391. The trackbed approaching its site from the south first crosses a drainage channel by a bridge of stone—presumably a Croesor Tramway relic. The widening of the formation for the station, with its passing loop, is very short, suggesting that long trains and much traffic were never envisaged. It lies on a low embankment; below this on the west side, the corrugated iron station building was built at ground level, and there, in a field, it remains.

Grass on the trackbed is sparse enough to reveal traces of ballast and a few decayed remains of wooden sleepers (track on this section was not lifted until about 1949), and opposite the concrete pillar for the water tank the trackbed is still coated, tar-like, with oil which dripped from locomotives standing there and then congealed.

One visualises the driver oiling round, while the fireman takes water and the train fills up with tourists bound for the scenic wonders of Aberglaslyn.

7/16 Portmadoc New Station, built c. 1923 for the Welsh Highland Railway on the course of the Croesor Tramway, was for a few years the Porthmadog terminus of both WHR and Festiniog trains. This is its site, at grid reference SH 571391. The corrugated iron station building still stands at the foot of the embankment, and the concrete pillar for the tank from which locomotives took water can be seen in the distance.

ACKNOWLEDGEMENTS

Many people have kindly helped with this book, both by providing information, and by providing facilities to take photographs. I am particularly grateful to the following:

J. Acklam (Derwent Valley Railway); I. M. Atkinson (Steamtown); J. Bodner (The Holiday Fellowship Ltd); G. Campion (SLOA); R. A. Clark and staff at Beamish; Dr. J. Coiley, P. W. B. Semmens and staff at the NRM; R. Clegg (Midland Railway Trust); M. J. Draper (SVR); A. Hall-Patch (Science Museum); G. D. Hinchcliffe (Steamtown); Bernard Kaukas (BR); A. H. Lawson (Corris Railway Society); R. G. Manders (North Western Museum of Science & Industry); Capt. P. Manisty (ARPS); A. R. Meek and staff at Belvoir Castle; W. S. Mitchell; C. E. Mountford (Bowes Railway); Alex Murray (BR); W. Newby (Edge Hill); R. M. Palk (Narrow Gauge Railway Museum); J. B. Radford (Midland Railway Trust); Connie Redmond (Travellers-Fare); J. Searson (BR); J. N. Slater (Railway Magazine); S. B. Smith, M. Vanns. D. de Haan and staff at Ironbridge; J. B. Snell (RH & DR); J. D. Storer (Royal Scottish Museum); D. H. Ward (BR); D. C. Williams (SVR); S. J. Woodward and staff of GWR Museum, Swindon.

I am also grateful for the assistance of officials of the Department of the Environment, the Welsh Office, the Scottish Development Department, the Royal Commission on Ancient & Historical Monuments in Wales, the Royal Commission on Ancient & Historical Monuments of Scotland, Durham County Council, Gwynedd County Council, Tyne & Wear County Council, and the National Coal Board.

D. Rendell has done his usual excellent work in developing and enlarging photographs; and I am grateful too to my wife and family for their patient support.

APPENDIX

Addresses of principal railway museums, preserved railways and preservation groups

Association of Railway Preservation Societies Ltd, c/o North Norfolk Railway, Sheringham, Norfolk, NR26 8RA.

Bala Lake Railway, Llanuwchllyn, Bala, Gwynedd.
Beamish North of England Open Air Museum, Stanley, Co. Durham.
Birmingham Railway Museum, Warwick Road, Birmingham.
Bluebell Railway, Sheffield Park Station, Uckfield, East Sussex, TN22 2QL.
Bowes Railway, Tyne & Wear Industrial Monuments Trust, Sandyford House, Archbold Terrace, Newcastle upon Tyne, NE2 1ED.
Bressingham Steam Museum, Bressingham Hall, Diss, Norfolk.
Bulmer Railway Centre, H. P. Bulmer Ltd, Whitecross Road, Hereford.

Corris Railway Society: Hon. Secretary, 165 Gynsill Lane, Anstey, Leicester, LE7 7AN.

Dart Valley Railway (both lines), The Station, Buckfastleigh, Devon, TQ11 0DZ.
Dinting Railway Centre Ltd, Dinting, Glossop, Derbyshire.
Dowty Railway Preservation Society, Northway Lane, Ashchurch, Tewkesbury, Glos. GL20 8JR.

East Somerset Railway Co. Ltd, Cranmore, Shepton Mallet, Somerset.
Edge Hill Railway Trust Ltd, PO Box 23, Liverpool, L69 7AD.

Festiniog Railway Co., Harbour Station, Porthmadog, Gwynedd, LL49 9NF.

Glasgow Museum of Transport, 25 Albert Drive, Glasgow, G41 2PE.
Great Central Railway (Main Line Steam Trust Ltd), Loughborough Central Station, Great Central Road, Loughborough, Leicestershire.
Great Western Railway Museum, Swindon, Wiltshire.
Great Western Society, Didcot, Oxfordshire, OX11 7NJ.

Industrial Railway Museum, Penrhyn Castle, Llandegai, Bangor, Gwynedd.
Ironbridge Gorge Museum Trust, Ironbridge, Telford, Salop, TF8 7AW.
Isle of Man Railways, Terminus Buildings, Strathallan Crescent, Douglas, Isle of Man.

Keighley & Worth Valley Railway, Haworth Station, Haworth, Keighley, West Yorkshire, BD22 8NJ.
Kent & East Sussex Railway, Tenterden Town Station, Tenterden, Kent, TN30 6HE.

Lakeside & Haverthwaite Railways, Haverthwaite Station, Nr. Ulverston, Cumbria, LA12 8AL.
Lochty Railway, Balbuthie, Kilconquhar, Fife.
London Transport Museum, Covent Garden, London WC 2.

Merseyside County Museum, Land Transport Gallery, William Brown Street, Liverpool L3 8EN.
Middleton Railway Trust Ltd, Garnet Road, Leeds, LS11 5TJ.
Midland Railway Trust Ltd, Butterley Station, Ripley, Derby.
Monkwearmouth Station Museum, North Bridge Street, Sunderland, SR5 1AP.

National Railway Museum, Leeman Road, York, YO2 4XJ.
Nene Valley Railway, Wansford Station, Old North Road, Stibbington, Wansford, Nr Peterborough, Cambridgeshire.
North Norfolk Railway, Sheringham Station, Sheringham, Norfolk, NR26 8RA.
North Road Station Museum, Darlington, Co. Durham.
North Western Museum of Science & Industry, 97 Grosvenor Street, Manchester, M1 7HF.
North Yorkshire Moors Railway, Pickering Station, Pickering, North Yorkshire.

Railway Preservation Society of Ireland, Whitehead Excursion Station, Whitehead, Co. Antrim, Northern Ireland.
Ravenglass & Eskdale Railway, Ravenglass, Cumbria, CA18 1SW.
Romney, Hythe & Dymchurch Railway, New Romney, Kent, TN28 8PL.
Royal Scottish Museum, Chambers Street, Edinburgh EH1 1JF.

Science Museum, South Kensington, London SW7 2DD.
Scottish Railway Preservation Society, Wallace Street, Falkirk, Stirlingshire.
Severn Valley Railway (Holdings) Ltd, The Railway Station, Bewdley, Worcestershire, DY12 1BG.
Steam Locomotive Operators' Association, 44 Stafford Road, Lichfield, Staffordshire WS13 7BZ.
Steamport Southport, Derby Road, Southport, Lancashire, PR9 0TY.
Steamtown Carnforth, Warton Road, Carnforth, Lancashire, LA5 9HX.
Strathspey Railway, The Station, Boat of Garten, Inverness-shire, PH24 3BH.

Talyllyn Railway, Wharf Station, Tywyn, Gwynedd, LL36 9EY.
Timothy Hackworth Museum, Shildon, Co. Durham.

Welsh Highland Light Railway (1964) Ltd, Gelert's Farm, Madoc Street West, Porthmadog, Gwynedd.
Welshpool & Llanfair Light Railway, The Station, Llanfair Caereinion, Powys.
West Somerset Railway, The Railway Station, Minehead, Somerset.
Worth Valley Railway—see Keighley & Worth Valley Railway.

SELECT BIBLIOGRAPHY

General

Barrie, D. S. M., (edited by), *The Derwent Valley Railway* Oakwood Press, Blandford, 1978

Baxter, Bertram, *Stone Blocks and Iron Rails* David & Charles, Newton Abbot, 1966

Bellwood, John, and Jenkinson, David, *Gresley and Stanier, A Centenary Tribute* HMSO, London, 1976

Bonavia, Michael R., *The Organisation of British Railways* Ian Allan, Shepperton, 1971

Boyd, James I.C., *The Festiniog Railway* Oakwood Press, Blandford, Vols I and II, 1975

Boyd, James I. C., *Narrow Gauge Railways in Mid-Wales* Oakwood Press, Lingfield, 1965

Boyd, James I. C., *Narrow Gauge Railways in South Caernarvonshire* Oakwood Press, Lingfield, 1972

Brown, G. A., Prideaux, J. D. C. A., and Radcliffe, H. G., *The Lynton & Barnstaple Railway* David & Charles, Dawlish, 1964

Butcher, Alan and Leigh, Chris, *Railways Restored 1980* Ian Allan, Shepperton, 1980

Carlson, Robert E., *The Liverpool & Manchester Railway Project 1821–1831* David & Charles, Newton Abbot, 1969

Conroy, J. C., *A History of Railways in Ireland* Longmans Green & Co., Harlow, 1928

Crombleholme, Roger and Kirtland, Terry, *Steam '80* George Allen & Unwin, London, 1980

Desaguliers, J. T., *A Course of Experimental Philosophy* London, 1734

Didcot Railway Centre Great Western Society Ltd, Didcot, 1979

Ellis, Hamilton, *British Railway History 1830–1876* George Allen & Unwin Ltd, London, 1954

Ellis, Hamilton, *British Railway History 1877–1947* George Allen & Unwin Ltd, London, 1959

Ellis, Hamilton, *The Midland Railway* Ian Allan Ltd, Shepperton, 1955

Ewans, M. C., *The Haytor Granite Tramway and Stover Canal* David and Charles, Newton Abbot, 1966

The Great Western Railway Museum Swindon Borough of Thamesdown Museums and Art Galleries, Swindon

Hadfield, Charles, *The Canals of South Wales and the Border* David & Charles, Newton Abbot, 1977

Hadfield, Charles, and Biddle, Gordon, *The Canals of North West England* David & Charles, Newton Abbot, vols I and II, 1970

Hadfield, Charles, and Norris, John, *Waterways to Stratford* David & Charles, Newton Abbot, 1968

(N.B. The above three books contain much information about tramroads and early railways in their respective areas.)

Jarvis, Adrian, and Morris, Len, *Lion* Merseyside County Museums, Liverpool, 1980

Klingender, Francis D., (edited and revised by Elton, Arthur) *Art and the Industrial Revolution* Paladin, St Albans, 1975

Lead, Peter, *The Caldon Canal and Tramroads* Oakwood Press, Blandford, 1979
Lee, Charles E., *The First Passenger Railway* The Railway Publishing Co. Ltd, London, 1942
Lee, Charles E., *Narrow Gauge Railways in North Wales* The Railway Publishing Co. Ltd, London, 1945
Lewis, M. J. T., *Early Wooden Railways* Routledge & Kegan Paul Ltd, London, 1970
Lewis, M. J. T., *How Ffestiniog got its Railway* Railway & Canal Historical Society, Caterham, 1965

Marshall, C. F. Dendy, *A History of British Railways down to the year 1830* Oxford University Press, Oxford, 1938
Marshall, C. F. Dendy, *A History of Railway Locomotives down to the End of the Year 1831* Locomotive Publishing Co. Ltd, London, 1953
Morgan, Bryan, *Railway Relics* Ian Allan, Shepperton 1969

Paine, E. M. S., *The Two James's and the Two Stephensons* David and Charles, Dawlish, 1961

Radford, J. B., *Midland Railway Centre Locomotives and Rolling Stock* Midland Railway Trust Ltd, Ripley, 1977
Rees, Paul, *Railways began here . . . Stations of the Liverpool & Manchester Railway on Merseyside* Edge Hill Railway Trust, Liverpool, 1980
Rimmer, A., *The Cromford & High Peak Railway* Oakwood Press, Lingfield, 1971
Ripley, D., *The Peak Forest Tramway* Oakwood Press, Lingfield, 1972
Rolt, L. T. C., *George and Robert Stephenson* Penguin Books, Harmondsworth, 1978
Semmens, P. W. B., *Exploring the Stockton & Darlington Railway* Frank Graham, Newcastle upon Tyne, 1975
Simmons, Jack (edited by), *Rail 150, The Stockton & Darlington Railway and What Followed* Eyre Methuen, London, 1975
Simmons, Jack, *The Railways of Britain* Routledge & Kegan Paul London, 1965
Smiles, Samuel, *The Lives of George and Robert Stephenson* Folio Society, London, 1975
Somerville, Christopher, *Walking Old Railways* David & Charles, Newton Abbot, 1980

Warn, C. R., *Waggonways and Early Railways of Northumberland* Frank Graham, Newcastle upon Tyne, 1976
Webster, Norman, W., *Britain's First Trunk Line The Grand Junction Railway* Adams & Dart, Bath, 1972
Williams, D. C., *Severn Valley Railway Stock Book* Severn Valley Railway Co. Ltd, Bewdley, 1980

Young, Robert, *Timothy Hackworth and the Locomotive* Shildon 'Stockton & Darlington Railway' Jubilee Committee, Shildon, 1975
Dates given are those of editions consulted. In many instances there are earlier or later editions, and other publishers.

Periodicals

Railway Magazine
Railway World
Steam Railway
Steam World
Industrial Past
Industrial Archaeology
Industrial Archaeology Review
Popular Archaeology

INDEX

Bold page numbers indicate illustrations